Enterprise-Wide Risk Management: Developing and Implementing

Enterprise-Wide Risk Management: Developing and Implementing

Edited by

Jean-Paul Louisot, Ingénieur Civil des Mines, MBA, ARM, MIRM, RWW
Professor of Risk Management Université Paris 1 Panthéon Sorbonne et ENSIB

Christopher Ketcham, CPCU, CFP®, CIC, CRM
Senior Director of Knowledge Resources
AICPCU/IIA

First Edition • Second Printing

American Institute for Chartered Property Casualty
Underwriters/Insurance Institute of America
720 Providence Road, Suite 100
Malvern, Pennsylvania 19355-3433

First Edition • Second Printing • February 2010

Library of Congress Control Number: 2009931865

ISBN 978-0-89463-390-4

Foreword

American Institute for Chartered Property Casualty Underwriters/Insurance Institute of America (the Institutes) are not-for-profit organizations committed to meeting the evolving educational needs of the risk management and insurance community. The Institutes strive to provide current, relevant educational programs in formats that meet the needs of risk management and insurance professionals and the organizations that employ them.

The American Institute for CPCU (AICPCU) was founded in 1942 through a collaborative effort between industry professionals and academics, led by faculty members at The Wharton School of the University of Pennsylvania. In 1953, AICPCU coordinated operations with the Insurance Institute of America (IIA), which was founded in 1909 and remains the oldest continuously functioning national organization offering educational programs for the property-casualty insurance sector.

The Insurance Research Council (IRC), founded in 1977, is a division of AICPCU supported by industry members. This not-for-profit research organization examines public policy issues of interest to property-casualty insurers, insurance customers, and the general public. IRC research reports are distributed widely to insurance-related organizations, public policy authorities, and the media.

The Institutes' customer- and solution-focused business model allows us to better serve the risk management and insurance communities. Customer-centricity defines our business philosophy and shapes our priorities. The Institutes' innovation arises from our commitment to finding solutions that meet customer needs and deliver results. Our business process is shaped by our commitment to efficiency, strategy, and responsible asset management.

The Institutes believe that professionalism is grounded in education, experience, and ethical behavior. The Chartered Property Casualty Underwriter (CPCU) professional designation offered by the Institutes is designed to provide a broad understanding of the property-casualty insurance industry. Depending on professional needs, CPCU students may select either a commercial or a personal risk management and insurance focus. The CPCU designation is conferred annually by the AICPCU Board of Trustees.

In addition, the Institutes offer designations and certificate programs in a variety of disciplines, including the following:

- Claims
- Commercial underwriting
- Fidelity and surety bonding
- General insurance
- Insurance accounting and finance
- Insurance information technology
- Insurance production and agency management
- Insurance regulation and compliance
- Management
- Marine insurance
- Personal insurance
- Premium auditing
- Quality insurance services
- Reinsurance
- Risk management
- Surplus lines

You can complete a program leading to a designation, take a single course to fill a knowledge gap, or take multiple courses and programs throughout your career. The practical and technical knowledge gained from Institute courses enhances your qualifications and contributes to your professional growth. Most Institute courses carry college credit recommendations from the American Council on Education. A variety of courses qualify for credits toward certain associate, bachelor's, and master's degrees at several prestigious colleges and universities.

Our Knowledge Resources Department, in conjunction with industry experts and members of the academic community, develops our trusted course and program content, including Institute study materials. These materials provide practical career and performance-enhancing knowledge and skills.

We welcome comments from our students and course leaders. Your feedback helps us continue to improve the quality of our study materials.

Peter L. Miller, CPCU
President and CEO
American Institute for CPCU
Insurance Institute of America

Preface

The Institutes, through their Center for the Advancement of Risk Management Education (CARME), have joined with the Risk and Insurance Management Society, Inc. (RIMS) to bring you a unique professional development experience. *Enterprise-Wide Risk Management: Developing and Implementing* is designed to introduce enterprise-wide risk management (ERM) concepts that prepare the student to implement an ERM project and/or to assist other stakeholders in the implementation process.

Enterprise-Wide Risk Management: Developing and Implementing assumes an understanding of the fundamentals of risk management. Therefore, the student should have the Institutes' Associate in Risk Management (ARM) designation or the equivalent experience before considering this content. This program's content also assumes that the student has an MBA or equivalent understanding of finance, strategy, economics, management, culture, and other concepts associated with business administration.

Within ERM's framework is the same six-step risk management process described in the Institutes' ARM program. However, ERM enhances the ARM process in three ways: (1) ERM establishes an organization's internal and external contexts at the outset, (2) ERM requires communication and consultation with all stakeholders, and (3) ERM adds a decision step prior to risk treatment in which executive management determines whether residual impact is within the organization's risk tolerance and/or appetite. If it is, the action is to monitor results. If it is not, the action is to choose the appropriate risk management techniques (treatment or response).

An ERM framework includes the risk management process, but it is designed to accomplish more than traditional risk management. ERM enables an enterprise to graft risk management concepts onto its strategic plans and culture. Traditional risk management often operates as a separate function within an organization's silos. ERM is distributed throughout an organization to enable risk owners and risk centers to optimize risk taking. However, ERM would not be effective without the support and engagement of senior executives. They are responsible for inculcating the culture with ERM competencies and for aggregating the distributed risk to build a risk portfolio. This allows them to produce a risk-optimized strategy that incorporates the effects of risk into strategy and vice versa.

The contents of *Enterprise-Wide Risk Management: Developing and Implementing* can be summarized as follows:

- Chapter 1 introduces the advantages of ERM and compares it to traditional risk management.

- Chapters 2, 3, and 4 examine the first step in the ERM process, in which an organization establishes its internal and external contexts. Chapter 2 discusses the relationship between these contexts and key organizational attributes. Chapter 3 places ERM within a strategic planning context, while Chapter 4 explains the role of business and economic intelligence.

- Chapters 5 and 6 explore the risk assessment process. Chapter 5 details how an organization can identify and analyze risk exposures, while Chapter 6 examines the role of organizational resources and management, departments, risk centers, and uncertainty modeling in this process.

- Chapters 7 and 8 explain risk treatment in the context of risk reduction, beginning with an examination of the levels of disruption, or extreme volatility, that may affect an organization's operations and the management of risks to reputation. Chapters 9 and 10 discuss risk finance in an ERM context.

- Chapters 11 and 12 cover the monitor and review step, which entails governance, compliance, and auditing.

- Chapters 13 and 14 emphasize the importance of communication and consultation with all stakeholders to successful ERM implementation. Chapter 13 discusses risk ownership by internal and external stakeholders. Chapter 14 applies project management techniques in the implementation of ERM and change management in general.

- Chapter 15 is a comprehensive business case study that describes the establishment of ERM within an enterprise.

We would like to acknowledge the contributions of RIMS and its members, several of whom are listed as contributors to this text. We thank them for their support during the development of this course.

For more information about the Institutes' programs, please call our Customer Service Department at (800) 644-2101, e-mail us at customerservice@cpcuiia.org, or visit our Web site at www.aicpcu.org.

Jean-Paul Louisot

Christopher Ketcham

Contributors

The American Institute for CPCU and the Insurance Institute of America acknowledge with deep appreciation the contributions made to the content of this text by the following persons:

Richard Berthelsen, JD, MBA, CPCU, AIC, AU, ARe, ARM

Laurent Condamin, ARM, Ingénieur de l'Ecole Centrale des Arts & Manufactures de Paris

Richard Connelly, PhD

Mary Ann Cook, MBA, CPCU, AU, AAI

Cheryl Ferguson, EdD, CPCU, AU, AAI, API, AIM

Carol A. Fox, ARM

Nancy Germond, MA, ARM, AIC, ITP

Christophe Girardet, DEA en Statistiques, DESS en Ingenierie Mathematique, ARM, EFARM

James Kallman, PhD, ARM, RF

Valerie Ullman Katz, MBA, CPCU, ARM, CBCP

Melissa Leuck

Pamela Lyons, BA, FCIP, CRM

Michael J. Moody, MBA, ARM

Ann E. Myhr, CPCU, ARM, AU, AIM, ASLI

Patrick Naïm, ARM, Ingénieur de l'Ecole Centrale des Arts & Manufactures de Paris

Charles Nyce, PhD, CPCU, ARM

Donald R. Oakes, PhD, CPCU, ARM

Kevin Quinley, CPCU, ARM, AIC, AIM, ARe

Jenny Rayner

Bertrand Robert

Kathleen J. Robison, CPCU, AU, ARM, AIC, CPIW

Hugh Rosenbaum

Liz Taylor, MIRM, FBCI

Guillaume Tissier, DESS Droit et Affaires Internationales

Marilyn B. Wade, ARM, CRM

Larry Warner

Eric Wieczorek, MBA, ARM, ARe

Contents

Chapter 1

The Advantages of Enterprise-Wide Risk Management — 1.1

Improving Strategic Decision Making With ERM — 1.3

Traditional Risk Management Versus ERM — 1.11

ERM in Approaching Business Uncertainties — 1.19

Major Risk Management Frameworks and Standards — 1.25

Summary — 1.32

Chapter 2

Establish Internal and External Contexts: Risk Culture and Attitude, Goals, and Sustainable Development — 2.1

The Influence of Organizational Culture on Risk Attitude — 2.3

Align Individual Objectives and Organizational Strategic Goals — 2.12

Risk Attitudes and Departmental Objectives — 2.18

Sustainable Development — 2.20

Summary — 2.23

Chapter 3

Establish Internal and External Contexts: ERM and Strategic Planning — 3.1

Strategic Development Process and Types of Business Strategies — 3.3

Developing ERM Goals Aligned With Strategic Goals — 3.9

A Risk Maturity Model — 3.23

Analyzing an Organization's Internal and External Contexts — 3.27

Conducting a SWOT Analysis — 3.34

Summary — 3.41

Chapter 4

Establish Internal and External Contexts: Incorporating Business and Economic Intelligence — 4.1

Economic Intelligence—ERM Program Application — 4.3

Elements of a Business Intelligence System — 4.8

Business Intelligence Systems—Enterprise-Wide Risk Management Implementation Steps — 4.15

Business Intelligence Systems—IT Governance and Outputs — 4.24

Business Intelligence Systems—Presenting the Case for ERM — 4.31

Summary — 4.36

Chapter 5

Risk Assessment: Exposure Analysis — 5.1

Exposure Spaces and Risk Assessment — 5.3

Impact—Role for Exposure Analysis and Evaluation — 5.16

Applying the Exposure Spaces Model — 5.22

Summary — 5.37

Chapter 6

Risk Assessment: Management Departments, Risk Centers, and Uncertainty Modeling — 6.1

Management Departments — 6.3

Risk Centers and Risk Owners — 6.7

Methods and Limitations of Uncertainty Modeling — 6.12

Risk Quantification Case Study—Woodworking Workshop — 6.23

Summary — 6.45

Chapter 7

Risk Treatment: Reacting to Disruptions	7.1
Levels of Disruption	7.3
Managing Risk to Reputation	7.7
Activities to Prepare Executives and Managers to Face Disruptions	7.16
Mitigating Risk Through Business Continuity Planning	7.22
Scope and Phases of Strategic Redeployment Planning	7.26
Summary	7.30

Chapter 8

Risk Treatment: The Supply Chain and Crisis Communication	8.1
Supply Chain Risk Management	8.3
Crisis Communication	8.7
Recommending Risk-Appropriate Mitigation Tools	8.10
Summary	8.18

Chapter 9

Risk Treatment: Risk Financing	9.1
Indigo Company Case —Evaluating an Investment Proposal	9.3
Limitations of Cash Flow Analysis in Decision Making	9.13
Importance of the Risk-Return Relationship	9.15
Portfolio Selection and Optimizing Risk Taking	9.17
Polytech Company Case—Cost of Capital and Optimal Capital Allocation	9.29
Summary	9.37

Chapter 10

Risk Treatment: Alternative Risk Transfer and Derivatives	10.1
Purpose and Functions of Derivatives and Alternative Risk Transfer (ART) in Risk Financing	10.3
Case Study: Winding Down a Captive Insurer	10.13
Summary	10.22

Chapter 11

Monitor and Review: The Role of Governance and Compliance in ERM	11.1
Integrating Governance and Compliance With Enterprise Risk Management	11.3
Governance and Enterprise Risk Management	11.5
Compliance Issues in Enterprise Risk Management	11.9
Ethics and Social Responsibilities in Enterprise Risk Management	11.15
Summary	11.22

Chapter 12

Monitor and Review: Assurance in ERM	12.1
Review and Monitoring for Continuous Improvement	12.3
Assurance and Risk Management	12.6
ERM to Meet Financial Rating Agencies' Expectations	12.9
Summary	12.13

Chapter 13

Communicate and Consult: Risk
Ownership and Communication With
Stakeholders   13.1

The Importance of Risk Ownership by
Internal Stakeholders   13.3

Communication With Stakeholders   13.12

The Importance of Risk Ownership by
External Stakeholders   13.18

Developing an ERM Business Case   13.25

Determining an Organization's Risk Criteria   13.33

Summary   13.38

Chapter 14

Communicate and Consult:
Project Management   14.1

Project Management Plan Development
and Implementation   14.3

Managing Risks in a Project   14.11

Organizational Change Management Steps   14.20

Implementing ERM—Continuous Change   14.27

Summary   14.35

Chapter 15

Comprehensive ERM Business Case Study   15.1

Amiable Footwear, Inc. Case Study   15.3

Summary   15.36

Index   1

The Advantages of Enterprise-Wide Risk Management

Educational Objectives

After learning the content of this chapter and completing the corresponding course guide assignment, you should be able to:

▶ Explain how an organization can improve its strategic decision making by incorporating enterprise-wide risk management (ERM).

▶ Contrast traditional risk management and ERM.

▶ Explain why ERM is an effective approach to use to face business uncertainties.

▶ Summarize the major risk management frameworks and standards.

Outline

Improving Strategic Decision Making With ERM

Traditional Risk Management Versus ERM

ERM in Approaching Business Uncertainties

Major Risk Management Frameworks and Standards

Summary

The Advantages of Enterprise-Wide Risk Management

Enterprise-wide risk management (ERM) offers many advantages over traditional risk management. There also are myriad ways in which the two methods differ. As ERM evolves, the role of those who manage ERM programs within their organizations is gradually becoming more defined. Some organizations that operate in an ERM environment have given their risk manager the title of Chief Risk Officer, although this title has not been widely adopted. This text uses the lower-case term "chief risk officer" to refer to the person in charge of risk management in an ERM environment and the term "risk professional" to refer to other persons associated with risk management in an ERM environment.

ERM improves an organization's strategic decision making by addressing threats and opportunities in a way that integrates risk management with the strategic planning process. ERM is a systemic approach to managing all of an organization's uncertainty (that is, key risks—threats and opportunities) in order to maximize shareholder value by optimizing risk taking. Traditional risk management considers only hazard and operational risks that can affect an organization. By using an ERM approach to manage business uncertainties, organizations can enhance their decision making and improve risk communication.

IMPROVING STRATEGIC DECISION MAKING WITH ERM

To be effective and improve an organization's likelihood for success, ERM must be intertwined with the way an organization is managed. Integrating ERM into strategic decision-making processes is key to its implementation. ERM is not exclusive to the corporate world. Sole proprietorships, partnerships, government and its institutions, not-for-profit organizations, non-governmental organizations (NGOs), and all other forms of enterprise have benefited from integrating ERM with strategy.

ERM can improve an organization's strategic decision making and enable it to become more strategically confident by allowing it to address threats to its existence and optimize opportunities. An organization can realize this improvement by readily integrating ERM into its strategic planning process and by addressing legal and regulatory issues related to ERM at a high level of planning.

Improving Strategic Decision Making

ERM improves an organization's strategic decision making by producing high-quality information that is essential to the organization's survival. ERM helps boards and executives make better decisions that can render their organizations less vulnerable to failure and better equipped to survive changes in the external environment.

Business model
The core aspects of an organization, including its vision, mission, strategies, infrastructure, policies, offerings, and processes.

Strategic planning is the process by which an organization's board and executives develop, refresh, and refine its strategies in line with its view of the future. The reason for developing a strategic plan is the recognition that an organization's current **business model** will not survive indefinitely. Risks to the business model can arise from changes in competition, technology, the market, and customers' demands. An organization that incorporates ERM with its strategic planning process improves its decision making in several ways, including these:

- It can address potentially devastating threats.
- It can exploit opportunities by incorporating them into its current business model or completely reinventing a new model that will successfully carry it into the future.
- It can use ERM as a process to manage unwanted variations from expectations.

Therefore, strategic planning that incorporates ERM can help ensure the continuation and success of the organization.

Integrating ERM and Strategic Planning

The ERM process framework requires an organization to establish its internal and external contexts, assess risks, choose appropriate treatments, and then monitor the treatment and the ERM plan. Within all steps of the process are the engagement of and communication with the organization's stakeholders. An organization that integrates ERM with its strategic planning process increases the likelihood that it will adequately address risks. To integrate ERM, an organization's board and executives can follow this process:

1. Develop ERM goals (establish the internal and external contexts)
2. Identify risks (risk assessment)
3. Analyze, evaluate, and prioritize critical risks (risk assessment)
4. Treat critical risks, considering priority (risk treatment)
5. Monitor critical risks (monitor and review)

ERM Process

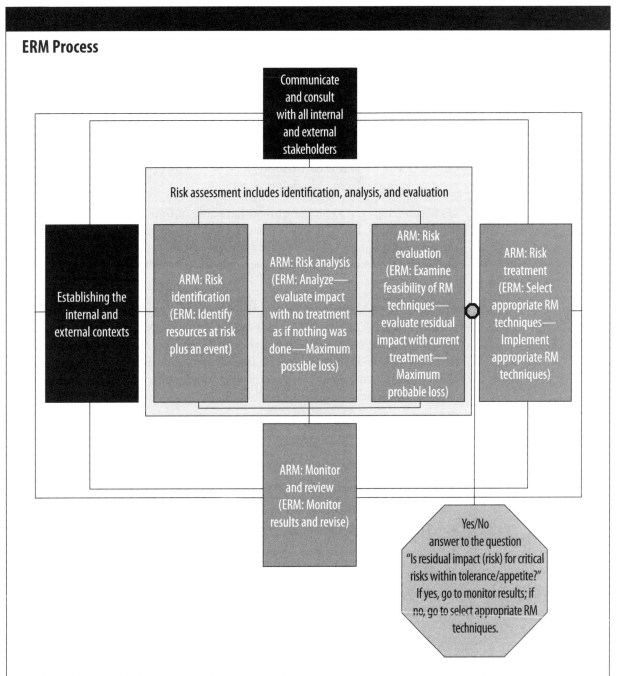

Within ERM's framework is the Associate in Risk Management (ARM) six-step risk management process: identify, analyze, examine feasibility of risk management techniques, select appropriate risk management techniques, implement selected risk management techniques, and monitor and review. However, ERM enhances the ARM six-step process in three ways: (1) ERM establishes internal and external contexts of the enterprise at the outset, (2) ERM requires communication and consultation with all stakeholders, and (3) ERM adds a decision step prior to risk treatment that asks the risk manager to determine whether residual impact is within risk tolerance/appetite. If within risk tolerance, the action is to monitor results. If not within risk tolerance, the action is to choose the appropriate risk management techniques (treatment).

The "identify risks" step in the risk assessment process should reveal many risks to the enterprise. The enterprise must evaluate these risks based on how critical they are to the organization's strategy or even its survival. Assessing, identifying, treating, evaluating, and monitoring critical risks is ERM's prime directive. An organization's determination of what it considers critical is part of the process of establishing its internal and external contexts. For example, a government institution may have zero tolerance for the risk of terrorist attacks on its infrastructure, leading to both an increase in intelligence and infrastructure hardening. A corporation may consider minor differences in the cost of raw materials as constituting a critical competitive risk that requires treatment in the form of hedging.

Over time, new risks emerge while others fade in importance. The enterprise must engage the ERM process continuously in order to maintain a current understanding of both the risks that can affect the organization and their potential for positively and negatively affecting expected outcomes.

Develop ERM Goals (Establish the Internal and External Contexts)

The first step in integrating ERM with strategic planning is to consider goals for ERM as part of the organization's business model. Annually, the board and executive team develops or reviews the organization's vision statement, mission statement, strategic objectives, and financial projections. During this process, the board and executives should also develop the organization's ERM goals.

An organization's ERM goals are based on several considerations:

- The organization's risk appetite
- Why the organization is establishing the ERM program
- The business or organizational need for an ERM program
- The intended scope of the ERM program
- How ERM will assist the organization in meeting its strategic goals
- How the organization defines ERM
- Whether the organization has a function- or department-focused culture or a collaborative culture and how that will affect ERM implementation

An organization's ERM goals will guide the decisions that are made in the steps that follow and provide structures within the organization that support assessing, treating, and monitoring risks.

Sample ERM Goals

- Identify opportunities for and threats to achieving organizational goals
- Incorporate planning to take advantage of opportunities and mitigate threats to the organization
- Anticipate and reduce deviations from expected outcomes
- Anticipate and recognize emerging risks
- Improve business resiliency and sustainability
- Drive consistency in risk taking
- Optimize risk taking, considering appetite and tolerance
- Reduce earnings volatility
- Improve risk management competencies throughout the organization
- Encourage proactive management behavior in treating risks
- Achieve greater stakeholder consensus for risk management
- Increase management accountability and risk-based performance management
- Establish a consistent basis for risk-based decision making and planning
- Enhance the health and safety of employees, customers, and their communities
- Design and enhance appropriate management controls to more effectively and efficiently reduce defects and minimize loss
- Boost internal and external stakeholder confidence and trust
- Enable better-informed governance
- Improve external transparency and risk disclosure
- Comply with relevant legal and regulatory requirements and international norms
- Establish cross-functional and organizational awareness of risks posed in specific geographies

Analyze, Evaluate, and Prioritize Critical Risks (Risk Assessment)

The board and executives next direct an examination of internal and external threats to the organization's mission, strategies, and goals. Such threats are identified by noting changes that can undermine the organization, as well as changes that present opportunities, in areas such as these:

- Competition
- Customer demographics or behaviors
- Technology
- Economy
- Politics and regulation
- The organization's ability to meet regulatory requirements

Asking "what if" questions is an effective method an organization may use to identify risks to strategies. For example, "What risks will result if. . ." could precede each of these items:

- Favorable exchange rates make our products more competitive in Europe?

- Frost in Florida decreases crop yield for our major competitors?

- A competitor emerges in our market that undercuts our prices?

- Regulations change that double the amount of time needed to develop our products?

- Technology changes make our leading product irrelevant?

- Consumers demand a "greener" product?

- Our company's unique manufacturing competencies are needed for an emerging product?

Each risk to strategy should be considered because it may affect the organization's success and sustainability. The impact of risk to strategy may manifest gradually rather than having immediate consequences. Therefore, identifying and evaluating trends is important in the assessment process.

After risks to strategy have been identified, the "criticality" of the risk to the organization is determined so that the organization can prioritize risks for treatment. There are many approaches to quantifying criticality, but most include measurements of impact upon the resources and goals of the enterprise and its stakeholders. Frequency combined with valuation is also a consideration, but a low-frequency/high-impact risk that cannot be completely avoided requires careful consideration. For each critical risk identified, potential triggers or warning signs should also be identified. At a minimum, an organization should identify its top five risks, consider their likelihood, and target them for treatment and monitoring.

Treat Critical Risks, Considering Priority (Risk Treatment)

Building answers to the "what if" questions from the assessment process is an effective way to initiate treatments to address the risks identified. Based on the likelihood (low, medium, or high) of the risk identified, the organization might initiate action to address a threat or to seize an opportunity.

Practical techniques for treating risks to strategy can be placed into these categories:

- Avoid—Use alternative approaches that eliminate the cause of the risk or its consequences

- Accept—Accept the risk by planning for ways to deal with the uncertainty if it occurs

- Transfer—Assign the responsibility to manage the risk to a third party

- Mitigate—Initiate activities to reduce the probability, impact, or timing of a risk event to an acceptable risk tolerance

- Optimize/exploit—Develop actions to optimize positive consequences to achieve gains

Monitor Critical Risks (Monitor and Review)

Risks to strategy are periodically monitored by identifying trends, triggering events, and warning signs during the assessment phase for each risk identified. Reporting may be periodic or on an exception basis, depending on the likelihood of occurrence and the potential impact that the risk poses.

Examples of Treating Risks to Strategies

What risks will result if...	Likelihood	Treatment
A competitor emerges in our market that undercuts our prices?	High	Avoid—Lobby to prevent regulatory changes that will allow the competitor to enter the market
		Mitigate—If the competitor does enter the market, launch a marketing campaign that highlights our product's superior features
Regulations change that double the amount of time need to develop our products?	Low	Accept—If this occurs, address the time needed to develop products
Technology changes make our leading product irrelevant?	Medium	Mitigate—Initiate plans to diversify our products into distinctly different technological areas
Consumers demand a "greener" product?	Low	Mitigate—Study comparable "green" alternatives for our processes in case this becomes an issue
Our company's unique manufacturing competencies are needed for an emerging product?	High	Optimize/exploit—Contact the developers of the emerging product to seek a collaborative approach
Favorable exchange rates make our products more competitive in Europe?	Medium (periodic fluctuations)	Optimize/exploit—Increase marketing campaigns and direct as much inventory as practicable toward the European market
Frost in Florida decreases crop yield for our major competitors?	High	Optimize/exploit—In addition to capitalizing on inevitable higher prices, negotiate with competitors' supermarkets for increased shelf space for our product

Monitoring risks to strategy is complex, because the triggering events must generally be identified from a variety of sources, including, for example, industry newsletters, regulatory announcements, and surveys. For risks that pose a potentially high severity and likelihood, an organization may foster relationships with key individuals in positions to know when changes are imminent that will trigger conditions that could result in an event. With such information, the organization can be prepared to launch treatments.

Emerging Legal and Regulatory Requirements Regarding ERM

Standards and guidelines regarding ERM as it is applied to strategic management are emerging. For example, rating agencies, specifically Standard & Poor's (S&P), view risk management in strategic decision making as an important keystone to an organization's planning and have expectations that focus on ERM's strategic applications. The international risk management framework ISO 31000:2009 includes guidelines regarding the risk management process.[1]

Standards, which define acceptable practices, methods, and processes, are not legal requirements in themselves. However, they may become mandatory when a government enacts them as legislation.

To ensure that emerging regulatory requirements are considered and documented when ERM is applied to strategic decision making, an organization's chief risk officer should search for requirements related to risk management in several areas:

- Management's view of the organization's most important risks, including the likelihood and potential severity or impact of such risks
- The frequency of key risks and the process used to identify key risks
- The influence of risk sensitivity on liability management and financing decisions
- The role of risk management in strategic decision making
- The culture of risk management in the organization as identified by communication systems, frameworks, roles, policies, and metrics applied

The organization's executives and board of directors should always consider that compliance with standards is not a substitute for sound risk management throughout the organization; rather, ERM can accomplish this.

TRADITIONAL RISK MANAGEMENT VERSUS ERM

Traditional risk management (referred to as RM) considers only hazard and operational risks that can affect an organization. ERM expands an organization's risk focus to include financial and strategic risks, allowing it to account for all eventualities that can affect its ability to achieve its goals.

There are four major differences between RM and ERM:

- Risk categories
- Strategic integration
- Performance metrics
- Organizational structure

Risk Categories

Both RM and ERM agree that, while risk can be quantified to some degree, it can only be estimated. The need to accurately measure risk in an effort to reduce uncertainty is common to all risk management frameworks, but beyond these points, the RM and ERM frameworks diverge.

Traditionally, risk can be classified as either **pure risk** or **speculative risk**, and further categorized as hazard risk, operational risk, financial risk, and strategic risk.

Pure risk
A chance of loss or no loss, but no chance of gain.

Speculative risk
A chance of loss, no loss, or gain.

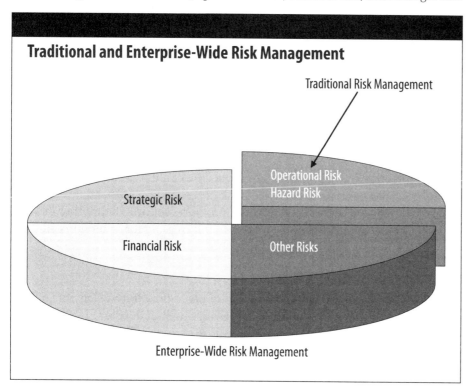

Traditional and Enterprise-Wide Risk Management

Traditional Risk Management

Operational Risk
Hazard Risk
Strategic Risk
Financial Risk
Other Risks

Enterprise-Wide Risk Management

Traditional risk management is concerned with pure risk, where there is no upside or positive outcome possible other than the status quo. An example of such risks would be hazard risks, which are pure risks that include damage to property from perils such as fire and explosion or losses stemming from accidents and injuries to employees or customers. Pure risks can also include operational risks that arise out of service, processing, or manufacturing activities.

Traditional risk management focuses on preventing or reducing potential losses and on compensation for losses that do occur. Preventive measures for hazard risks include the use of warning labels, process flow alterations, and other engineering considerations. Sprinkler systems, first aid training, and efficient product recall procedures are examples of pure risk loss mitigation strategies.

In contrast, ERM considers all risks that an organization faces, regardless of their source or potential outcomes. Both pure risk and speculative risk, which can be commonly categorized as financial, strategic, and some operational risks, are included. Financial risks include interest rate risk, competitive risk, inflation, and market-timing risks, among others. Strategic risks include management decisions regarding new products, emerging competitors, and planning issues. Examples of operational risks include supplier disruptions or periods of power loss during the failure or overload of the electrical grid. Another risk not normally considered by RM is risk to reputation.

ERM emphasizes the interrelationships between pure and speculative risk, while RM focuses only on pure risk. Then, ERM seeks to optimize risk taking in relationship to strategic goals, while RM seeks to prevent or reduce risks related only to losses.

ERM also considers "upside" risk—the risk that the organization will outperform its strategic goals. Examples of upside risks include situations in which a business venture experiences an unexpected increase in revenue or market share. What opportunities or threats does this variation from the expected present to the venture?

For example, the development of a new vaccine could present to a governmental health organization the upside risk of not having to spend its entire budget. It could use these funds to better promote wellness, fight other diseases, or even reinvest the funds in the general treasury for other purposes.

Strategic Integration

Traditional risk management is normally involved only in the elements of the organization's strategy that deal with pure risk and hazard risks. ERM, however, is integrated with the entire organization's strategy. By linking risk to the entire enterprise, the organization decouples its financial, strategic, operational, hazard, and other risks from individual operational silos and addresses them within strategy as a whole. Thus, ERM considers the global array of risks that affect the organization.

This global array can be represented by a three-dimensional depiction of attributes known as the exposure spaces model. The attributes are resources, events, and impacts. On the horizontal x-axis are the various resources of the enterprise that may change in value. The impacts—the actual consequences or changes in value of the resources—are shown on the vertical y-axis. The third dimension, the z-axis, shows the causes of the changes in value. ERM uses the exposure spaces model to consider the range of potential impact from positive to negative. Once this range is established, its estimated effect on resources can be contrasted against desired strategic changes in resource value so that appropriate risk treatment can be applied to minimize variation from the desired value.

Strategic Integration—An Illustration

LowCost, a regional airline, has three strategic objectives:

- Maintain its low-cost status

- Continuously improve its on-time arrival metrics

- Maintain its environmentally friendly reputation

Using a traditional risk management strategy, the airline would have given the fuel-hedging responsibility to the finance department and the management of risk at fuel storage facilities to the risk manager.

After adopting an ERM approach, LowCost challenged the organization to develop a hedging plan in relationship to the organization's strategy as a whole. Elements evaluated for LowCost included:

- The carrying, storage, and insurance costs of maintaining multiple storage facilities associated with the purchase of large amounts of fuel

- The adverse impact of a major fuel spill or fire in a metropolitan storage facility on its environmental reputation goal concomitantly with the cost of having to purchase more expensive fuel after the loss, which would affect its low-cost goal and, if layoffs are required, its on-time arrival goal

- The strategic implications for low-cost and on-time strategy if the hedging basis or timing risk is greater than expected

After assessing both the upside and downside risks of a hedging program within the strategic goals of the organization, LowCost adopted a hedging and fuel inventory risk management plan that optimized risk within and among the three enterprise strategic objectives. As a result, LowCost discovered that its previous traditional risk management plan, which considered risk independently in operational and financial risk silos, had underestimated the risk to the enterprise's low-cost and on-time arrival objectives.

Exposure Spaces Model

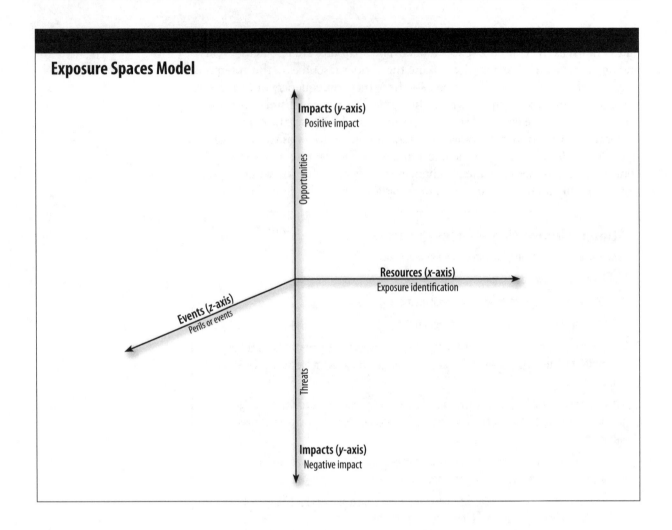

RM Versus ERM: An Example

XYZ Enterprises and ABC Industries have similar problems. Management at XYZ, employing traditional risk management techniques, asked its risk manager to minimize the cost of a possible loss caused by pure risks. The traditional risk manager for XYZ Enterprises identified fire as a major peril that could affect the business by causing loss to property and business income over time. To combat the possibility of loss by fire, the traditional risk manager calculated the cost benefit of deploying fire-resistant structures, sprinkler systems, and less flammable processing chemicals in relationship to insurance and retention costs. In addition, the traditional risk manager considered a multiple-location strategy versus a one-location strategy as it related to the frequency and severity of fire loss and the entry of competitors to the market after a full shutdown in a single-plant strategy.

Engaging ERM, management at ABC considered not only how it would manage the pure risk of fire cost effectively, but also factored in the implications of operational efficiencies as they relate to span of control, the availability of workers, the ability of management to effect a continuous process improvement program, and the effect of competitive entry in a multi-location configuration as opposed to a single-plant operation.

XYZ's traditional risk management plan split the plant into five locations to minimize the pure risk associated with fire to no more than 20 percent of production capacity should one location burn. However, XYZ's traditional risk management process did not consider the effect of such measures on the process efficiency of the organization and the resulting cost increases that might make its products less competitive—the speculative risk. While XYZ's plan may prevent competitive entry following the sudden loss of all or most of its production, the cost inefficiencies of the five-location operation may lead to unanticipated entry by more efficient competitors regardless of fire losses.

ABC's ERM plan divided the operation into two plants and concluded that it could operate in shifts to generate lost capacity if one location burned. The plan produced operating efficiencies associated with larger plant structures to optimize ABC's need to reduce cost of production and to provide the spread of risk necessary to slow or prevent competitors' entry into the market brought about by a catastrophic event at a singular location.

Thus, while both the traditional risk management and ERM programs deployed spread of risk as a risk management strategy, the enterprise risk manager assessed the holistic impact on the organization from the perspective of both pure and speculative risk with a goal not simply of minimizing or eliminating risk but of optimizing risk in relationship to the organization's strategic goals of competitive advantage. In summary, ERM focuses on achieving strategic objectives for both pure and speculative risk, not just the operational need to compensate for expected losses.

Performance Metrics

Success in traditional risk management can be measured both as an activity and as a result. For example, a traditional risk management plan for an organization that employs a considerable amount of manual labor might include objectives for reducing worker injury costs and incidents in addition to an activity metric involving the number of safety meetings held. This approach assumes that reducing incidents will reduce the number of injuries. This reduction in injuries will affect product costs and duty of care to employees (result) over the long term. Also assumed is a direct link between the number of safety meetings and the extent of training (activity) and the number of worker injuries.

However, a certain amount of risk is unavoidable in business; eliminating all risk would be tantamount to terminating the organization's operations. ERM seeks to optimize risk taking in relationship to strategic goals. Optimization is both an eventuality and a process through which the organization searches for the equilibrium between risk and outcome in relationship to strategic goals. The enterprise then manages the organization toward that equilibrium. ERM asks, "How do risk management activities relate to the organization's strategic needs, and how should we measure success?"

Organizational Structure

The traditional risk manager generally reports to an organizational department such as finance, operations, or legal. Quite often, the responsibility for pure risk management may be localized within a risk management department, which then orchestrates the risk management plan as a central authority. While some responsibilities for risk management may be delegated to others, they are generally only those responsibilities involving pure risk. Thus, a local plant manager may be responsible for both hazard identification and conducting safety meetings in the facility. Conversely, in ERM, risk management responsibility is decentralized and integrated into all levels of the organization.

Chief risk officer
A generic term for the senior risk professional engaged in ERM in an enterprise; distinct from "Chief Risk Officer," a title given to some risk professionals who report to senior management.

Alternatively, the enterprise risk manager—often called a **chief risk officer**—may report to the chief executive officer (CEO) or the board of directors and act as a facilitator of and an educator about the ERM process and serve as a coach to other risk owners in the enterprise.

As facilitator, the chief risk officer engages the organization's management in a continuous conversation that establishes risk strategic goals in relationship to the organization's strengths, weaknesses, opportunities, and threats (SWOT). Unlike traditional risk management, ERM engages all the organization's stakeholders in the risk management process. Thus, the "enterprise" in ERM becomes the organization itself and its stakeholders, which include employees, management, board of directors, suppliers, customers, partners, community, and the government or regulators. The chief risk officer's responsibility in the strategic process is to help the organization develop tools that identify and manage events and perils that may cause variation from the achievement of specific strategic goals.

As an educator and coach, the chief risk officer helps the enterprise create a risk culture in which individual department heads and project managers are identified as "risk owners." Risk owners are then given tasks and responsibilities for identifying and managing variation from the achievement of organizational strategic goals. In the fully integrated ERM organization, attending to and addressing risk become part of every job description, every project, and every department. Successful risk management of strategic objectives becomes both an evaluation measurement and a success measurement.

An organization with a fully integrated ERM program develops a sophisticated but user-friendly communication matrix that moves information throughout the organization, laterally through peers and similar departments, and among internal and external stakeholders across the enterprise. Communications include dialogue and discussions that occur locally or among levels as a result of the development of personnel competencies that identify potential risks and communicate them to others.

The establishment of valid metrics and the continuous flow of cogent data are as important in this communication structure as the keen eyes of an observer trained to identify risk or its potential. These matrices and metrics are carefully woven into reporting structures that engage the entire organization—from individual risk owners to external stakeholders to senior management and the board—in an effort to identify emerging risk in relation to and in context with specific and aggregate strategic goals. They are also involved in quantifying the success of treatment of previously identified risks.

The process of ERM is both iterative and recursive—iterative in that the risk management process is engaged to identify and manage each discoverable risk, and recursive in that the risk management process is revisited regularly to maintain its optimization in relationship to strategic goals. As existing risks are successfully managed, new risks emerge that must be addressed. In other circumstances, existing risks evolve into something for which a previous treatment is no longer effective. When strategic goals change or evolve, entire risk management strategies may change as formerly important risks no longer exist and risks never before managed emerge to the forefront.

Beyond Traditional Risk Management

	Traditional Risk Management	Enterprise-Wide Risk Management	
Risk Defined	Operational Risk Pure risk—only loss, no gain Perils only Threats only Cost of risk containment	All risks. Risks that can produce positive or negative results.	Events Threats and opportunities Creating value while adhering to values
Risk Linked to Strategy	Rewards both activities and results	Links rewards to results and results to strategic needs. Risk management is aligned with strategy.	Optimize risk taking Preserving value; adding value
Enterprise Wide	Considers only those parts of the organization affected by operational risk	Considers global risk, including: Supply chain. Crisis management.	Reputation Disturbances Involves all internal and external stakeholders Rating agencies
Common Language	Uses insurance industry terms and jargon	Uses a common language developed by standards making organizations and government agencies.	
Elements of a Risk Culture	Traditional risk manager often without C-level authority or responsibility—not linked to corporate strategy other than operational risk	CRO—Interaction with board—C-level authority and responsibility that are linked directly to corporate strategy. Risk centers with risk owners. While ERM is a process, project management techniques can be used in the initial implementation of ERM.	Communication and consultation Building the business case within the organization Understanding and changing risk perception throughout enterprise Audit and self-assessment Portfolio approach to risk Stakeholder involvement in process
Exposure Spaces	Management of perils—pure risk—loss only	Exposure to any conceivable event or fact and resulting impact positively or negatively—variation from the expected.	
Information Systems	Risk Management Information System (RMIS)	Business intelligence (BI) systems integrate enterprise data flows and generate analytic information for risk management decision making, internal controls testing, and credit evaluation needs.	

ERM IN APPROACHING BUSINESS UNCERTAINTIES

In today's global, often volatile business climate, organizations must deal with business uncertainties in a thorough, systematic manner. They may do so by adopting an ERM approach, which transcends traditional risk management.

Traditional risk management focuses on hazard risks and long-established risk management techniques—avoidance, prevention, reduction, transfer, and retention. It restricts risk management to a middle-management function that is primarily responsible for purchasing insurance and making traditional risk management decisions.

An organization that has adopted an ERM approach monitors risks, threats, and opportunities that arise from many sources. This approach provides two important benefits:

- Enhanced decision making
- Improved risk communication

Enhanced Decision Making

Whether it is a profit-driven organization, a not-for-profit organization, a charity, or a governmental entity, an organization must manage competing interests to achieve its strategic goals. An ERM approach allows an organization to systematically explore new opportunities for economic efficiencies while it manages threats that stem from internal and external contexts. It does so by focusing on managing all of an organization's key or critical risks—its threats as well as its opportunities—in a manner that optimizes its value.

ERM provides a means for an organization to identify and select among alternative risk responses. Rather than consolidating risk management responsibility at the senior-management level (which slows the decision-making process and sacrifices potential corporate advantages to organizational gridlock), ERM enhances the organizational decision-making process by giving all decision makers in the organization access to its total risk picture.

When threats and opportunities are understood and risk taking is optimized strategically, managers may make better decisions, which in turn builds their confidence for decisions on future projects. This improved decision making enables an organization to quickly meet emerging marketplace challenges and provides several additional advantages:

- Increased profitability (or, for those organizations where profitability is not an issue, economic efficiency)
- Reduced volatility
- Improved ability to meet strategic goals
- Increased management accountability

Increased Profitability (Economic Efficiency)

An ERM approach increases an organization's profitability because strategic decisions involve more than preparing only for adverse outcomes. Properly implemented, ERM goes beyond evaluating insolvency at preset confidence levels. ERM allows organizations to engage in additional business opportunities by allocating resources through rational decision making at the local level. When an organization adopts an ERM approach, every strategic decision made at every level is sounder, which helps to further ensure economic efficiency. Therefore, over time, organizations with a sound ERM process in place will show higher earnings.

Historically, an organization's shareholders and the media tend to focus on quarterly profits and losses. An organization that adopts an ERM approach monitors systemic risks inherent in the organization that can adversely affect its long-term financial outlook. When an organization adopts an ERM approach, unexpected occurrences or variations cause much less disruption because the organization has already incorporated the possibility of such occurrences or variations into its decision-making process. Even natural disasters can be less disruptive to an organization that has built supply chain resilience into its operational model.

For example, an organization may have to decide whether it should continue to sell a product that is highly profitable but that also has the potential to produce a higher level of liability claims. In making this decision, the organization should consider that, ideally, business momentum in a unit that has an above average rate of return on risk should be increased, because the unit produces higher profits relative to units that may perform well but that generate liabilities. ERM is the framework that any organization could use in its decision-making process to aid in achieving increased profitability (economic efficiency) in all operating units.

Reduced Volatility

In addition to maintaining cash flows and balancing its budget, an organization must manage its cash flow to ensure an adequate pipeline of capital to meet challenges and to explore strategic growth opportunities. How organizations approach this aspect of risk management differs due to variations in internal characteristics such as the current environment, technology, competition, and regulatory climate. Organizations like the Red Cross, which rely heavily on their reputation to garner financial support, tend to be more risk averse than, for example, a pharmaceutical company that has extensive research and development expertise.

When an organization decides to embark on a new venture, the venture must be sufficiently capitalized to allow the organization to capitalize the increased cost of risk associated with it. For instance, the Red Cross may experience a decline in donations during a recession, posing a risk that it may not be able to provide needed services during a disaster and the risk that it could incur threats to its reputation in addition to the risks associated with having to take capital from its endowment to provide services. However, if the organization evaluates the risk only at the project level, it may miss the broader implications of that risk.

For example, suppose an apparel manufacturer outsourced the manufacture of one of its clothing lines to an offshore manufacturing site. The clothing line became enormously successful because the offshore site's lower labor costs made the clothes affordable. However, when the apparel manufacturer performed its initial cost/benefit analysis, it failed to consider the risks associated with outsourcing to the offshore site, which included significant use of child labor. When these child labor issues were made public, the clothing line was plagued by stinging press reviews, causing sales of the line and collateral lines of clothing to plunge.

In this situation, the manufacturer's cash flows would be significantly reduced, not just by sales attrition, but also by the funds expended for public relations damage control. The effects of these types of cash flow reductions could spiral through the organization, reducing the cash flow the organization has to embark on new ventures. If the organization had adopted an ERM approach, it would have incorporated the risks associated with the offshore site's use of child labor into its cost/benefit analysis of the venture.

ERM provides a systematic framework that allows organizations to deploy capital through organization-wide decision making, which ultimately results in stable earnings projections to fund future projects. If an organization focuses solely on risk avoidance or risk transfer, opportunities to use ERM to optimize economic efficiency through acquisition, mergers, exploring new product lines, or other avenues may be missed.

Improved Ability to Meet Strategic Goals

ERM provides for organization-wide involvement in the strategic formulation and decision-making process. This process examines factors in the internal and external environments to identify risks that would impede growth and achievement of established goals.

Factors considered when establishing strategic goals include competitors, the availability of substitute products, customers, and the supply chain. These considerations are especially important in today's increasingly global community, where a disruption in one system can cause widespread disruption to other organizations.

Consider the importance of supply acquisition. Organizations closely manage their vendor relationships to ensure a steady and inexpensive supply of raw materials or goods. However, they increasingly rely on single-source vendors and vendors located abroad. Lean supply chains can drive down prices. However, supply-chain disruption can cause economic chaos for organizations that depend on the supply chain's competitive advantages. What happens if the main supplier faces problems of its own, such as a raw materials or labor shortage; cash-flow problems; or, in the case of foreign providers, political instability? ERM can help the organization uncover potential risks related to vendor relationships and establish contingency plans within the decision-making process. When used effectively, ERM can minimize variation through thorough risk identification and assessment, thus improving the organization's ability to meet its strategic goals.

Increased Management Accountability

While the ERM process is represented at the highest level of an organization with the appointment of a Chief Risk Officer (CRO), those closest to a particular risk are in the best position to evaluate and manage it. Therefore, the ERM approach must be embedded in corporate culture. When this occurs, the board and senior executives establish the organization's overall mission, vision, and strategic goals, but each manager is responsible and accountable for decision making about risks within his or her individual unit. The responsible manager is often called a risk owner, someone who is responsible for managing risks from a specific risk center or operation. Distributed responsibility and accountability for risk at the risk center level are features that distinguish ERM from traditional risk management. They also have contributed to the failure of some ERM implementations in which local risk owners were not permitted or would not accept responsibility and accountability for risks within their purview.

Consider the example of Société Générale, a large European financial services organization. Recently, a low-level futures trader who was experienced in back-end operations cost the company $7.2 billion when fictitious trades he engineered spiraled out of control—the largest banking fraud in history. As a result, the entire European banking industry and its risk management systems were suddenly in jeopardy. If Société Générale had adopted an ERM approach, it might have avoided this fraud. ERM increases management accountability, leading to improved corporate practices and greater managerial understanding of and consensus regarding corporate strategy.

Improved Risk Communication

ERM allows organizations to develop systems that drive information throughout the organization, eliminating the barriers created by "information silos," a term used to describe a situation in which access to critical knowledge about risks, corporate strategies, and the organizational framework is limited to a number of key personnel.

ERM also encourages an organization to widely communicate its risk management approach across all of its layers. This includes making all managers aware of the need to identify obstacles that could interfere with achievement of the organization's strategic goals. As part of the ERM approach, the organization establishes a method to gather information organization-wide and develops a framework for analyzing and communicating that information.

Improved organization-wide communication results in fewer surprises for managers who could otherwise be caught without adequate information or full knowledge of the gravity of risk. This communication relies on all employees operating in accordance with the same corporate values. Value-driven ERM must be instituted using an ethical philosophy that is embedded in the organization, guiding and monitoring all decision makers' actions throughout the organization.

Strong communication can also result in greater management consensus and improved acceptance by both internal and external stakeholders.

Management Consensus

ERM improves management consensus by creating a corporate culture that embraces risk as an additional component of each decision. By empowering all managers to consider risk optimization and the cost of risk, ERM provides them with complete information about the potential effects of a decision, including its downsides and upsides. Managers who can successfully gauge threats and opportunities act with confidence because they can appropriately evaluate the alternatives associated with any course of action. This builds a sense of management by consensus, as opposed to the traditional hierarchal model of management, in which a series of decisions is driven from the top down.

ERM most effectively improves management consensus if it has been integrated throughout the organization. For this to occur, upper management must lead the initiative and motivate all employees to embrace ERM. The organization also must include in its overall performance evaluation indicators of the quality of its risk management. These indicators include documentation of risk optimization activities as well contributions to the organization's total cost of risk. Such action encourages risk ownership through all levels of the organization.

Stakeholder Acceptance

An organization that has effectively incorporated ERM is also better able to gain the acceptance of both internal and external stakeholders.

ERM improves acceptance by internal stakeholders by building a spirit of cooperation among management, which subsequently instills confidence among all employees. Increasing the spirit of cooperation among management begins with managers' understanding that the way they manage risk will have a positive impact on the organization, which, in turn, will benefit them personally. Projecting the reduced cost of risk to the organization through ERM ensures that all managers are held to the same standards. As an organization begins working toward a unified view of risk and rewards, ERM becomes the vital link that guides the organization toward economic efficiency.

A strong ERM program also encourages the buy-in of an organization's external stakeholders by establishing management strategies that protect the organization's reputation and assets. Reputation management is critical in today's world of instant communication. Experts estimate that an organization's intangible, reputation-related assets may be worth several times more than its tangible assets. Therefore, an ERM approach encourages managers to take stock of more than dollars and cents and begin to benchmark behavioral metrics.

When crises occur, they tend to develop quickly. Therefore, organizations must have a crisis management approach in place to deal with adverse events, whether they are caused by natural forces or human error. Pre-event reputation-related risk exposures may be complex. Because the threat to an organization's reputation can come from diverse areas, organizations increasingly are outsourcing aspects of crisis management to public relations teams that help coordinate post-event communications. Protecting the organization's reputation and dealing effectively with crisis management are critical in maintaining the confidence of external stakeholders.

No risk management plan, however, is foolproof. An organization always will face some level of risk and must therefore evaluate the amount of risk it is willing to embrace. A key aspect of ERM is the conscious decision to accept or manage risk.

RM Versus ERM

Category	RM	ERM
Operational risk	Yes	Yes
Financial risk	No	Yes
Strategic risk	Limited to operational strategies	Yes
Strategic integration	Operational only or none—technical risk management	Enterprise-wide
Performance metrics	Activities and results	Metrics appropriate to the eventuality and risk
Organizational penetration	Limited integration: risk handled in silos; operational responsibilities delegated to departments or retained by risk manager	Systemic integration: risk owners at every level; job descriptions; all risks belong to all, not segregated in any one silo
Outcomes	Minimize; mitigate; eliminate risk	Optimize risk

MAJOR RISK MANAGEMENT FRAMEWORKS AND STANDARDS

Some standards, such as ERM standards, are not compulsory or certifiable. Still, compliance with these standards demonstrates that an organization is following best practices. When an organization applies ERM frameworks and standards, it also can more effectively implement ERM and prepare for aspects of ERM that may become compulsory.

The risk management processes organizations apply have received increasing regulatory and private scrutiny because risk drives growth and opportunity as well as the potential downside of loss. ERM frameworks and standards provide an organization with approaches for identifying, analyzing, responding to, and monitoring risks (threats and opportunities) within the internal and external contexts in which it operates. Compliance with the assumed best practices represented by the frameworks and standards demonstrates that an organization is properly managing risk.

How an organization applies external frameworks and standards depends on its nature. Some risk management frameworks and standards (ISO 31000:2009, BS 31100, COSO II, AS/NZS 4360, and FERMA) are not compulsory unless a client or customer contractually requires them. They are, however, regarded as best practices for risk management implementation.

Other frameworks and standards are required. For example, U.S. public companies subject to securities laws and related matters must comply with the Sarbanes-Oxley Act of 2002 (SOX). Similarly, European banks are subject to Basel II, while European insurance companies are subject to Solvency II.

ISO 31000:2009

ISO 31000:2009 is a 2009 publication issued by the International Organization for Standardization, a body that establishes international standards in many areas of business. It includes guidelines and principles for implementing risk management and is supported by a glossary and documents that describe implementation methods.

ISO 31000:2009 provides an international standard for risk management as well as a generic approach to risk management applicable within any industry sector. It focuses on commonly accepted principles, such as meeting goals and the importance of risk communication. Overall, the standard emphasizes that risk management is integral to an organization's structures, strategies, and goals.

ISO 31000:2009 consists of three major parts: principles, a framework, and processes for managing risks.

> **ISO 31000:2009 Summary**
>
> ISO 31000:2009 consists of three major parts: principles, framework, and processes for managing risks. Principles are rooted in risk management and are designed to generate value and continuously scan and react to the environment. The framework consists of elements based on program design, implementation, and monitoring. The processes necessary for risk management emphasize deliberative communication, context, risk evaluation and treatment, and follow-up.

ISO 31000:2009 is a generic guidance document that must be supplemented with terminology, requirements, guidelines, and tools specific for an industry and/or a country. ISO/IEC Guide 73:2002 provides such terminology. The IPPC directive addresses environmental issues, while ISO 14001 covers information technology. Although ISO 31000:2009 is not certifiable, some of the other ISO standards are, such as ISO 14001.

BS 31100

In 2008, anticipating ISO 31000:2009, the British Standards Institution (BSI) published British Standard (BS) 31100 as a code of practice for risk management. The code establishes principles and terminology for risk management and provides recommendations for the model, framework, process, and implementation of risk management.

BS 31100 is intended to be a scalable standard that can be used by individuals responsible for risk management activity in organizations of all sectors and sizes as a basis for understanding, developing, implementing, and maintaining proportionate risk management. Application of the standards depends on the organization's context and complexity. The standard has four primary goals:

- Ensuring that an organization achieves its goals
- Ensuring that risks are managed in specific areas or activities
- Overseeing risk management in an organization
- Providing "reasonable assurance" on an organization's risk management

COSO II

The Committee of Sponsoring Organizations of the Treadway Commission (COSO) published the COSO Enterprise Risk Management—Integrated Framework (known as COSO II or COSO ERM) in 2004. COSO II defines ERM as a process driven from an organization's board of directors that establishes an organization-wide strategy to manage risk within its risk appetite.

COSO II provides an effective mechanism for initiating a dialogue with an organization's board and its senior executives about establishing ERM goals as part of the strategic management process. It does not delve into the details of risk management approaches and processes. Rather, it focuses on threats to the organization and application of controls. Therefore, COSO II's intended audience is an organization large enough to require examination of risk appetite and board direction of ERM strategies.

AS/NZS 4360

Risk Management, a joint Australian/New Zealand Standard for ERM known as AS/NZS 4360, was published in 2004 as a generic framework for managing risk. AS/NZS 4360 is designed for directors, elected officials, chief executive officers, senior executives, line managers, and staff across a wide range of organizations:

- Public sector entities at national, regional, and local levels
- Commercial enterprises, including companies, joint ventures, firms, and franchises
- Partnerships and sole practices
- Nongovernment organizations
- Voluntary organizations such as charities, social groups, and sports clubs

This variety of organizations requires an adaptable risk management approach that is easy to understand and implement. Therefore, AS/NZS 4360 is intended to provide only a broad overview of risk management. Organizations are expected to interpret this guide in the context of their own environments and to develop their own specific ERM approaches.

AS/NZS 4360 builds consultation and communication into the ERM process and includes the entire organization in a collaborative environment. It thoroughly describes process steps with examples to facilitate implementation. It is accompanied by two documents that aid in its implementation:

- HB 436-2004—Risk Management Guidelines, Companion Guide AS/ NZS 4360 helps implement the standard in an organization.
- HB 158-2006—Delivering Assurance, based on AS/NZS 4360 Risk Management, was developed jointly by risk managers and auditors to help auditors fulfill their obligation to audit risk management according to the standard.

COSO II Summary

Intended Audience	Organization of sufficient size to examine risk appetite at the board level
Concepts	ERM is: • A process, which is ongoing • Effected by people at all levels of an organization • Applied in strategy setting • Applied across the organization at every level and unit • Designed to identify potential events that will affect the organization within its risk appetite • Able to provide reasonable assurance to the organization's board of directors • Geared to the achievement of objectives in overlapping categories
Components	ERM has components integrated with the management process: • Internal environment • Objective setting • Event identification • Risk assessment • Risk response • Control activities • Information and communication • Monitoring
Objectives	ERM is geared to achieve these types of objectives: • Strategic—high-level goals, aligned with and supporting the organization's mission • Operations—effective and efficient use of resources • Reporting—reliability of operational and financial reporting • Compliance—compliance with applicable laws and regulations

Source: Committee of Sponsoring Organizations of the Treadway Commission.

The Standards Australia/Standards New Zealand Joint Technical Committee on Risk Management has approved the adoption of ISO 31000:2009 as AS/NZS/ISO 31000:2009 and the transition from AS/NZS 4360 when it becomes available. The only difference between the two documents is that the introductory section of AS/NZS/ISO 31000:2009 discusses the transition from 4360 to 31000.

Singapore, Austria, and Canada have their own frameworks, which liberally incorporate concepts and steps from existing frameworks. Other countries, states, or provinces are likely to adopt ERM over time. Individual jurisdictions will implement a modified version of an existing framework or closely imitate another country's framework. In France, for example, a noncompulsory implementation guide was to be published by Association Francaise de Normalisation (AFNOR), ISO's French affiliate, before the end of 2009.

FERMA

The Federation of European Risk Management Associations (FERMA) consists of national risk management associations, individual risk managers from Central European countries, and representatives from health organizations, educational sectors, and public sectors. FERMA adopted the Risk Management Standard, which was published in the United Kingdom in 2002. The standard has several elements:

- The establishment of consistent terminology
- A process by which risk management can be executed
- An organized risk management structure
- Risk management goals

The standard, which is intended for public and private organizations, recognizes that risk has both an upside and a downside. Its components allow organizations to report compliance with best practices.

Basel II and Solvency II

Basel II was issued by the Basel Committee on Banking Supervision[2] in 2004 to provide recommendations on banking laws and regulations. It established an international standard that banking regulators can use when creating regulations regarding the amount of capital banks need to keep in reserve to guard against the financial and operational risks they face. This standard is intended to protect the international financial system from problems that might arise if a major bank or a series of banks were to collapse.

Basel II establishes risk and capital management rules designed to ensure that a bank holds capital reserves appropriate to the risk the bank assumes through its lending and investment practices. The greater the volatility of the bank's portfolio, the greater the amount of capital the bank needs to hold to safeguard its solvency.

Solvency II, developed by the European Commission in 2007 (sometimes referred to as "Basel II for insurers"), consists of regulatory requirements for insurance firms that operate in the European Union. It facilitated the development of a single market in insurance services in Europe while providing adequate consumer protection.

Basel II and Solvency II Summary

	Basel II	Solvency II
Intended Audience	Banks in the international market	Insurance companies in the European Union
Purpose	Basel II rules endeavor to: • Ensure that capital allocation is more risk sensitive • Separate operational risk from credit risk, and quantifying both • Align economic and regulatory capital more closely to reduce the scope for regulatory arbitrage	Solvency II rules endeavor to: • Reduce the losses suffered by policyholders in the event that a firm is unable to meet all claims fully • Provide supervisors early warning so that they can intervene promptly if capital falls below the required level; and • Promote confidence in the financial stability of the insurance sector
Concepts	Basel II uses a "three pillars" concept: 1. Maintenance of minimum capital requirements based on credit risk, operational risk, and market risk 2. Supervisory review by regulators for the first pillar 3. Greater stability in the financial system through increased disclosures by banks	Solvency II uses a "three pillars" concept: 1. Quantitative requirements such as the minimum amount of capital an insurer should hold 2. Governance and risk management of insurers, as well as supervision of insurers 3. Disclosure and transparency requirements
	Source: Basel Committee on Banking Supervision	Source: European Commission

Sub-Frameworks

There are other frameworks that are not considered to be ERM frameworks but that provide specific industries and sectors with guidance. These sub-frameworks are likely to proliferate as governments and regulators grapple with systemic risk issues that could affect whole economies or specific sectors. Such sub-frameworks include these:

- Directive IPPC 96/61/CE, dated September 24, 1996 (Integrated Pollution Prevention and Control)—Imposes on all member countries of the European Union a common integrated approach to assessing the environmental impact of highly polluting industries

- ISO 14001:2004 (Environmental Management Systems Requirements with Guidance for Use)—Proposes a method to include environmental management within the overall management processes of an organization

- OSHAS 18001 (Occupational Health and Safety Assessment Series)—Proposes a certification and evaluation process for an organizational health and safety program compatible with other international management systems (including environment and quality)

- EN ISO 17776:2000 (Petroleum and Gas Industries—Offshore Production Installations)—Provides guidelines on tools and techniques for hazard identification and risk assessment

- ISO 17666:2003 (Space Systems Risk Management)—Proposes an integrated approach to managing risks associated with space projects and compatible with best practices for managing such projects

- ISO 14971:2007 (Medical Devices—Application of Risk Management to Medical Devices)—Became EN ISO 14971:2009 when the European Centre for Normalization opted to make it a European standard for the managing of risk throughout the life cycle of medical devices

- ISO/EIC 27000 (Information Technology—Security Techniques—Information Security Management Systems—Overview and Vocabulary)—New information security standard published jointly by the ISO and the International Electrotechnical Commission

SUMMARY

ERM improves an organization's strategic decision making by addressing risks essential to the organization's existence. Threats and opportunities are addressed in a process that integrates ERM with the strategic planning process. To integrate ERM, an organization's board and executives can follow this process:

1. Develop ERM goals (establish the internal and external contexts)
2. Identify risks (risk assessment)
3. Analyze, evaluate, and prioritize critical risks (risk assessment)
4. Treat critical risks, considering priority (risk treatment)
5. Monitor critical risks (monitor and review)

Emerging legal and regulatory issues related to ERM can be addressed at a high level of planning; however, compliance with standards should not be considered a substitute for an ERM policy.

Traditional risk management usually considers only operational risks that can affect an organization. ERM identifies the existence of hazard, operational, financial, strategic, and other risks such as risk to reputation; develops an understanding of their interrelationships; and then estimates variation over time to determine the potential effect on the enterprise. ERM seeks to optimize a risk management strategy that is integrated into the entire organization.

ERM is a systemic approach to managing all of an organization's key business risks and opportunities in order to optimize shareholder value. In using an ERM approach to manage business uncertainties, organizations can enhance their decision making and improve communications.

ERM frameworks and standards establish best practices that demonstrate that an organization is properly managing risk and can fulfill risk management-related contractual obligations. Public companies that are subject to the securities laws apply particular frameworks and standards. Other frameworks and standards are not mandated unless a client or customer establishes the standards as a requirement in a contract, but are recognized as best practices for the implementation of risk management.

CHAPTER NOTES

1. International Organization for Standardization, *Editing Committee Draft, Pre-ISO/FDIS 31000* (Geneva, Switzerland: International Organization for Standardization, 2008).
2. The Basel Committee on Banking Supervision is an institution created by the central bank governors of the Group of Ten (G10) nations (Belgium, Canada, France, Italy, Japan, the Netherlands, the United Kingdom, the United States, Germany, and Sweden).

Establish Internal and External Contexts: Risk Culture and Attitude, Goals, and Sustainable Development

Educational Objectives

After learning the content of this chapter and completing the corresponding course guide assignment, you should be able to:

▶ Explain how an organization's attitude toward risk is influenced by organizational culture.

▶ Describe the need and the methods for aligning individual objectives and organizational strategic goals.

▶ Explain how an organization's risk attitudes influence its departmental objectives.

▶ Describe sustainable development.

Outline

The Influence of Organizational Culture on Risk Attitude

Align Individual Objectives and Organizational Strategic Goals

Risk Attitudes and Departmental Objectives

Sustainable Development

Summary

Establish Internal and External Contexts: Risk Culture and Attitude, Goals, and Sustainable Development

CHAPTER 2

Chapters 2, 3, and 4 examine the first step in the enterprise-wide risk management (ERM) process as depicted in the ERM process diagram on page 1.5:

1. Establish the internal and external contexts

2. Risk assessment—identification, analysis, and evaluation

3. Risk treatment—selecting and implementing appropriate risk management techniques

4. Monitor results and revise

5. Communicate and consult with all internal and external stakeholders

These steps are specific to ERM and may differ from other processes and related steps (including traditional risk management) discussed in this work. Chapter 2 continues the discussion of the relationship between external and internal contexts and applies it to organizational culture. Organizational culture influences an organization's attitude toward risk. Having goals that are consistent with each other and with the organization's mission and vision is essential for an organization to be successful. Organizational success also depends on the presence of a risk attitude that is balanced between aggressive and conservative to achieve sustainable development.

THE INFLUENCE OF ORGANIZATIONAL CULTURE ON RISK ATTITUDE

An organization's culture is a reflection of the organization's staff. Culture defines the organization, enables its success, and helps to provide for its future.

An organization is defined by the shared beliefs, values, and accepted behaviors of its staff members. Organizational culture is expressed both internally and externally, including through the treatment of employees, customers, and partners; the manner in which information flows throughout the organization and is communicated to stakeholders; the quality of decision-making processes; new product development; and the management of risk.

An organization's attitude toward risk is influenced by organizational culture, and vice versa, in an ongoing interrelationship. For example, to achieve innovation-related **goals**, an organization must have a culture that encourages risk taking. This means that it must not only focus on being able to respond to future stakeholder needs but also have a culture that facilitates the risk taking

Goal
A high-level organizational aspiration usually associated with strategy.

required to innovate—a risk-seeking culture. A culture that supports risk taking in turn influences risk management by integrating the awareness of a risk culture into the overall risk management plan.

These are the essential elements of the influence of organizational culture:

- Purpose of organizational culture
- Cultural drivers of risk taking and risk innovation
- Too much versus too little risk

Purpose of Organizational Culture

An organization's culture reflects the personality or the norms and attitudes of the organization. A corporate hierarchy or government bureaucracy does not create or change organizational culture. Rather, the members of an organization—its employees—create, sustain, and modify its culture. A fully developed organizational culture creates a sense of shared meaning and shared experiences throughout the organization that helps guide decision making.

An organization's culture cannot be prescribed in a written document. It is developed and nurtured within the organization and embedded on a subconscious level. Organizational culture is the sum of the organization's experiences both past and present, its business philosophy, and its values. It reflects the organization's written and unwritten rules, its formal code of conduct, and the actual code of conduct as exhibited in daily decisions and behaviors. In essence, organizational culture is the glue that binds the organization as a cohesive unit.

ERM integrates an organization's risk strategies across departments, business units, and processes. While the chief risk officer functions as a coach for supporting and enabling those individuals throughout the organization who have responsibility for managing the organization's risks, everyone within the organization is obligated to assist the chief risk officer in effectively identifying, quantifying, and addressing the risks within their respective areas. This requires ERM competencies to be embedded in the organizational culture.

Underlying Bases of Organizational Culture

Beliefs, values, and behaviors are the bases of organizational culture. Beliefs are the practices and concepts that employees in the organization accept as true. Assumptions are formed from these beliefs that ultimately drive behavior. Types of corporate cultures (as shown in the "Types of Corporate Cultures" exhibit) can vary based on a number of factors. Government institutions and bureaucracies often have distinct cultures, and one agency may have a completely different culture from another. These differences are attributable to a combination of leadership, personnel, policy, legislation, politics, and the nature of the agency's mission.

Types of Corporate Cultures

An organization's corporate culture can vary based on the beliefs, values, and behaviors that are considered norms. Norms can vary based on factors including geographic location, political environment, level of uncertainty avoidance, and societal characteristics. A risk manager should understand different types of business cultures in order to successfully navigate through them.

Type of Culture	Characteristics
Adaptive	Culture in which the core value is the ability to adapt and change, particularly in reaction to dynamic external conditions
Inert	"Dead" or static culture that is unable or unwilling to change
Networked	Culture characterized by social networks of small, creative teams that might not have long-term loyalty to the organization
Mercenary	Culture in which ruthless business operations are dedicated to work and winning, but in which cultural sociability is low
Fragmented	Culture characterized by loose alliances of independent employees (for example, attorneys or a physicians' group practice) and in which both sociability and loyalty are low
Communal	Culture embodied in organizations that have both high loyalty and sociability and that often self-identify as a "family" of workers

Adapted, in part, from Richard Bowett, "Organisation: Building a Positive Corporate Culture," tutor2u.net/business/organisation/culture_more.htm (accessed May 15, 2009).

Values within the organization are exhibited in two ways: through the goals of the organization that are based on its values and through the manner in which the organization pursues those goals.

Behavior is determined by organizational values. The organization's employees establish and expect all staff to exhibit a certain norm or standard of behavior based on values and assumptions. Organizations must challenge themselves to push beyond accepted norms related to risk and determine whether there are assumptions regarding risk that should be modified.

Culture and Management Functions

Many layers of culture may exist within an organization. For example, an organization may have a home office culture influenced by senior leadership or a departmental culture that expresses the uniqueness of a specific business unit in contrast to the organization. Additionally, many subcultures may exist within an organization, or cultural units may exist based on department, profession, job function, geographic location, and so forth. One way of examining organizational culture is based on the management function (planning, organizing, leading, controlling, or allocating) applicable to an issue or action.

Often, these management functions and the roles attached to them can shape levels of risk appetite:

Objective
A tactical or operational-level aspiration.

- Planning—Managers throughout all layers across the organization are encouraged to participate in **objective** setting in relationship to the organization's strategic goals. The chief risk officer reaches out across the enterprise to all aspects of the organization. He or she engages all key participants to assist in creating and revising the organization's risk management goals.

- Organizing—Management and the chief risk officer establish the risk management process throughout the organization by effective allocation of resources, proper determination of the risk activities, and identification of those roles responsible for managing the activity. The activities flow in a logical manner with accountability.

- Leading—The chief risk officer assumes a managerial role within his or her own department by managing its functions and daily operations. The chief risk officer assumes a leadership role within the organization by communicating the risk management process comprehensively and frequently to all whose cooperation is needed for successful ERM.

- Controlling—The chief risk officer monitors and evaluates the timeliness and effectiveness of the organization's risk management activities and communicates this information to the appropriate stakeholders.

- Allocating—Management allocates scarce resources to optimize organizational performance and risk taking in accordance with the organization's specific strategies.

The risk management function is normally on the staff level. The chief risk officer does not have production duties but advises those who do. He or she is responsible for training and assisting others in the technical risk transfer and risk optimization functions and also for the risk identification, quantification, management programs, and plans used by all managers throughout the organization. These responsibilities are fulfilled using solid technical and leadership skills in planning, leading, organizing, controlling, and allocating. When ERM concepts engage an organization's culture and become part of it, the probability of the success of the risk management process increases significantly.

Patterns of Values and Behaviors

As an organization continually reinforces its desired values and behaviors, those values and behaviors become embedded within it. Senior executives are responsible for fully articulating and supporting the values of the organization, which then establish patterns for employee behavior. A sustained focus on values informs behavior by explaining why and how decisions are made and activities are performed. One way such focus can be sustained is through a comprehensive internal communications plan.

Once a risk professional has identified the organizational culture and cultural units (for example, a culture that varies by specific departments), he or she should review the values and behaviors of each unit related to the risk management process. The values reflect patterns that support acceptable organizational outcomes.

For instance, a pharmaceutical company's research and development (R&D) department may have as a value or goal, "We will engage in constant and continual innovation for the benefit of our patients." Behavioral patterns form from the cultural values that support pursuit of the organization's outcomes, such as an R&D department manager's support of a collaborative environment in which trial-and-error decision making is acceptable as long as lessons are learned from the errors. Alternatively, the United States Department of Homeland Security's strategic plan has as its mission, "One Team, One Mission, Securing our Homeland" which also supports a collaborative effort within the entire agency but within a single strategic goal of security for the country.

As part of the chief risk officer's review of values and behaviors, he or she can ask questions such as, "What is the unit's risk tolerance level?," "Has the unit defined its parameters of acceptable risk?," "Does the unit adequately identify, assess, and evaluate risks?," and "Are the values and behaviors related to the risk management process of each cultural unit in sync with the organization's?" By understanding the patterns of risk values and behaviors throughout the organization, the chief risk officer can take the actions necessary to implement a successful organizational risk management process.

Evidence and Support of Culture

The cultural support for ERM is evidenced by the risk behaviors that the organization and its business units exhibit. These can range from ad hoc behaviors, in which the risk management process is used for singular risk events as they occur (such as changes to labor laws), to fully assimilated behaviors, in which senior management embraces, directs, and leads the risk management process through ownership and accountability.

To be effective, assimilation of ERM into the organizational culture must be a gradual process. The process must be implemented through an integrated, cooperative mode of communication, education, training, coaching, and feedback. The organization must be encouraged to repeatedly use the ERM system in order to achieve desired outcomes. Once management has become skilled at using the process and experiences its benefits—such as being able to control and direct risk decision making in alignment with organizational goals—assimilation of ERM into the organization's culture has begun.

Challenges With Organizational Culture

When implementing an ERM process throughout an organization, a risk professional may face numerous culture-related challenges. An organization's culture is developed over time and, therefore, may not respond immediately to ERM practices. Some cultures are risk averse and value transferring or avoiding as much exposure to risk as possible (notwithstanding the costs involved). This risk-averse mindset consequently poses limitations on budgeting, marketing, and product development. Other organizations consider themselves leading innovators and have a culture in which a heightened risk appetite or risk-seeking bias is acceptable. Regardless of whether the culture is risk seeking or risk avoiding, a critical goal of ERM is to optimize risk in relation to strategic goals and within the risk-taking nature and ability of the organization.

In times of change, the chief risk officer can assist the organization by using risk management practices appropriate to the new circumstances. For example, in times of organizational change (whether driven by, for example, the economy, marketing strategies, or restructuring), ERM can help by, for instance, using a holistic internal communications plan to accelerate the organization's capability to adopt new values and behavior patterns.

Changes to organizational culture can stall when the change effort encounters an attitude of "This is the way we've always done things around here." When this attitude is embedded in an organization or a work unit, the chief risk officer faces adversity even if he or she has the support of senior management. The new behaviors required to support a risk management culture must become shared values and accepted patterns of typical behavior—the norms. Without newly established norms, the post-implementation part of the risk management process will begin to degrade as senior management turns its attention to other projects, incorrectly believing that the ERM process is complete.

As shown in the "Risk Attitude Continuum" exhibit, an organization's approach to risk can be viewed along a dynamic continuum. Based on an organization's risk attitude (which may be characterized as avoiding or seeking, or could fall somewhere in between those extremes), risk optimizing may fall anywhere on the continuum. Risk optimization's position on an organization's risk attitude continuum shifts as the organization's risk portfolio changes or evolves. Additionally, the size of each zone within an organization's continuum depends on the organization's attributes. For example, the risk attitude of a financial services company specializing in derivatives might fall closer to the right side's risk-seeking extreme than a savings institution's risk attitude, which might fall closer to the left side's risk-avoiding extreme.

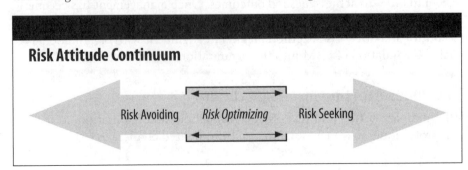

Risk Attitude Continuum

Risk Avoiding   *Risk Optimizing*   Risk Seeking

Cultural Drivers of Risk Taking and Risk Innovation

The typical drivers of an organization's risk culture are connected to its risk appetite. For example, a company can be a risk-seeking organization, such as a venture capital firm or a biotech company, or a risk-averse organization, such as a utility or a government agency that distributes entitlement benefits and services.

Organizations today are operating during a time of accelerated business, environmental, and technological development. For example, the accelerating rate of technology is apparent given the length of time required to produce and market these technologies to a global audience of at least 50 million people:

- Radio: 38 years
- Television: 13 years
- Internet: 4 years
- iPod: 3 years
- Facebook: 2 years

Given the accelerating rate of change, organizations should consider not only the consequence of the opportunities and threats already apparent to them in today's marketplace, but also the consequence of risk that is unknown or emerging. What might those opportunities and threats be, and how much time will organizations have to react to them?

A culture of innovation is essential for many organizations' survival, not to mention their ability to succeed. The pressure to innovate and to be risk seeking can be a driver of risk culture. Many of today's organizations must be future focused to remain competitive. They must allocate resources to the development of new products and new services and develop new uses for existing products. These future-focused activities must be completed in increasingly short time spans, requiring an organizational culture that embraces risk at an appropriate level and the innovation that can lead to success.

In looking to the future, a degree of uncertainty must always be considered. Risk professionals must examine both the threats and opportunities inherent in uncertainty. Threats constitute downside risks and are defined as a chance of harm or loss. Uncertainty also presents opportunities, such as the chance for a pharmaceutical company to introduce a blockbuster drug developed as a consequence of a costly research and development process.

To develop behavioral patterns that lead to innovation, an organization must have a culture that encourages appropriate and informed risk taking.

Innovation: Internal Versus External Drivers

An organization's ability to innovate is influenced by both internal and external drivers. Internal drivers are the conditions and forces within the organization that influence the culture. These are examples of internal drivers:

Risk attitude

The manner in which an organization and its stakeholders collectively perceive, assess, and treat risk.

- Resource allocation—distribution of available resources to risk opportunities that are consistent with goals
- **Risk attitude**
- **Risk appetite**
- **Risk tolerance**
- Employee rewards—compensation for innovative behavior; failure is not punished, and lessons learned influence future decision making

External drivers are the conditions and forces that exist outside the organization that support or hinder innovation. These are examples of external drivers:

Risk appetite

The events or perils and levels of impact an organization intends to retain, treat, and monitor.

- Political—government regulation
- Social—labor availability on both a skills and a knowledge basis
- Economic—capital requirements and capital availability
- Technological—development and rate of change

Innovation: Positive Versus Negative Drivers

Risk tolerance

The level of residual risk that an organization and its stakeholders are willing to bear within a given strategic context.

Senior management's attitude toward innovation and the associated risks can create either positive or negative drivers that influence innovation and risk culture. These are examples of positive drivers:

- Future-focused direction and planning
- Willingness to reallocate resources that support yesterday's successful products and/or services in favor of future products and/or services
- Embrace of risk by increasing risk appetite and modifying risk tolerance
- Rewarding employees for taking risks; whether or not the result is successful, the lessons learned are beneficial
- An environment that supports teamwork and collaboration
- An open communication process

These are examples of negative drivers:

- Satisfaction with the status quo
- Attitude of complacency and lack of awareness of vulnerability to future changes
- Protecting current products and services
- Avoiding risks associated with innovation
- Maintaining current level of risk appetite and risk tolerance
- Rewarding employees only for being successful
- Creating silos within the work environment
- Limited communication processes

Innovation: Too Much Risk Versus Too Little Risk

One question that risk professionals and senior executives within an organization must ask themselves is, "What is the appropriate amount of risk that we should assume when undertaking innovation?" Too little risk taking hinders innovation, which can result in a poor economic outlook for the organization and perhaps even threaten its survival as a going concern. Too much risk taking can be just as crippling by chaotically expending the organization's resources only to receive minimal or no return.

An organization must achieve a balance (its optimized risk) between assuming too much risk and too little risk by engaging in risks that are consistent with the organization's culture and its stated goals while simultaneously practicing fiscal responsibility. Consideration of the level of risk assumed should include an estimate of the return that could be generated.

To optimize its risk, an organization should be diligent in its investigation of new or potential innovations. These investigations should thoroughly explore the upside and downside of the risks involved. For example, organizations should attempt to plan for "outlier" occurrences that have a high impact on the organization and its business practices but that are very difficult to predict, such as technological or scientific discoveries or events of significant historical magnitude, such as the fall of the Berlin Wall or the terrorist attacks of September 11, 2001. With the information obtained through this investigation, costs, timeframes, and the optimum or critical process path for delivery of the innovation can be determined.

Risk and innovation are intertwined. Innovation is nearly always accompanied by a degree of risk. Only by being willing to take risks can an organization innovate. To do this, it must have a culture that embraces risk, aligns risk with the organization's goals, and properly manages the process to optimize return.

ALIGN INDIVIDUAL OBJECTIVES AND ORGANIZATIONAL STRATEGIC GOALS

An organization's strategic goals should be consistent with each other and with its mission and vision. This consistency or "alignment" means objectives and goals should fold upward, building on each other into a type of hierarchy that helps fulfill the organization's vision, mission, purpose, and strategy.

The risk management function can be used to help align risk management goals across the organization, but only if it is perceived as creating value as opposed to as a hindrance. ERM requires that all staff in an organization take personal responsibility for, participate in, and endorse the concept of aligning risk management goals. The chief risk officer must coach executives to promote a culture of risk consciousness and line managers to consistently utilize ERM practices and concepts.

Risk professionals should consider various methods when aligning risk management goals across the organization:

- Executive direction versus operational realities
- Risk management as a value creation proposition versus a hindrance
- Drivers and motivators for all staff
- Energizing line managers' interest in risk management

Executive Direction Versus Operational Realities

An organization's board of directors or executive management establishes its direction by developing and endorsing a mission and vision, values statement, or statement of purpose. Also, the executive directors establish the organization's strategy by defining the types of products and services it will offer, its production or service methodology, target market, and the financial parameters of operation. They also set the organization's rules of conduct, including governance, compliance, and management of risks. These actions are all performed at a high organizational level as the senior executives develop an overview of the risk framework for the organization, including an overview of the strategic impact of risk.

An organization's executives and management typically establish direction using three levels of objectives and goals:

- Strategic goals—established at the board or executive level; broad-based and conceptual; give the organization direction
- Operational objectives—established at the staff management level; functional; cut across all departments
- Tactical objectives—established at the line management level; specific tasks; related to producing the organization's products and services

Executive direction should cascade down the organizational hierarchy through both staff and line areas to the front line, operational employees who are involved with providing an organization's actual productions and services. At each level, moving from strategic to tactical, the objectives and goals become more specific and detailed to appropriately address each level's scope of responsibility. This allows for the inclusion and/or adjustment of operational realities. An organization's leadership must convince those throughout the organization who "own" the risk why it is vital that they create value through ERM practices. For example, executive direction at the strategic level could include plans for the opportunities (as well as threats) presented to a manufacturer that considers purchasing a second manufacturing facility. How can all the functional areas within the manufacturing company contribute value to the organization by providing information from their disciplines (for example, human resources and sales) that leads to a better purchasing decision? Executives can drill down to the operational level to address issues related to multiple departments, managers might consider the current type of machinery used in the new production facility and its effect upon the product quality and production safety. At the tactical level, managers might examine whether the new plant's machinery needs to be upgraded and whether new workplace procedures should be put in place.

In this manner of aligning direction and planning, all departments' and all employees' objectives fold upward into fulfilling the organization's strategic mission and purpose, thus aligning all types of goals.

Executive Goals

The executive management team's goals are conceptual, broad-based, and define the acceptable level of risk tolerance and risk appetite within the organization. The executives' strategic goals set the direction for the operational and tactical objectives developed by the remainder of the organization. Executives allocate the resources necessary to fulfill objectives and goals at all levels.

Executives have responsibility for developing and achieving strategic goals because these goals are attained through the application of leadership skills rather than the performance of specific tactical tasks. For an organization to succeed, it is critical that its strategic goals are deployed and understood at each of its levels. Use of a detailed executive summary outlining the strategic plan accompanied by specific action items assists an organization's operational staff in understanding strategic goals.

Risk Management Role

An organization's chief risk officer acts as a motivator and coach for both executives and staff in an organization, illustrating to them the value of supporting an ERM program and the benefits that they can derive from it. The chief risk officer is also responsible for assisting the executives in setting goals that first consider all dimensions of risks and then consider the goals in conjunction with the organization's risk appetite. This review process helps executives establish, with the chief risk officer's assistance, appropriate risk management operational objectives for the organization. The chief risk officer occupies a staff management position; that is, he or she manages a specialized function that cuts across and affects all departments of the organization. The chief risk officer does not have front line responsibility for developing, producing, marketing, or servicing the organization's products and services. Instead, the chief risk officer serves in an advisory role to line managers, who are responsible for developing operational objectives.

When a risk professional assists line managers in setting risk management-related objectives, the daily operational realities faced by the line managers must be considered. The risk management objectives must be perceived by the line managers as being practical, realistic, and achievable. These perceptions are very important, as risk professionals are dependent on the organization's employees to use the risk management plan and is held accountable for any objections raised by line managers as they attempt to achieve their risk management objectives. For example, if a risk professional advises a line manager to maintain a risk register as part of daily operations, he or she must take responsibility for ensuring the line manager has the appropriate resources and tools available to maintain the register.

Line Manager's Role

A line manager has front-line responsibility and accountability for the products and services an organization offers to its customers. These responsibilities and accountabilities include such areas as new product development, production processes, and sales. The line manager has formal responsibility for how people and resources are utilized on a daily basis. For example, a line manager may need to redeploy workers from one project to another in order to meet a delivery deadline. The front line manager is responsible for ensuring that a risk is properly managed.

A line manager develops objectives targeted at the tactical level because he or she must carry out the specific tasks necessary to contribute to achievement of the organization's strategic goals. The chief risk officer has the responsibility of providing the guidance and leadership necessary to encourage the line managers to incorporate the risk management objectives into their department's tactics. This is why line managers are commonly called risk owners.

Risk Management as a Value Creation Proposition Versus a Hindrance

The risk management function can provide a platform for an organization's leadership to create value throughout the organization by reducing uncertainty. Additionally, risk management enables management and staff to accurately identify and assess the threats and opportunities that confront the organization. ERM allows executives to clearly understand risks and risk impacts, thus enabling them to accurately plan, determine proper resource allocation, protect capital, and ensure stakeholders' interests. An ERM perspective thus allows the line managers to contribute to organizational value as they efficiently execute the risk strategy and adapt their tactics and tasks to curb threats and enhance opportunities. The risk management function is then viewed as fulfilling a role that enhances the value of the organization rather than as presenting a hindrance.

As society and government demand greater governance and transparency, the degree of regulation imposed upon organizations continues to expand. Regulatory compliance thus has become extremely important to organizations as a risk that must be managed. When focusing his or her efforts on compliance, a risk professional can be perceived by the organization as operating in a defensive mode within a legal environment or being required to do things in a certain manner so the organization's practices remain "legal"—perhaps at the cost of producing a profitable product or service. In such instances, through ERM, the chief risk officer is responsible for enforcing controls and complying with audits.

The risk management function creates organizational value when it demonstrates the ability to reasonably predict future risk costs and trends, to offer focused information concerning both threats and opportunities, and to provide a balanced factoring of business risk (one that is neither too high nor too low). When an organization's risk management function is able to demonstrate these capabilities, ERM moves from a perception of hindrance to the reality of value creation, integrating management of risk into all levels of the organization's goals and objectives.

Drivers and Motivators for All Staff

Successful implementation of an ERM program requires that all staff in an organization take personal responsibility for, participate in, and endorse the concept. A risk professional must motivate executives to engage the organization in a cultural conversation about risk and, where appropriate, assign risk ownership and accountabilities. Next, the risk professional must motivate the managers and their staffs to embrace and consistently utilize ERM practices and concepts.

Motivating all staff members to practice ERM presents several challenges for the chief risk officer and the organization's leadership. For instance, in order for a manager to effectively motivate staff, he or she must increase the proportion of a staff member's actions that support the organization's risk management strategic goals and operational objectives (such as enrollment in a training program) and decrease the actions that detract from them (such as pressure to increase work hours in order to achieve an unrealistic production deadline). This requires removing internal and external conflicts wherever possible and establishing alignment between the organization's goals and the staff members' perceived organizational and personal needs.

The level that individual staff members occupy in an organization's structure may offer them a high level of motivational influence. For example, front line staff may be concerned about how their work will enable them to lead fuller personal lives through higher pay or more leisure time. Conversely, the executive staff may be more motivated by the organization's profitability, fulfillment of its basic mission, or ability to serve its stakeholders.

For a risk professional to successfully implement ERM within an organization, he or she should understand the various drivers and motivators (shown in the "Executive and Line Manager ERM Drivers" exhibit) for both the executives and the line managers within the organization. Such an understanding can enable a risk professional to enlist them as allies from a holistic, enterprise-wide perspective and generate value.

Executive and Line Manager ERM Drivers

Executives	Line Managers
Executives focus on strategic and broad-based risk control measures that increase operating efficiency, improve the quality of the organization's products and services, enhance employees' well-being, serve the general public, and define an efficient risk financing strategy that is aligned with the overall organization's finance strategy.	Line managers focus on specific, task-oriented risk control measures that allow them to perform their function effectively and efficiently. The risk control measures must be understandable and easily communicated to staff. The measures must also be perceived by staff as being realistic and achievable while meeting production or service and safety goals.
Proper identification of organizational risk • Accurate, timely, and reliable information and data • Balanced risk assessment for both threats and opportunities using appropriate risk criteria • Increased operating efficiencies • Enhanced governance	Fair allocation of risk management costs across the budget
Regulatory compliance	Safety and compliance procedures • Realistic for daily operations • Do not hinder the production and services process and delivery Provide incentives
Transparency	Risk data that are consistent and reliable
Quality improvements to and innovations of products and services • Profitability • Quality • Shareholder value • Stability	Realistic risk measurements
Employee and customer satisfaction	Pay increases and bonuses Clean and safe work environment

Energizing Line Managers' Interest in Risk Management

The potential for ERM to succeed within an organization is dependent upon the program being embraced and properly implemented by an organization's line managers. The degree to which and quality with which an organization's line managers implement ERM is directly related to their perception of both the positive and negative impacts of ERM on the daily operations of their units or departments.

In order to ensure the success of ERM within an organization, a risk professional must go beyond merely influencing a line manager to adopt ERM practices. Rather, the chief risk officer must energize the line manager to the extent that the line manager incorporates the organization's risk management goals into his or her tactical objectives. The line manager then becomes a "true believer" in the program—a true risk owner.

Risk professionals use various methods to energize line managers:

- They provide clear and focused communications of a shared risk management vision that includes specific goals.
- They mentor other employees to acquire the knowledge of the full risk impacts of activities, processes, and organizational relationships.
- They create an understanding of how a unit's activities contribute to risk management goals.
- They establish succinct, reliable, and credible measurements.
- They maintain needed information in a consistent, accurate, and accessible format.
- They provide the budget estimates required to support the necessary overall department activities and resources.
- They understand and apply the method used to fairly allocate risk management costs to the line manager's budget.
- They use ERM to facilitate process improvements that benefit, not hinder, daily operations.
- They create incentives and recognition for supporting ERM.

Risk professionals should understand that line managers whose responsibilities vary may be focused on achieving different risk management objectives. For ERM to succeed, risk professionals must include line managers in a collaborative planning process that provides a clear path toward a shared ERM vision that is fully aligned with the organization's goals.

RISK ATTITUDES AND DEPARTMENTAL OBJECTIVES

An organization's risk strategic goals should be aligned with its members' individual risk attitudes and each department's operational objectives. Executives and the board should strive to achieve a balance between risk-seeking and risk-avoiding (risk optimization) approaches in order for the organization to achieve its overall goals.

Every organization has an overall risk tolerance that reflects its readiness to bear both upside and downside risk after risk treatment. Individuals within an organization have their own risk tolerance levels based on their personal attitude toward risk. These personal risk attitudes directly affect departmental objectives through individual and group decisions. Similarly, every organization has an overall risk appetite. However, the risk attitudes and risk-taking abilities of individuals, departments, and the organization may not always be in alignment.

Risk decisions often are made and implemented by groups within an organization. The chief risk officer must work with these groups, champion a certain course of action, and manage a group's risk attitude dynamic to achieve the organization's objectives and goals.

Role of Risk Taking in an Organization

Managers must understand their organization's risk tolerance level, their own risk tolerance level, and the risk tolerance levels of any subordinates involved in activities that require risk-return evaluations and decisions.

The risk-return relationship is a critical component of an organization's strategic and financial decision making. In order for an organization's management to invest in projects that entail a higher degree of risk, it must be assured of higher returns. Conversely, an organization and its management should be satisfied with a lower rate of return on investments in projects that entail less risk.

Attitude Toward Risk

Attitude is intended to mean a way of thinking, of feeling. Attitude toward risk and perceptions of the environment directly influence risk behavior activities. For example, if a sharp decline in the stock market indices leads to a belief that a recession is imminent, many may not purchase stocks. However, a belief that the economy is robust and the indices' decline is an anomaly could lead one to believe that the decreased stock prices represent an ideal time to invest. Individual responses to risk can have a wide range of variations.

Because an organization consists of individuals, each of whom has a unique attitude toward or perception of risk, it encompasses a wide range of such attitudes or perceptions. Some of its individuals may voluntarily seek and assume new projects and initiatives. They view taking risks as a "great adventure." Others may prefer to continue to undertake the same, familiar activities. Such individuals do not enjoy venturing out of their "comfort zone."

An organization may include both types of individuals. The ideal risk attitude for a department depends on its function. For example, it is good for the research department to be creative, but not necessarily so for the accounting department.

There are three types of risk attitudes seen by risk professionals:

- Risk-seeking (risk-naive)
- Risk-avoiding (risk-obsessed)
- Risk-optimizing (risk-managed)

Risk-Seeking Attitude

Risk-seeking decision making tends to quickly seek a bottom-line explanation and to install an action plan/solution that anticipates positive results. Individuals with risk-seeking or risk-naive attitudes may underemphasize a risk's impacts, variances, and potential negative effects. They believe that the result of their risk decision will allow the organization to reap significant rewards worth the risk (both upside and downside) presented. They view risk-taking as an adventure that they actively seek.

Entrepreneurs, salespersons, product developers, and researchers, for example, often embody a risk-seeking attitude. However, individuals in an accounting department or those responsible for operating a nuclear power plant, for example, may not.

Risk-Avoiding Attitude

Individuals with risk-avoiding attitudes are at the opposite end of the risk continuum relative to those with risk-seeking attitudes. They overemphasize risk or are "obsessed" with risk—typically downside risk—and seek methods of transferring it to another entity to avoid it altogether. They prefer to continue traditional methods of business operations rather than innovate. For example, if the individuals producing the electric typewriter had maintained a risk-avoiding attitude, they would never have started manufacturing word processors, even as their business declined into bankruptcy.

Risk-Optimizing Attitude

A risk-optimizing or risk-managed attitude balances characteristics of both the risk-seeking and the risk-avoiding attitudes. Individuals with risk-optimizing attitudes assess risk strategically, based on an organization's vision, mission, goals, values, and beliefs. They weigh the risk-reward relationship while realistically evaluating potential outcomes and consequences and are selective regarding risks that they ask the organization to assume. Although risk attitudes and perceptions can vary, organizations should seek to employ executives and staff who are risk optimizers.

Turning Risk Management into a "Can-Do" Philosophy

Organizational decisions often are made by groups rather than by a single individual (a departmental task force or safety committee, for example). A risk professional must work with these groups and champion a course of action. When the group makes a decision, it must then implement it.

The various risk attitudes of a group of individuals form the group's risk attitude. Generally, a group's risk attitude shifts from conservative toward aggressive. One reason this shift occurs is that, as more information becomes available, uncertainties are better understood and assessed. Another reason is that stronger individuals who tend to be greater risk takers assume group leadership. Also, because a group makes a risk decision, no single individual is responsible for the outcome. This causes the group as a whole to act more aggressively.

To turn risk management into a "can-do" philosophy throughout an organization, the chief risk officer must manage the risk attitude shift within the group dynamic. The chief risk officer must encourage and guide the shifting of the group's risk attitude to one that is appropriate and balanced.

SUSTAINABLE DEVELOPMENT

Sustainable development directly affects an organization's ability to achieve its goals. Governments and societies influence elements of sustainable development.

By practicing sustainable development, an organization strikes a balance by using social, environmental, and economic elements to meet its current needs without compromising the ability of future generations to meet their needs.

One model of sustainable development first suggested by a leading researcher in the corporate responsibility movement, John Elkington, consists of three major, interrelated, and dependent elements:

- Social—the well-being of society
- Environmental—all natural resources utilized, altered, affected, or made into waste
- Economic—the production, distribution, and consumption of goods and services

These elements may also be referred to as social well-being, environmental protection, and economic growth, respectively. Each is driven by the needs and expectations of multiple stakeholders—groups who have vested interests in the organization's activities. Note that this model is not the definitive version of sustainable development; other models and possible elements also exist.

Sustainable Development Defined

Sustainable development is a balanced use of resources that fuels economic growth while fulfilling social needs. It protects the environment without compromising the ability of future generations to meet their needs and works to ensure that current decisions made and/or programs undertaken have positive consequences for future generations. By contrast, unsustainable development occurs when resources are consumed faster than they can be replaced.

When sustainable development's social well-being and economic growth elements are balanced, equitable financial distribution exists in the present. However, future negative environmental protection impacts could exist when the concern for the present overshadows potential negative consequences on the environment.

Similarly, a balance between the social well-being and environmental protection may come at the expense of economic growth. This scenario may prove to be unbearable for future generations.

In order to achieve a balance between economic growth and environmental protection, negative impacts may occur to social well-being. Certain products that society does not want to voluntarily purchase may be mandated, or jobs may be lost as plants close because the cost to refit for environmental protection is prohibitive.

These are three levels of sustainability:

- Not sustainable—Resources are consumed faster than they can be replenished.
- Steady state—Equilibrium exists, as resources are replenished at the same rate as they are consumed.
- Growth state—Resources are replenished at a greater rate than they are consumed.

To achieve and maintain a successful sustainable development program, an organization must link the program to its overall strategic planning. For example, an organization may need to resolve the differences among competing goals and stakeholders if some stakeholders do not wish to support sustainable development. An organization can attract stakeholders because of its sustainable development program or it could lose stakeholders, a downside to this approach.

Issues arise regarding sustainable development as to who determines society's current wellness needs; the rate of natural resource utilization that allows those resources to replenish; and the ideal amount, timing, and location of economic growth. Because each element consists of multiple variables and dependencies, implementing a corrective action could result in many unfore-seen consequences for future generations.

Challenges Posed by Sustainable Development

Over the past decades, the idea of sustainable development has grown to the point where it is now recognized by societies around the world. Today, most organizations, whether they are for-profit, not-for-profit, governments, or non-governmental organizations (NGOs), must examine how they are reacting to the concept of sustainable development and what they are doing to achieve it. For many organizations, sustainable development poses two major challenges. The first challenge is to go beyond the financial goals of the organization. The second is to reconsider who are their stakeholders.

Going Beyond the Prime Financial Goals of the Organization

A primary business goal of many organizations is to protect, preserve, and grow its capital base while providing investors with reasonable short- and long-term returns on investment. By reaching these goals, the organization achieves only part of its own sustainable development. Broader goals, including nonfinancial goals, are realized when an organization achieves its strategic plan economically and efficiently. In contrast, governmental organizations do not have profitability goals in the way that publicly held businesses do. Nevertheless, sustainability in this context considers the effective and efficient use of operating budgets and the relevancy of the mission of the institution to the current needs of its stakeholders and citizenry.

Only recently have organizations incorporated social well-being and environmental protection into their capital and investment goals. Organizations are recognizing that they do not exist in a vacuum, but are interrelated and dependent upon people, the environment, and governmental entities. Because of this dependency, it is in an organization's self interest to use both human and natural resources with care to ensure its continued availability.

Though all organizations can pursue sustainable development, the ability to make a difference in society as a whole varies by sector, organization size, and the manner in which it prioritizes its sustainable development goals. Organizations must seek the best balance between actions undertaken for their own financial self-interest and those undertaken for the good of society. Some organizations have undertaken major efforts at waste reduction in their production processes, which has resulted in both a significant cost savings and a positive return on investment (ROI).

However, an organization cannot obtain sustainable development alone. If its competitors do not undertake measures to provide for social well-being and protection of the environment, its products and/or services could be under-priced. As a result, the organization's market share could be reduced and the viability of the organization impaired.

Environmental concerns have resulted in stricter regulations. These can affect economic growth for some organizations if they require infrastructure enhancements or updates that draw down an organization's capital base and thus restrict economic growth.

Reconsidering Stakeholders

An organization's stakeholders are those that are directly or indirectly affected by its operations. Traditionally, stakeholders include shareholders, investors, customers, employees, and suppliers.

When an organization adopts the concept of sustainable development, the scope of stakeholders is widened to include all groups that have a vested interest in its operations. Included as stakeholders are regulators, as well as the community and/or communities where the organization operates, sells its products, and obtains its natural and human resources. This adds a higher level of accountability for the organization.

Each stakeholder group has its own needs and expectations. As their number increases, so will the conflicts among their differing needs and expectations. The community where the product is produced may expect the environment to be protected in a way that would require costly changes in the organization's infrastructure. To accomplish this, the product's purchase price might have to be increased against the expectation of the customers. While the employees as part of the community might favor protection of the environment, they might also fear a loss of jobs if customers purchase fewer products due to the increase in price.

Effectively balancing stakeholders' needs and expectations is a complex challenge for an organization. The fact that the needs of stakeholders are continually evolving adds to its complexity. Organizations pursuing sustainable development therefore need to continually monitor, balance, and adjust accordingly.

SUMMARY

The culture of an organization is defined by the shared values, beliefs, and accepted behaviors of its staff members. An organization expresses its culture in its daily internal operations and in its external interactions. To optimize organizational performance, organizations must be future focused and aware of the various drivers that influence innovation. Innovation does not come without risks, and each organization should find a risk balance that is consistent with its organizational goals.

Risk professionals should consider various methods when aligning risk management goals across the organization:

- Executive direction versus operational realities
- Risk management as a value creation proposition versus a hindrance

- Drivers and motivators for all staff
- Energizing line managers' interest in risk management

Risk professionals work together with executives and staff at the strategic, operational, and tactical levels to ensure that risk management objectives are integrated into organizational planning. The chief risk officer must motivate the organization's leadership to promote a risk-based culture and to motivate them to consistently utilize ERM practices and concepts.

Risk attitudes directly affect an organization's departmental objectives through individual/group risk making decisions. There are three types of risk attitudes:

- Risk-seeking
- Risk-avoiding
- Risk-optimizing

Organizational decisions often are made by groups rather than by a single individual (a departmental task force or safety committee, for example). To turn risk management into a "can-do philosophy" throughout an organization, the chief risk officer must act as a coach and manage the risk attitude shift within the group dynamic.

Sustainable development is a balance of social, environmental, and economic elements that meets current needs and expectations without compromising the ability of future generations to meet their needs. Organizational sustainable development emphasizes economic growth (among other nonfinancial benefits) but does so in a balanced manner while maintaining present and future stakeholders' social well-being and conducting operations for environmental preservation and protection.

CHAPTER NOTE

1. "Department of Homeland Security Strategic Plan," United States Department of Homeland Security, September 16, 2008, www.dhs.gov/xabout/strategicplan (accessed August 4, 2009).

Establish Internal and External Contexts: ERM and Strategic Planning

Outline

Strategic Development Process and Types of Business Strategies

Developing ERM Goals Aligned With Strategic Goals

A Risk Maturity Model

Analyzing an Organization's Internal and External Contexts

Conducting a SWOT Analysis

Summary

Educational Objectives

After learning the content of this chapter and completing the corresponding course guide assignment, you should be able to:

▶ Summarize the strategic development process and the types of business strategies organizations use.

▶ Summarize how an organization aligns its enterprise-wide risk management (ERM) goals with its strategic goals.

▶ Explain how a risk maturity model (RMM) can be used as an ERM performance scorecard.

▶ Summarize the process for analyzing an organization's internal and external contexts (in general and as applied to risk management).

▶ Given information about an organization's business strategies, conduct a SWOT analysis to evaluate its strategy.

Establish Internal and External Contexts: ERM and Strategic Planning

The roots of an organization's success lie in its business strategy. However, even the best plans can be undermined by unforeseen events. When an organization applies enterprise-wide risk management (ERM) to its strategic planning, it can use an understanding of the threats and opportunities present in its internal and external contexts to develop strategic goals that account for associated risks and optimize risk-taking.

STRATEGIC DEVELOPMENT PROCESS AND TYPES OF BUSINESS STRATEGIES

The concept of **strategic management** originated from the practical concepts armies used to win wars. Within the competitive business environment, strategic management evolved to encompass the actions that organizations take to achieve their long-term goals.

Strategic management provides direction, focus, and consistency of action throughout an organization, enabling it to fulfill its long-term goals. Through strategic management, all of an organization's activities are aligned.

Strategic management is the responsibility of an organization's senior-level executives, who lead the process of devising its **vision statement**, **mission statement**, and goals with oversight from the board of directors. Executives then use these elements to develop policies and allocate resources.

The strategic management process entails three interdependent stages:

- Strategy formation—creating the plan
- Strategy implementation—putting the plan into action
- Strategy evaluation—checking the results to determine whether the plan is working as envisioned

This discussion of strategy uses terms such as management, boards of directors, and other business terms. Words such as cabinet officers, leaders, governors, trustees, and others could be substituted in a government or not-for-profit environment. "Fulfillment of regulatory responsibility" or other such terms could also be used to replace "business plan" or "business strategy."

Strategic management
The coordination of interrelated activities of functional areas of a business to achieve an established purpose.

Vision statement
The aspirational description of what an organization will accomplish in the long-term future.

Mission statement
A broad expression of an entity's goals.

Strategy Formation

In the strategy formation stage, senior-level executives and the board develop strategies by following a three-step process.

First, they perform an internal analysis of the organization and an external analysis of competitors, current and prospective customers' needs, and the current and anticipated economy and government regulations. They commonly use the SWOT (strengths, weaknesses, opportunities, and threats) technique to perform this analysis.

SWOT Analysis Table

	Strengths	Weaknesses
Internal	List assets, competencies, or attributes that enhance competitiveness. Prioritize based on the quality of the strength and the relative importance of the strength.	List lacking assets, competencies, or attributes that diminish competitiveness. Prioritize based on the seriousness of the weakness and the relative importance of the weakness.
	Opportunities	**Threats**
External	List conditions that could be exploited to create a competitive advantage. Prioritize based on the potential of exploiting the opportunities.	List conditions that diminish competitive advantage. Prioritize based on the seriousness and probability of occurrence.
	Note strengths that can be paired with opportunities as areas of competitive advantage.	Note weaknesses that can be paired with threats as risks to be avoided.

In considering how receptive the market would be to its products and services and its competitive position within the market, an organization may categorize its opportunities as those that it "could," it "can," and it "should" exploit. With this approach, the framework for a high-level strategic plan begins to emerge.

Second, the executives develop long-term strategies commensurate with that framework, while considering the organization's vision and mission statements. They then assist the manager to develop short-term corporate objectives that are aligned with the strategies. These objectives address the organization's financial needs.

Strategic Plan Drafting and Refining

The development of an organization's strategic plan by senior management is important because it directs the activity of the organization for a year or multiple years. When drafting and redrafting a strategic plan, executives may include some or all of these analyses:

Suitability of the Plan

Analysis of the suitability of the strategic plan questions how it will work for the organization and in the current and future marketplace.	• Can the strategic plan be accomplished? Can the needed changes in processes, products, knowledge, and personnel be successfully implemented and managed? Will the entire organization support the strategy?
	• Is the strategy appropriate for the marketplace? Are there environmental factors that would render the strategy ineffective? Will the strategy create a product or service different from those of competitors so that customers will purchase the organization's products or services instead?

Feasibility of the Plan

Analysis of the feasibility of the strategic plan examines resource allocation, cost, and impact. Resources include personnel, knowledge, information, money, and time.	• Cash flow issues—What initial investment is needed? Is the cash available? If not, what will it cost to obtain it?
	• Break-even point—How much time will pass between the point of initial investment and when the product/service produces enough profit to recover the initial investment? Is it acceptable?
	• Net present value (NPV)—What is the NPV of the investment in projects proposed in the strategic plan, and is it acceptable? How do the NPVs of proposed projects compare, and do they indicate that some projects should be included while others are eliminated?
	• Resource allocation—What additional resources are needed? Can they be easily obtained from outside sources, or must they be internally developed? What is the time frame for becoming productive?

Acceptability of the Plan

The strategic plan should produce anticipated results or returns for the organization's stakeholders (shareholders, employees, and customers).	• Return—For shareholders, will the strategy result in an increase in stock prices? How will employees individually benefit from implementing the strategy (such as better pay, career advancement, enhanced job functions, increased knowledge base)? For customers, will the product/service be improved while it remains at an acceptable price?
	• Risk—What are the risks inherent in the strategies? What happens if the strategy does not work as well as planned or even fails? How much risk is the organization willing to take? What risks does it want to avoid? If the product or service proposed is more successful than anticipated, can the organization meet the increase in demand?
	• Reactions—How will each group of stakeholders react to the changes created by the strategy? What will be the impact of the reaction?

Third, the executives reach agreement on the actions needed to achieve the strategies. This agreement details the "who," "what," and "when" responsibilities for the selected actions.

Strategy Implementation

Strategy implementation, sometimes also called execution, is the process of making the strategies work. This stage is more difficult to complete and requires more time than the strategy formation phase. While senior executives are responsible for creating strategy, the entire organization is responsible for its implementation. Strategy implementation involves five steps, which are usually the responsibility of mid-level managers:

- Create a documented roadmap of the specific processes, tasks, and responsibilities necessary to disseminate the corporate strategies throughout the organization.
- Communicate information regarding the strategies clearly, frequently, and completely throughout the organization.
- Assign specific responsibilities, tasks, authority, and accountability throughout the organization.
- Allocate adequate resources for successful implementation. Resources include finances, staff, training, time, equipment, data, and technology.
- Manage variances between the goals and the mid-year results, and make necessary adjustments to achieve the goals.

Strategy Evaluation

The accomplishment of senior-level goals often requires significant effort and may be derailed by unexpected circumstances. Strategy evaluation involves comparing plans to results as a year progresses.

As a result of the evaluation, some plans may be reformed, and/or the manner in which they are implemented may be adjusted. The evaluation may indicate that results are off target in ways that cannot be addressed through moderate adjustments. Or, it may reveal that the plan's concepts were not completely connected in the implementation phase, requiring an adjustment to the implementation approach. Further, unexpected outside economic forces may make the achievement of a strategic plan impractical or impossible.

Types of Business Strategies

Strategic plans encompass a variety of organizational activities. Because organizations vary widely, every organization requires its own approach. Strategies can be categorized based on the levels at which they are carried out within an organization, how they relate to the development stage of the organization, and how they align with the general approach that an organization adopts.

Organizational Levels

Different kinds of strategies are carried out at various levels within an organization. Strategies at all levels should be aligned to support the organization's overall mission and vision. On any given day, employees may participate in implementing multiple strategies simultaneously. These are the most prevalent types of organizational strategies:

- Corporate strategy represents the highest strategy level for a diversified organization. It determines the types of businesses or activities the organization will undertake and their acceptable level of profitability or economic efficiency. The implementation of a corporate strategy may lead to divestitures of less profitable business units and acquisitions of others (or the elimination of inefficient government agencies or merger with other authorities or agencies).

- Business strategy may be implemented by a single operation or, in the case of a diversified corporation, a strategic business unit (SBU). In a for-profit operation, it encompasses plans for remaining competitive and profitable over the long term. In a not-for-profit or government agency, strategies are designed for the efficient use of resources and for meeting established performance goals.

- Functional strategy is carried out by individual departments performing specific organizational functions. Examples include marketing efforts and new product development.

- Operational strategy relates to a department's narrowly defined day-to-day business activities. Operational strategies include workflows and production processes.

Development Stage Models

Corporate strategies can be complex and can encompass many decisions, each of which has a vast range of potential outcomes. Because of the broad scope of corporate strategies, decisions may be categorized as strategies based on the organization's development stage.

Growth strategies are designed to improve an organization's status. Status measurements generally include increases in sales, market share, revenue, stock price and/or profits. These are examples of types of growth strategies:

- Market penetration concentrates on improving production efficiencies and capturing a larger share of the available market with a limited product or service. For example, an organization could engage in a branding campaign to build market share and draw customers from competitors.

- Vertical integration focuses on assuming operations formerly performed by suppliers and/or functions performed by others in the distribution of products or services.

- Diversification entails entering different geographic markets or adding new products or services, such as a traditional four-year college's addition of adult degree completion programs to its offerings or a government agency's development of additional expertise and increased staff to handle more customers as it expands its geographic reach into additional states or provinces.

Stability strategies seek to maintain an organization's current position. Some organizations, satisfied with their current industry position, products, profits, and growth, may not want to risk committing resources to future potential growth. Therefore, they devise strategies to maintain their current position indefinitely.

An organization uses retrenchment strategies when it must reduce the amount of products or discontinue the services it offers. Types of retrenchment strategies include these:

- Turnaround—A temporary across-the-board cost-cutting measure to improve the organization's future strength. Strategies may include reducing personnel, selling assets, reducing the number of products or services offered, or constricting the geographic market area.

- Divestiture—The selling or closing of a unit within the organization in order to reduce business losses. Governments generally do not divest themselves of agencies, but they may eliminate agencies or departments through sunset laws or reductions in funding. Governments also can outsource certain activities.

- Bankruptcy—Legal protection in order to restructure debt to a manageable level and deal with creditors.

- Liquidation—The process a business or business unit undergoes when going out of business.

General Approaches

Two general, but distinct, approaches to strategic planning are the industrial organizational approach and the sociological approach.

The industrial organizational approach bases strategic planning on the maximization of profit through competition, economies of scale, and effective resource allocation. Strategic plans involve activities that enhance returns to shareholders.

The sociological approach focuses primarily on human interaction. It is based on the assumptions that people behave rationally and in a way that will satisfy their needs and that less than optimal profit is acceptable. An organization applying this approach would direct its strategic plans toward the quality of the organization's interaction within its community and the quality of services it provides to employees and members. The sociological approach is favored by many governmental agencies and not-for-profit institutions, because they need to satisfy stakeholders other than shareholders and economic efficiencies, not profitability, are integral to their strategy.

DEVELOPING ERM GOALS ALIGNED WITH STRATEGIC GOALS

Organizations that have adopted an ERM approach must align their ERM goals with their strategic goals as part of their planning process.

ERM has gained credibility as a viable discipline as organizations have adopted practices described in national standards,[1] international initiatives,[2] and voluntary internal control and governance guidelines.[3] ERM focuses on an organization's overall business goals, its risk tolerance, its risk appetite, and its culture.

Typically, an organization goes through three stages to integrate its strategic plan with an ERM approach:

1. Develop ERM goals that are aligned with strategic goals

2. Adopt an ERM-based approach

3. Apply risk criteria

When planning an organization's strategic goals, senior management and the board focus most attention on the upside of risk in order to seek opportunities to enhance stakeholder value.[4]

Well-managed organizations recognize the value of incorporating ERM into their strategic planning process. By aligning ERM goals with strategic goals, an organization can balance enhancing and protecting stakeholder value without focusing exclusively on upside or downside, such as failures in risk management practices that led to the collapse of companies once considered unassailable.

ERM helps management assess and reduce uncertainties associated with strategic planning. When considering the connection between ERM and corporate strategy, board members want to know what "success" looks like.

Within its strategic planning process, an organization evaluates its mission, vision, and enterprise strategy in the context of its core values. Risk criteria can include costs and benefits, legal and statutory requirements, socioeconomic and environmental factors, the concerns of stakeholders, priorities, and other considerations. The criteria an organization chooses are directly linked to its culture, values, competencies, and influences. The strategic process, driven through a series of scenario planning activities, is an important component of this evaluation.

Risks include potential threats to achievement of the organization's mission and strategy as well as opportunities for gain. Examples of external market and macro forces might include, depending on the organization itself, social/political, market/economic, competitors, customers, or technology. The organization identifies these forces (or risks) and assesses them based on the ranking of their relevance, degree of certainty, and importance to its base strategy. This generally occurs within a strategic scenario planning workshop setting. Scenarios drive potential alternative strategies, thereby testing the base case strategy for adaptability. The organization's leaders take these risks into account in determining the success and adaptability of the organization's business strategy, thereby gaining more thorough knowledge and consideration of key uncertainties.

Potential deliverables from a strategic scenario planning workshop might include these:

- Strategic risk map

- Scenarios based on key uncertainties

- Prioritized list of important organizational trends (that is, those forces that are relevant and important, but are certain)

Scenario planning outcomes should include articulated implications and consequences to the base case strategic plan, including expected financial deviations, derived from the various scenarios in the long-range strategic plan. This should occur before operational planning and budgeting. Operational planning and budgeting addresses the internal context in greater depth. Through scenario planning, the organization and/or business unit(s) can assess required changes in the base case strategy if different scenario elements occur. The inclusion of scenario planning in the strategy development allows for adaptability, to the extent possible. Scenario planning's primary purpose is to prepare an organization for what may occur in the future (allowing it to become proactive rather than reactive).

Success is measured by comparing the value the organization was attempting to create and capture with expected outcomes. Such success measurements may include customer satisfaction, organizational efficiencies, talent management, degree of regulatory compliance, or financial achievements.

The "Success Trajectory" exhibit graphically shows how mission, vision, and strategy, combined with ERM and enhanced strategic planning, can be used to develop a risk optimization approach over an extended period.

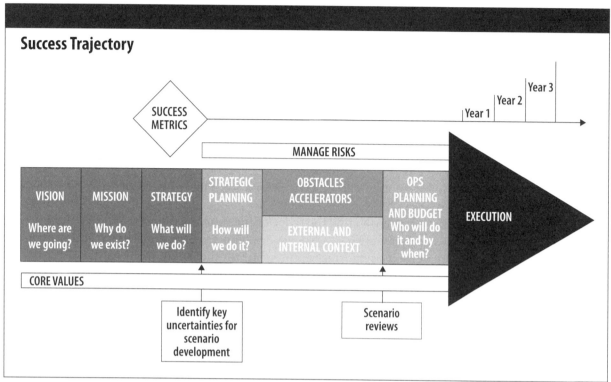

© Convergys 2009. Reprinted with permission.

The process of developing corporate strategy involves three steps:

1. Define the vision, mission, and core values
2. Articulate the strategy
3. Consider risks to strategy

Define the Vision, Mission, and Core Values

To establish strategic goals, an organization must first understand its mission, vision, and core values. This understanding is also fundamental to aligning ERM with established strategic goals.

An organization usually clarifies its vision and mission in its strategic planning documents. An organization's vision articulates its "destination." Its mission is a clear statement addressing why it exists and what it must accomplish. An organization's core values define its internal and external behavior in all business dealings.

For example, the Coca-Cola Company states, "Our vision guides every aspect of our business by describing what we need to accomplish in order to continue achieving sustainable growth."[5] Dow Chemical Company describes its vision as "To be the largest, most profitable, most respected chemical company in the world."[6] Dow's stated mission is "To constantly improve what is essential to human progress by mastering science and technology."[7] Pharmaceutical company Novo Nordisk's vision statement is "We will be the world's leading diabetes care company."[8]

Note that each of these organizations' vision and mission statements is unique regarding how leadership views the organization and its role in its market.

Articulate the Strategy

Once its vision, mission, and core values are defined, an organization must articulate the strategic goals that support its stated vision and mission.

An organization's vision is its destination, an expression of desired future conditions based on its mission. The goals provide a roadmap to achieve the vision. Understanding the scope of the strategy—and the external macro and micro environment—is the responsibility of an organization's strategy planning team. It is imperative, therefore, for the chief risk officer to collaborate closely with members of the strategy planning team to align the organization's ERM goals with its overall strategic goals. Inherent in any strategy is a careful analysis of the organization's competitors, its position relative to its competitors, and market forces.

Understanding and anticipating the impact of competitors' activities, whether existing or potential, on an organization's price point(s) and customer demand lays the foundation for evaluating the organization's capabilities against existing and emerging market forces. These include the threat of new entrants, the threat of substitute products or services, the bargaining power of current and potential customers, and the bargaining power of suppliers. These competitive analyses are typically the domain of an organization's strategic development team. An organization must also understand market force risks, emerging disruptive technologies, and the impact of changes in supply and distribution chains in order to identify, mitigate, and exploit strategic risks.

All organizations, not just for-profit enterprises, must consider the ramifications of competition. For example, governments and other institutions may have competition from other agencies or departments or from the business community. Senior leadership in an agency may determine that it is less costly to provide needed services through outsourcing. The bargaining power of a federal agency may dwarf that of a local agency, leading to a reduction in services needed from the local agency. As another example, competition for research professionals, grants, and other research funding is keen at Class A research universities. The risk of losing a top research professor to another institution can be a significant threat for a university, but it is an opportunity for the other institution attracting him or her.

The primary factors that determine competitive advantage in the profit equation for demand are product price and quantity. How does the organization make its products and/or services more attractive than those of real or potential competitors? That is, how can it create greater value? For example, an organization should determine whether it can differentiate its products in a manner that increases demand to a point at which more customers are willing to pay a premium price for them.

The objective of competitive advantage is to achieve and maintain a leading market position through superior advertising and branding, first-to-market innovation, or technologies that disrupt the market, such as Apple's iPhone. The key to competitive advantage is controlling the knowledge that supports innovative products or services, as well as controlling the assets that maximize profits arising from innovations. The risk of losing such assets could be detrimental to an organization's sustainability.

The primary drivers for competitive advantage in the profit equation for efficiency are cost and quantity. Reducing costs through efficiencies gained in sourcing, manufacturing, operations, labor, packaging, distribution, service delivery, sales, and administration all serve to increase competitive advantage, assuming that pricing remains stable. Driving down costs while driving up value for consumers can open new markets.

While driving down costs is important, so is increasing revenue. For example, to enter a new market, a company with a low cost structure may actually increase the price of its product to match others in the market because that sector's consumers perceive a correlation between the higher cost and quality. A government agency that shows that it can operate efficiently may convince legislatures and administrations that it can do more or expand its authority with more budget dollars.

Often, the role of the risk practitioner is to collaborate with the strategic planning team to embed questions related to competitive advantage with the strategic planning process and/or to validate the value statements contained in the strategic planning documents.

Consider Risks to Strategy

After articulating its strategy and establishing a plan to gain a competitive advantage, an organization must consider strategic risks that could affect its ability to sustain its established competitive advantage. To do so, it must examine its internal and external contexts and possibly revise its underlying assumptions accordingly.

Shareholder Value Articulation Questions

1. How does this particular strategy create value?

    a. Is this product/service one that people are willing to pay for?

    b. At what price points?

    c. What uncertainties are clients/customers facing that may change their perception of the value of our product/service?

2. How does the strategy capture and/or protect shareholder value?

    Value is captured when an organization profits from the products and/or services it offers.

    a. How and to what extent do we profit from the products/services we offer?

    b. How does this strategy protect current shareholder value?

    c. How critical is this strategy to achieving our corporate goals—on a scale of 0-3, with 3 being absolutely critical (that is, the organization can't survive unless we execute this strategy)?

    d. How will our existing capabilities enable us to execute this strategy?

3. How will we deliver shareholder value?

    a. What strategic controls will we use, how, and by when?

        *   Increase price?

            Increasing price over competitors suggests that an organization's product and/or service can be differentiated to such an extent that customers are willing to pay more for its product or service than for a competitor's product.

        *   Reduce cost?

            External pressures may result in increased costs. Specially fabricated parts for complex products, sole suppliers, energy costs, and unfavorable currency fluctuations are just a few examples of externally driven conditions or events that affect the cost to produce products and/or services. On the other hand, if an organization can build efficiencies into its product or service to drive down cost better than its competitors, it can capture more market share.

        *   Push out quantity?

            Complementary to reducing cost in order to capture additional market share (thereby increasing quantity), an organization can push out quantity by tapping markets in alternative industries, linking the product and/or service to complementary product and service offerings, approaching non-traditional buyers, and reaching unexplored consumers through alternative channels.

        *   Create additional demand?

            Creative or focused marketing typically is what organizations think of to create additional demand. However, investing in unique organizational competencies that cannot be easily imitated, traded, or stolen and that are not so expensive that they do not yield an adequate return is an alternate way to create additional demand for an organization's products or services.

        *   Combination

            An organization's strategies will often utilize a combination of these controls to create, capture, and deliver value.

Internal context includes resources such as people, systems, processes, and capital needs. For example, an organization might gain a competitive advantage by using a new technology that others can't easily duplicate or by exploiting unique internal capabilities. However, if, for example, an organization's competitive advantage lies in its unique internal values and culture of delivering superior customer service, failure to maintain that culture diminishes the value proposition and gradually diminishes the organization's competitive advantage. In such an instance, the underlying assumption is that employees will always maintain the original values that defined the original competitive advantage. Therefore, as a result of its examination of its internal context, the organization must establish a process to assess the ongoing effectiveness of such underlying assumptions.

External context includes the social, regulatory, cultural, competitive, financial, and political environments in which an organization operates. Because these external conditions can significantly affect its ability to successfully implement its strategy, an organization must recognize possibilities such as market changes, consumer preferences, financial trends, or unexpected events that could affect the implementation of its strategy.

An organization must also anticipate the capacity required to retool in a timely fashion to meet emerging demands. For example, if an organization's products or services are affected by new home-building trends, it is important to recognize that population declines in the geographic region served may undermine any competitive advantage the organization may have gained. The underlying assumption is that the population in the geographic region will continue to grow at current rates. In order to sustain its competitive advantage, the organization must periodically test this assumption and respond appropriately when changes are detected.

An organization's analysis of its internal and external contexts in its strategic risk assessments must align with the internal and external contexts addressed in its strategic plan. Each of the organization's business or resource units must articulate measurable expected outcomes for each specific business strategy. For risk-adjusted allocation purposes, it helps to prioritize business strategies in order of their importance in meeting corporate goals. Once the specific business strategy is defined, along with the expected outcome(s), the business unit owner can identify the major opportunities or threats to the achievement of the expected outcome(s) and the area(s) of impact. Further, the risk practitioner must understand the context of strategy planning in creating and sustaining organizational value in order to link and embed consideration for uncertainties that may undermine the organization's overall mission and vision.

Once the competitive analysis has been completed and organizational value has been fully articulated, the organization should align its mission, vision, culture, and strategy. In developing goals for both strategy and ERM, four important characteristics help define success:

- They must be achievable.
- They must be implementable.
- They must be measurable.
- They must be time-limited.

This is a variation of the SMART (simple, measurable, achievable, realistic, and timely) model. While strategic goals may be simply stated, they are often complex and far reaching in scope; thus the traditional model was not used in this context.

For example, a strategy's measurable stated outcome might be, "Over the next three years, we will drive annual sales growth by x percent; achieve annual margin growth of xx percent; expand the core business by developing new, exciting technology that meets the needs of the xyz market; and drive internal costs down by yy percent through internal technology deployment and cost reductions." A charitable food bank may have as its strategic goal, "Feed all who grace our doorstep and ask for food."

Adopt an ERM-Based Approach

When adopting an ERM-based approach to strategy, risk practitioners must understand the primary components of the organization's strategy by business unit, line of business, and/or resource unit within the broader corporate and segment strategies and how to align them with the organization's vision, mission, and cultural values.

Why ERM at Mars, Inc.?

This is an example of how ERM was initially established at Mars, Inc.

Senior management sought:

- A methodology to determine what is actually achievable by business units in the context of corporate performance objectives

- To improve alignment and accountability around the pursuit and execution of each business unit's goals and objectives

- To foster a risk discussion mentality among business unit management teams

- A mechanism that enables managers to knowledgably and comfortably take risks in order to achieve growth goals that exceed overall market growth

- A tool to objectively track performance

Therefore, the objective of ERM is to provide Mars with a proven, sustainable framework to proactively understand and deal with complex business risks, both tangible and intangible, existing and emerging, across the entire organization.

Senior management identified and agreed upon the following major drivers for ERM success at Mars:

- Create value

- Leverage Mars' unique strengths

- Work with existing organizational structure

- View risk as opportunity

- Encourage alignment and accountability

Therefore, the risk management function assists the organization's strategic development organization in articulating the organization's strategies, focusing on its core values, while including the four critical goal characteristics: achievable, implementable, measurable and time-limited.

The process of integrating a specific strategy with ERM involves six steps:

1. In order to identify strategic risks, the organization articulates the measurable expected outcome for the specific strategy.

2. The strategy is then prioritized according to its importance in meeting corporate goals.

3. To strengthen mitigation approaches, major challenges and risks are identified that would affect the business strategy.

4. Current mitigation or optimization activities are noted for the identified threats and opportunities.

5. Potential mitigation or optimization activities are identified from a value protection and creation standpoint that will further improve effectiveness in managing the threats and opportunities.

6. The management team evaluates the effectiveness of the potential mitigation activities in reducing the challenges and risks or in optimizing the success for this strategy and notes the results in a template depicting the risk profile.

Another approach management may adopt to integrate strategy and ERM is to conduct a risk assessment workshop that encompasses three activities:

*   Management votes on the effectiveness of the current mitigation activities.

*   Management votes on the expected effectiveness of potential, proposed mitigation activities.

*   Management discusses the value of closing the mitigation gap while business units/segments receive guidance for including implementation steps for the additional mitigation efforts in their operational business plans, and execution is incorporated into the operations plan.

The outcome of such a workshop is a measurable risk profile and a practical method that business unit owners can use to estimate the success of their strategies and that involves investing in activities that increase the odds of a successful strategy. Documenting these activities means that they can be monitored by management with visible board oversight. Management can act quickly if the activities do not achieve the desired results.

Mars, Inc. Template for Strategic Risk Analysis

Differentiation/Innovation **Expected Outcome:** Drive annual sales growth by xx%, achieve margin growth of xx% and expand the core business by _____ that meet the needs of the XYZ market and drive internal costs down by xx% through _____ deployment and cost reductions **1**	**Risk Profile** **6**	60/80
	Priority Level **2**	1

Challenges, risks and impact (P, C, D, Q)	Current Mitigation Activities	Potential Mitigation Activities
• Limited number of _____ (Q) • Intense price competition (P) • Few XXX customers (D,Q) • Future growth will be driven by _____ (D,C) **3**	• xx new ideas in pipeline leveraging local and global resources • Strategy around acquisitions • Enforce standardized product development process **4**	• Increase demand in XXX customers by xxx • Push multiple installations through alliance partnerships • XXXX **5**

P   Price
C   Cost
Q   Quantity
D   Demand

1. In order to identify strategic risks (and their associated definitions, as needed), first articulate measurable expected outcome for the specific strategy.

2. Prioritize strategy by importance in meeting corporate goals.

3. Identify the major challenges and risks that the strategic risks present to the business strategy (area of impact).

4. List current mitigation activities for the challenges and risks.

5. Identify potential mitigation activities that will further improve management effectiveness of the challenges and risks.

6. Management Team evaluates the effectiveness of the (current)/(current + potential) mitigation activities in reducing the challenges and risks for this strategy (see next slide).

The Risk and Insurance Management Society (RIMS) provides its members with practical tools for implementing ERM. One of these tools is the ERM planning template, which was created by practitioners for practitioners. The "Mars, Inc. Template for Strategic Risk Analysis" exhibit is one adaptation of the ERM planning template. Its six steps mirror those in the ERM planning template:

1. Identify risks to strategy
2. Prioritize
3. Identify challenges, risks, and impacts
4. Review current mitigation activities
5. Review potential mitigation activities
6. Evaluate the effectiveness of the mitigation strategies

The "Risk Assessment Workshop: Mars, Inc." exhibit depicts the profile of the effectiveness of current mitigation and the mitigation gap that may be reduced by the adoption of the potential mitigation strategies and other discoveries that were identified in the workshop.

Risk Assessment Workshop: Mars, Inc.

Strategic risks—placing the "bet" to close the risk mitigation gap (tie performance to how well risk is managed)

1. **Current mitigation effectiveness:** the degree to which actual current mitigation efforts will enhance or protect the value to be captured based on the strategic risk assessment.

2. **Potential mitigation effectiveness:** the degree to which the potential mitigation level, assuming reasonable resources, will increase the value impact from managing the risk.

3. **Mitigation gap:** the difference between current and potential effectiveness of the mitigation efforts; potential opportunities for management to improve its current mitigation efforts will focus here.

   - **Balance investment** in current and potential risk mitigation efforts against the value capture in Operational Business Plan.
   - **Incorporate execution** of risk mitigation activities in Operations Plan.

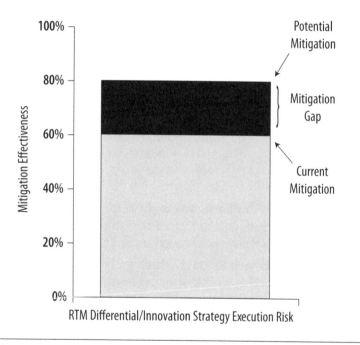

Because every organization integrates ERM differently, there are no wrong answers to the template's questions, only answers that apply to the specific organization. The time an organization spends completing the template provides the foundation for a sustainable and strategic ERM program.

Apply Risk Criteria

Risk criteria
Reference standards, measures, or expectations used in judging the significance of a given risk in context with strategic goals.

Risk criteria can include costs and benefits, legal and statutory requirements, socioeconomic and environmental factors, the concerns of stakeholders, priorities, and other considerations. The criteria chosen are directly linked to the organization's culture, values, competencies, and influences.

When determining relevant risk criteria, an organization should consider these factors:[9]

- Its comfort level in accepting risk (appetite for risk)
- The nature and types of consequences that can occur
- Its definition of unacceptable risk
- How "likelihood" will be defined and depicted
- The immediacy of the risk and development of the consequence
- Impact measured in financial or operational terms
- Impact to its reputation and/or sustainability
- How combinations of risks could affect it

Risk Governance Structure

To promote risk management effectiveness in reducing uncertainty and managing potential variations from expected outcomes in achieving its strategy, an organization should incorporate a risk governance structure, regardless of which recognized standard, guideline, or framework it chooses to adopt or modify.

At a minimum, the risk governance structure should specify these elements:

- Who ultimately is responsible for oversight of the organization's ERM framework, its key practices, and related critical risk monitoring (for example, the board of directors, through its audit committee)
- Who is responsible for setting the risk strategy, the implementation and execution of the company's risk management standards, practices, and activities, as well as for defining the organization's risk appetite and tolerances (for example, the executive management team)
- Who retains authority, accountability, and responsibility for day-to-day risk management and reporting of risks within their areas of responsibility, such as lines of business, business units, and functional unit heads (risk owners)
- That risk management functional areas are responsible for enabling executive management and risk owners to carry out their respective responsibilities[10]

- Which of the risk management functional areas is authorized by the board or executive management to execute and be responsible for developing, directing, and implementing the risk management framework and the necessary activities entailed in that effort

Detailed roles and responsibilities for each of these governance areas can and should be articulated in the organization's enterprise risk management policy and/or standards documents. Risk reporting by the risk owners—at whatever frequency required by management and depending on the risk itself—can be included in the normal reporting mechanisms that already exist within the organization. Generally, the risk management functional area with the greatest reach and influence plays the key pivotal role of driving the ERM process and framework as a business discipline throughout the organization. Since Internal Audit is charged by the board with reviewing (and reporting on) the effectiveness of management's risk controls (including ERM program effectiveness), its need for independence may make it unadvisable for it to assume the dual responsibility of ERM program execution. One benefit of establishing such a governance structure and risk reporting arrangement is that risk tolerance discussions and resource allocation decisions can be made through an existing and organized risk oversight process.

One method an organization may use to measure progress toward its ERM goals is application of a risk maturity model.

A RISK MATURITY MODEL

ERM is an ongoing process aimed at identifying and monitoring organizational threats and opportunities. A well-implemented ERM program will provide continuous improvement for the organization. An important component of continuous improvement is measuring results and monitoring progress with tools such as a risk maturity model (RMM) to ensure that goals are achieved.

ERM is a process, not a piece of equipment. ERM cannot simply be installed in an organization, turned on, and expected to produce the desired output. An ERM program's effectiveness must be monitored throughout the organization in order to realize the full value and benefits of the ERM program. A RMM provides the framework for setting goals and for measuring progress toward those goals.

The RIMS Risk Maturity Model

To improve continually, it is essential for an organization to conduct periodic self-assessments to measure key ERM improvement indicators. An objective and consistent measurement tool with best practice elements and standards should be used for this purpose. The Risk and Insurance Management Society (RIMS) has developed a measurement tool meeting these qualifications: the RMM for ERM.

A RMM can be thought of as an organization's risk management performance scorecard. It reviews risk management performance throughout the organization, supplies feedback on improvement efforts, and provides knowledge for making better decisions.

There are two major components of the RIMS RMM:[11]

- Attributes—organizational characteristics that drive business value
- Maturity levels—descriptions that measure each attribute's key drivers, ranging from nonexistent to Level 5: leadership

Attributes

The RIMS RMM takes into account member best practices and effective goal setting while identifying organizational elements and characteristics that indicate the strength and competency of risk management. The elements and characteristics consider the viewpoints of all stakeholders and encourage a consensus on priorities and tactics. Attributes are measured to determine the degree to which the organization's total management team has both adopted and supported ERM throughout the organization.

The RIMS RMM lists seven attributes and their key drivers:[12]

- ERM-based approach—Executive support is one of the most important components of success. Support must go beyond regulatory compliance aspects and include all processes, functions, business lines, roles, and locations. Communication and coordination between the internal audit, compliance, information technology, control, and risk management functions are also assessed within this attribute.

- ERM process management—The ERM process should be followed throughout the organization to identify, assess, evaluate, treat, and monitor and review potential risks affecting the business process, both from within and from outside. Qualitative and quantitative methods, tools, and models should be utilized for this purpose.

- Risk appetite management—Throughout an organization, management should understand the trade-offs between the risk and reward and opportunities and threats faced. Leadership should be accountable for their risk-reward decisions.

- Root cause discipline—When a challenge to a process (whether business or bureaucratic) arises, the organization should consistently determine and measure the root cause(s). The process should also be reviewed to determine both where and how it was affected by the challenge and how to reduce the variation from expectation that resulted. All variables should be considered: people, external environment, systems, and processes; both singularly and in multiple combinations.

Risk Maturity Model

Attributes	Maturity Levels					
	Level 5: Leadership	Level 4: Managed	Level 3: Repeatable	Level 2: Initial	Level 1: Ad hoc	Nonexistent
	Key Drivers: Degree of …					

1 Adoption of ERM-based approach

- Support from senior management, Chief Risk Officer
- Business process definition determining risk ownership
- Assimilation into support area and front-office activities
- Far-sighted orientation toward risk management
- Risk culture's accountability, communication and pervasiveness

2 ERM process management

- Each ERM Process step (see definition)
- ERM Process's repeatability and scalability
- ERM Process oversight including roles and responsibilities
- Risk management reporting
- Qualitative and quantitative measurement

3 Risk appetite management

- Risk-reward tradeoffs
- Risk-reward-based resource allocation
- Analysis as risk portfolio collections to balance risk positions

4 Root cause discipline

- Classification to manage risk and performance indicators
- Flexibility to collect risk and opportunity information
- Understanding dependencies and consequences
- Consideration of people, relationships, external, process and systems views

5 Uncovering risks

- Risk ownership by business areas
- Formalization of risk indicators and measures
- Reporting on follow-up activities
- Transforming potentially adverse events into opportunities

6 Performance management

- ERM information integrated within planning
- Communication of goals and measures
- Examination of financial, customer, business process and learning
- ERM process goals and activities

7 Business resiliency and sustainability

- Integration of ERM within operational planning
- Understanding of consequences of action or inaction
- Planning based on scenario analysis

Source: RIMS Risk Maturity Model (RMM) for Enterprise Risk Management, Risk and Insurance Management Society, 2006, p. 9.

- Uncovering risks—The organization should consistently collect and analyze data from multiple sources to document threats and opportunities. Multiple data sources should be used, including the experiences and expertise of both internal and external professionals, internal and external databases, and electronic files.

- Performance management—The organization's mission and vision should balance the financial goals, customer needs, business processes, and learning and growth perspectives. Performance management refers to how well the mission and vision are executed, along with the flexibility and timeliness with which the organization addresses changes in its strategic plans.

- Resiliency and sustainability—The resiliency and sustainability aspects of the ERM process should be incorporated throughout an organization's operating plan. As part of planning, an organization should consider future potential risk situations (both threats and opportunities) that might affect its economic efficiency or operations. Various scenarios involving the risk situations should be mapped out and analyzed according to their impact on the organization's continued viability and ability to fulfill its vision and mission.

Maturity Levels

Maturity levels are similar to developmental stages and allow an organization to self-assess its ERM process and set targets for improvements. By using maturity levels, the RIMS RMM recognizes that the implementation of an effective ERM program can only occur over an extended period of time. Using this model, the organization can document its progress over the span of several years. There are six maturity levels:[13]

- Nonexistent—The organization has not yet implemented an ERM program.
- Level 1: Ad hoc—The organization utilizes the risk management process for singular events.
- Level 2: Initial—The organization is in the early stages of risk management process implementation.
- Level 3: Repeatable—The risk management process is beyond the early stages of implementation. It is being used regularly, and each business unit and department consistently repeats the process.
- Level 4: Managed—The organization's management is skillful in utilizing the ERM process to detect, control, and direct decisions concerning organizational risks.
- Level 5: Leadership—Senior management and the board not only embrace the ERM process but also direct and lead the organization by assimilating ERM into the culture with ownership and accountability.

Key drivers of each attribute are analyzed and measured to establish the maturity level based on the organization's ERM activities.

As an organization develops and implements its risk management process, the maturity level for each attribute may differ. The measured maturity level for each attribute serves as an outline for the next step of continuous improvement. They guide the organization toward achieving a mature ERM process.

ANALYZING AN ORGANIZATION'S INTERNAL AND EXTERNAL CONTEXTS

An organization's analysis of its internal and external **contexts** is a key prerequisite for its assessment and management of risks.

The world is reaching a consensus on an optimal process for managing risk. Standards bodies, governments, risk trade associations, academics, and professional associations are working together to develop a consistent, logical method for risk management. For example, in 2009, the International Organization for Standardization (ISO) circulated a proposed ISO/DIS 31000: *Risk Management—Principles and Guidelines on Implementation*. In 2005, Australia/New Zealand (AS/NZS) document HB4360: *Handbook, Risk Management Guidelines—Companion to AS/NZS 4360:2004* was issued.

The ISO standard recognizes that before managing risk, an organization must understand its context (also referred to as environment). Similarly, the AS/NZS standard asserts that

> . . .establishing the context defines the basic parameters within which risks must be managed and sets the scope for the rest of the risk management process. This is important to ensure that the objectives defined for the risk management process take into account the organizational [internal] and external environment.[14]

An organization therefore begins its risk management process by assessing the internal and external environments in which it operates, evaluating and organizing relevant **stakeholders**, articulating the organization's goals, specifying its **values**, and supporting the organizational culture of risk management with appropriate competencies. After performing these activities, the organization is prepared to develop a risk management department, risk teams, and committees. It may then draft a risk management policy based on the organization's goals. These steps are the building blocks of establishing the organization's risk culture, understanding **risk perceptions**, and defining its **risk position**.

Context
The environment in which an organization seeks to achieve its goals.

Stakeholder
Any individual or organization that is directly or indirectly involved with or affected by an organization's decisions and activities.

Values
Those outcomes that satisfy stakeholders, including economic performance, social justice, and environmental stewardship.

Risk perception
Given their values and goals, the manner in which individuals and organizations observe and perceive volatile situations.

Risk position
A party's risk appetite plus risk tolerance; the willingness to pay to accept volatile projects and pay to transfer volatile situations to third parties.

Assessing the Internal and External Environments

Marketing managers and risk management professionals use the SWOT method to analyze their organization's external and internal environments and learn about the organization's risk management context.

External Environment

The external environment includes several categories that represent opportunities for and threats to the organization:

- Physical environment—In real estate, the axiom for controlling risk is "location, location, location." Indeed, an organization's location is a source of much variability. An organization in San Francisco is concerned with earthquakes, but not with hurricanes; an organization in New Orleans is concerned with hurricanes, but not with earthquakes. Another physical environmental challenge is the potential impact of climate change.

- Social environment—Society, with its cultural norms and values, expects an organization to manage its risks. Often, these expectations are expressed through political actions, such as the formation of nongovernment organizations (NGOs). The competitive environment within a society also influences the organization's risk management.

- Legal environment—Government regulations, statutes, and case law impose mandates for desired risk control. A multinational organization must understand and comply with the various local, state/provincial, national, and international mandates to which it is subject.

- Economic environment—The macroeconomic influences on an organization are systemic and nondiversifiable. Nevertheless, an organization must be aware of business cycles, employment conditions, and levels of gross national output in order to make realistic long-range plans (for example, the impact of hard and soft insurance markets).

Internal Environment

The internal environment includes four categories that represent the organization's strengths and weaknesses:

- Product environment—The demand for products and services is constantly in flux. New, innovative products are continuously introduced to satisfy demand. An organization must relentlessly monitor demand and supply to remain competitive.

- Operations environment—How an organization creates its goods and services regularly changes. Examples include changes in logistics, supply-side risks, operations management, inventory control, manufacturing processes, and distribution systems. Financial managers may change the organization's capital structure in response to changes in the operations environment.

- Technology and information systems environment—Methods change by which an organization collects, stores, evaluates, and communicates information. Such changes can enhance decision making.

- Cognitive environment—Each individual perceives risks differently at various times. Similarly, as a business grows, its aggregate perception of risk changes. This perception is reflected in the organization's culture, values, and risk policies. Organizations frequently monitor these factors in order to appropriately respond to risks.

The Stakeholder Model

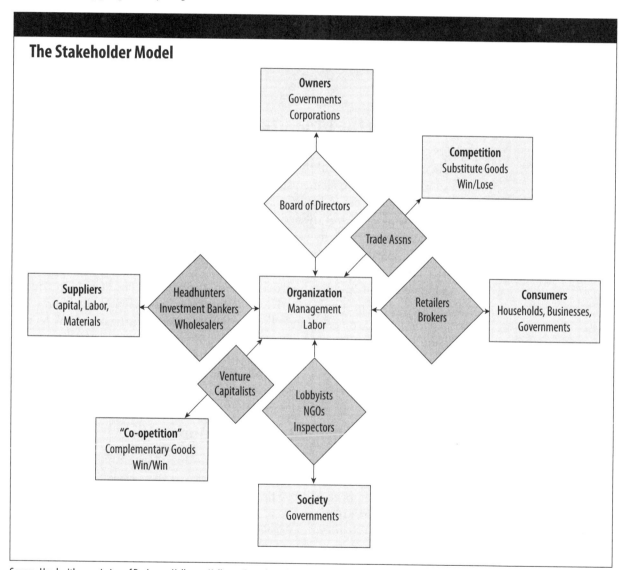

Source: Used with permission of Dr. James Kallman, Kallman Consulting Services.

Evaluating Key Stakeholders

Some organizations believe their greatest asset is people. An organization's key personnel include managers, such as the chief executive officer (or cabinet officer, president, governor, or prime minister), chief risk officer, or front-line manager. Other key employees include salespersons for key accounts and laborers with specialized skills and knowledge. Key people, such as suppliers, consumers, intermediaries, and members of NGOs or trade associations, also work outside the organization. They are key because they hold a stake in the organization's success.

A risk management professional identifies key stakeholders and evaluates their response to the organization's risks. This helps define the risk management context.

Articulating the Organization's Goals

A good chief risk officer is a good listener. He or she interacts with the board of directors to understand the organization's long-term strategies, communicates with senior management (also referred to as the C-suite) to understand operating objectives, and learns about short-term tactics from front-line managers and workers. After these consultations, the chief risk officer articulates the organization's goals in a single document, presents the document to each group for confirmation, and revises it when necessary. Next, the risk management professional ensures that the organization's goals are synchronized and aligned. That is, subordinate short-term tactical goals must support their single-period operational objectives, all objectives must support the appropriate long-term strategies, and all strategies must support the organization's mission statement. This critical step in ERM is necessary to eliminate any isolated departments (silos) not aligned with the entire organization. Finally, the risk management department, like others, must develop its own goals. These include pre-loss and post-loss goals.

Specifying the Organization's Values

Triple bottom line
The expansion of the traditional reporting framework to take into account ecological and social performance in addition to financial performance.

An organization exists to accomplish certain values. Governmental organizations attempt to provide efficient and effective services. For-profit corporations attempt to achieve financial returns for investors. ERM recognizes that no organization has a single focus. All organizations aspire to multiple values. Organizations seek a "**triple bottom line**."[15] That is, they pursue economic performance values, social justice values, and environmental stewardship values; or, simply stated: profit, people, and planet. Many Fortune 500 organizations have adopted the triple bottom line to create long-term sustainability.[16] An organization's desired total value is defined at the highest levels, often by a board of directors, while the total value is defined as a combination of several important attributes. Some organizations use the triple bottom line to define their organization's value statement. There are three values of the triple bottom line:

- Economic performance—profit
- Social justice—people
- Environmental stewardship—planet

Every organization that uses the triple bottom line assigns different priorities to each of the basic values. A weighted average formula describes these priorities. Risk managers are familiar with the weighted average cost of capital as one method to estimate the average price of external funds. The weighted average value equation (WAVE) is a similar model:

$$V = W_{EP} \times S_{EP} + W_{SJ} \times S_{SJ} + W_{ES} \times S_{ES}$$

where:

V = the organization's total value

W_{EP} = the proportional weight of economic performance

S_{EP} = the score of economic performance

W_{SJ} = the proportional weight of social justice projects

S_{SJ} = the score of social justice projects

W_{ES} = the proportional weight of environmental stewardship policies

S_{ES} = the score of environmental stewardship policies

The sum of the weights must be 100 percent. Common scoring schemes use a five- or seven-point scale; the higher the score, the more positive (upside) the impact. For example, assume a for-profit corporation's board of directors decides its value weights are:

$$W_{EP} = 60 \text{ percent}, W_{SJ} = 25 \text{ percent, and } W_{ES} = 15 \text{ percent}$$

Next, the board evaluates the organization's performance and assigns scores for these three values:

$$S_{EP} = 6, S_{SJ} = 3, \text{ and } S_{ES} = 5$$

The company's total value score is this:

$$V = (.60 \times 6) + (.25 \times 3) + (.15 \times 5) = 3.6 + .75 + .75 = 5.1$$

The board will determine whether this score is high enough to achieve the desired total value for its stakeholders.

Integrating Risk Management With an Organization's Culture

An organization should integrate risk management with all of its practices and processes so that it becomes part of the organization's culture. Every process should include a risk assessment. For example, risk management should be a part of the board's strategic planning, the C-suite's policy development, and mid-level managers' business planning.

One way to achieve this is to establish responsibility, authority, and accountability for managing risks. This is accomplished by specifying risk owners, providing cost-effective risk solutions, and requiring timely and accurate reports. Moreover, a risk culture is enhanced by establishing performance metrics and outcome assessments followed by appropriate levels of recognition; reward; correction; and, if necessary, sanctions.

A robust risk management culture must be continuously maintained to remain effective. This means allocating the necessary resources of people, money and materials, and time. Budgets for money, materials, and time must be reasonable and feasible; cost allocation models must be fair, acceptable, and compatible with other budgets.

The Organization's Risk Perceptions

An ERM-related challenge is understanding the context within which key stakeholders perceive risks. How individuals perceive situations, how they frame them into a familiar context, how they filter out what they perceive as extraneous, and how they communicate their perceptions to other workers are key issues. Risk perceptions vary due to differences in individuals' values, needs, assumptions, concepts, and concerns. Individual risk perceptions may be influenced by legal or regulatory requirements. Because individuals' perceptions have a significant impact on decisions, it is important that those perceptions are identified, recorded, and taken into account in the decision-making process.[17] Group dynamics demonstrate how individuals withhold or modify their own risk perceptions in response to group pressures. The perceptions and values of various external stakeholders must also be considered when risk policies are established and communicated.

The Organization's Definition of Materiality

Materiality
The measure of a significant variance from an expected outcome.

An event or outcome is material to an organization if its occurrence has a significant impact on achieving the organization's goals. **Materiality** must be defined at the organization's highest levels. Often the definition will be stated as a proportion of some other value—that is, as a ratio. For example, a university's board of regents may define a material change in revenues as any value greater than 15 percent of total revenues. Alternatively, a corporation's board of directors may define a material risk as one that is associated with any variation greater than 10 percent of total assets. This critical part of ERM helps the entire organization understand the organization's risk management context.

The Organization's Risk Position

An organization should clearly articulate its risk position so everyone in the organization knows what variability is acceptable. An organization's risk position (risk philosophy or risk attitude) consists of two components: its risk tolerance and its risk appetite, which establish a critical context for its risk management program. A sample risk philosophy might look like this:

Sample Risk Philosophy

The organization will align its risk management practices with its overall vision, mission, and strategy and embed risk competencies into the management practices of every group or department leader in order to:

- Avoid risks that could materially affect the value of the organization

- Contribute to economic efficiency

- Take risks that the company can manage in order to optimize returns

- Balance risk and reward against the impact and cost of managing risks for the organization

- Provide transparency of the organization's risks through internal and external reporting

An organization's risk philosophy should be explicit and reinforce its stated core values (for example, integrity). Incorporating enterprise risk management considerations into daily business practices will also serve to reinforce an organization's core values and its ethical business practices.

An organization's risk attitude is part of its cultural makeup and may swing from one end of the continuum (aggressive risk-taker regardless of consequences) to the other end of the continuum (risk aversion regardless of the potential gains that may be made otherwise). In reality, organizations operate at various places along this continuum, depending on circumstances and individual perceptions of what it is willing to accept or tolerate. How well an organization manages its risk appetite by applying and monitoring its risk tolerance(s) is key to determining the success of an ERM program. ERM helps organizations to understand and strive to develop a risk optimization strategy within their risk appetite.

Risk Attitude Continuum

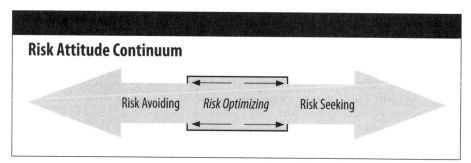

Risk Avoiding   *Risk Optimizing*   Risk Seeking

Risk appetite could be considered the aggregate amount of risk a company is willing to accept in pursuit of its mission, vision, business objectives, and strategic goals. Risk appetite is directly related to an organization's culture, risk management competencies, and business plans. Appetite, the "fuel capacity" that allows the organizational "engine" to operate, should be in alignment with the growth and profitability goals established by the organization.

The organization's appetite for risk and return should be based on strategic and business objectives and be described in measurable terms and aligned with the key performance metrics used to manage business performance.[18]

Risk tolerance is the specific maximum level of risk that, if exceeded, may imperil not only the organization's strategy and operational objectives, but also, in the aggregate, threaten its very survival. Tolerances, the "brakes" that keep the organizational "engine" from going off the tracks, must be fully understood, controlled, and monitored to prevent a seemingly inconsequential decision from becoming a "train wreck."

CONDUCTING A SWOT ANALYSIS

A SWOT analysis can improve an organization's planning process and the resulting outcome, particularly if those participating in the process ask and find answers to difficult questions and represent a variety of perspectives. An organization can use SWOT analysis to evaluate whether its business strategies will contribute to the organization's success.

A SWOT analysis, which is used to examine an organization's internal and external environments, is not an end in itself but a step in action planning. The results of a SWOT analysis can change over time. Therefore, the first step in conducting an evaluation of business strategies is to complete a current SWOT analysis. The current analysis is then used to examine the organization's business strategies, placing emphasis on the issue that has prompted the evaluation. The strategies can then be evaluated to determine whether they are appropriate in guiding the operations of the organization to its goals and objectives.

Case Facts

To evaluate an organization's strategies, a reviewer or a team of reviewers will need information about the organization's internal and external environment, and the organization's strategic goals. An understanding of the purpose of the evaluation will help narrow its focus.

The overall question to be answered is, "Will this organization's current operations still allow it to achieve its strategic goals, or is a change of operations required?"

Grandmother's Daycare—Internal and External Environment

Grandmother's Daycare began as a single daycare facility thirty years ago and has expanded into a multistate corporation with more than fifty facilities. The corporation operates on its founding principles: to provide nurturing, safe, sanitary, and secure daycare for children ranging from newborn through kindergarten ages. The corporation has an extensive employee screening and training process to ensure that the safety and well-being of the children in its care continues to rank first within the daycare industry. Registered nurses and licensed security guards are on staff at each facility. As a result, Grandmother's Daycare has the best record for child safety and health of all corporations of its kind.

The need for quality child care has increased steadily over the past thirty years. However, in the last ten years, preschools have become popular. This popularity has been bolstered by research showing that children are receptive to learning at an early age and that children under age five learn some language skills more easily than older children. Preschools are more expensive than traditional daycare, but they focus on beginning educational experiences at the earliest age possible. Preschools frequently hire licensed teachers as caregivers who also provide education. The facilities may include computers for the children's use, educational games, the incorporation of a second language, and a structured learning environment.

Grandmother's Daycare—Goals

An organization's goals provide the overall context for what the organizations seeks to achieve and the specific milestones that are used for planning activities.

The goals of Grandmother's Daycare have remained fairly consistent for the last ten years. Metrics are established annually based on these goals:

- Increase profits by 5 percent per year
- Meet or exceed customers' daycare needs as determined by an annual survey
- Comply with all legal requirements in operating daycare facilities
- Operate as a community member by contributing time, effort, support, and charitable giving

Grandmother's Daycare—Business Strategies

A business strategy defines an organization's long-term goals. Based on its mission to be the "daycare leader by filling an essential need in child care," Grandmother's Daycare has developed business strategies that define its activities and actions.

Grandmother's Daycare—Business Strategies

1. Customer Focus—We will strive to meet customers' wants and needs for child care by providing a safe, sanitary, and secure environment. To accomplish this, we will:

   - Maintain hiring standards that include a background check for all employees that includes financial and criminal records as well as psychological and aptitude testing

   - Establish protocols for determining primary and secondary contacts to restrict the parties to whom children will be released from the facility

   - Maintain professionally trained staff members providing security and health services at each daycare facility

   - Conduct a daily visual inspection and a monthly intensive inspection of each facility

2. Solution Focus—We will meet parents' changing needs by providing after-hours and weekend child care.

   - Establish and maintain a process for parents to arrange for extended care hours

   - Respond flexibly to parents' needs for care hours as practically as possible

   - Develop additional on-call staff members who can respond to extended after-hours child care needs

3. Fiscal Focus—We will safeguard Grandmother's Daycare as a financially prudent organization.

   - Establish an annual operating budget

   - Determine annual fee for services that does not increase by more than 3 percent per year

   - Invest prudently for capital expenditures

Issues That Prompted the Evaluation

Grandmother's Daycare continued to grow and expand until about five years ago. More recently, the facilities have maintained children until the age of three within their care; however, the number of children over age three has steadily declined, and the rate of decline is accelerating. Because of this decline, Grandmother's Daycare has failed to achieve its profit goals for the last two years.

SWOT Analysis Table

	Strengths	Weaknesses
Internal	List assets, competencies, or attributes that enhance competitiveness. Prioritize based on the quality of the strength and the relative importance of the strength.	List lacking assets, competencies, or attributes that diminish competitiveness. Prioritize based on the seriousness of the weakness and the relative importance of the weakness.
	Opportunities	**Threats**
External	List conditions that could be exploited to create a competitive advantage. Prioritize based on the potential of exploiting the opportunities.	List conditions that diminish competitive advantage. Prioritize based on the seriousness and probability of occurrence.
	Note strengths that can be paired with opportunities as areas of competitive advantage.	Note weaknesses that can be paired with threats as risks to be avoided.

Case Analysis Tools and Information

To evaluate business strategies for Grandmother's Daycare, some information is required:

- A current SWOT analysis
- A list of the organization's business strategies
- An explanation of the business issue that has prompted the evaluation
- A list of the organization's goals and objectives that relate to the business issue

Case Analysis Steps

Evaluating an organization's strategies involves a series of decision-making steps. Following these steps minimizes the effort required by focusing on the issues, strategies, and desired outcome:

1. Conduct a current SWOT analysis of the organization's internal and external environments

2. Determine the business strategies relevant to the business issue that generated the need for the evaluation

3. Evaluate the relevant business strategies using the SWOT analysis

SWOT Analysis Process

One method of conducting a SWOT analysis is through a group activity that involves an organization's managers and is organized by a facilitator.

Brainstorming

- If the group is large, the facilitator may divide the managers into smaller groups to encourage participation.

- Through brainstorming, factors are listed under each of the SWOT headings.

- This activity will produce many factors randomly organized under each SWOT heading.

Refining

- To make the list easier to examine, similar items are clustered together.

- Items of high importance are noted under each of the SWOT headings.

Prioritizing

- Strengths are ordered by quality and relative importance.

- Weaknesses are ordered by the degree to which they affect performance and by their relative importance.

- Opportunities are ordered by degree and probability of success.

- Threats are ordered by degree and probability of occurrence.

- Strengths that require little or no operational changes and can be paired with opportunities are designated for potential action to maximize competitive advantages that entail low risk.

- Weaknesses that can be paired with threats are designated in the prioritized list for potential action to minimize consequences that entail high risk.

Conduct a Current SWOT Analysis

The SWOT analysis process is a methodical assessment of the organization and its business environment. During a SWOT analysis, each of the aspects of the business is examined. In most cases, the analysis will be carried out by a group of people involved in planning and decision-making for the organization.

What does the SWOT analysis of Grandmother's Daycare reveal?

The SWOT analysis reveals that Grandmother's Daycare faces a high-risk threat because it has not met its customers' changing needs by providing preschool education, and competitors have an edge in the preschool market. Considering the enrollment drop that Grandmother's Daycare is experiencing, is it reasonable to assume that parents are withdrawing their children from daycare services and enrolling them in preschools with structured learning environments. This apparent problem can be confirmed by surveying the parents who have withdrawn their children from Grandmother's Daycare, but this reason is a plausible conclusion. A review of the annual survey sent to customers will reveal whether the right questions are being asked to discover emerging needs or whether the survey focuses only on the daycare services the organization has traditionally offered.

SWOT Case Table

	Strengths	Weaknesses
Internal	Strengths are apparent in the organization's reputation and record: • Excellent reputation for child safety and health. • Thirty years of experience and success. • Quality in the hiring and training of staff members. • Specialist in the focus of care for young children. • Children under age three are a strong existing clientele.	Weaknesses have emerged in the types of services that the organization has not developed and the needs it is not meeting: • Lack of response to the changing interests in early education. • Lack of trained staff, equipment, and knowledge in delivering childhood education. • Dated focus in meeting the clients' needs. • A corporate name that sounds antiquated.
	Opportunities	**Threats**
External	Opportunities provide potential actions that the organization can exploit in meeting the needs of its current and potential clients: • Quality staff members can be retrained in preschool education. • Possibility of adding state-of-the-art equipment without the burden of existing capital investments. • Ability to add services for children to an existing slate of excellent safety and care. • Ability to rebrand the corporation through a new name and image.	Threats have surfaced because customers' needs are being met by the organization's competition: • Competitors have a significant edge in the preschool market. • Competitors are experienced in education and have facilities in place. • Preschools continue to draw children from ages three through five away from traditional daycares. • Traditional daycares are viewed as warehouses for children rather than educators.
	Note that the strengths the organization has had in hiring quality staff members can be paired with the opportunities for retraining in preschool education.	Note that the weaknesses in the lack of response to customers' changing needs can be paired with threat of the competitors' edge and experience in the preschool market.

However, the SWOT analysis also reveals that Grandmother's Daycare has a low-risk competitive opportunity in having staff that can be retrained to provide preschool education.

Determine Business Strategies to Be Evaluated

The organization's business strategies are its long-term approach toward attainment of its goals and objectives. Organizational strategies consist of planning, organizing, execution, and control activities. Business-level strategy is specifically focused on gaining a competitive advantage in the market.

Because an organization's strategies can be extensive, it is helpful to narrow the focus of the examination by understanding the business issue that has prompted the evaluation. The strategies relevant to the issue can then be targeted for evaluation.

Which business strategies have bearing on the failure of Grandmother's Daycare to meet its profit goals for the last two years?

Assuming that the apparent problem that parents are withdrawing their children to enroll them in preschools can be confirmed, the organization's first business strategy is in error and should be examined.

Business Strategies to Be Evaluated

1. Customer Focus—We will strive to meet customers' wants and needs for child care by providing a safe, sanitary, and secure environment. To accomplish this, we will:

    1.3 Maintain professionally trained members providing security and health services at each daycare facility

---

Evaluate Relevant Business Strategies

After an organization's internal and external circumstances and its business strategies have been examined, the next step is to determine whether a change in course is required to achieve the organization's goals.

Will the current business strategies for Grandmother's Daycare continue to be the most effective approach toward attaining its goals, or should its business strategies be changed?

The organization's customer focus strategies will not guide it toward the achievement of its goal to "increase profits by 5 percent per year." Also, it is likely that the organization is not meeting another of its goals: to "meet or exceed customers' daycare needs as determined by an annual survey." It is possible that the survey being used is an inadequate method of determining customers' changing needs for child-care services and that it should be enhanced and augmented with additional measures for assessment.

If the organization changes its strategies to offer preschool education, additional changes might be required:

- The organization might have to change its name from "Grandmother's Daycare" to a name that more closely reflects the new focus. A **rebranding** of the organization might also be required.
- Staffing should incorporate employees trained in preschool education.
- Capital expenditures must incorporate educational equipment, such as computers.
- The surveying process must change to better capture information about the type and scope of education that the parents seek.

Rebranding
The process of creating an organization's marketing identity with a product or service.

SWOT Case Correct Answer

Grandmother's Daycare has failed to meet its profits goals for the last two years because the retention of children ages three years and older is declining. A SWOT analysis indicates that parents have a need to attain preschool education for their children that is not being met by Grandmother's Daycare, and preschool organizations are meeting those needs.

Using that information to evaluate its strategies, Grandmother's Daycare must change one or more of its customer focus strategies in order to meet its goals. On the plus side, the organization has a low-risk opportunity to retrain its staff members to provide preschool education.

SUMMARY

A business strategy enables an organization to produce planned outcomes. Strategic plans provide direction, focus, and consistency of action throughout the organization. The strategic management process has three interdependent phases:

- Strategy formation
- Strategy implementation
- Strategy evaluation

Businesses may have multiple and varied types of strategies based on levels within an organization, development stages of the organization, and general approaches.

An organization must embed ERM within its strategic context as a common starting point for development and maturation as a business discipline. It may accomplish this by developing ERM goals that are aligned with strategic goals, adopting an ERM-based approach, and applying risk criteria.

Organizations implement the ERM process over time. When an organization is committed to achieving the full value and benefits of ERM, measuring ERM effectiveness and improvements throughout the organization is critical to success. For this purpose, RIMS has developed the RIMS RMM, an objective and consistent measurement tool for self-assessments. This model reviews risk management performance throughout the organization, gives feedback on improvement efforts, and provides knowledge for making better decisions.

Analyzing an organization's internal and external contexts entails assessing the organization's external and internal environments, evaluating its key stakeholders, developing the risk management department and teams, articulating its goals, specifying its values, and establishing a culture of risk management.

A SWOT analysis is a structured examination of an organization's internal and external environment as a prelude to action planning. When used to evaluate an organization's business strategies, SWOT analysis focuses on the event that prompted the evaluation. The results of the business strategies relevant to the cause of the event are examined to determine whether those strategies will be effective in achieving the organization's goals.

CHAPTER NOTES

1. These include the AZ/NZS 4360; Red, Blue, White, and Orange books from the National Research Council (NRC) of the United States; British Standards Institute 31000; and the Canadian Standards Association (CSA).

2. Such as ISO/31000: 2009 and IRGC.

3. Such as the Treadway Commission's COSO ERM guidelines, the Turnball Report, and the Cadbury Report.

4. In a for-profit organization, shareholders are the prime stakeholders.

5. "Mission, Vision & Values," The Coca-Cola Company, www.thecoca-colacompany.com/ourcompany/mission_vision_values.html (accessed March 17, 2009).

6. "Our Company," The Dow Chemical Company, www.dow.com/about/about-dow/vision.htm (accessed March 18, 2009).

7. "Our Company," The Dow Chemical Company, www.dow.com/about/about-dow/vision.htm (accessed March 18, 2009).

8. "Our Vision," Novo Nordisk A/S, www.novonordisk.com/about_us/NovoNordisk-Way-of-Managment/NN-way-of-management-our-vision.asp (accessed March 18, 2009).

9. Based in part on ISO/DIS 31000:2009, AU NZS 4360, and RIMS Risk Maturity Model (RMM) for ERM.

10. Risk management functional areas may include, but are not limited to, Global Risk Management, Internal Audit, Business Continuity Planning, Legal, Compliance, Privacy & Security Office, IT Risk Management, and Financial Risk Management.

11. Risk and Insurance Management Society, RIMS Risk Maturity Model (RMM) for Enterprise Risk Management (New York: RIMS, 2006), p. 7.

12. RIMS Risk Maturity Model (RMM) for Enterprise Risk Management (New York: RIMS, 2006), pp. 8–9.

13. RIMS Risk Maturity Model (RMM) for Enterprise Risk Management (New York: RIMS, 2006), p. 9.

14. Risk Management Guidelines: Companion to AS/NZS 4360, Standards Australia/Standards New Zealand (Sydney, AU/ Wellington, NZ), 2004, p. 27.

15. John Elkington, *Cannibals with Forks: The Triple Bottom Line of 21st Century Business* (New Society Publishers, 1998) and "Towards the sustainable corporation: Win-win-win business strategies for sustainable development," *California Management Review*, vol. 36, no. 2, pp. 90–100.

16. Dan Anderson, *Corporate Survival* (iUniverse, 2005), p. 120.

17. For additional details, see ISO/DIS 31000, p. 9, and AS/NZ HB 4360, pp. 19, 22, and 29.

18. RIMS Risk Maturity Model (RMM) for Enterprise Risk Management (New York: RIMS, 2006), p. 8.

Direct Your Learning

Establish Internal and External Contexts: Incorporating Business and Economic Intelligence

Educational Objectives

After learning the content of this chapter and completing the corresponding course guide assignment, you should be able to:

▶ Describe the importance of economic intelligence as applied to enterprise-wide risk management (ERM) program goals.

▶ Describe business intelligence system functions that apply to ERM.

▶ Describe the phases in the implementation of a business intelligence (BI) system for an ERM program.

▶ Describe the governance and output elements of information technology (IT) BI systems as they relate to ERM program goals.

▶ Given the assignment of presenting an ERM case to management, recommend the BI systems, information technology (IT) governance practices, and risk outputs that benefit an organization.

Outline

Economic Intelligence— ERM Program Application

Elements of a Business Intelligence System

Business Intelligence Systems— Enterprise-Wide Risk Management Implementation Phases

Business Intelligence Systems—IT Governance and Outputs

Business Intelligence Systems— Presenting the Case for ERM

Summary

Establish Internal and External Contexts: Incorporating Business and Economic Intelligence

Effective enterprise-wide risk management (ERM) programs require information (intelligence) about a broad array of economic, political, and competitive factors that affect an organization's management strategies and objectives. Well-developed economic intelligence (EI) and business intelligence (BI) systems and information technology (IT) governance are important tools and methods that help enable an ERM program, which in turn benefits the organization by allowing for better-informed decision making.

ECONOMIC INTELLIGENCE—ERM PROGRAM APPLICATION

Economic intelligence data gathering is vitally important for organizations that want to control their exposure to risk, protect their proprietary technologies and strategies from competitors, and enhance opportunities that may arise.

To optimize risk-taking, effective ERM programs require intelligence about a broad array of economic, political, and competitive factors that affect an organization's management strategies and objectives. The discipline of EI blends and analyzes the macro data available from public and private sources with expert risk assessments to produce informed perspectives on potential loss events. For example, data that indicate certain demographic shifts (such as an increase in elderly population) may be assessed as affecting the rate of demand for an organization's goods or services (such as a municipality's need for more local health clinics and senior services).

This external context of risk analysis enables an organization to develop and correlate risk response plans that prepare it for a variety of external conditions. It also translates external data into risk management information that is used to detect potential threats and opportunities from the competitive environment and for deploying internal controls to protect organizational assets. For example, EI may allow a distributor to anticipate a recession, leading it to assess its internal buying strategies accordingly. This could cause it to place stronger controls on inventories and limit new purchases to products its customers deem essential.

Economic intelligence
The information used to evaluate changes in macroeconomic information for production, distribution, and consumption of goods and services with country data on labor, finance, and taxation that affect risk management decisions.

EI for an ERM program is applied through three integrated methods:

- EI data gathering
- EI risk investigation
- EI monitoring

Economic Intelligence Data Gathering

EI data are gained from a wide variety of private and public data sources that provide quantitative tracking information (audit reports, risk control measures, and action items) and qualitative tracking information (customer service or field representative notes). For example, ERM program managers use EI sources to establish indicators for timelines for analysis of external trends, such as current economic conditions, or the marketplace adoption of a potentially disruptive technology (for example, the "smart phone's" encroachment on the portable global positioning system market). The analysis of such data may reveal leading or lagging indicators that affect management decisions.

Additionally, organizations use EI not only to make determinations about current strategy, but also to make projections that affect future strategic planning. Decision making regarding the political, economic, cultural, human, and competitive environments is influenced by EI.

EI methods can gather and integrate data from three types of sources:

- Public—freely available sources such as the Bureau of Labor Statistics
- Proprietary—fee-based information services such as Bloomberg
- Private—confidentially held sources of information analyses (such as a consultant hired to provide a detailed view of EI on the market share potential of introducing a totally electric-powered car)

For instance, decision makers in the pharmaceutical industry use EI to combine population demographics (public), prescription fulfillment data (proprietary and competitive), and product analysis (private) to define threats and opportunities related to growing market share in a given class of treatment.

Public information used in EI, also referred to as open source intelligence, is easily obtainable, but can require powerful search engines to refine it. Open source intelligence consists of various kinds of information:

- Country geographic structures and location codes—demographic information
- Government organizations and related responsibilities and activities—regulatory and policy-making information
- Market segment activity—customer and prospect information
- Corporate sector activity—business and industry sector information
- National income statistics—personal income and outlays information

- Money and banking activity—financial markets information
- Foreign trade activity—balance of payments, trends in goods and services information
- Public finance activity—government initiatives, public-private partnerships information
- Energy production and consumption—supply and demand information
- Infrastructure project activity—improvements and finance source information
- Agriculture production and consumption—supply and demand information
- Crime—trending, geographic, and demographic information

Economic Intelligence Risk Investigation

The purpose of EI risk assessment and analysis is to reveal trends and opportunities and to determine potential relationships between external and internal exposures. Any positive correlations from the data are aligned with risk investigation and analysis. This analysis process uses BI systems information to align risk exposures with business categories (such as roles, functions, processes, and lines of business) and subcategories that show the root causes or effects of the risk exposure.

EI data are mined to identify metrics that provide risk indicators that can, in turn, affect potential loss events. EI data are applied to metrics developed by the organization. The information obtained as a result of the data analysis is used for risk investigation. EI metrics used for risk identification and assessment include these examples:

- Population size—to assess levels of demand for goods and services
- Employment—to assess economic cycles
- Labor costs—to assess employment categories for goods and services
- Prices—to assess production cycles and demand
- Tariffs—to assess government policies and protectionism affecting trade
- Consumption rates—to assess changes in demand
- Patents—to assess changes in technology and related applications
- Regulations—to assess changes in compliance control requirements
- Regulatory fines—to assess penalties for regulatory violations
- Criminal activities—to assess threats and risk control vulnerabilities
- Environmental disasters—to assess catastrophic event potential

Potential losses or threats, as well as potential gains or opportunities, are also analyzed using EI modeling. EI modeling methods create what-if analyses of potential threats to the organization's assets, resources, and competitive positioning. For example, an EI model can be created to help an organization formulate its strategy related to the appropriate combination of private and

Business intelligence (BI) systems
The enterprise information management technologies designed to plan and control the decision-making information flows that affect upside and downside risk analysis and extract, transform, and load systems data into an integrated structure.

Key performance indicator (KPI)
A financial or nonfinancial measurement that defines how successfully an organization is progressing toward its long-term goals.

Key risk indicator (KRI)
A financial or nonfinancial metric used to help define and measure potential losses.

public financing for a new project or the viability of potential new-product initiatives.

The outcomes from these models help establish the foundation for preparing contingency plans and stress tests for potential risk response strategy scenarios. For example, in 2009, stress tests were developed by the United States Federal Reserve and the U.S. Treasury Department to assess the viability of large banks. These stress tests considered a number of EI factors to determine whether the banks could weather change within target parameters without becoming insolvent.

The scope and depth of EI risk investigation and analysis are based on determining the breadth of risk types and risk issues that affect senior management's goals. EI analysis is used to assess the degree to which external factors affect all potential loss exposures in an organization's ERM program. However, EI analysis is only as good as the data that are being analyzed. If stress tests, for example, do not consider outlier possibilities or combinations, then they may not detect significant risks to the organization. The timing of EI reporting is important. An organization may want to add monthly reporting indices or even more frequently measured indices to important quarterly EI reports in order to discover variation in a more timely fashion.

Economic Intelligence Monitoring

Business intelligence (BI) systems are used to convert the EI information gathered into monitoring reports. Monitoring reports capture risk information and relate it to **key performance indicators (KPIs)** and to **key risk indicators (KRIs)** to enable drill-down analysis from senior management's goals to root-cause factors. Senior management and/or those individuals in the organization who perform specific business functions are accountable for providing "sign-offs" attesting to the completeness of EI risk identification and action items.

Generic Examples of Risk Types and Risk Issues That Assist in Evaluating Specific Causes of Risk

Risk Type	Risk Issue
Strategic risk	• Competitive positioning
	• Gross domestic product decline
	• Interest rate risk spreads
	• Bankruptcies/foreclosures
	• Unemployment
	• Product and service offerings
Compliance risk	• Product and service standards
	• Ethical standards
	• Employment practices
Financial risk	• Credit rating
	• Foreign exchange
	• Capital adequacy
	• Erroneous reporting
Operational risk	• People
	• Processes
	• Systems
Environmental risk	• Property and premises
	• Safety
	• Weather conditions

EI risk investigation, analysis, and intelligence monitoring typically follow risk frameworks (with risk types and risk issues) that can vary by organization.

These are examples of executives who are accountable for EI identification of emerging risk issues:

- Marketing senior executive—identifies competitors
- Senior sales executive—identifies customers
- Purchasing senior executive—identifies suppliers
- Compliance senior executive—identifies regulations
- Customer service senior executive—identifies service issues
- IT senior executive—identifies systems applications

ERM program leaders monitor risk analysis inputs (such as general ledger account data with alerts linked to a change in percentage or value trend for a specific time period) on emerging or evolving conditions to update risk response decisions and contingency plans. Major retailers examine EI relative to their purchasing records. If the economy is moving into a period of recovery, the retailer might consider devoting more floor space and advertising to higher-value goods such as appliances. It may consult previous periods of recovery to determine the extent to which appliances were purchased by its customers or the retail industry.

Changes revealed by ERM program monitoring are delegated to the appropriate risk owner within the organization that has risk oversight accountability for specific risk centers.

These are generic examples of roles within an organization and their oversight accountabilities:

- Chief executive officers—responsible for internal controls
- Auditing senior executive—responsible for internal controls testing
- Legal senior executive—responsible for corporate policies
- Human resources senior executive—responsible for organization position controls
- Finance/accounting senior executive—responsible for the integrity of the general ledger accounts structure

An organization's management has a responsibility to monitor the ERM program's effectiveness and ensure that the data gathered via the application of EI are relevant and accurate. Relevance and accuracy of information can be confirmed by comparing the information to best practices benchmarks, by having the information evaluated by internal or external experts, and by having the findings analyzed and correlated. Additionally, the relevance and accuracy of the information can be supported through data monitoring controls and risk notification logs. For example, when a percentage change in data occurs that exceeds the allowable range, the proper risk owners are immediately notified.

ELEMENTS OF A BUSINESS INTELLIGENCE SYSTEM

An organization's BI systems integrate enterprise-wide data flows to improve risk management decision making, internal controls testing, and credit evaluation. BI systems also facilitate transparent data management, which supports **corporate governance** objectives for accountability in monitoring performance reporting, regulatory compliance, and data integrity.

BI systems **extract, transform, and load (ETL)** data from multiple sources into an integrated performance management framework to ensure that there are consistent definitions and calculations in business reporting and analysis. That is, BI systems obtain raw data from many sources that then must be

Corporate governance
The mechanisms and procedures that determine how corporations are run.

Extract, transform, and load (ETL)
The extraction of data from multiple sources, transformation of the data so it conforms with the organization's needs and standards, and loading of the data into an accessible database or data management system.

transformed into information that is useful to the organization and that meets its reporting structure and needs. This information is entered into databases from which it may be delivered to risk owners through standard reports or unique searches. These are the primary BI system functions that apply to ERM practices:

- Performance management scorecards
- BI information user roles
- BI reports
- BI data mining and risk notifications
- Master data management

Performance Management Scorecards

Performance management scorecards summarize performance status information from multiple source systems. They enable management to monitor both changes in financial results and progress toward key operational targets that are linked to strategic plans and goals. ERM grafted onto an organization's strategic plan links operational objectives and organizational goals and allows an organization to confirm the performance accountability of its management.

For example, human resources might use performance management scorecards in a learning management system (LMS) to record and track existing competencies and competencies gained through training and education. This LMS could also identify required competencies of risk owners and record personal development goals for each in order to reduce competency gaps or to provide guidance in hiring persons with the required competencies.

Performance management scorecards generate reports showing metrics that are designated as either KPIs or KRIs. KPIs define and measure progress toward organizational goals. KRIs support the development of risk management criteria for measuring the impact of potential or actual losses. Senior managers and the board demonstrate the application of corporate governance practices to policy review and approval processes when they use performance management scorecard reports.

Performance management scorecard reports document that risk thresholds have been applied to monitoring KPIs. Risk thresholds measure variances from expected results (for example, from an organization's stated risk appetite in a specific area such as interest rate risk). Scorecard "warning lights" are applied to reports to create visual alerts for yellow-light (moderate risk exposure) and red-light (extreme risk exposure) situations that warrant drill-to-details review of root cause issues that may affect contingency plans and resource allocation decisions. For example, a senior executive's "dashboard" warning indicators ("dashboard" in this context refers to a BI software application that provides real-time performance data, including those related to unusual exceptions to performance) might change as a 120-day moving average of a key ratio approaches a risk threshold. To illustrate, an average temperature dashboard for a large retailer may reveal that autumn has been warmer than expected, which might indicate the need for it to start the Christmas sale of winter coats even earlier.

Scorecard reports present indices and ratios expressed as **benchmarking** metrics that compare industry results and risk assessment calculations. These metrics include key financial ratios that financial institutions and governments use to assess capital adequacy and comparable **risk factors**.

Performance management BI is designed to allow users to penetrate the various levels of detail of financial management reports to the underlying metrics that show the risk analysis of **leading indicator** (those that, for example, anticipate the direction in which the economy is heading) and **lagging indicator** (those that, for example, help explain how long an economic downturn or upturn will continue) relationships. For example, substantiating a lower reserve amount for obsolete inventories (a strategic goal) could be validated by the information obtained through the analysis of purchase order trends and work-in-process statistics (operational objectives). Examples of performance management scorecards used by organizations include those for financial management, revenue management, expense management, and long-term asset management.

Financial KPIs produced through BI systems represent a systemic control for replicating the formulas used in KPI calculations. KPI calculation verification documentation tied to financial management scorecards is used to confirm internal controls for testing the metrics that underlie the financial reporting of net income, return on assets, and other key financial ratios used in benchmarking risk exposures. The "Performance Management Scorecards—Financial" exhibit is an example of a financial scorecard.

Benchmarking
The process of comparing results to industry standards or best practices.

Risk factors
The quantitative and qualitative criteria used in the evaluation of the relative loss exposure levels in financial accounts, workflow processes, and risk events.

Leading indicator
A predictor of change at the beginning of an economic cycle.

Lagging indicator
A consequence of change at the end of an economic cycle.

Performance Management Scorecards—Financial

Financial management scorecard reports include metrics that show specific goals for revenue growth, profitability, asset efficiency, and ERM index.

Financial Management

| Revenue Growth (%) | Contribution Margin (or Profitability) (%) | Financial Management | ERM Index |

Revenue scorecards link external data and internal performance metrics to organizational structure and processes. Items that might be included in a revenue scorecard are revenue; sales representative performance; customer satisfaction; opportunities by product line; and, for a municipality, sales tax revenue. Revenue scorecard metrics link to the revenue strategies of the organization, providing an added source of competitive advantage. The drill-down from financial reporting to operational analysis shows workflow monitoring across the customer transaction life cycle. For example, new product sales and market share growth can be measured in depth and according to established metrics. The "Performance Management Scorecards—Revenue" exhibit is an example of a revenue scorecard.

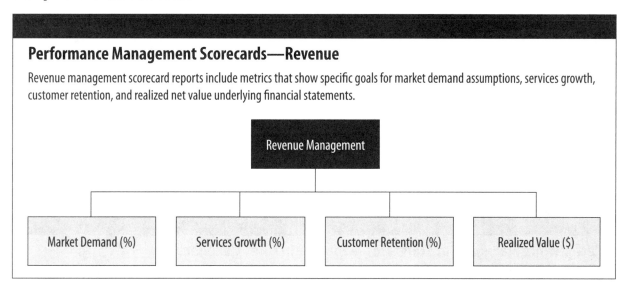

Performance Management Scorecards—Revenue

Revenue management scorecard reports include metrics that show specific goals for market demand assumptions, services growth, customer retention, and realized net value underlying financial statements.

Revenue Management

| Market Demand (%) | Services Growth (%) | Customer Retention (%) | Realized Value ($) |

Operational expense scorecards, for example, show supply chain management controls across the processes that transform raw materials or third-party services into finished goods or value-added services for customer requirements. For example, in an ERM environment in which business goals are aligned with known opportunities and threats, financial reporting scorecards may show that rising vendor costs in a critical area are a direct result of the death of an experienced buyer. However, because this risk had been anticipated and a long-term training strategy and robust recruiting program had been previously implemented, the rising vendor costs fall within an acceptable range. The "Performance Management Scorecards—Operational" exhibit is an example of an operational scorecard.

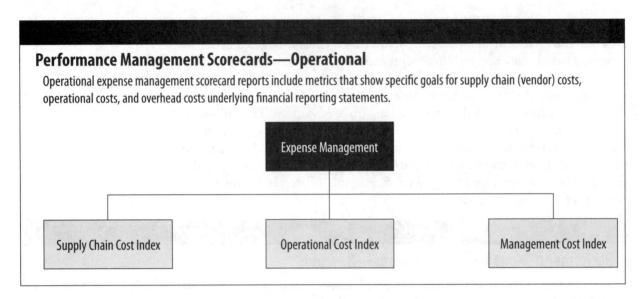

Performance Management Scorecards—Operational

Operational expense management scorecard reports include metrics that show specific goals for supply chain (vendor) costs, operational costs, and overhead costs underlying financial reporting statements.

Long-term asset management scorecards may show how resource expenditures are evaluated from a capital investment perspective. The macro-to-micro analysis from financial reporting may show life-cycle tracking for tangible and intangible assets. The "Performance Management Scorecards—Long-Term Asset Management" exhibit is an example of a long-term asset management scorecard.

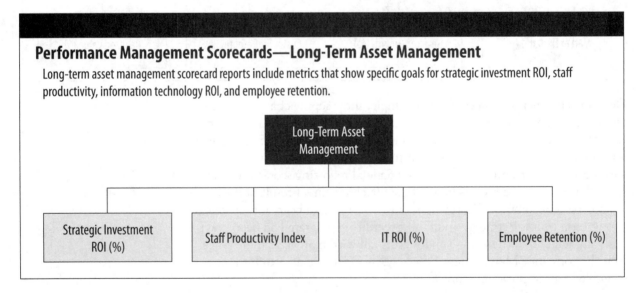

Performance Management Scorecards—Long-Term Asset Management

Long-term asset management scorecard reports include metrics that show specific goals for strategic investment ROI, staff productivity, information technology ROI, and employee retention.

Performance management scorecards help ensure that management information is synchronized and risk-assessed for consistency with strategic goal planning and controls.

BI Information User Roles

Business intelligence information user roles define sets of workflow activities that individuals must complete for the organization to achieve its goals. **Active directory** controls administer user group role assignments, monitor workflow processes, and log those who access the controls. This information management structure creates technical links between people and workflow processes by granting access privileges according to user role(s). For example, an individual user may have one or more business roles (financial, human resources, or administration functions) that can be grouped with similar users. In such an instance, active directory controls would grant required levels of system access for the user groups rather than for each individual in a particular group.

Financial information user group membership is used to plan and control appropriate **segregation of duties**. Use of this plan and control process demonstrates that appropriate internal controls exist over inputs, outputs, and changes to the general ledger system. Financial information user roles include processes for identifying these user roles:

- Managers responsible for general ledger account analysis
- General ledger account reconcilers
- General ledger reconciliation approvers
- General ledger reconciliation confirmers

Functionality of BI report administration is used to assess whether the access that employees in different work functions and job types have matches their risk management program sign-off accountability. This process uses **decision role analysis** to match competency reviews with planning and control of authorized staffing levels.

Decision roles are based on the fusion of job type and work function assignments. They classify information user roles from a risk analysis perspective.

Job types classify levels of organizational decision-making authority and use a classification structure that identifies these user groups:

- Senior executives who have policy management oversight responsibilities
- Executives who have management planning and control responsibilities
- Managers who have supervisory responsibilities
- Professional/ technical workers who have operational control responsibilities
- Administrative workers who have administrative control responsibilities

Business intelligence information user roles
The functional and organizational parameters used to evaluate how information requirements relate to job responsibilities.

Active directory
A security management component used on the Windows platform to manage the identities and relationships that make up network environments.

Segregation of duties
The processes that ensure that no one individual has the physical and system access to control all phases (authorization, custody, and record keeping) of a business process or transaction.

Decision role analysis
A process that determines what kinds of decisions are needed, where in the organizational structure those decisions should be made, and to what extent each manager should be involved.

In addition to the job type dimension, work function is a dimension that classifies job requirements by employment categories. Work functions can include these classifications:

- General management
- Finance
- Sales
- Marketing
- Legal
- Risk management
- IT systems

When developing BI information user roles in the context of workflow activities and responsibilities, information user decision-making responsibilities are divided into three access review levels for assessing risk management accountability and data privileges:

- Primary decision roles, which originate or complete transactions and have direct impact on expense
- Contributory decision roles, which are responsible for quality control activities and risk monitoring of work that originates in other work functions
- Status decision roles, which are responsible for certifying business results and releasing external reports that cover their areas of organizational responsibility

Information access controls are effectively defined for risk management analysis when information roles are identified for all organization positions and people who affect workflow process activities and/or management reporting integrity.

Business intelligence reports
The multidimensional slices of information that connect system users to performance scorecards and analytics for enterprise-wide decision making.

Dimensional design
A business intelligence method used to convert transaction data into hierarchical structures for enterprise-wide decision analysis.

BI Reports

Business intelligence reports are vehicles for drilling down from performance goals to key details that underlie performance and risk control decisions. BI reports use **dimensional design** (for example, a product code) that links metrics (quantitative data) to hierarchical structures (for example, product batch code, product type code, product subtype code) for summarizing data attributes into risk analysis categories. To illustrate, in a manufacturing company, return on investment (ROI) of a particular product type can be linked to marketing and finance. A consistent approach to dimensional design demonstrates that there is IT governance focus on enterprise-wide risk issues and decision areas that align facts across organizational areas into a unified process for enterprise-wide risk analysis. Examples of BI reports include BI external reports, BI planning reports, and BI analysis reports.

BI External Reports

Regulatory mandates for greater transparency impose requirements on organizations to prepare financial reports and footnotes in an open source eXtensible Business Reporting Language (XBRL) for balance sheet, income statement, and cash flow reporting. XBRL tags link metrics for specific periods to industry **metadata** templates for footnotes and dimensional roll-up structures (instance documentation). Regulatory reporting in XBRL expands the public information available on other organizations that can be used to create BI analysis for evaluating **performance benchmarking** comparisons of industry results and risk appetites. XBRL electronic information exchange reinforces data standards for communicating with regulators, financial services providers, customers, and vendors. Change management notifications (changes in reporting structures) and organization accountability information (audit trails) are direct evidence of XBRL's continuous controls.

BI Planning Reports

Financial results forecasts and budget plans are expressed in BI reports using a scenario plan to tag multiple projections for the same financial periods. Scenario analysis shows that the baseline budgets approved by management and the board of directors include financial contingency plans that anticipate different market conditions.

BI Analysis Reports

BI analysis reports show how a drill-down-to-details review of root cause performance issues will cover the highest priorities in an organization's ERM oversight processes. Examples of BI analysis report content include results analysis drill-down-to-details dimensions for these areas:

* Time drill-down that relates events to relevant time periods

* General ledger (GL) account drill-down that relates financial monitoring to balance sheet details

* Organizational head count drill-down that relates staffing levels and staffing mix analysis to budget planning and control centers

* Competencies drill-down that relates job performance requirements to workflow process risk analysis

* Risk drill-down that relates risk frameworks to specific risk exposures

* Regulations drill-down that relates compliance requirements to specific regulations

* Policy drill-down that relates policy type oversight to specific policies

* Customer drill-down analysis that relates revenue recognition and payment risk to customer invoice aging details

* Vendor drill-down that relates expense monitoring to supplier performance risk and vendor invoice fulfillment details

Metadata
The data about data that provide context for analyzing transaction facts with efficient structures for grouping hierarchical information.

Performance benchmarking
A process for comparing results to comparable organizations and best practices.

BI Data Mining and Risk Notifications

Data mining
The process of extracting hidden patterns from data that is used in a wide range of applications for research and fraud detection.

Notification log
A control document used to monitor risk threshold alert messages sent to system users.

BI **data mining** reports extract hidden patterns from underlying transaction data. For example, data errors and process irregularities that occur that could affect an organization's value and reduce its assets can be detected. A data mining report's inventory shows the breadth of risk management activity for detective controls to prevent fraud.

BI risk notifications are messages sent to key personnel when risk tolerances for specific events are exceeded. **Notification log** monitoring shows evidence of how ERM is applied at the appropriate senior management oversight levels.

KPI notifications for strategic goals are assigned to senior-level managers who have primary responsibility for presenting KPIs and related risk tolerance issues to the board of directors for strategic goals review and approval.

KRI notifications for potential losses are assigned to employees who are responsible for monitoring potential losses in specific drill-down-to-detail analysis reports that roll up to affect aggregate results.

Risk evaluation responsibilities are linked to BI report utilization audits of information role responsibilities. Thus, audit findings revealing that specific areas of the organization are underperforming or are exceeding risk tolerances can be addressed. This practice reinforces IT governance oversight of risk monitoring issues, the application of automated controls to corporate governance practices, and data security administration.

Master Data Management

Master data management
A set of processes and tools that consistently defines and manages the nontransactional data entities of an organization; also called organization reference data.

BI data warehouses are staging points for organizing metrics and data tables into the most efficient structures for extracting timely and accurate BI reports. Each BI dimension in BI reports serves as a **master data management** checkpoint for testing the information reliability and roll-up accuracy of facts extracted from multiple source systems into unified consensus on the status of results and plans.

The goal of master data management is to reduce the use of potentially inconsistent versions of the same master data across the enterprise. BI data management testing is used to identify problems that can include poor data quality management practices, inconsistent data classification controls, and gaps in data reconciliation activities.

BUSINESS INTELLIGENCE SYSTEMS— ENTERPRISE-WIDE RISK MANAGEMENT IMPLEMENTATION PHASES

A BI system provides an organization with the building blocks for its ERM program, enabling it to convey critical risk exposure information to its senior executives and board of directors. The BI system allows the organization to link detailed analyses back to a broader governing authority and to gain consensus on root cause issues.

When establishing internal and external contexts for ERM, BI system implementation can be used to integrate financial reporting transparency requirements and risk notification accountabilities for identifying potential losses and managing risk control activities. An ERM program requires that information be reliable, valuable, and consistent throughout the organization. Thus, BI as a tool can be used to implement ERM. There are five phases in BI system implementation, which can be linked to the steps in the ERM process:

1. Enterprise risk identification—This correlates with ERM's establishing the internal and external contexts and assessment steps.

2. Risk information mapping—This correlates with ERM's assessment step.

3. ERM program evaluation—This correlates with ERM's assessment step.

4. ERM information compliance—This correlates with ERM's implementation step.

5. BI reports for risk control roles and notifications—This correlates with ERM's communicate and consult and monitor and review steps.

BI essentially provides organizations with the tools to gather data and to produce the reports necessary to better identify threats and opportunities and enable ERM.

BI ERM Implementation Phases

Phase 1. Enterprise Risk Identification
Organizations identify and prioritize emerging risk exposure issues
Use risk frameworks to connect data sources to enterprise risk information maps
Relate risk exposures to responsibilities and competencies

Phase 2. Risk Information Mapping
Connects enterprise risk information source applications to business reporting
cycles and process responsibilities for managing risk control

Phase 3. ERM Program Evaluation
Roll-up information resulting from the BI analysis generates performance
management scorecard indicators
Active monitoring of ERM decisions
Enables ongoing ERM program evaluation at senior management levels

Phase 4. ERM Information Compliance
Monitors key financial and transactional data
Creates baseline information for testing ERM analysis and auditing internal
controls
Uses XBRL standards for financial reporting—regulatory compliance

Phase 5. BI Reports for Risk Control Roles and Notifications
Creates reports for assigned risk control roles
Creates notifications of deviations from expected results
Links KRI metrics and risk control roles

Enterprise Risk Identification

In the enterprise risk identification phase of BI implementation, the organization prioritizes the emerging risk exposure issues that affect performance management goals, credit evaluation, and regulatory compliance standards. BI risk information needs are prioritized through top-down risk factor review of the hazards and drivers associated with the organization.

Risk frameworks connect relevant enterprise data sources to enterprise risk information maps that show how well risk exposures relate to organization decision-making responsibilities and competencies.

These are examples of risk frameworks:

- Insurance risk types established by underwriters to define and manage insurance policy coverages
- Risk types established by the Committee of Sponsoring Organizations (COSO) of the Treadway Commission for Sarbanes–Oxley (SOX) compliance audits
- Basel II risk types established by the Bank for International Settlements (BIS) for assessing capital adequacy
- Risk types established by the Office of the U.S. Comptroller of the Currency (OCC) for assessing banking controls
- ISO Standard 31000:2009

Enterprise risk issues are reported in annual statements and public documents. BI systems create hierarchies for drilling down to risk frameworks from risk categories to identify the best set of enterprise risk issues that provide guidance for assessing internal controls and risk response decisions. Risk categories and risk types vary by organization.

Generic Examples of Risk Categories

These are generic examples of risk categories with risk types that point to specific BI risk exposures:

- Strategic risks—external economic and political events, interest rate volatility, competitive positioning, product/service offering changes
- Compliance risks—product and/or service standards, ethical standards, employment practices
- Financial risks—credit rating, foreign exchange, capital adequacy, erroneous reporting
- Operational risks—people, processes, systems
- Environmental (or hazard) risks—property and premises, safety, weather conditions

---

The roll-up of risk information from risk categories and types creates a BI risk analysis dimension that is inserted into enterprise-wide risk analysis reports. Each dimension in risk exposure analysis reports is linked to a senior executive who has the ERM competencies and status oversight responsibility for assessing potential volatility and confirming that controls are in place to manage risks. At each hierarchical level, from line managers to executives, risk owners are responsible for sign-offs that are completed based on agreed-upon standard measures.

These are examples of BI dimensions and executives who might be tasked with confirming the completeness of risk identification oversight for their areas of responsibility:

- Internal controls—general management senior executive
- Internal control assertions—audit senior executive
- Risks—risk management senior executive

- Corporate policies—legal senior executive
- Regulations—compliance senior executive
- Organization positions—human resources senior executive
- Systems applications—IT senior executive
- General ledger accounts—finance/accounting senior executive

Risk Information Mapping

Once an organization has identified its enterprise risks, the risk information is mapped. Risk information mapping connects, or "maps," enterprise risk information source applications to business reporting cycles and process responsibilities for managing risk control activities at specific points in the organization. Risk mapping is usually rendered graphically in a two-dimensional matrix according to likelihood of event and impact.

ERM program leaders work with IT department managers to document the information inputs, communication responsibilities, and distribution timing requirements for ERM program participants. ERM documentation covers analysis of loss event reporting and KRI information that detects deviations from expected results for KPIs.

Risk information maps are developed for all the business areas that affect the organization's strategic value chain. Senior executives sign off on the data calculation accuracy and monitoring accountabilities for the KPIs and KRIs that match their respective organizational authority and competencies.

Examples of KPIs used in risk information mapping include the financial ratios that banks, investors, and regulators use to benchmark performance relative to comparable organizations.

Illustrative, Generic Example of an Excerpt From an ERM Risk Analysis

Risk Type	Risk Category	Enterprise Risk	Outcome
Compliance	Audit deficiency	Inadequate or ineffective controls	Theft
Environmental	Pollution	Environmental damage	Restoration expense
Financial	Credit	Access to funding	Bankruptcy
Operational	Data security	Inadequate or ineffective data security	Cost of breach
Strategic	Market demand	Services volume escalation	Programs expense

Risks are then assessed and scored according to level of risk (for example, on risk likelihood and severity scales of one through five), with KPI drill-down components included that drive the score.

Executives who are assigned related accountabilities identify risk thresholds for each KPI and KRI to create notification alerts for yellow-light (moderate risk exposure) and red-light (extreme risk exposure) situations. Risk thresholds are performance ranges that measure variances from expected results to highlight positive or negative trends (calculation formula rules for some KPIs and KRIs are shown in the next exhibit). Risk notifications may trigger contingency plans that respond to extreme risk events; they represent the different levels of disturbance the organization is experiencing.

KPIs, KRIs, and Calculation Formula Rules

KPIs and their calculation formula rules include these areas of measurement:

Financial management

- Operating margin: operating income divided by net sales

- Net margin: net income divided by net sales

- Return on assets: net income divided by average assets

- ERM risk index: average risk exposure levels across ERM program areas

Staffing management

- Revenue productivity index: income divided by staffing head count

- Employee retention: percentage change in base period head count after employee turnover

Operations management

- Inventory turnover: cost of goods sold divided by average inventory

- Capacity utilization: actual unit output divided by potential unit output

KRIs include the metrics that are used to identify abnormal patterns and exceptions to policy. KRIs and their calculation formula rules include these areas of measurement:

- Percentage change from prior period—current result divided by prior period (day/month/quarter/year)

- Budget variance percentage—current result divided by expected result

- Aged accounts receivable—unpaid customer invoice amounts greater than "X" days that may affect bad debt reserves

- Aged accounts payable—unpaid vendor invoice amounts greater than "X" days that may result in legal action

BI Program Evaluation

In an ERM context, BI analysis roll-up information creates performance management scorecard indicators that document active monitoring of ERM decision issues and enable ongoing evaluation of the ERM program at senior management levels.

The enterprise risk management risk index metric is an aggregate measure that shows the scope of ERM program design and the drill-down paths to accountability for risk management evaluation and reporting details. These risk assessment factors are ERM index components:

- Inherent or initial risk—The potential maximum loss (PML) rating (alternatively called possible maximum loss), or exposure score, identifies risk issues with high levels of inherent risk. BI analysis shows risks and related workflow process points that require detailed loss event severity evaluation. The PML exposure score is used to identify general ledger accounts that represent a potential material risk to reporting the organization's financial results. Potential loss calculation details are reported to the board of directors and discussed in the context of stress testing and financial statement footnotes that provide explanations of strategic risks.

- Impact and likelihood risk—Risk matrix ratings of risk likelihood and risk impact assess financial loss tracking activity, the risk response decisions to retain, and whether to mitigate or transfer specific exposures. BI analysis reports of risk probabilities show their relationship to insurance policy layers for primary and excess coverage limit decisions.

- Residual risk—Residual risk ratings target unmitigated exposures. The documentation of internal control activities, contingency plans, and audit assertions are the evidence of risk controls' effectiveness for low-exposure index scores. BI analysis allows the organization to evaluate its people, processes, and systems. The information obtained from the evaluation provides documentation for root cause analysis and management accountability at specific control points in the organization.

- Recovery risk—Net recovery risk exposure ratings target loss controls and information about restoration activity and litigation activity that influence case reserves, balance sheet liabilities reserves, and loss adjustment expenses. For example, the restoration costs after a hurricane may be greater than expected due to scarcity of construction materials and contractors.

The appropriately designated senior executives use BI recovery report information to drill down on loss events to verify reserve estimates that affect their areas of responsibility and take appropriate risk response action at the risk financing level.

ERM Information Compliance

BI systems enable organizations to establish baselines for accountability, transparency, and audit integrity of key financial and transactional data across the enterprise and to promptly communicate risk assessment results.

Regulatory standards for XBRL (extensible business reporting language) financial reporting provide direction for mapping financial statement data to standard taxonomies defined by industry. Public companies are responsible for mapping current period information to their roll-up structures for income statements, balance sheets, and cash flow analysis. Footnotes to financial statements are organized into metadata tags that explain accounting assumptions and risk disclosure issues.

ERM managers monitor administrative logs that show the extraction and transformation of the source data that is transformed into BI and XBRL reports. XBRL is a worldwide XML-based standard for gathering, analyzing, and producing financial data. Information is input once and can be converted to many different delivery formats. This information is used to show that IT governance practices are tracking any baseline changes in report structure, source systems, and calculation rules that affect audit testing benchmarks. Master data management practices align BI information updates with the maintenance of the dimensional relationships that join enterprise relationships across data tables.

A BI audit administrative monitoring log includes these types of content:

- Report assignment by authorized user (risk event participants)
- Report cycle notifications
- Report events submitted by users (risk event participants)
- Assignment review and validation by job function and role
- Changes in period-to-period reports (for example, weekly sales or monthly accounting reports)

BI Reports for Risk Control Roles and Notifications

The last phase in BI ERM system implementation is creating BI reports for risk control roles and notifications. For example, BI administration audits provide the basis for monitoring how well report utilization matches ERM role responsibilities for enterprise risk monitoring, drill-to-details analysis, and timely reporting.

The organization roles dimension is linked to key reports to create a systematic method for assigning people to evaluate risks associated with deviations from expected results. Examples of these risk monitoring assignments appear in BI reports used for managing financial results and customer or vendor relationships. The linking of KRI metrics and roles creates the elements for managing risk alert notifications. BI administration creates log reports that show the timing of report information generation and risk notification to responsible roles. This information is used to confirm that ERM is a continuous process embedded in business processes, competencies, and risk management culture—the "**tone at the top**."

Tone at the top
The environment an organization's senior executives create by clearly communicating expectations to employees and other stakeholders, leading by example, linking governance with transparency, and encouraging ethical behavior.

BUSINESS INTELLIGENCE SYSTEMS—IT GOVERNANCE AND OUTPUTS

BI system outputs align IT governance practices with ERM performance goals and internal controls.

IT BI governance frameworks have become an essential managerial requirement for organizations subject to the Sarbanes-Oxley Act of 2002. IT governance assessments reinforce compliance with industry standards for management of threats to IT investments that can affect information integrity, operational continuity, and fraudulent activity prevention. IT governance oversight of automated controls provides baseline documentation of systemic procedures to anchor internal controls audit testing.

IT Governance and CobiT Processes

CobiT (Control Objectives for Information and related Technology) is an IT governance framework that establishes guidelines that an organization's IT department can use to implement IT best practices, measure IT processes, and ensure that its IT strategies are consistent with its overall business plan.

Four domains exist within the CobiT framework to address IT risks and activities that must be managed:

- Plan and Organize (PO)—Provides direction to solution delivery (AI) and service delivery (DS)

- Acquire and Implement (AI)—Provides the solutions and passes them to be turned into services

- Deliver and Support (DS)—Receives the solutions and makes them usable for end users

- Monitor and Evaluate (ME)—Monitors all processes to ensure that the direction provided is followed

Of the four CobiT domains, several processes within two of the domains are used as a baseline for auditing IT governance:

- PO4—Define IT processes, organization, and relationships

- PO5—Manage IT investment

- PO9—Assess and manage IT risks

- ME2—Monitor and evaluate internal control

- ME4—Provide IT governance

Source: IT Governance Institute, CobiT 4.1 Excerpt (Rolling Meadows, Ill.: IT Governance Institute, 2007), pp. 12–13.

BI system outputs integrate IT governance activities with performance goals and ERM program objectives for these physical (brick and mortar) and virtual (Internet) IT strategic areas:

- IT investment management
- IT asset controls
- IT application management/configuration services
- Data management/enterprise information modeling
- System administration/security management
- Business continuity planning/IT disaster recovery

Output elements such as performance scorecard reports and IT audits link the organization's risk controls for information and related technology to executive-level governance and decision making. While compliance is only one output of BI, it is one of the key tools that are used to enable an ERM program.

IT Investment Management

IT investments are managed through BI scorecard reports that align IT goals and budgets with enterprise performance management review processes. An enterprise performance management review allows the organization to manage its IT investments by using the BI system to drill down to user roles, KPIs, and root cause analysis.

IT investment management's KPIs cover financial metrics and related operational indicators, such as these:

- IT transaction volume (For instance, is volume high, moderate, or low?)
- IT capacity utilization (For example, how well is IT productive capacity being utilized?)
- IT systems uptime percentage (For example, is optimal uptime percentage being maintained?)
- IT system re-start response times (For instance, are objectives being met?)
- IT audit rating (Evaluate audit ratings and make adjustments to processes as required.)
- IT project return on investment (ROI) (Is ROI being realized? If not, examine drill-down details.)
- IT data gathering and decision-making framework appropriateness (For instance, are the appropriate data being consistently captured and analyzed to drive KPI reporting?)

BI reports analyze IT investments by aligning the structural relationships between IT goals, risk factors, internal controls, and actual performance. IT elements are evaluated through drill-to-detail dimensions that monitor performance metrics for IT assets, system applications, workflow process impact, and people.

IT strategies are managed through reports that place IT projects and management priorities into the enterprise risk evaluation oversight processes. These reports enable management to plan and control IT investments through portfolio risk analysis of capital and resource allocation decisions to achieve project management goals. For example, an organization can use BI reports to test specific budget scenarios before it implements budget changes.

IT Asset Controls

BI reports drill down from balance sheet analysis to IT asset-type information and related internal controls. Asset management reports include relevant content for aligning IT program activities with financial planning and control. This process covers asset status information about preventative, predictive, routine, and unplanned support activities.

Hierarchal Goal Pathway

This pyramid illustration shows how the hierarchal relationship from underlying functions or decision areas such as product management, marketing, and sales drives operational goals and, ultimately, the financial goals of the organization. KPI data are gathered throughout the IT BI system, informing strategic goals set at the enterprise level, operational goals set at the functional level, and the decision-making areas within those functions.

Source: Adapted from R. Moisimann, P. Moisimann, R. Connelly, M. Dussault, and C. Bedell, *The Performance Manager* (Ottawa, Canada: Cognos, Inc., 2008).

Together, these IT programs contribute to goals for these areas:

- Asset cost reduction
- Asset utilization
- Operational risk management
- Asset life cycle planning
- Asset tax depreciation documentation compliance

For example, balance sheet analysis could develop asset control information regarding the balance and structure of financial funding options and resources. As the balance sheet, capital adequacy, or income statements are analyzed, drill-down variances to goals can be assessed, such as efficiency at utilizing assets, and delivery on operational planning targets.

IT Application Management/Configuration Services

BI reports create profiles of IT system application control activities across all management reporting cycles. This information is used in assessing standards for software application development, purchase decisions, outsourcing practices, IT staffing competencies, and vendor selection. IT governance documentation covers these processes:

- Application development (For example, ensure new software complies with business model and established standards.)
- Application user acceptance testing (For instance, assess applications using various scenarios. That is, do users have required competencies?)
- Application support (For example, determine the levels of IT support required to manage applications.)
- Application change management (For example, respond to change requests and improve controls in order to comply with governance standards.)

BI analysis also enables IT management to relate configuration management plans for maintaining consistent software performance functionality for organizational work responsibilities.

For instance, the effectiveness of IT application management controls is measured through Capability Maturity Mode (CMM) standards. The CMM is a growth model that is used to design and refine an organization's software development process based on a multi-level path of increasingly organized and more mature system processes. ISO 9000 CMM standards set parameters for software application management controls that cover expectations for these areas:

- Procedures that cover all key business processes
- Monitoring processes to ensure effectiveness
- Recordkeeping documentation
- Quality control preventative and detective activities
- Contingency plans
- Continuous improvement management

IT application management analysis information is a key component for supply chain management auditing requirements. Industry standards (such as ISO 28003:2007) provide the frameworks for relating IT application management controls to vendor certification processes that are essential to ERM.

Data Management/Enterprise Information Modeling

Data management and information modeling activities are designed to ensure enterprise information integrity. BI supports enterprise data management and information modeling through systemic analysis of information supply chains. This provides an integrated framework for linking data sources to data management decisions and data delivery quality standards. Information supply chains provide the data necessary to support existing decision making and model future decision scenarios—for example, ensuring that the IT budget is prioritized to support ongoing investment BI systems that support the ERM framework.

Information supply chains are built by mapping IT assets into the supply chains that connect to user requirements. This enables management to monitor the information demand, quality controls, strategic priorities, and performance metrics that connect users to data sources.

Information supply chain oversight underscores the importance of management programs for master data management to ensure consistent data integrity across all organization areas and the importance of different areas of the organization working together to obtain the data required. BI design review is used to assess relational structures for aligning performance management metrics with the correct data tables and hierarchies that are stored in data warehouses. Information supply chain evaluation provides the basis for testing consistency and cost effectiveness for retrieving data related to these items:

- Ad-hoc queries
- Analysis
- Management reporting
- Performance scorecards
- Risk notifications

Executive Decision Making and Master Data Management

Executive management uses data management and information modeling to support performance, risk, and compliance goals. Data gathered from these three primary decision areas drive the outputs that executive management uses to obtain a comprehensive view of business performance and to make the decisions necessary for effective planning or target resetting.

Executive Management Decision Making	
Performance	Financial management—Performing to shareholder expectations
	Operational revenue management—Driving revenue growth effectively
	Operational expense management—Managing operational expenses effectively
	Long-term assets management—Managing long-term assets effectively to drive future revenue and expense controls
Risk Management	Managing the risks required to sustain performance
Compliance Management	Complying with regulatory and governance requirements

Source: Adapted from R. Moisimann, P. Moisimann, R. Connelly, M. Dussault, and C. Bedell, *The Performance Manager* (Ottawa, Canada: Cognos, Inc., 2008).

System Administration/Security Management

BI provides enterprise oversight analysis of system administration practices and data security controls. Senior managers ensure that security management control responsibilities are reviewed to keep data safe from corruption and ensure that information access is properly controlled throughout the enterprise.

Data security audits of information practices include oversight of internal control activities for these areas:

- Disk encryption
- Data and system backups
- **Data masking**
- System log-in password controls
- Single sign-on access rights
- Data security laws and regulation

Data masking
Software application that hides sensitive information by replacing it with plausible camouflage data.

BI system auditing functionalities are applied to internal controls for data security administration. Evaluation of user roles for risk management responsibilities is synchronized with light directory application protocol (LDAP)/ user group active directory (AD) management procedures to ensure that audit trails are in place for preventing and/or analyzing loss events. BI system auditing functionalities can capture these data:

- Log-in history
- Operations selected by user
- Report creation and execution
- Report usage by user group
- Report usage by role
- Report usage by person
- User session details

For example, a BI system can produce a security audit report assigning audit issues uncovered to the managerial functions that will carry out the audit recommendations. Auditees' progress on the audit recommendations can be updated online and in real time. Notification is provided to senior management when existing recommendations are due, updated, or overdue.

Business Continuity Planning/IT Disaster Recovery

BI analysis relates IT disaster recovery plan documentation to workflow processes and organizational responsibilities. BI reports show that risk management oversight and testing of contingency activities should be defined for these items:

- IT applications
- Data management
- Systems hardware
- Communications networks
- Infrastructure and facilities

Contingency testing priorities are established as part of the management's enterprise risk evaluation process. BI creates analytic links to generate financial risk analysis of potential losses and reserves for IT risk events. For example, an organization's business continuity plan should have a disaster recovery component that is tested, using BI systems, along these dimensions:

- Are the proper function roles assigned to tasks?
- Are the proper business continuity steps in the correct order of operation?
- Are post-incident actions designed to minimize damages and expense?
- Are the designated contingent resources subject to changes in availability over time?
- Are possible variables included in the plan with cost and function assigned to each?

Business continuity and disaster recovery analysis provide information that adds important details to procedural guidance for backup and recovery implementation. BI data warehouses provide the facilities to store key information for records retention compliance requirements.

BUSINESS INTELLIGENCE SYSTEMS—PRESENTING THE CASE FOR ERM

A risk management professional may be called upon to justify or make the case for implementing BI systems in his or her organization as part of a larger ERM program. An ERM program that includes BI produces the evidence that senior management and regulators require to document that corporate governance and enterprise risk control practices are integrated across organizational silos.

Organizations that are subject to the Sarbanes-Oxley Act, AS/NZS 4360, ISO 31000:2009, and/or other industry or regulatory reporting standards are required to demonstrate that certain internal controls and risk management processes are in place. Risk management evaluation criteria defined by Standard & Poor's (S&P) provide a generic framework that can be applied when presenting financial results to any rating agency or regulatory organization that assesses ERM program effectiveness. Companies that use integrated risk programs, including BI systems, to factor risk assessment into management planning and decision making earn higher ratings that lower their cost of acquiring and managing capital.

Additionally, senior management can use BI-based documentation to support compliance reporting standards; it demonstrates financial transparency and the systemic application of ISO (International Organization for Standardization) ERM certification principles.

The business case for a BI approach to ERM can be established across several benefit areas:

- IT governance practices for benchmarking of enterprise risk information calculations
- Risk management culture accountability
- Risk factor evaluation for emerging risks
- Enterprise risk controls validation
- EI and risk model testing
- Enterprise risk management program assessment

IT Governance Practices for Enterprise Risk Information Benchmarking

IT governance practices for BI enable and implement the ERM framework that supports the organization's enterprise-wide goals. For example, to ensure that an organization is in compliance with industry regulations, metrics for data gathering and documentation of adherence to governance practices (such as defining specific audit periods) are established and monitored systemically. Reports generated from the data are then used to benchmark transparency internally with business operations and externally with stakeholders.

A BI reporting framework satisfies regulatory compliance recommendations, showing independent replication of underlying transaction data and operational baselines for auditing changes in internal control methods. These practices are documented for best practice review and confirmation of automated control procedures for management information reporting. For example, the relevant CobiT (Control Objectives for Information and related Technology) process for auditing is ME2 (monitor and evaluate internal control).

To prepare a BI ERM case that includes enterprise risk information for benchmarking, the management team must highlight the data-gathering and reporting features from BI systems that eliminate redundant or ineffective activities. BI systems maintain a repeatable operational process for gathering and verifying ERM information. One method of providing appropriate operational controls over information reporting is to implement XBRL standards for management reporting.

The use of XBRL demonstrates that systemic controls are applied to aligning financial results with organizational roll-up structures and financial statement footnotes. XBRL uses BI methods to organize metrics and dimensions (such as roles, reporting periods, or reporting relationships) that reinforce enterprise-wide master data management integrity. XBRL tagging relates localized information to industry-specific metadata tags that use a global open source data structure as the basis for consistent reporting.

For example, XBRL provides a database-like framework that facilitates the exchange of data between proprietary systems. Data are defined in terms of the appropriate taxonomy required for a specific regulatory or industry report, such as submitting 10-Ks or 10-Qs to the SEC. If an organization does not adopt XBRL, then an appropriate system of data definitions and controls must be constructed that bridges the information silos within the enterprise.

Risk Management Culture Accountability

Risk management culture accountability is reflected in how BI is used to establish and manage ERM oversight roles. The chief executive officer (CEO) and chief financial officer (CFO) of public corporations have an annual reporting responsibility to certify the integrity of internal risk controls. The presentation of the ERM case illustrates to regulators that risk management principles originate at the top of the business's hierarchy, where a tone is set that emphasizes the importance of managing risk enterprise-wide as part of each person's daily work activities. BI systems, IT governance, and risk outputs can form the basis of a key document demonstrating that the organization supports and is accountable to a risk management culture.

When internal controls are imported into a BI data repository, they create a central point for aligning ERM activities with management reporting. BI report dimensions regarding risks, policies, general ledger accounts, and organizational positions serve as a data management drill-down cornerstone in assessing whether adequate risk mitigation controls are embedded in daily and monthly control activities.

As part of the analysis required to prepare an ERM case, a function or roles dimension can be used to filter reporting results viewed by management. For example, roles can be sorted according to functions performed by the "responsible manager," the "financial reconciliation reviewer," and the "management approver." Management can then confirm that roles at every organizational level are accountable for managing risk and that checks and balances exist that reinforce the integrity of information-gathering practices.

Risk Factor Evaluation for Emerging Risks

An organization's senior management and board of directors are responsible for risk management oversight, including identification and evaluation of emerging risks. Traditional management reporting explains risk factors in narrative text documents that supply basic description. In contrast, BI relates risk analysis to the enterprise data structure. This enables management to evaluate how different risk types affect potential losses in workflow processes and financial results. For example, a change in a company's sales growth would have different implications for areas such as staffing, workflows, budgeting, and business development. The breadth of risk issues included in BI analysis shows the scope of emerging risk issues that have been taken into account when financial and operational planning projections are made.

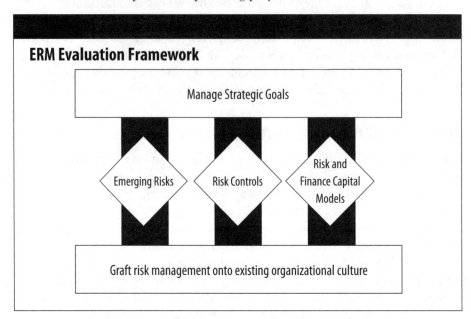

The depth of risk factor BI analysis shows how the ISO 31000 ERM standard is applied to risk response decision-making practices. BI data structures create the organizational links that show the underlying processes that support risk assessment and related action plans.

Structuring a BI program from an ERM design orientation means that the board and management at multiple levels of an organization are able to view risk management and business performance goals across multiple, interdependent perspectives. When the case is made for an ERM program with BI systems-based validation, these reviews produced by IT are among those that can be used to link processes with risk assessment:

• BI inherent risk review shows how financial loss analysis is associated with loss event identification control activities.

• BI loss event likelihood and severity review show how risk matrix analysis leads to risk management decisions for risk retention and insurance coverage.

• BI residual risk review shows how risk control activities and contingency plans focus on risk remediation.

• BI net recovery review shows how loss events are related to financial reserves and litigation activity controls.

Enterprise Risk Controls Validation

An ERM BI case analysis can be used to demonstrate to management where, throughout the enterprise, risk management processes link to the automated or manual control activities that are designed to prevent or detect potential losses. The BI drill-to-transaction detail reports generated validate that the identified risks are assessed and managed using the proper risk controls. This review of risk events and risk controls covers all processes in the organization and shows levels of internal controls, including delegation of responsibility. Each activity that is backed by a monitoring report provides the basis for assessing whether management has correctly and competently interpreted the causes of potential loss events. ERM with BI enables an organization to implement 360-degree closed-loop risk reporting from key parties throughout the risk management network.

An ERM risk controls review creates ERM case decisions about the methods of automated testing that are most effective to optimize internal controls design and audit examination methods. For example, a review of an organization's finance processes might reveal a simpler, more efficient, and more consistent way to deliver detective controls information to business unit managers.

The timeliness and precision required to capture and assess risk information affects how risk tolerances should be set and how risk notification communications should be scheduled. For example, the optimal automatic triggering controls should be determined when risk tolerances are set; the level of an activity or type of event requiring notification of persons in accountable roles might vary from one area of the enterprise to another. KRIs are developed in BI reporting so that critical metrics can be aligned with drill-to-detail information that highlights data outliers and abnormal transactions.

Economic Intelligence and Risk Model Testing

When the case is made to management that the organization should adopt an ERM program with BI, another supporting reason is the benefit such a system can offer in terms of using the BI to translate EI into risk model testing.

Risk modeling or "stress" testing of risk scenarios is a financial services regulatory compliance requirement that affects risk management planning in all businesses. Risks related to EI drive the need for organizations to show that they have multiple plans prepared to deal with changing conditions. To conduct stress tests, a framework for evaluation is developed, risk assessments and expert knowledge are used to generate planning scenarios, internal and external data are included in the scenarios, and KRIs are used to hone identification of potential losses.

BI organizes scenarios into a structure with financial attributes that compares actual scenario results with annual budget plan variances for corresponding time periods. Additional forecasts can be added to a given scenario. As the results change and adapt to the new scenarios, evidence is produced that can document that the alternative plans developed respond to changing conditions. The thresholds for identifying abnormal transactions are set in advance for discussion with auditors and regulators.

BI planning reports use "what-if" functionality to create an inventory of stress tests that respond to changes in economic growth scenarios and interest rates. The information generated by the stress tests can be used as a decision-making aid for senior management and the board of directors during the preparation of investor guidance statements and strategic planning alternatives.

Enterprise Risk Management Program Assessment

An ERM case presentation to management can illustrate how enterprise risk assessment is reflected in the goals, organization accountability, and risk threshold assessments that are reported in senior management's guidance statements. An ERM risk index assessment is constructed to show that there is systemic review of risk factors. From this systemic review of risk factors a determination is made of how potential losses are vetted in financial reports and footnotes. For example, senior management identifies material risks and general ledger accounts that can have a significant effect on overall results to protect the interests of shareholders and other key stakeholders who rely on the integrity of transparent reporting information.

BI is used in financial reporting to calculate KPIs for ratios and other metrics that serve as planning and control indicators. BI ERM practices validate that calculations based on information supplied from internal data sources can be replicated and tested independently. KPI calculation formulas may be reported in public documents. For example, an organization might report the calculation it uses to determine its receivables, the average number of days an account is delinquent, or a receivables turnover rate. Benchmark calculations for KPI metrics compared across industries are particularly important in ERM case presentations used to confirm planning effectiveness, reporting transparency, and financial integrity.

BI drill-down analysis of an ERM index KPI can confirm that people with the appropriate competencies and role responsibilities are using valid analytic reports to forecast potential losses, mitigate losses, and verify financial reporting integrity.

Board Responsibility for Testing Enterprise Risk Management Governance Standards

Among the emerging uses of BI with ERM is the assessment of the health of financial institutions and the use of federal regulations. The rapid economic decline in all economies and markets that began late in the first decade of the twenty-first century will forever be associated with broad financial risk management failures on the part of businesses, institutions, and governments globally.

Consequently, many financial experts and economists are predicting an eventful period of regulatory policy and legislative changes that will lead to the institutionalization of governance practices and active board involvement in how organizations identify and manage systemic and event-driven risks.

Regulatory bodies are proposing greater accountability for maintaining ERM governance standards at the board of directors oversight level. The U.S. Securities and Exchange Commission rules are expanding risk assessment requirements as part of public financial reporting procedures. Board endorsement and sign-off on an organization's ERM program will be evaluated in the context of three management principles now firmly incorporated into national policy objectives:

- Accountability
- Transparency
- Audit integrity

Business review content presented to board committees can be tested by BI audits of the facts and data sources that underlie financial statements, footnotes, and risk factor statements. Organizations that use BI in ERM presentations are able to identify the organization's risk owners who have direct responsibility for maintaining relevant corporate governance and ERM documentation.

Making the Case for ERM and BI

Making the Case	Benefits
• Present the ERM case analysis to the organization's senior management team for adopting an ERM program with BI.	• Creates an enterprise-wide culture of risk management.
• Link the outputs of ERM to regulatory compliance requirements.	• IT monitors activities and events and applies risk controls.
• Recommend the benefits of ERM and BI that can be realized through IT applications.	• IT governance practices for risk information benchmarking (provide a framework for compliance and comparison).
	• Risk management culture accountability (oversight roles and responsibilities).
	• Risk factor evaluation for emerging risks (identify and evaluate emerging risks and link processes with risk assessments).
	• Enterprise risk controls validation (links processes, controls, and roles).
	• Business intelligence and risk model testing (stress testing, scenario planning).
	• Strategic risk assessment (roll-up to macro view of how risk affects executive-level decision making).

SUMMARY

To optimize risk-taking, effective ERM programs require intelligence about a broad array of economic, political, and competitive factors that affect an organization's management strategies and objectives.

EI for an ERM program is applied through three integrated methods:

- EI data gathering
- EI risk investigation
- EI monitoring

BI systems integrate enterprise-wide data flows and generate analytic information for risk management decision making, internal controls testing, and credit evaluation, all of which support the organization's corporate governance goals. These are the primary BI system functions that apply to ERM practices:

- Performance management scorecards
- BI information user roles
- BI reports
- BI data mining and risk notifications
- Master data management

BI implementation aligns ERM program monitoring responsibilities into a closed-loop system for executive oversight and drill-to-details analysis of ERM. There are five BI ERM implementation phases:

1. Enterprise risk identification
2. Risk information mapping
3. ERM program evaluation
4. ERM information compliance
5. BI reports for risk control roles and notifications

BI system outputs integrate IT governance activities with risk management analysis and ERM program objectives for these physical and virtual IT strategic areas:

- IT investment management
- IT asset controls
- IT application management/configuration services
- Data management/enterprise information modeling
- System administration/security management
- Business continuity planning/IT disaster recovery

A risk manager may be called upon to make the case to senior management for implementing an ERM program with BI. BI ERM cases should recommend these applications and benefits:

- IT governance practices for enterprise risk information benchmarking
- Risk management culture accountability
- Risk factor evaluation for emerging risks
- Enterprise risk controls validation
- EI and risk model testing
- Enterprise risk management program assessment

CHAPTER

5

Risk Assessment: Exposure Analysis

Educational Objectives

After learning the content of this chapter and completing the corresponding course guide assignment, you should be able to:

▶ Describe the exposure spaces model within the context of risk assessment.

▶ Describe the role of impact in analyzing and evaluating exposures.

▶ Apply the exposure spaces model to a given risk scenario.

Outline

Exposure Spaces and Risk Assessment

Impact—Role for Exposure Analysis and Evaluation

Applying the Exposure Spaces Model

Summary

Risk Assessment: Exposure Analysis

Chapters 5 and 6 discuss the risk assessment process, which starts with identifying and analyzing risk exposures. This is the second of enterprise-wide risk management's (ERM) steps, as depicted on the ERM process diagram on page 1.5:

1. Establish the internal and external contexts
2. Risk assessment—identification, analysis, and evaluation
3. Risk treatment—selecting and implementing appropriate risk management techniques
4. Monitor results and revise
5. Communicate and consult with all internal and external stakeholders

Risk managers can use the exposure spaces model to describe the various attributes of a risk, including resources, events, and impacts. An event can result in changes in resources that may have significant consequences, or impacts, on an organization's risk profile. The many possible variations of these impacts are evaluated as part of exposure analysis. A case study in this chapter applies exposure analysis to a hypothetical fact situation.

EXPOSURE SPACES AND RISK ASSESSMENT

The **exposure spaces model** is a concept risk management professionals use to describe the multiple attributes that constitute a risk. These include the **resources** that may change in value, the **events** that cause a change in a resource's value, and the **impacts** of the change.

In the early days of risk management, only the downside of risk was considered. ERM, however, is a holistic and speculative approach to risk management that includes the upside of risk. Therefore, additional terms are required to fully describe a risk. These terms are the dimensions that constitute the exposure spaces model:

- Resources
- Events
- Impacts

Exposure spaces model
A three-dimensional representation of resources, events, and impacts that is used as a risk assessment tool.

Resource
Any element that can change in value or level.

Event
An occurrence or series of occurrences that causes a change in a resource's value or level.

Impact
A positive or negative consequence or change in value or level of a resource.

Exposure Spaces Model

A risk can be thought of as a combination of multiple attributes: resources, events, and impacts. The exposure spaces model is a three-dimensional representation of these attributes. The exposure spaces model is intended to be used as a risk identification tool only. It has no application to risk treatment or the other steps in the ERM process beyond identification, although it may be used to develop a response when resources and events intersect (identification plan) and can be used to envision a risk's impact (third axis).

Exposure

Loss exposure
Any condition or situation that presents a possibility of loss, whether or not an actual loss occurs.

An exposure or, more precisely, a **loss exposure**, exists when something of value is subject to a condition that may cause a loss. Referring to the exposure spaces model, a loss would be a change in value, which would be indicated on the y-axis. This axis illustrates the impact or consequence on a resource.

For example, a manufacturer's factory is an asset that may decrease in value and therefore is a loss exposure. Key employees are another example of a loss exposure, as they may become injured or ill. The manufacturer may have a legal liability exposure as the result of a lawsuit. Finally, the manufacturer may have a net income exposure as the result of a direct loss to the factory, the injured employee, or the lawsuit.

This definition of "loss exposure" served risk management professionals well as long as they were charged only with managing the downside of risk. But in today's ERM environment, risk management professionals are increasingly charged with managing the upside of risk. Therefore, a new definition was needed to more accurately reflect the current global and speculative approach. The concept of exposure spaces includes the possibility that a resource may increase in value. For example, a firm may invest in an asset, hoping that its value will increase. Alternatively, the firm may hire an executive, hoping that his or her value will increase.

Resources (x-Axis)

The x-axis in the exposure spaces model represents the resource at risk. In ERM, both loss exposures and speculative projects are referred to as resources. Often, a loss exposure and a speculative project are the same resource. For example, a building can be regarded as an exposure because it may experience a loss in value due to a fire. The same building may have a gain in value caused by increased demand for buildings of its type at its location. Alternatively, an executive may be an exposure in that he may be injured at work. The same executive may gain in value because he has obtained additional education.

Resources are divided into several categories because the impacts that apply to each resource category are different. Understanding the specific type of resource (and its related dimensions of causes and impacts) helps risk management professionals better manage those resources.

Events (z-Axis)

On the z-axis of the exposure spaces model are events that cause change in value of a resource. The events can also be referred to as perils and sources. A loss exposure will have a loss in value because of a peril. A speculative project will have a gain in value because of a source. The many causes of changes in value vary depending on the type of resource.

For example, human resource losses are caused by the perils of death, disability, retirement, or termination. Financial resource losses may be caused by consequential or contingent losses to other resources.

Speculative projects may gain value because of various sources. For example, human resources may gain value because of additional knowledge, experience, or education acquired. Information resources may gain value because of demand.

The first two dimensions (the x- and z-axes) of the three-dimensional exposure spaces model are illustrated by the "Resources and Events of the Exposure Spaces Model" exhibit. These two dimensions do not depict the impact from variation (both positively and negatively) attributable to risk associated with these resources.

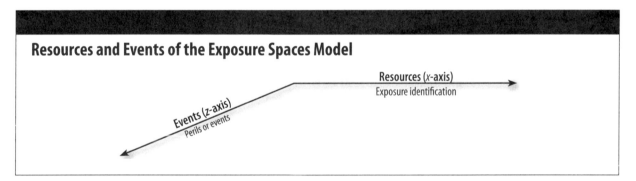

Resources and Events of the Exposure Spaces Model

Resources (x-axis)
Exposure identification

Events (z-axis)
Perils or events

Impacts (y-Axis)

On the y-axis of the exposure spaces model are impacts, which are the consequences or change in value of a resource. Impacts may be positive or negative. In the "Resources, Events, and Impacts of the Exposure Spaces Model" exhibit, negative impacts are shown as threats, while positive impacts are shown as opportunities.

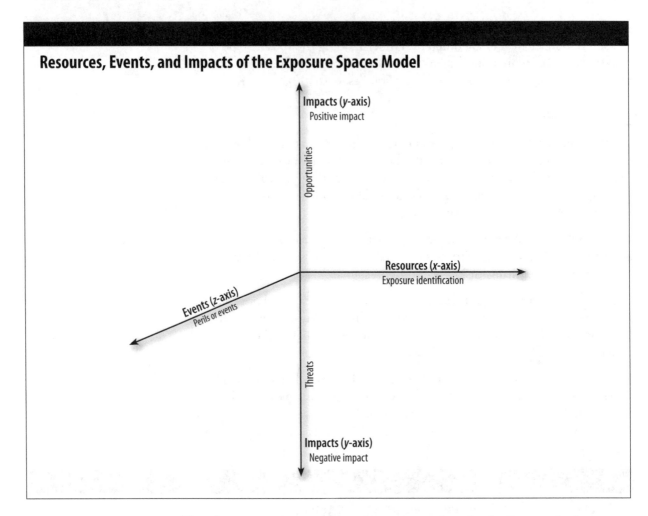

Resources, Events, and Impacts of the Exposure Spaces Model

The change in value is measured using several methods. One method suggests that losses are often both direct and indirect. The direct loss to an organization's human, technological, or financial resources is significantly compounded by indirect losses. These indirect losses include loss of production, lost revenues, increased expenses, and decreased earnings. Some analysts suggest the ratio between indirect and direct losses is, on average, four to one. For example, for every dollar directly lost for medical human resource expenses, another four dollars are lost in productivity, lost wages, and decreased earnings.

Another method of measuring impact is in terms of primary and tertiary damages. Primary damage is the loss impact to the organization and its resources. Tertiary damage is the loss impact on all third parties and the environment. Tertiary damages may result from breaches of contract, legal liabilities, or fiduciary indiscretions.

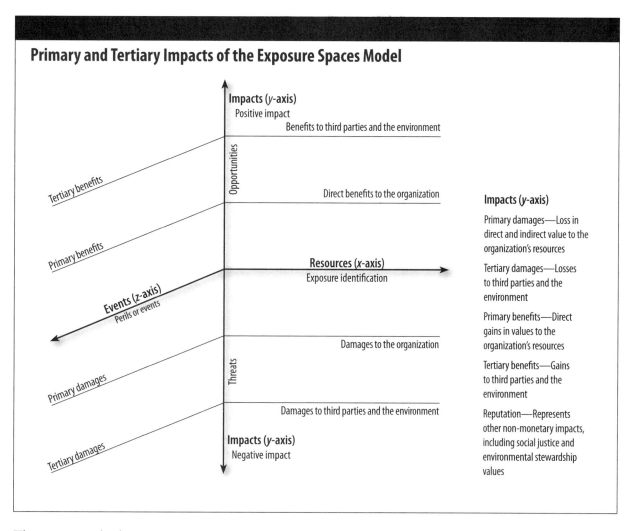

Primary and Tertiary Impacts of the Exposure Spaces Model

Impacts (*y*-axis)
Positive impact
Benefits to third parties and the environment

Opportunities

Tertiary benefits

Direct benefits to the organization

Primary benefits

Resources (*x*-axis)
Exposure identification

Events (*z*-axis)
Perils or events

Damages to the organization

Threats

Primary damages

Damages to third parties and the environment

Impacts (*y*-axis)
Negative impact

Tertiary damages

Impacts (*y*-axis)

Primary damages—Loss in direct and indirect value to the organization's resources

Tertiary damages—Losses to third parties and the environment

Primary benefits—Direct gains in values to the organization's resources

Tertiary benefits—Gains to third parties and the environment

Reputation—Represents other non-monetary impacts, including social justice and environmental stewardship values

The concept of value in ERM assumes much more than a simple monetary change. Although the economic value of a resource is a critical value, and often the most important one, other impacts are important to society as well. All of an organization's goals are not necessarily translated into financial terms; instead, reputation, social responsibilities, and environmental impacts must be also taken into account. The consequences of many events can be simultaneously measured according to three impacts or values: economic performance, social justice, and environmental stewardship. These three values of profit, people, and planet are regarded by many Fortune 500 companies as essential components of a balanced ERM portfolio that helps these firms create a "triple bottom line."

The three-axis exposure spaces model is a simplistic representation of reality, but it can provide a competitive advantage for organizations. It can identify concentrations of risk that have attributes common to certain resources, events, and impacts that previously were not apparent. Known concentrations of risk directly affect an organization's risk appetite and can help an organization guide its research into possible negative or positive risk correlations before its competitors discover them.

The exposure spaces model can also be used to identify outlier event risks whose potential loss impact is significant, but whose probability of occurring is small. If an organization determines ten 1-percent probability outlier event risks, it may conclude that there is a 10-percent probability of one of them occurring during a given time period.

Classes of Resources

ERM focuses on six loss exposure categories, which are intended to include all resources that an organization may or will have, acquire, lease, borrow, or use:

- Human resources
- Technical resources (tangible assets)
- Information resources
- Partner resources (or key business relationships)
- Financial resources
- Free resources

Human Resources

Human resources are all the personnel linked to an organization as employees or contractors. For many organizations, their most valuable resource is the people who work for them because their physical and mental labor adds value to the organization. The specific experiences and competencies of an organization's personnel are assets, although they are not always assessed and valued in the organization's financial statements.

Factors that directly affect the productivity of personnel, such as health, compliance with safety procedures, and work habits, should be carefully monitored by, for example, a front-line supervisor or a risk management professional. Furthermore, the exposures associated with personnel should be investigated in terms of key person and labor costs. Key persons—those who are critical to the continuous successful operation of the organization—should be identified. Possible substitutes for each key person should also be identified. Labor costs should be compared to those of the organization's competitors or to those of other organizations in the same industry. To keep prices competitive, the organization's labor costs cannot be too high, and to prevent valuable personnel from leaving the organization, labor costs cannot be too low.

Knowledge management
A strategy for capturing and assessing information so that everyone in an organization is able to access the information needed.

In many organizations, **knowledge management** is a high priority. An organization that practices knowledge management gathers, organizes, shares, and analyzes the collective knowledge, expertise, and ideas of its personnel.

Knowledge management involves a synergistic combination of data, information technology, and human creativity. This pooling of knowledge allows an organization to move beyond the boundaries of its current practices, products, services, and structures and to respond more innovatively to the complexities of the business environment. Knowledge management supports competence and adaptation to a changing environment and, therefore, survival.

Technical Resources (Tangible Assets)

Technical resources, for the purposes of this discussion, are all the tangible physical assets under the direct control of an organization. They include assets such as buildings, equipment, and tools. The legal status of those assets is an element to consider. The organization may own or rent certain property rights of some physical assets. It may also simply store property for a third party in a **bailment**.

If an organization owns an asset, there are fewer restrictions on how it can manage it than if the asset is rented or is part of a bailment. An organization is also likely to be legally responsible for damages caused by more perils if it owns a given asset.

It is essential for risk management professionals to understand the depth and breadth of control the organization can exert over an asset when managing the risks to which it is exposed and when exploiting the benefits that can be derived from those risks.

Information Resources

Information resources include all the information that flows throughout an organization, whether electronically, on paper, or even as ideas not yet recorded in permanent form. This information may concern the organization itself, such as (1) the organization's financial statements, which may be required to be publicly disclosed or (2) trade secrets regarding its internal processes, which are protected from disclosure by intellectual property laws. Disclosure is an important consideration because an organization wants to protect the value of this resource. Disclosure of certain information, such as a trade secret, can make it much less valuable.

Information may also be related to others, such as customers or competitors.

Information may be obtained through publicly available sources, as with **open source intelligence**, or through sources that are private but that may be available to the organization, such as patients' medical records in a hospital.

Risk management professionals should be aware that others, possibly competitors, may try to obtain their organizations' information resources through criminal acts such as theft of trade secrets, bribery, or blackmail. These acts can collectively be referred to as **industrial espionage**.

Bailment
The temporary transfer of a property's custody.

Open source intelligence
The act of using publicly available sources to find, select, and acquire information that can be analyzed to produce actionable intelligence.

Industrial espionage
The use of secretive methods to obtain private information for a competitive or an economic advantage.

Partner Resources (or Key Business Relationships)

This resource involves relationships with others outside an organization, without which the organization either could not operate or could not operate as efficiently. The relationships could involve another organization that is "upstream," such as a supplier, service provider, or contractor, or they could involve another organization that is "downstream," such as a distributor or customer.

Key business relationships must be identified clearly if the dependencies in the supply chain and distribution chain are to be treated with a risk management technique. This is particularly true for organizations that have outsourced some or all of their production tasks.

Financial Resources

Cash flow
The cash receipts coming in minus the cash payments going out over a set period of time.

Financial resources comprise all the financial streams that flow into and out of an organization (often referred to as **cash flow**). Financial streams flowing in are often sales revenue and investment income. Financial streams flowing out include expenses incurred to generate sales revenue, such as producers' commissions or underwriting expenses.

Financial resources can be short term—such as cash, other liquid assets, and financial obligations that are due within the current accounting period—or long term, including capital, reserves, project financing, and the portion of debt that is repaid over a period of time longer than the current accounting period.

A thorough risk analysis includes an assessment of the risks associated with the organization's financial strategy and the balance it has struck between risk and return.

Free Resources

Free resources, received from the environment without direct financial compensation, do not appear in an organization's accounting records (and are therefore called "free"). A complete analysis of an organization's resources must take into account the organization's noncontractual exchanges with the environment.

The term "environment" has broad application in this context, and each type of environment should be investigated:

- The physical environment comprises the air, water, and earth.
- The political, legal, and social environments require examining aspects of life conditions, societal organization, and cultural differences.
- For the competitive environment, a risk management professional must look at aspects of current competition, technological advances being made, shifts in customers' tastes, and available substitutes for the organization's products or services.

It is important to understand that free resources are not actually free. Someone eventually pays the price for the resources that are consumed. Economists theorize that any voluntary transaction between a buyer and seller benefits both parties, reasoning that if either party did not benefit from the exchange, that party would refuse it. However, the exchange can have additional effects—called externalities—on third parties not directly involved in the exchange. Externalities can be negative or positive.

A negative externality occurs when society incurs costs as a result of the private transaction between the buyer and the seller. Here are several examples of negative externalities:

- Burning oil, gas, and coal as part of manufacturing a product, resulting in pollution
- Overfishing by one fishing company, depleting the fish population and affecting the catch of other fishing companies

Negative externalities can result in too much of a product being made because not all costs created by the transaction are assessed against the buyer and seller. Using the pollution example to illustrate, if a manufacturer's costs to produce a product were increased to include the cost of cleaning up the pollution it creates, the number of products it could produce or sell would be decreased.

A positive externality occurs when society benefits as a result of the private transaction between the seller and the buyer. There are several examples of positive externalities:

- Homeowners who upgrade their landscaping and siding benefit their neighbors by improving the property values in the area.
- An auto repair garage removes CFC (chlorofluorocarbon) and replaces it with another refrigerant to recharge a customer's air conditioner, which has the added benefit of reducing the destructive effect of CFC on the atmospheric ozone layer.

Positive externalities can result in too little of a product being made because not all benefits are enjoyed by the buyer and seller who create the transaction.

It is crucial for any organization planning to diversify and enter a new market with local production to be aware of its needs for free resources, as they may not be available in the prospective locations or countries involved.

Classes of Events

When classifying events that could affect an organization, managers must examine whether a given event is an internal event that occurs within the organization or is an external event that occurs outside the organization. Managers may also classify an event according to its cause. Causes of events fall into four categories, which are intended to include all possible events that can affect an organization:

- Economic events
- Natural events
- Industrial events
- Human events

Economic Events

Events that are caused by dramatic changes in the overall economic environment can create unexpected opportunities for or threats to an organization. Such events could include fluctuations in foreign currency exchange rates, the performance of global markets, technological advancements, or the bankruptcy of an organization's largest competitor. Shifting commodity costs, such as variations in the price of oil or other raw materials, could require rapid reevaluation of organizational strategy to protect assets. The most effective way to manage potential events related to the economy involves developing accurate forecasting models and establishing monitoring systems to track trends in domestic and global economies. Most economic events can be addressed strategically. When ERM is grafted onto an organization's strategy, strategy and risk management become inextricably linked.

Natural Events

Natural events are generally weather related, such as windstorms, hurricanes, and flood. Events such as earthquakes and volcanic eruption also are considered natural events even though they are not weather related. Natural events often happen suddenly and are outside the control of humans. Therefore, traditional loss prevention methods aimed at reducing frequency are not appropriate. However, pre-event and post-event loss reduction methods are often effective in reducing the severity of losses related to natural events. Pre-event loss reduction methods include properly designing a building to reduce the effect of potential natural events and locating operations in areas that are less prone to natural disasters. A well-designed contingency plan and emergency procedures are examples of post-event loss reduction methods.

For some natural events, such as floods or hurricanes, a warning period may precede the impact of the event, during which an organization can take precautions to reduce loss severity. The length of the warning period significantly influences the available loss reduction methods. For example, if flooding is forecasted, a manufacturing operation could move equipment and other property to another location outside the threatened area. Few early warning systems or forecasting methods anticipate other natural events, such as earthquakes.

Industrial Events

Events that arise from the overall activity within an organization can be referred to as industrial events. These events may or may not result from human interaction and include fire, machinery breakdown, building collapse, pollution, vandalism, theft, injuries to workers or members of the public, and similar types of events.

Sometimes, industrial events can also be categorized as hazard risks that may result in a reduction in the organization's value due to an accidental loss (such as a major fire at the organization's headquarters). Because these events can be categorized as nonsystematic or diversifiable risks affecting only some individuals or businesses, they are well suited for treatment through the traditional insurance mechanism. Loss exposure analysis can be used to project expected loss frequency and loss severity levels. Based on these projections, appropriate risk financing techniques, such as transfer and retention, can be put into place.

Human Events

Human events are closely related to industrial events, and the two are often difficult to distinguish. Human events fall into two general categories: involuntary and voluntary.

Involuntary human events result from an error, an omission, or negligence (for example, a fire started by a carelessly discarded cigarette). The most appropriate treatments for such events are systems and procedures that control the consequences of involuntary human acts. In the case of the discarded cigarette, regulations prohibiting smoking and procedures for proper disposal of smoking materials would be appropriate risk control methods.

Voluntary human events result from conscious and deliberate acts of individuals or groups. Some of these acts, such as vandalism or arson, are intended to cause harm, while others are not. An example of a well-intentioned voluntary act that results in unintended harm is a software programmer who independently alters code with the intent of improving its performance but instead inadvertently creates major systems problems for his employer.

The ideal treatment for many voluntary human events is prevention. Organizational policies and procedures can be designed to deter employees from engaging in acts that could cause either intentional or unintentional harm. Additional techniques such as using keycards, passwords, inventory controls, and security measures can also be effective. Many voluntary events that are intended to cause harm are also illegal and are punishable by imprisonment, fines, or other legal action. Such punitive measures may also assist in deterring others from committing voluntary acts that cause intentional harm.

Complete Exposure Spaces Model

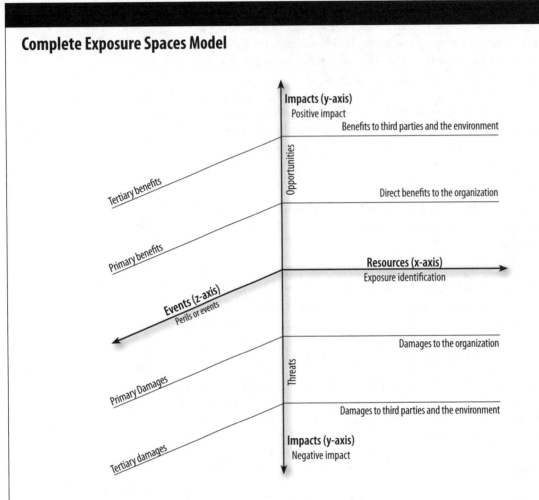

Exposure Spaces Symbol Key

Resources (*x*-axis)

H—Human resources, internal stakeholders

T—Technology resources, property, or assets

Inf—Information resources, intellectual capital

P—Partner resources, external stakeholders

Fin—Financial resources

Free—Free resources, resources not connected directly to economic transactions

Events (*z*-axis)

E—Economic events

N—Natural events

Ind—Industrial events caused by human construction

Hinv—Involuntary human events caused by mistakes

Hv ("Smart Alec")—Voluntary human events caused by intentional acts/modification

Hv (criminal)—Voluntary human events caused by criminal actions

Impacts (*y*-axis)

Primary damages—Loss in direct and indirect value to the organization's resources

Tertiary damages—Losses to third parties and the environment

Primary benefits—Direct gains in values to the organization's resources

Tertiary benefits—Gains to third parties and the environment

Reputation—Represents other non-monetary impacts, including social justice and environmental stewardship values

Using an Exposure Assessment Tool

Once the concepts of risk dimensions have been mastered, the risk management professional has a better understanding of the resources that may change in value, the reasons or causes of the change in value, and the impacts of the change in value. Given these parameters of risk in the exposure spaces model, a risk management professional can develop a **risk register**. This portfolio of resources, causes, factors, and impacts provides a systematic approach to risk management and facilitates the optimal implementation of solutions.

A risk register is a "living" document that is continually updated and used to track and monitor risk. It allows the risk professional to view events in a larger context while focusing on the more essential individual risks to an organization. Therefore, it is an essential tool for managing portfolios and implementing rational decisions, leads to sound governance, and contributes to compliance with international risk regulations.

Risk register
A tool developed at the risk owner level that links specific activities, processes, projects, or plans to a list of identified risks and results of risk analysis and evaluation and that is ultimately consolidated at the enterprise level.

Sample Risk Center Register

Risk Center Risk Register

Risk Owner _____   Date _____

Item	Risk Owner (of component parts, if applicable)	Resource Risk Scenario	Potential Impact (Opportunity/ Threat)	Risk Level 1=Minimum 2=Low 3=Medium 4=High 5=Maximum	Risk Treatment (Present)	Proposed Improvement Action (Future: Include target date and responsible party if not risk owner)	Next Review Date
1.							
2.							
3.							
4.							
5.							

The risk register is a versatile tool that can perform multiple functions and may be customized according to the needs of a particular organization. Columns may be added to the risk register that include factors, inherent level of risk, and current level of risk. For example, an organization's leadership may occasionally agree to tolerate a risk that is greater than the residual risk it normally accepts. A risk register may be used to quantify and track such instances. Additionally, a risk register can also be used to report risk to stakeholders and to provide assurance and compliance with risk management and associated governance and compliance controls.

IMPACT—ROLE FOR EXPOSURE ANALYSIS AND EVALUATION

In order to achieve its long-term strategies and short-term objectives, an organization must place resources at risk of loss. However, losses to various resources can have multiple and divergent impacts. An organization with an ERM approach must simultaneously consider all substantive impacts to achieve optimal success in obtaining its goals.

In an ERM context, impact is the quantitative and qualitative consequence of a change to a resource's value, which can also be referred to as a change to a resource's level. When the resource is a loss exposure, the impact is a negative consequence to the organization's total value. When the impact may be a positive consequence to the organization's value, the resource is a speculative project.

It is important to understand the effects of individual impacts, because a negative impact can impair an organization's ability to achieve its goals, while a positive impact can make the realization of an organization's goals more likely. The impact of change in a resource's value is a component of the organization's total value. The process of describing the value changes related to impacts includes using quantitative and qualitative measurements.

Describing Impact

An impact may be positive (an upside risk), negative (a downside risk), or both, and it can be financial and nonfinancial. Some impacts are direct, affecting the organization's assets. Other impacts are indirect—the consequence of, or contingent upon, another event.

A key consequence of a volatile event is the impact on the organization's goals. For example, a hospital's goal may be continuous operations. But the impact of a fire may be that attaining the goal is not possible. An organization exists for specified reasons. A thorough impact analysis must include a consideration for the impact on the organization's goals.

Upside of Risk Versus Downside of Risk

Risk is the variation from the expected outcome over time. The variation may be greater or less than expected. When the impact is a positive gain, the event is a speculative project or on the upside. The upside of risk is that the organization may outperform its strategic goals. The downside of risk is that the event may affect a loss exposure and the organization will incur a loss greater than expected.

Financial Impact and Nonfinancial Impact

The financial impacts of an outcome are frequently the most important consequences for an organization. However, the organization also needs to be concerned with the non-financial, qualitative impacts (such as impact on the organization's culture, impact on the organization's stakeholders, and impact on its reputation) if it hopes to achieve its goals. Likewise, not-for-profit organizations and governments, which are less concerned with financial gain, require some financial gains in order to maintain liquidity and the ability to provide nonfinancial services to their constituencies.

Direct Versus Indirect Impact

Event outcomes can affect the organization directly if the organization sustains a change in value to one of its resources. For example, the value of an internal stakeholder (an employee) may go up or down. Likewise, a technology resource may go up or down in value because, for example, it becomes obsolete when a newer, more productive software program becomes available. However, the organization does not have to incur a direct impact to be affected by an event. The organization is said to have an indirect impact if it has a contingent relationship with another organization. For example, assume an organization's inventory (and consequently its revenues) are contingent upon receiving a steady shipment from a supplier. Further assume the supplier suffers a loss to its warehouse from a fire. The supplier suffers a direct loss, and the organization suffers an indirect loss.

Levels of Impact

In addition, the consequences can be viewed as being primary or tertiary impacts. Primary impacts are those that affect the organization's resources; these are positive outcomes from opportunities taken and negative outcomes caused by threats. Tertiary impacts are those that affect third parties. Positive tertiary impacts result in opportunities for partners, suppliers, customers, society, and the environment. Negative tertiary impacts result in threats and losses to these same parties.

Primary Impact

Primary impact
The positive or negative consequences of a random event that affects an organization itself, the value of its resources, and the achievement of its goals.

A **primary impact** creates direct consequences for an organization. It may be a positive (upside) or a negative (downside) impact.

A primary impact is considered to be upside when the impact enhances the ability of the organization to achieve its goals. One example is a month of sales greater than expected. Upside impacts involve evaluating opportunities.

A primary impact is considered to be downside when the variation from the expected outcome is negative. If losses are greater than planned for in the budget, the impact may be an operating loss. Downside impacts involve evaluating threats.

Tertiary Impact

Tertiary impact
The positive or negative consequences of a random event that affects an organization's stakeholders, including third parties linked to the organization as well as society, the environment, and externalities.

Tertiary impacts affect third parties. They may be positive (upside) or negative (downside) impacts.

A tertiary impact is considered to be upside when the affected parties enjoy gains that result from the risk. These parties include business partners and society in general.

An upside tertiary impact can present opportunities for partners or certain stakeholders to enjoy gains that result from the risk. For example, if sales are greater than expected for an organization, then its supplier will also enjoy greater sales.

An upside tertiary impact can also cause positive impacts for third parties and positive externalities for the environment. For example, society benefits when a firm enjoys profits and other positive outcomes from the upside of risk because the organization pays additional taxes and might decide to contribute to charities.

A tertiary impact is considered to be downside when events have a negative impact for third parties, partners, and the environment. Should an organization suffer a loss in sales, then its supplier will also lose sales. These contingent losses can represent a significant impact for partners who are part of the organization's procurement network.

A downside tertiary impact can also cause negative externalities for third parties and for the environment. For example, a manufacturing firm may create a defective product that harms a consumer, resulting in a lawsuit against the manufacturer, which is a primary impact, and the retailer who sold the defectively manufactured product, which is a tertiary impact. Additionally, if the manufacturer emits harmful pollution into the air, water, or land while making the product, the expense of addressing it is an economic downside that affects all of society. The costs of these downside externalities can be enormous.

Measuring Impact

The impact on resources is measured in quantitative and qualitative aspects. The quantitative aspects are expressions of frequency, magnitude, expected value, variation, and time. The qualitative aspects include the effects on culture, stakeholders, and goals.

Frequency

The frequency, or count, is the number of times an impact is observed in a sample from a specific population. When related to the total possible number of observations, it produces the relative frequency or probability of that event. This ratio depicts the odds of an event's occurring, and when the probabilities of all possible outcomes are displayed together, they create a probability distribution. In this way, the probability of exceeding a profit threshold, a loss value, or another goal can be described in detail.

For predicting outcome frequencies, past performance may not be a valid indicator of future results. So, risk analysts combine the past information with their intuition and professional experience to predict future outcomes. A problem with predicting frequency values is that people are usually very inaccurate. They tend to overestimate the probability of gains and underestimate the probability of losses. Therefore, risk management professionals should temper their predictions accordingly.

Magnitude

The magnitude of an impact is the degree of change in a resource's value and level that occurs as a consequence of an event. When an impact is a negative change in a resource's value and level, the degree of the negative impact should be analyzed. When the impact is a positive change, the degree of the positive impact should also be analyzed. As with frequency measures, future values are estimated based on past observations and tempered with professional experience. Measures of the change in values are often stated in terms of measures of central tendency. These measures help the analyst know what to expect—or predict—for future scenarios. There are many measures of central tendency. The most common include the arithmetic mean (average), the mode (most common), and median (middle) values. Any of these measures may be more appropriate than others in various scenarios. A key factor in deciding which measure of central tendency to use in a forecast is the shape of the probability distribution.

Within magnitude is the dimension of timing. Timing concerns when an event occurs, which can affect magnitude. A fire that strikes a restaurant in a seaside resort community in November may not produce the same impact (loss of revenue) as it would in July. Duration of an event is also a factor. For example, a sudden leak from an above-ground fuel storage tank may be discovered before any pollutants enter the groundwater. Alternatively, an underground storage tank may leak for years without detection, affecting large areas.

Application to Exposure Spaces

The most important consequence for many organizations is achieving an optimal economic performance. For loss exposures, this is achieving the smallest possible loss values. For speculative projects, it is achieving an optimal financial measure—often profit. While this concept sounds simple and straightforward, in practice, measuring the quantitative impacts on resources can be very challenging.

Exposure spaces include resources that are divided into specific categories:

- Human resources—internal stakeholders
- Technical resources—property or assets
- Information resources—intellectual capital
- Partner resources—external stakeholders
- Financial resources—financial streams flowing in or out of an organization
- Free resources—economic externalities

In considering human resource (HR) loss exposures, measuring special damages is a matter of adding up medical bills, lost wages, and other specified costs. Measuring general damages, however, can be very subjective because they are based on, for example, pain and suffering, which does not have a specific economic value and varies considerably from person to person. Moreover, measuring the impact of indirect (consequential) losses is also difficult because these losses may not be recognized for quite some time, if ever.

When considering human resources as speculative projects, various proxies are used to estimate the increase in value. Some possibilities are a decrease in employee turnover or increased production.

Impacts that affect technology resources (such as property and assets) can also be difficult to measure. Asset values may be measured using several methods (RC, ACV, market value, and so forth). Similarly, the impact, or change in the asset's value, can be measured in a variety of ways, such as a reduced ability to produce income or a diminution in value. Consequently, the overall impact could be a subjective assessment.

Impacts that affect information resources are also estimated based on expected future contributions of the intellectual capital. If the resource is stolen or compromised, the loss of earnings associated with this information resource may never be quantified to its full extent. Proxies are used to estimate the business interruption loss or expected net present value of the resource.

Impacts regarding financial resources, such as a firm's ability to secure a loan, have recently become relevant for many organizations. Macroeconomic events can make obtaining bank loans, selling commercial bonds, or issuing new stock either very easy or difficult.

The impacts that affect free resources may occur immediately or may develop over many years. For example, the impact of a firm emitting pollution may not be noticed or addressed for decades. Once discovered, these losses can have retroactive claims and assessments. However, positive impacts also can be slow to be appreciated. For example, the City of Cincinnati's Pollution Prevention Program has been in effect since 1992, yet only recently have the city's accomplishments been publicized. The quantitative impact can be measured in reduced energy consumption, lower waste disposal costs, and increased recycling participation.

Qualitative Impacts

Qualitative impacts are each equally important in assessing the overall impact to resources. Organizations fail to complete their impact assessment if they consider only quantitative (frequency and magnitude) impacts. Qualitative impacts can completely overshadow the quantitative impacts. There are three basic types of qualitative assessments:

- The impact on the organization's culture
- The impact on the other stakeholders
- The impact on the organization's goals

Perhaps the most important qualitative impact is how a change in value to a speculative project or loss exposure affects the organization's employees. Frequently, managers focus on the bottom line of profit or economic efficiency and fail to consider how an event will affect their employees. Negative impacts include increased turnover, difficulty in recruiting new employees, or decreased production.

Positive consequences include employee loyalty and a willingness to work extra hours or exert extra effort for the firm.

Qualitative impacts on other stakeholders are also significant. Adverse responses to an event could result in higher supplier prices and restricted supplies of capital or raw materials. Possible negative non-governmental organization (NGO) reactions include boycotts and sudden negative Internet publicity that affects an organization's reputation. Governments could increase scrutiny, regulation, or penalties. The impact of an event on demand for the organization's goods and services could be significant. Positive impacts, however, include higher scores from rating agencies and other voluntary compliance standards associations. For example, complying with quality standards could earn an ISO 9000 award[1] and increase business opportunities.

The qualitative assessment must also include an analysis of the impact of changes in resource values on the organization's goals. A loss to some resources may have an insignificant impact on long-term strategies, but a major loss to another resource may force a complete reevaluation of the organization's goals. Impacts should be evaluated in terms of effects on both the organization's goals and its values. For example, a positive macroeconomic event may render a firm's current profit goals outdated.

Certain financial goals could be affected by both macro- and microeconomic changes. Consider a firm with a goal of continuity of operations. The question is rarely that of an absolute continuity, but rather how long an interruption the organization can tolerate. The longer the tolerable downtime, the lesser the investment necessary to mitigate the threat. However, when public service is at stake, the tolerance may be very limited—a hospital, for example, needs electricity without interruption.

Partnering with what were once considered adversaries has proved to be an effective technique for achieving strategic goals. Likewise, environmental stewardship policies can result in positive or negative impacts. For example, pollution liability suits can have catastrophic impacts for a firm, while compliance with international standards, such as ISO 14000, can generate positive goodwill and reputation, consumer satisfaction, and greater profits.

APPLYING THE EXPOSURE SPACES MODEL

This case study is based on the "Tire Fire Case Facts Applicable to All Organizations" as well as the case study facts specific to each organization. To successfully complete this case study, you should understand three concepts:

- Exposure defined
- Using an exposure assessment tool
- Exposure spaces model

High-Level Steps for Case Analysis

This case study applies the exposure spaces model to each of the three organizations involved in the "Tire Fire" case, by following two steps that consist of several sub-steps.

For each organization, the first step involves applying the exposure spaces model to the facts specific to the organization by identifying these factors:

- Essential resources of the organization (at least one from each resource class)
- Events affecting the organization
- Impacts to the organization, third parties, and environment for each event identified

The second step involves analyzing the organization's ERM plan in the aftermath of the fire by answering two questions:

- What were the strengths and weaknesses of the organization's ERM plan in dealing with the effects of the fire on the internal and external stakeholders?
- What corrections can be made to the plan to address the more pressing weaknesses?

Exposure Defined

An exposure or, more precisely, a loss exposure, exists when something of value is subject to a condition that may cause a loss. Referring to the exposure spaces model, a loss would be a change in value, which would be indicated on the y-axis. This axis illustrates the impact or consequence on a resource.

For example, a manufacturer's factory is an asset that may decrease in value and therefore is a loss exposure. Key employees are another example of a loss exposure, as they may become injured or ill. The manufacturer may have a legal liability exposure as the result of a lawsuit. Finally, the manufacturer may have a net income exposure as the result of a direct loss to the factory, the injured employee, or the lawsuit.

This definition of "loss exposure" served risk management professionals well as long as they were charged only with managing the downside of risk. But in today's ERM environment, risk management professionals are increasingly charged with managing the upside of risk. Therefore, a new definition was needed to more accurately reflect the current global and speculative approach. The concept of exposure spaces includes the possibility that a resource may increase in value. Financial analysts refer to any financial position that may change in value as a "project." Because an ERM project's value may increase, decrease, or stay the same, the project is often referred to as a speculative project.

For example, a firm may invest in an asset, hoping that its value will increase. Alternatively, the firm may hire an executive, hoping that her value will increase.

The Tire Fire Case Facts Applicable to All Organizations

At about 1:30 AM on April 17, 20XX, a fire erupted at Wheeler's Tire Disposal, Inc. This corporation, wholly owned by Walt Wheeler, operates a large scrap tire disposal yard in the Ribiera Riverside section of Friendship City, a major metropolitan area in the eastern United States. Walt's company also has a similar, but somewhat smaller, tire disposal yard in each of two other cities; one is fifty miles north of Friendship City; the other is eighty miles south of the city. Wheeler's uses a combination of chemical, grinding, and crushing processes to recycle scrap tires into a variety of rubber-based raw materials, which it sells wholesale as its major source of revenue.

Because of their rubber, petroleum, and complex chemical content, tires give off great heat when burned. They also produce intense, billowing, acrid smoke, especially when they have been mounded into towering piles. Such piles had crowded Wheeler's lot for several months before the fire, prompting many neighboring property owners to complain that Wheeler's operations created an illegal environmental hazard. Most of the tires burned during the six hours the fire was out of control or during several subsequent days before the fire was completely extinguished.

Harold's Heavy-Duty Equipment Company is immediately adjacent, somewhat downhill, and usually downwind from Wheeler's Tire Disposal. For three months before the tire fire, Harold, the owner, had been complaining to city, state, and federal authorities that the noise and fumes from Wheeler's disposal yard interfered with Harold's ability to do business and endangered the health of the company's employees and customers. Occasionally, oil released during Wheeler's tire processing ran down onto Harold's property. That flow of oil became a virtual flood on the day immediately following Wheeler's fire.

The local office of the federal Environmental Protection Agency (EPA) agreed with Harold's and other complaints. Before the fire occurred, the EPA had ordered Wheeler's to cease its tire disposal activities at the Friendship City location as of April 18 and to clear all scrap tires from the lot as soon as possible thereafter. The April 17 fire complicated enforcement of the EPA's order. Therefore, Friendship City Fire Department officials speculated publicly that the fire almost certainly had been intentionally set.

Many skeptical observers noted that if Wheeler himself did not set the fire, then other possible arsonists—whether strangers or Wheeler's relatives, friends, or enemies—had done him a great favor, helping him out of a difficult business and legal situation and letting him appear as an innocent victim of a crime. Nonetheless, an adjuster for Wheeler's commercial package property, business interruption, and liability insurer telephoned Walt a few days after this speculation appeared in the media. The adjuster told Walt that the insurer was considering issuing a reservation of rights letter before defending any fire-related liability claims against Wheeler or his company and was contemplating denying all property coverage because of arson allegedly committed by, or at the direction of, the insured.

Part of Wheeler's Friendship City tire disposal yard lay beneath an interstate highway that passes above the streets of the city on a series of overpasses. Consequently, the intense heat rising from the burning tires buckled the steel girders supporting the aging overpass and snapped the steel reinforcing rods in its roadbed. Federal and city authorities closed this section of the interstate for five weeks until the overpass could be repaired, and as a result, commuters were forced to find new routes or transportation alternatives.

The fire, together with its fierce heat and noxious smoke, imposed accidental losses on hundreds of individuals and organizations. This study focuses on losses to three of the affected entities: Wheeler's Tire Disposal, Inc.; Harold's Heavy Duty Equipment Company; and Schneller's Transport, a common carrier shipping from Friendship City.

First Step, Wheeler's Tire Disposal: Applying the Exposure Spaces Model to the Facts Specific to the Organization

Applying the exposure spaces model to Wheeler's Tire Disposal entails identifying the company's essential resources; events affecting the company; and impacts to the company, third parties, and the environment.

Essential Resources of the Company

In ERM, there are six classes of resources: human, technical, information, partners, financial, and free. For Wheeler's Tire Disposal, these resources were identified in each class:

*   Human—owner Walt Wheeler, general manager Fred Jones, and the company's other employees
*   Technical—buildings, equipment, scrap tire inventory, and bags of catalytic chemicals
*   Information—the knowledge and skill of how to use a combination of chemical, grinding, and crushing processes to recycle scrap tires into a variety of rubber-based raw materials
*   Partners—major suppliers of scrap tires and the wholesale buyers of Wheeler's recycled rubber raw materials; the clinical psychologist who treated Walt Wheeler
*   Financial—revenue the company earned from the sale of its product; expenses incurred to produce the product
*   Free—the air pollution the company discharged before, during, and after the fire occurred, at least until the state and federal environmental protection agencies began enforcing statutes against the company; the flood of oil onto the neighbor's property until the neighbor sued the company for damages

Wheeler's Tire Disposal

Of all those suffering losses from this fire, Walt Wheeler's enterprise was the one most directly affected, with these immediately apparent losses:

- The fire totally destroyed the buildings, equipment, and scrap tire inventory at the company's Friendship City lot. It also consumed many bags of the catalytic chemical that Wheeler's used in its on-site chemical processing of scrap tires. Only a few isolated sections of walls, such as the foundations (which were below ground), and some of the wiring and piping, remained intact.

- Wheeler's Tire Disposal and Walt Wheeler, personally, were sued by many neighboring and distant organizations for interfering with their businesses. Wheeler's own employees submitted workers compensation claims for fire-related injuries, and federal and state environmental agencies brought suit for violations of various statutes. Friendship City sued to recover part of the fire department and police department costs incurred for extinguishing the fire, rerouting traffic, and maintaining order in a situation that, the city contended, Wheeler's could have prevented by conducting its business with reasonable care.

- The property was so badly damaged and the fire became the subject of so much civil and criminal litigation that Walt Wheeler decided not to reopen a Wheeler's Tire Disposal facility in Friendship City. This decision reduced the company's revenues by more than it reduced the company's expenses, thus lowering its overall net income.

- Adverse national publicity about the tire fire threatened Wheeler's with loss of several of its major suppliers of scrap tires and many of its wholesale buyers of its recycled rubber raw materials.

- Dealing with the aftermath of this fire consumed almost all of Walt Wheeler's time and energy for the rest of the year. His family, friends, and business associates described Walt as having become obsessed with defending his personal honor against rumors that he was an arsonist and with fighting against what Walt called the "injustice of insurers' denying legitimate claims." Consequently, at the urging of the company, Walt took a six-month leave of absence from the company to undergo the care of a clinical psychologist. Wheeler's Tire Disposal retained several consultants, including a risk management expert, to advise it until Walt was able to return as the company's chief executive.

- Early the following year, members of a youth gang, complete strangers to Walt and his company, confessed to setting the fire as a way of celebrating an important victory by their school's basketball team. Only then did public and police suspicion against Walt, and the insurer's doubts about his claims, disappear. By about fifteen months after the fire, Walt was able to resume his normal work at the two remaining tire disposal locations.

- The general manager of Wheeler's Friendship City lot, having become overstressed by the pressures of coping with this fire and with the adverse publicity, some of which focused on him, resigned within a month of the fire. Even after Walt regained control of the company, he and his family agreed that the risk management consultant hired during Walt's absence should stay on indefinitely.

Events Affecting the Organization

The events that affected the value of the organization's resources fall into one of four classes: economic, natural, industrial, and human.

While the fire did have an economic impact, it was not caused by the economy and therefore should not be classified as an economic event; nor were the company's losses caused by a natural event (such as lightning). The fire was caused by arsonists.

The company's losses could be considered to have been caused by either or both of the last two classes: industrial and human. Industrial events can be categorized as traditional hazard risks, including fire, building collapse, pollution, vandalism, and injuries to workers and to members of the public. Human events are perhaps the most direct cause of this fire. This class includes voluntary human events that result from conscious and deliberate acts of individuals and groups. The criminal act of a youth gang setting fire to the tires as a way of celebrating an important victory of their school's basketball team is clearly a human event.

Impacts to the Organization, Third Parties, and Environment

In an ERM context, impact is the quantitative and qualitative consequence of a change to a resource's value.

The change in the value of Wheeler's resources as a result of the fire was almost universally negative. The industrial and human events destroyed the Friendship City plant's buildings, equipment, and scrap tire inventory. Also lost were bags of catalytic chemical. These losses should be easy to quantify by adding up the replacement cost of each item.

Wheeler's also was hit with a barrage of legal claims: from other organizations for interfering with their businesses, from its own employees bringing workers compensation claims for fire-related injuries, from federal and state environmental agencies for violation of various statutes, and from the city to recover some of the fire and police costs incurred extinguishing the fire. The legal claims are difficult to quantify, as a judge or jury is likely to decide the amounts to be awarded on a subjective case-by-case basis.

The company also decided not to reopen its Friendship City plant, resulting in loss of future sales revenue it might have otherwise earned. This loss amount can be estimated based on previous years' net income generated by the Friendship City plant, projected to what it would have been for future years.

Other losses cannot be so easily quantified: the damage to the company's reputation that resulted from the negative publicity; the loss of production resulting from the distraction and stress the fire caused for Walt Wheeler for fifteen months; and the loss of the company's general manager, Fred Jones, a key employee, which was likely a contributing factor in the decision not to reopen the Friendship City plant.

If any benefit to the company resulted from the fire, it may have been the permanent addition of a risk manager.

Second Step, Wheeler's Tire Disposal: Analyzing the Company's ERM Plan in the Aftermath of the Fire

In this step, the strengths and weaknesses of Wheeler's ERM plan are analyzed in relation to the fire and corrections are suggested.

Strengths and Weaknesses of Wheeler's ERM Plan

The strengths of the organization's ERM plan are difficult to discern, primarily because Wheeler's apparently had no such plan in place during the loss. However, the organization had taken several helpful risk management actions. One was to diversify its locations. With two other locations, even though one location suffered a catastrophic loss, the organization was still able to produce its product and stay in business.

Another action the company took was to seek help for the owner after his productivity fell due to the stress of the loss. The company also sought the counsel of several consultants to replace the expertise lost while Walt was unavailable. The company's purchase of insurance is also a strength; because Walt recognized that he had exposures that were best transferred to an insurer, he purchased a commercial package policy and business interruption insurance.

Wheeler's risk management activities had a number of weaknesses. The company allowed tires to accumulate into towering piles that not only created an environmental hazard but were apparently an attractive nuisance for teenagers to burn. The company's relationship with its neighbor, Harold's Heavy-Duty Equipment Company, was not amicable before the fire because of fumes, noise, and the oil seepage from Wheeler's premises onto Harold's property. Because of these oil seepages, it may have been reasonably foreseeable that a fire would result in a flood of oil.

The company's reputation with the state and federal environmental agencies was also a weakness, as evidenced by the number and types of complaints they received about the company from neighboring businesses and the company's lack of remedial responses. It was also reasonably foreseeable that if the piles of tires under the overpass caught fire, the road above would be damaged. In addition, the company experienced difficulty replacing the managerial expertise after losing the services of its owner and general manager. Finally, the security of the plant's premises was questionable. It was apparently easy for the youths to enter the premises, start the fire, and then leave undetected.

Corrections to Address the More Pressing Weaknesses

Wheeler's could make several corrections to address the more pressing weaknesses of its ERM approach. The first correction would be to create an ERM plan. The risk manager now on staff can champion this project through to completion.

The ERM plan should include a disaster recovery plan (DRP), which would address immediate needs in the event of a loss, such as protocol for responding to the news media. Appropriate media responses might have prevented fire department officials' speculation that Walt had started the fire himself, which in turn might have prevented the company's insurer from denying coverage. Appropriate responses might also have prevented some of the claims or lawsuits that resulted from the fire or reduced the settlement or jury award amounts of those that were not prevented.

Media responses could have included Wheeler's expression of concern for its neighbors and other victims of the fire, a statement pointing out that the company is also a victim and will suffer significant losses, an indication of willingness to fully cooperate with the fire investigation, and an assertion that determined arsonists are difficult if not impossible to defend against completely.

A business continuity plan (BCP) could also be added to the ERM plan. The BCP would facilitate transfer of critical responsibilities when one or more of the company's key employees became unavailable.

Reduced reliance on free resources would also create less conflict with state and federal environmental protection agencies and the company's neighbors. The ERM plan should address ways to prevent the release of noxious fumes and the flow of oil onto the neighbor's property. The costs of these preventive environmental measures should be included in the price of the company's product.

The location of the tires should also be reconsidered. The tires should be placed away from structures that would sustain extensive losses if damaged, such as overpasses.

Finally, the premises' security should be addressed. Measures to restrict access to the tires and other combustible materials, such as use of a security guard, surveillance equipment, and higher and stronger fencing, will reduce the frequency of similar losses.

First Step, Harold's Heavy-Duty Equipment Company: Applying the Exposure Spaces Model to the Facts Specific to the Organization

Essential Resources of the Company

For Harold's Heavy-Duty Equipment Company, these resources were identified in each ERM resource class:

- Human—Harold and his employees.

- Technical—The company's buildings and its inventory of electrical generators, bulldozers, and other earth moving equipment.

- Information—The knowledge and skills needed for the company to rent or sell its clients the large, heavy, yet portable machinery in its inventory with the competency the clients have come to expect and trust. Otherwise customers would go to a competitor.

- Partners—The clients to which the company rents or sells its inventory.

- Financial—The cash flowing in and out of the company, including the revenues it receives from renting or selling the products in its inventory, as well as the company's expenses, such as the mortgage payment for the building that warehouses its inventory.

- Free—The decrease or increase in the value of the environment. Harold's company does not engage in activities that caused harmful substances to be released into the environment; therefore its use of free resources is considerably more limited than it is, for example, for Wheeler's Tire Disposal.

Harold's Heavy-Duty Equipment Company

Harold's business is located immediately next to and downwind from Wheeler's. The equipment Harold's rents and sells—large, portable electrical generators, bulldozers, and other earth-moving equipment—sustained serious property damage, resulting in income losses to Harold's because of Wheeler's fire. In addition, Harold himself became partially but permanently disabled after the fire. More specifically, the losses included these:

- Heat and smoke damage rendered much of Harold's equipment unsuitable for commercial use.

- The day of the fire and for several days thereafter, about 10,000 gallons of petroleum, released during the uncontrolled burning of tires on Wheeler's lot, flowed each day onto and over Harold's property and equipment. Extensive cleanup—and in some cases, disposal of unsalvageable property—was required. The oil damaged storm drains and contaminated the underlying water table, possibly permanently.

- Many of Harold's employees were sickened by the thick cloud of smoke they encountered when reporting for work on April 17, qualifying them for workers compensation benefits, for which Harold and his workers compensation insurer are liable.

- From April 17 to May 20, the Friendship City fire and police departments barricaded all the streets for three blocks around Wheeler's while they investigated the fire and determined the condition of the overhead interstate highway. Consequently, for over a month Harold was unable to reach his one place of business, and as a result, he lost substantial revenue and several long-standing customers. During the time his business was closed, many of his expenses (such as property taxes and mortgage payments on his building and some of his equipment) continued to accrue.

- The acrid smoke Harold first encountered on the morning of the fire lingered over the following few days, during which he tried to do business despite the police and fire department presence. The smoke greatly aggravated his emphysema. After two decades of working twelve-hour days to build his company, Harold (age fifty-five) was no longer able to stand or do other work for more than four hours a day because of his emphysema.

Events Affecting the Organization

The four classes of events that affect the value of the organization's resources are economic, natural, industrial, and human.

The smoke, heat, and oil damage the company incurred was not caused by the economy; therefore, it was not an economic event. The damage was also not caused by a natural event such as a windstorm. It was caused by an industrial event. The smoke, heat, and oil originated from outside the company, but the company's resources were negatively affected when those harmful elements came onto the company's premises.

Two human events also occurred. First, the youth gang's arson, although directed at Wheeler Tire Disposal, set into motion an unbroken chain of events that resulted in damage to Harold's as well. Second, Wheeler's failure to provide adequate security on its premises, as well as its storing of tires under the overpass, affected Harold's company.

Impacts to the Organization, Third Parties, and Environment

The change to Harold's Heavy-Duty Equipment Company's resource values was universally negative. The heat and smoke damage to its inventory was caused by industrial and human events. The amount of the loss would be relatively simple to determine by adding the selling prices of the equipment that was to be sold to the rental income that would have been generated over the useful life of each piece of rental equipment.

The fire also caused a flood of oil that contaminated the underlying water table. If the contamination is determined to be permanent and water is necessary for Harold's occupancy of the premises, the impact of the loss may be the cost to relocate to an uncontaminated site.

The smoke sickened Harold's employees and Harold himself. Workers compensation will pay the employees' medical expenses, lost wages, and rehabilitation costs. However Harold's health has been permanently compromised, and the company will have the services of this key person for less than half the time he formerly contributed.

The fire department closed the roads needed to access Harold's business for a month, forcing him to shut down his business. This resulted in loss of revenue and several longstanding customers.

Second Step, Harold's Heavy-Duty Equipment Company: Analyzing the Company's ERM Plan in the Aftermath of the Fire

In this step, the strengths and weaknesses of Harold's Heavy-Duty Equipment Company's ERM plan are analyzed in relation to the fire and corrections are suggested.

Strengths and Weaknesses of Harold's ERM Plan

The strengths of the company's ERM plan, to the extent that it may have had one, are not evident. It is not clear what risk management activities the company performed, other than to buy workers compensation insurance for its employees (which is normally required by law).

The weaknesses of the company's ERM plan are many.

There is no evidence that Harold had insured his inventory for the types of events that resulted from the fire. Therefore, when his inventory was destroyed, his only recourse was to demand payment from Wheeler's insurer. The insurer was reluctant to pay, in part, because of its suspicion that Walt Wheeler committed arson.

Although Harold knew in advance of the fire that oil from Walt's business flowed downhill onto his property, he took no action to place a protective barrier between the properties. Further, because he did not diversify his locations, he was forced to close, at least temporarily, when his sole location became inaccessible. A separate location can increase costs substantially and result in other inefficiencies, and Harold's does not have the sales to warrant such an arrangement. A less expensive alternative would have been to purchase business interruption insurance to protect the business from these types of events. Harold apparently did not do so.

Finally, Harold had no successor ready to replace his expert leadership. Because his emphysema was aggravated by the smoke from the fire, his company must now conduct its operations with its leader present for only four hours a day.

Corrections to Address the More Pressing Weaknesses

Corrections were suggested for each of the weaknesses identified in the company's risk management plan. After the loss of his inventory, Harold is likely more receptive to the option of insuring it for similar losses in the future. Harold may want to take a more direct approach to protect the premises from the threat of oil from Walt's uphill property. Because Walt has been forced out of business at his Friendship City location, the threat of an oil flood in the future may be reduced or eliminated. However, determining whether any such threat remains will require investigation.

Harold should also consider transferring the risk of being shut down as a result of similar future events by purchasing business interruption insurance. Harold may also want to consider adopting a BCP to ensure a successor for him or other key employees.

First Step, Schneller Transport Company: Applying the Exposure Spaces Model to the Facts Specific to the Organization

Essential Resources of the Company

For Schneller Transport Company, these resources were identified in each ERM resource class:

- Human—the Schneller family and the company's employees
- Technical—the company's offices, storage warehouses, and the trucks used in the business of being a common carrier
- Information—the Schneller family's knowledge of shipping routes and facilities in and around the Friendship City region
- Partners—the supplier of the rental trucks the company had to use to address the sharp increase in shipping orders from customers

- Financial—costs of advertising, hiring additional drivers, rental fees for additional trucks, added insurance, and higher fuel expenses
- Free—air pollution generated by the company trucks' exhaust and the pollution generated by disposal of used truck tires

Events Affecting the Organization

The four classes of events that affect the value of Schnellers' resources are economic, natural, industrial, and human.

The company did not suffer a loss as a direct result of the fire. Instead, the company saw an opportunity to sharply increase its sales revenue. Traditional risk management would not have found this opportunity relevant. However, ERM does. In this case, however, the rapid increase in business was poorly managed, resulting in a net loss of income. The cause of this loss—poor management decisions—was neither an economic event nor an event caused by nature. It was also not an industrial event, because it was not caused by some traditional hazard peril. It was a human event, undertaken intentionally, but leading to unintended consequences.

Schneller Transport Company

Schneller Transport Company, owned by the Schneller family, is a general, common carrier shipping firm in Friendship City. Its offices and storage warehouses are far from Wheeler's. It operated for more than fifteen years before the fire at Wheeler's.

Based on the Schneller family's knowledge of shipping routes and facilities in and around the Friendship City region, the company tried to seize the opportunity created by the general transportation difficulties that followed in the fire's wake. The company advertised in various national media that, despite the fire at Wheeler's, Schneller could assure both present and prospective customers that it would make prompt deliveries into, out of, and through Friendship City. Despite its optimism, Schneller's ambitious promises caused it to incur several losses from Wheeler's fire:

- Schneller received more new business than it expected. To fulfill its advertised promise, the company had to hire more drivers, rent additional trucks, and incur extra expenses, such as added insurance costs and higher fuel costs. Trying to meet new customers' needs stretched Schneller's resources to the point that some of its established customers observed that they received less than the usual good service they had come to expect from the company, and they went elsewhere for transport services. As a result, the company's overall profit margin dropped significantly.

- Asking its employees—some of them new and all of them overtaxed by overtime work—to cope with this new volume of business contributed directly to many employee errors. These errors led to lost and misdirected shipments, bookkeeping mistakes, and highway accidents caused by driver error. Those mistakes led to many lawsuits against Schneller.

Impacts to the Organization, Third Parties, and Environment

The change to Schneller Transport Company's resources was universally negative despite the rapid increase in sales revenue. The company incurred increased costs for advertising, hiring additional drivers, rental fees for additional trucks, added insurance, higher fuel expenses, overtime salary expenses, and lawsuits due to driver errors in highway accidents.

Apart from unresolved lawsuits, the costs for each of these expenses can be readily determined. Harder to determine is the cost resulting from loss of established customers. The overall financial effect to the company is known: its profit margin dropped greatly.

Second Step, Schneller Transport Company: Analyzing the Company's ERM Plan in the Aftermath of the Fire

In this step, the strengths and weaknesses of Schneller Transport Company's ERM plan are analyzed in relation to the fire and corrections are suggested.

Strengths and Weaknesses of Schneller's ERM Plan

The strengths of the company's ERM plan, if it has one, are not clear. ERM is intended to address the opportunities presented to an organization. Schneller appears to have squandered the opportunity resulting from Wheeler's fire; however, it at least had the ability to recognize the opportunity. Further, despite the mistakes made with over-promising deliveries, the company was still able to make a profit, just with a lower margin.

The weaknesses of the company's ERM plan are poor management decisions made as the company tried to increase its production capacity. It is possible to have too much growth when it is compressed in too short a time period for the operations of the company to accommodate.

Corrections to Address the More Pressing Weaknesses

Corrections for the weaknesses in Schneller's ERM plan include management's being careful to match the sales increase to the production capacity increase. Management also should not be overly optimistic when promising delivery times and monitoring performance rendered to established customers, in order to continue the high quality of service customers have come to expect.

Table of Correct Answers

	Wheeler's Tire Disposal	Harold's Heavy-Duty Equipment Company	Schneller Transport Company
Resources	• Human • Technical • Information • Partners • Financial • Free	• Human • Technical • Information • Partners • Financial • Free	• Human • Technical • Information • Partners • Financial • Free
Events	• Industrial • Human	• Industrial • Human	• Human
Impacts	• Buildings, equipment, inventory destroyed • Legal claims • Future revenue lost from Friendship City location • Damage to reputation • Stress on owner, resulting in diminished contribution	• Inventory destroyed • Flood of oil contaminated underlying water table • Harold's and employees' health damaged by smoke	• Increased operating costs • Loss of established customers • Lower profit margin
Strengths	• Diversified locations • Sought expert help of consultants when needed • Purchased insurance to cover losses incurred	• Purchased workers compensation insurance	• Recognized opportunity • Was still able to make a profit despite mistakes
Weaknesses	• Towering piles of tires • Lack of attention to reputation prior to loss • Storing tires under overpass • Difficulty replacing management expertise • Inadequate premises security	• Uninsured inventory • No proactive treatment of oil flood risk • No diversity of location • No business interruption insurance • Difficulty replacing management expertise	• Poor management decisions when increasing operating capacity • Fast growth without sufficient planning
Corrections	• Create ERM plan • Create disaster recovery plan • Create business continuity plan • Reduce reliance on free resources • Relocate tires away from critical structures • Hire security guard • Install surveillance equipment • Erect higher, stronger fence	• Insure inventory • Erect barrier to catch oil flood • Insure business interruption • Create business continuity plan	• Match sales increase to the production capacity increase • Be realistic when promising delivery times • Monitor performance rendered to established customers to ensure continuing quality of services

SUMMARY

The exposure spaces model is a concept risk management professionals use to describe the multiple attributes that constitute a risk. These include the resources that may change in value (loss exposures and speculative projects), the events that cause change in value (perils and sources), and the impacts of the change (direct and indirect losses, social justice, and environmental stewardship). This three-dimensional model enables risk management professionals to describe situations more clearly to a broader audience.

Impact is the quantitative and qualitative consequence of a change to a resource. The impact may be positive (an upside risk), negative (a downside risk), or possibly both. Impacts are measured with regard to several attributes, including frequency, magnitude, expected value, variation, and time. Using this information, the risk manager should perform quantitative and qualitative analyses, which provide a more comprehensive understanding of the impacts.

One of the benefits of the exposure spaces model is that it facilitates identification of the strengths and weaknesses of an organization's ERM plan. Another benefit is that it helps the risk management professional identify corrections needed to address the more pressing weaknesses.

CHAPTER NOTE

1. ISO 9000 standards are available at www.iso.org/iso/iso_catalogue/management_standards/iso_9000_iso_14000.htm (accessed August 14, 2009).

Direct Your Learning

Risk Assessment: Management Departments, Risk Centers, and Uncertainty Modeling

Educational Objectives

After learning the content of this chapter and completing the corresponding course guide assignment, you should be able to:

▶ Describe how an organization structures itself according to management departments.

▶ Explain how an organization can more effectively manage its risks by creating risk centers that have risk owners.

▶ Describe the methods and associated limitations of modeling uncertainty.

▶ Given a case, apply Bayesian network probabilities, influence diagrams, and the expected values of utility.

Outline

Management Departments

Risk Centers and Risk Owners

Methods and Limitations of Uncertainty Modeling

Risk Quantification Case Study— Woodworking Workshop

Summary

Risk Assessment: Management Departments, Risk Centers, and Uncertainty Modeling

In an organization that has adopted enterprise-wide risk management (ERM), unit managers manage risk by using various methods of departmentalization and by considering how their department interacts with other departments. Risk centers result from dividing organizations into smaller component parts, and they enable organizations to most effectively manage a large number of diverse risks through empowering risk center managers, or risk owners. Organizations quantify and assess the dimensions of the uncertainty or risk by creating empirical models, which help management simulate, test, and predict outcomes and then learn from the data produced. A case study in this chapter allows the application of several methods of risk quantification.

MANAGEMENT DEPARTMENTS

Organizations that adopt an ERM approach often manage the risks associated with their organization's resources by structuring themselves according to management departments. These departments are based on four elements: specialization, standardization, coordination, and authority. These elements combine to allow for optimal quality and efficient completion of departmental tasks. For example, the human resources (HR) department has the authority to recruit, hire, train, promote, and dismiss employees. As such, it has standardized procedures and coordinates all of the organization's human resources activities.

Management departments may be categorized according to place, product, matrix, or function. Place departmentalization is used by organizations that have facilities in many different locations. Product departmentalization is often used by conglomerate corporations that have diversified product lines. Matrix departmentalization is a combination of function, place, or product structures.

Most organizations, however, use some form of functional departmentalization. Typical functional departments include human resources, sales and marketing, production, procurement and purchasing, information systems, finance, audit, and risk management. Each of these departments establishes individual goals and budgets. An ERM approach suggests that each department also consider two other elements: how actual outcomes vary from expected outcomes over a budgetary period, and the effects of their goals and activities on other departments.

Human Resources

Many organizations claim that people are their most important resource. Indeed, the physical skill and intellectual capital of the organization's personnel provide the basic ingredients for its success. While HR has the authority to manage employees, it must also have standardized procedures and coordinate all of the organization's human resource activities.

An effective HR department should consider the range of possible alternative outcomes relative to its expectations. For example, it may plan for an annual employee turnover rate of 15 percent. However, the actual rate may be lower under certain economic conditions. Alternatively, the actual rate may be higher during periods of low unemployment, when labor supply is scarce and employees secure higher-paying jobs. Other types of variation (risk) include variations in training program success, promotion expectations, and retirement rates. When the HR department creates goals and contingency plans for variation from expected outcomes, it optimizes its chance for success. HR should be most adept at managing its own risks.

Sales and Marketing

Every organization sells a product or a service. Not-for-profit organizations, for example, must promote and advertise their services. Governments must inform their constituencies of services. For-profit companies must advertise and sell their goods.

Marketing consists of four elements: product, price, place, and promotion. The sales and marketing department creates goals according to each of these elements. For example, the product element specifies the actual goods or services produced and how they satisfy customer demands. The scope of a product generally includes elements such as warranties and customer support. A product may fail to meet consumer needs or may exceed customer expectations. Thus, it is incumbent on the sales and marketing department to develop contingencies for variation from expected product, price, place, and promotion outcomes. That is, the sales and marketing department must practice risk management.

Production

The production (or operations management) department typically consists of four elements: process design, capacity scheduling, inventory management, and quality control. The department creates expected outcomes according to each element. It also should manage the variation for each element. For example, in process design, the department chooses the layout of work stations, flow of materials, and technology. When a machine breaks or an injury occurs at a work station, production must stop. The production department manager must have a contingency plan to ensure minimal impact in such situations that vary from expected outcomes.

Procurement and Purchasing

The purpose of this department (which may be a part of the logistics department) is to obtain raw materials for production in the most efficient and cost-effective manner possible. In some cases, the department is also responsible for delivering finished goods to customers. Maintaining sufficient, but not excessive, inventories can be critical to profitable operations. The procurement and purchasing department establishes a materials requirement plan to facilitate maintenance of an optimal inventory. Its challenge is to obtain consistent raw material quality, in the right quantity, at the right time. Any variation from these elements creates risks for which contingency plans must be made.

Information Systems

The information systems department manages an organization's information technology system and therefore often is the organization's most rapidly evolving department. Consequently, plans for computer hardware, software, transaction processing, database management, and reporting systems must be flexible and able to accommodate variation from expected outcomes. Unexpected changes can occur within even relatively short periods. For example, a new computer system may significantly increase the speed of transactions with customers. Alternatively, a new expert system may make decision making more efficient and give the organization a competitive advantage. Thus, the information systems department must practice risk management to ensure that it is prepared to exploit opportunities presented by such rapid changes.

Finance

Finance departments have traditionally practiced financial risk management. The volatility of asset and liability values may be addressed with products that include derivative instruments, securitization, and special purpose vehicles. Financial returns on assets are not guaranteed. Therefore, the finance department must manage variations from expected returns by using portfolio theory techniques such as diversification. It must also manage cash flows, because cash policies, credit policies, short-term investments, and dividend policy are critical elements of financial success. Planning for variation from the expected outcomes in each financial component is an essential part of a financial plan.

Audit

The audit department monitors, evaluates, and reports each department's output. It often uses qualitative and quantitative surveys to develop statistical control charts that illustrate how much the expected values in departmental budgets varied from actual mean values. The evaluation also includes a description of unusual observations, outliers, and any trends in the data. The audit department must present its reports to appropriate stakeholders in a clear fashion. Inherent in these tasks is the risk that the department will miss important observations, misinterpret data, and/or convey misunder-standings in its reports. Thus, the audit department should work diligently to control these risks and develop contingencies that alleviate potential misunderstandings.

Risk Management (RM)

In an organization that applies ERM, the RM department functions as a trainer and a facilitator. As a facilitator, the RM department helps other departments plan for risks. As a trainer, the RM department trains others to identify, measure, and organize their risks into a portfolio. The RM department helps other departments identify, measure, and evaluate possible solutions to problems posed by their risks. In addition, the RM department facilitates the RM functions of other departments.

Need for Global and Integrated RM

To achieve optimum performance, each unit or department of an organization should act in concert and in coordination with other departments within the organization and with partners outside it. Global RM refers to an organization is identifying and addressing risks across geographic barriers, such as those that exist between domestic and foreign operations within an organization or between an organization and a foreign partner. Integrated RM refers to the efforts of an organization to identify and address risks within a department or between departments.

Breaking Silos

Organizational departmentalization can increase efficiency and output, but its benefits may be limited if managers adopt a silo approach in which they focus solely on their own department. In an organization that applies ERM, all managers understand how all of the organization's departments relate to its portfolio of activities.

Financial portfolio theory indicates that managing a group of assets as a single entity yields less volatile returns than if the assets are managed separately. A hallmark of ERM is the incorporation of the portfolio theory concept into risk management. Specifically, if volatile resources are managed as a portfolio (rather than in silos), then the organization will be able to achieve its goals with less volatility.

For example, human resource managers should be familiar with the activities in the sales and marketing, production, and procurement departments. The departments other than HR have fluctuating personnel needs depending on such events as sales promotions, seasonal demand for the organization's prod-ucts, or the purchase of equipment that requires several additional employees to operate. By being familiar with the activities in other departments, the human resource managers can be more efficient and effective.

Integrating RM in Processes and Departments

All resources are subject to variation from their expected values over a time period; that is, all resources entail risk. For example, an organization may have a single-source supplier of a key material. Managing the partnership with this supplier may be critical to the organization's success. Applying an ERM approach in this scenario includes ensuring that the partner understands the organization's human resource constraints and that the organization understands the partner's human resource limitations. As another example, an organization's finance department must regularly monitor all other departments to ensure their financial budgets and assets are sufficient. An organization in which each department understands the risks (variations from expected outcomes) that exist in other departments improves its ability to succeed.

RISK CENTERS AND RISK OWNERS

Risk management within a small organization can be a relatively simple process; however, in large organizations that adopt an enterprise-wide risk management (ERM) approach, a risk management professional should use certain tools and methods to effectively identify and manage risk.

In an ERM framework, risk management professionals are charged with assessing risk across the organization using a holistic perspective. Risk managers should be aware that the term "risk" has several meanings and should not always be viewed as a negative. When an organization is divided into **risk centers** with **risk owners**, a risk manager should view risk through the multiple dimensions that encompass **exposure spaces**. These dimensions include resources, causes (including sources, perils, and hazards), and impacts.

Risk management professionals recognize that the number and diversity of the risks and opportunities an organization faces typically increase with the size and complexity of the organization. Additionally, risks and opportunities can differ according to the regions in which the organization operates and among its subsidiaries, operations, product lines, and business units. When an organization is divided into smaller component parts, with responsibility for particular risks or groups of risk assigned to specific individuals within each of those component parts, it can most effectively manage a large number of diverse risks.

An organization can create risk centers, each with a risk owner, by performing these steps:

1. Subdivide the larger organization into smaller, more manageable components called risk centers that each have risk owners.
2. Identify and assess the specific risks that each risk center faces.
3. Consolidate the individual risk assessments at the corporate level to assess and monitor the risks that the entire organization faces.

Risk center
A discrete unit within an organization, having a leader and specific objectives, and disposing of specific resources, at which level a particular risk (or group of risks) is most appropriately and effectively managed.

Risk owner
An individual accountable for the identification, assessment, treatment, and monitoring of risks in a specific environment.

Exposure spaces
The resources, events, and impact at each risk owner's level.

Subdivide the Organization Into Components

The first step in creating an organization divided into risk centers with risk owners is to examine its overall operations. Depending on the organization and how it is structured—for example, by geographic regions, subsidiaries, profit centers, product lines, or business units—it can be subdivided into its component parts or risk centers. Each risk center has a director, manager, or supervisor, and specific assigned objectives that it must meet in support of the organization's overall goals.

Subdividing the organization into its component parts has several advantages. It reduces the scope of risk analysis, making the process more user-friendly, particularly for those not experienced in risk management. It also allows for the involvement of operational managers, who have valuable knowledge and a different perspective from which to contribute to the risk analysis process. Additionally, it helps focus the analysis on the organization's strategic goals and operational objectives and the threats and opportunities that can directly affect those goals and objectives. And finally, it ensures that risks are managed at the most appropriate and efficient level within the organization.

For example, if an employee with specialized skills is essential to the achievement of a business unit's objectives, then the risk of losing that key employee is best managed within that business unit. Conversely, the risks associated with the administration of an organization's employee pension plan would be best managed at the corporate level, rather than the business unit level.

Once an organization's risk centers are identified, the risk management professional should recognize a risk owner, as appropriate, for each group of risks identified as being within the risk center's scope of authority and responsibility. Risk owners are responsible for ensuring that tasks including controlling, modifying, and monitoring of specific risks are completed. Risk owners are not necessarily responsible for performing actual risk management activities, but they must have the authority necessary to ensure that others carry out all the required tasks.

Risk Identification

Once the organization is subdivided into its component subsystems or risk centers, it must next identify and assess the risks that each risk center faces by listing the resources used by each risk center, the threats to which each of those resources may be exposed, and the opportunities that each may represent.

An organization may use a variety of tools to identify its resources and the risks and opportunities associated with them. Traditionally, these tools fall into one of these general categories:

- Risk assessment questionnaires
- Historical data and scenario analysis (when no historical data are available)

- Financial statements and underlying accounting records
- Other records and documents, such as advertising, packaging, user manuals, or human resources documents
- Flowcharts and organizational charts
- Personal inspections and interviews
- Expertise within and beyond the organization

Organizations use the information obtained with these tools to perform three useful methods of risk identification (though other methods may also be used): the simplified balance sheet method, the risk centers method, and interviews with risk owners. The identification and analysis of risks and opportunities at the organizational level helps direct and focus subsequent analysis at the risk center levels.

Simplified Balance Sheet Method

A balance sheet lists an organization's assets, liabilities, and resulting net worth as of a particular date. Because executives tend to base their assessment of an organization's financial condition on its cash position, the balance sheet can direct executive-level attention towards the importance of risk management at risk center levels.

The simplified balance sheet method of risk identification examines the balance sheet through four main categories: short-term assets, long-term assets, short-term liabilities, and long-term liabilities. For example, the balance sheet's list of assets can be used to identify property values (property is considered a long-term asset if it is intended to be held over one year) that are exposed to risk.

However, a flaw in the simplified balance sheet method is that it does not capture exposures that cannot be traced through the accounting system, such as those derived from the environment (for example, the availability of running water to power a hydro-electric plant). Additionally, the method focuses on the downside of a decrease in assets or an increase in liabilities by approaching risk from insurable loss perspective. This does, however, allow the organization's executives to visualize major threats to the organization's assets and the potential effects of those threats on net income.

Risk Centers Method

Risk managers can also identify an organization's threats and opportunities by closely examining an organization's risk centers and the resources the centers rely on—human, technical, information, partner, and financial.

Risk centers can be divided and subdivided down to elementary subsystems or micro-organization levels. The elementary subsystem is a "living" entity whose manager fulfills the organization's mission and goals with the assistance of available resources from among the five resource classes. Risks are identified, analyzed, and mitigated at the micro-subsystem level, the system level, and the organizational level. For example, an organization can be subdivided into business units, and the business units subdivided into departments.

The boundaries of risk centers are identified, and their resources are managed by risk center managers in coordination with other risk managers across the organization.

All the tools that can be used to identify and analyze risk at the organizational level (questionnaires, loss histories, financial and other documents, flowcharts and organizational charts, inspections, and internal or external experts) can be used at the risk center level. In particular, questionnaires are effective. The most effective approach, however, is an interview with risk owners (sometimes called field risk managers).

Interviews With Risk Owners

Risk owners are responsible for ensuring that their risk center's portion of the organization's ERM program is carried out. For example, a risk owner could be a department manager, a work team leader, or a factory floor supervisor. The risk owner has an understanding of how his or her unit or sub-unit operates and works with the risk management professional to uncover risks that were otherwise unidentified.

The risk management professional must maintain effective communication with a risk center's risk owners. When installing and supporting an ERM program, establishing a dialogue with field managers becomes a core mission of the risk manager. Thus, in conjunction with an on-site inspection, the risk manager should interview risk owners. For example, by virtue of the interview process, a risk manager could determine whether a chemical manufacturing plant has an emergency contact/communications plan in place. Or, the risk manager could identify an opportunity to the organization, such as the capability of modifying a production facility's processes in a way that conserves the organization's resources.

Interviewing risk owners enables risk managers to identify critical resource-related risks by probing the "how," "who," "where from," and "where to" elements of the organization's work processes, as well as the status and effectiveness of the organization's stakeholder communications plan. The interview process should elicit answers to strategic questions related not only to a loss of technical resources (such as a key raw materials supplier that suspends its operations) but also to a loss of human resources (such as a viral epidemic that infects large numbers of employees).

Conducting Risk Center Manager's Interview

GOALS

1. What are the goals of your department, service, business unit, or profit center?

RESOURCES

2. How are you organized?

3. Who is your staff, what are your buildings/workspace, equipment, and material?

4. Where are your products, raw materials, and information located?

5. Where do your products and information go?

6. What are your communication channels?

STRATEGIC QUESTIONS

7. Assuming your building (office, factory, etc.) burns tonight, destroying the building with all its contents—with no injury to your personnel—how would you be operational tomorrow, assuming your personnel are ready to work?

8. Assuming, on the other hand, that you have suffered no loss, but your personnel are not present (because of a labor strike or pandemic, for example), how would you be operational?

9. How is your organization's management structure and decision-making process designed to identify and respond to emerging opportunities?

HOW ARE YOU EQUIPPED TO MITIGATE THESE RISKS? (THREATS AND OPPORTUNITIES)

10. Immediately (pre-event mitigation)

    *   Prevention/protection
    *   Contractual risk sharing

11. When the event strikes (post-event mitigation)

    *   "Business continuity planning"
    *   "Crisis management and redeployment planning"

Consolidate Risk Assessments at the Corporate Level

The last step in creating an organization with risk centers and risk owners is to consolidate the risk assessments at the corporate level. While minor risks are managed at the risk center level, the more significant risks to the organization are consolidated at the corporate level. A risk may be deemed beyond the capacity of management by a risk center and therefore be consolidated at the corporate level if the risk owner cannot comprehend all the consequences of the risk and/or does not have the resources needed to appropriately address the risk's upside or downside. For example, a decision to change an everyday workflow process could be made at the risk center level. However, a decision to change a manufacturer's supplier of key component parts would most likely be made at the corporate level.

A tool that is commonly used to consolidate an organization's risk at the corporate level is a risk center risk register or a risk log (or simply a risk center log or risk register). A risk register links specific activities, processes, projects, or plans to a list of the identified risks and the results of the risk analysis and evaluation. Information on the status of the risk is also included. The risk register is a "living" document that is continually updated, revised, and used to track and monitor risk as an essential part of risk management activities. There is no "standard" risk register, as every organization uses different criteria for analysis.

METHODS AND LIMITATIONS OF UNCERTAINTY MODELING

To manage enterprise risk, practitioners need analytical tools to measure degrees of uncertainty and to predict how various factors and strategies can influence an organization's results.

Organizations quantify and assess the dimensions of the uncertainty of risk by creating empirical models. These models help management simulate, test, and predict outcomes and then learn from the data produced. Management uses the data produced from modeling to assist in many aspects of planning and strategic decision making.

A wide variety of risk modeling methods can be applied to any given risk. Each of these may be viewed as falling on a continuum based on the extent to which it relies on historical data, expert input, or a hybrid of the two.[1] A model's limitations partially determine when and how the model is used.

Most organizations use a basic version of an uncertainty model that links various inputs with key performance indicators (KPIs). No single organization is likely to use all of these modeling methods, and the methods are often customized to meet an organization's specific needs. Uncertainty modeling can be very organization-specific and highly detailed. The purpose of this discussion is to provide a basic description of each model and examples of how such models might be applied.

Methods Based on Historical Data

Certain techniques for modeling uncertainty are rooted in an analysis of past patterns and historical data. The leading risk modeling methods based on historical data feature these approaches:

- Empirical distribution
- Fit parameters of theoretical probability density functions
- Stochastic differential equations
- Extreme value theory
- Regression

Empirical Distribution

An empirical distribution estimates the theoretical probability distribution function of a set of many observed random variables (X_1, X_2, X_3, and so forth) from a sample (X_n). When constructing an empirical distribution, the most direct and simple approach is to assume that historical data fully define the probability distribution. In such cases, the analyst can then use the data to develop discrete probability distributions.

An empirical distribution often appears as a series of steps (as shown in the "Empirical Distribution" exhibit) resembling the cumulative distribution from which the sample is drawn. Organizations can use this model to estimate portfolio returns if the portfolio has generated sufficient valid and reliable historical data over time to develop credible inputs.

A drawback of the empirical distribution technique is that it assumes that the data gathered are complete and that the time span over which the data were collected includes the full spectrum of potential outcomes.

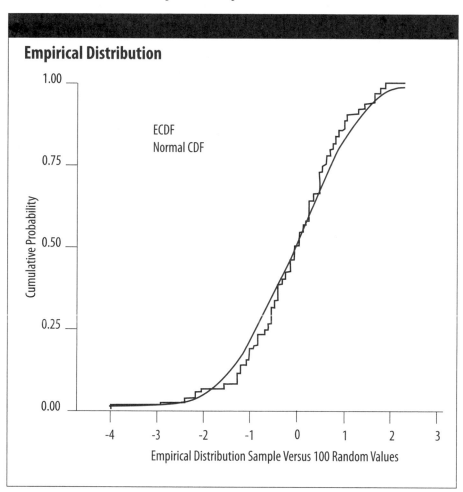

Empirical Distribution

ECDF
Normal CDF

Cumulative Probability

Empirical Distribution Sample Versus 100 Random Values

Fit Parameters of Theoretical Probability Density Functions

An option when using empirical distributions is to assume that a risk can be expressed as a theoretical probability density function. In such instances, an analyst uses data to estimate or "fit" the parameters of the theoretical distribution. For instance, in the case of property-casualty losses, claim frequency is often assumed to follow either a negative binomial or Poisson distribution. By contrast, claim severity is often assumed to follow a lognormal or a Pareto (or conditional claim or tail) distribution.

Stochastic Differential Equations

Stochastic differential equations (SDEs) express the difference (or change) between a variable's value (for example, interest rate) at time t and one time period later, $t + 1$. This difference is shown as a combination of a predictable change and an uncertain or a random (stochastic) change during the new time span. The random change is reflected as a random variable with a specified probability distribution (for example, a typical normal distribution). Starting with an initial value, an SDE is used to roughly determine a scenario in which a value changes over a forecast period, such as ten years. Hundreds or even thousands of scenarios can be produced this way. Scenarios can be summarized as probability distributions for each point in time over the forecast timeline and are then used by management to make predictions and strategic determinations.

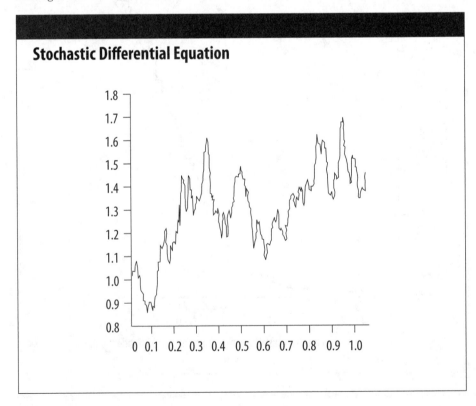

Extreme Value Theory

Extreme value theory (EVT) is a subset of the discipline of statistics. Rather than creating a model based on the assumption that values or returns are normally distributed, risk managers can use EVT to include extreme or rare deviations from the median of the probability distributions. As an analytical and a statistical tool, it aims to analyze probability distributions generated by processes. In the realm of risk, these processes may be natural forces such as erratic weather, one-hundred-year floods, or earthquakes. More recently, EVT stress tests have included finance and banking organizations' significant or "extreme" exposure to poorly performing collateralized debt obligations (securities such as bonds that are typically backed by pooled mortgages). For this reason, extreme value theory has utility in assessing risk from infrequently occurring but high-severity types of losses.

Regression

Regression is an analysis of the causal relationships among variables (for example, the effect of an increase in labor costs on product pricing). A regression mathematical model of product pricing, then, might include additional variables such as labor costs, as well as raw material and distribution costs.

A regression equation is a function of one or more predictors or "explanatory" variables (such as labor and raw material costs) used to develop the value of the "response" variable (for example, product pricing). Regression models provide risk managers and senior executives with information about the dynamic interactions of specific risk components so that the appropriate threats and opportunities are properly managed. For example, a production manager who anticipates a reduction in the cost of raw materials could use a regression model to determine an optimal product price.

Regression Model Example

For a commercial airline, fuel costs are a major variable operating expense. In addition to the price of fuel, the quantity of fuel needed varies with weather conditions, routes, airport conditions, and so forth. A regression model can be used to anticipate fuel needs.

Some of the major factors to consider in determining the amount of fuel needed during a given time period include the expected number of miles flown, the number of passengers per plane, and the average weight of passengers and cargo. This is a multivariate, linear regression model; in other words, one in which the dependent variable, F, is a linear combination of the parameters M, P, and W:

$$F = a + (b \times M) + (c \times P) + (d \times W),$$

where

F = Fuel amount needed (the response variable)

M = Miles expected to fly

P = Number of passengers per plane

W = Average weight of passengers and cargo

In this example, a is a constant and b, c, and d are coefficients that are multiplied by the predictor variables to calculate their effect on the response variable. Using regression analysis, the coefficients can be determined using historical data. Once the coefficients are determined and the regression model is shown as statistically significant, the model can then be used to estimate the amount of fuel needed in the future by inserting values for M, P, and W into the regression equation. In this case, another variable could be introduced in each period—for example, the price of kerosene (a component of jet fuel)—to establish a fuel cost forecast. Such a forecast can be used for budgeting or to establish a confidence interval to choose what risk can be transferred (for example, to an insurer, a reinsurer, or the financial markets).

Methods Based Primarily on Expert Input

Other methods of mathematical uncertainty modeling rely heavily on the input of those with expert knowledge. Risk modeling methods based on expert input feature these approaches:

- Preference among bets
- Judgments of relative likelihood
- Decomposition to aid probability assessment
- The Delphi technique

Preference Among Bets

The preference among bets modeling technique endeavors to convert expert opinion into probabilities. For example, one might ask an expert whether a particular event—such as regulatory approval of a new "blockbuster" medicine—is more likely than an event whose probability is known, such as the roll of six on a die. The model presumes that the sum wagered on the likelihood is modest to minimize any aversion to risk while simultaneously maximizing its subjective expected value.

Judgments of Relative Likelihood

Judgments of relative likelihood is a technique that experts use to assess the likelihood of event outcomes. For example, a model could be constructed to determine which of a basket of investments is most likely to provide the greatest return. One type of relative likelihood model is based on expert input about whether an event is (a) more likely, (b) less likely, or (c) equally likely relative to known probabilities.

However, sometimes expert input is influenced by an unintentional bias that causes the expert to characterize less familiar events as less likely and more familiar events as more likely. For example, an expert weather forecaster in the midwestern United States might be inclined to assess tornados as more likely (given an assumed familiarity with them in that region) and hurricanes as less likely.

Decomposition to Aid Probability Assessment

Those who are analyzing risk are often helped in the process by breaking down or "decomposing" an event or a portfolio (and its associated complex systems) into smaller, contingent causal events or components. This decomposition aids in probability assessment.

One way to depict interdependencies among known events (inputs), uncertainties and scenarios (intermediate variables), and an event of interest (outputs) is through an influence diagram. An influence diagram is a concise, mathematical, and graphical depiction of a decision-making process. Within an influence diagram are risk nodes. These represent contingent circumstances that might generate an outcome or event. Connecting arrows—also known as arcs of influence—illustrate relationships among nodes. By graphically depicting risks and their connections to certain outcomes, users can better envision the impacts of uncertainties.

Another way to use decomposition to aid in probability assessment is to employ a Bayesian approach. A Bayesian approach uses Bayes' Theorem, a formal equation for revising probabilities given the emergence of new information, data, or evidence. Another way to view Bayes' Theorem is to think in terms of revising a belief in hypothesis *A* in light of new evidence *B*, as expressed in this equation:

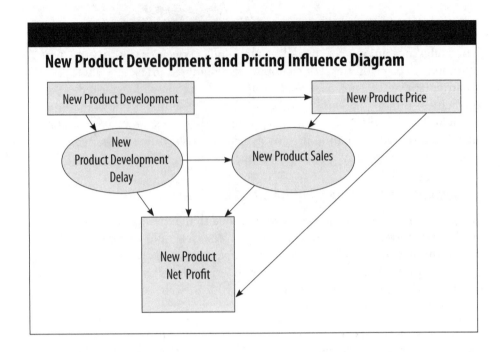

$$P(A/B) = \frac{P(B/A)\,P(A)}{P(B)}$$

P = Probability

A = A outcome

B = B outcome

Thus, as new information is introduced to the conditional probability, the probability is revised.

The Delphi Technique

The Delphi technique, named after the Oracle of Delphi in ancient Greece, is a method that attempts to move a group of experts toward a consensus opinion. Each individual expert in the group is asked a question. In isolation (face-to-face meetings are not required), the answers that each expert developed individually are reported to the entire group. The question is then posed again separately to the experts, who are instructed to consider revising their responses based on the results that were reported to the group. This question and response cycle continues for a predetermined number of rounds or until a consensus is achieved.

Hybrid Methods Based on Combining Historical Data and Expert Input

Other approaches to modeling environmental uncertainty blend elements of quantitative, historical analysis with elements of expert input. Hybrid risk modeling methods feature these approaches:

- System dynamics simulation
- Fuzzy logic
- Bayesian networks and influence diagrams

System Dynamics Simulation

System dynamics simulation is a modeling technique that overtly mimics or attempts to replicate dynamic cause/effect relationships of business, environmental, economic, and social systems. As a risk analysis tool, it embraces the use of available historical data, as well as the input of experienced managers, to produce simulation models. In turn, such models can help in developing probability distributions and running simulations such as a Monte Carlo simulation.

A Monte Carlo simulation (named after Europe's gaming capital) is a computer-generated series of "what-if" scenarios, including stress tests, that focus on specific risk factors in a project—such as revenues, gross margins, and costs—and define them as selected. A large number of values for each of these key factors are then randomly drawn from the random numbers relating to the probability distribution. For example, a Monte Carlo simulation can capture the effects of interest rate movements or changes in a portfolio.

The logic of Monte Carlo simulation methods is based on the law of large numbers—as the number of random drawings increases, the approximation moves closer and closer to the expected value of the phenomenon under observation.

Fuzzy Logic

Fuzzy logic is often used in modeling complex systems and interactions. Fuzzy logic takes complex, descriptive-language expert inputs and converts them to mathematical equivalents. For example, a window thermometer may show that the outdoor air temperature is 36 degrees Fahrenheit. Nevertheless, snow is falling. At the upper bounds of the atmosphere, the temperature is sufficiently low to generate snow. Is it "freezing" outside or not? What does it mean to say that it is "rather freezing" outside? Fuzzy logic developed in order to address such situations that are not entirely absolute or in which interpretations are subjective.

A fuzzy logic model is simple and flexible, and it can manage complex problems with nonlinear, incomplete data. Many experts consider fuzzy logic to be a useful tool in managing operational risks, because assessments of probabilities are often predicated on authoritative opinion and the risk environment contains many variables.

Bayesian Networks and Influence Diagrams

A Bayesian network is an important hybrid method that combines expert input and beliefs in a rational way. A Bayesian network has two fundamental elements:

- A causal graph that represents the structure of a domain
- A set of "local beliefs"—in other words, a set of local probability distributions, combined through the causal graph

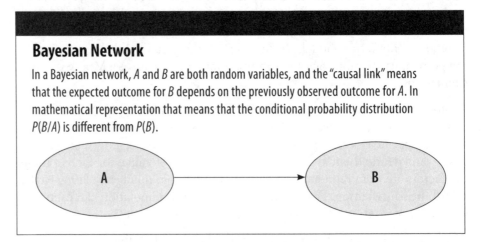

Bayesian Network

In a Bayesian network, *A* and *B* are both random variables, and the "causal link" means that the expected outcome for *B* depends on the previously observed outcome for *A*. In mathematical representation that means that the conditional probability distribution *P(B/A)* is different from *P(B)*.

Each Bayesian network includes these elements:

- Nodes and variables—Each node represents a variable (a variable with at least two possible outcomes). Although Bayesian networks could use continuous variables, discrete nodes are more typical. Furthermore, for a risk analysis step, the use of discrete variable (outcome values are grouped in classes) is generally appropriate and even recommended for improved communication on the models with the various nonspecialist stakeholders.

- Probabilities—All of the variables in the models are random; therefore, it is necessary to define a probability distribution for each of them. If not enough data are readily available in the organization's business intelligence (BI) systems, it is possible to use national statistics of the domain and/or expert opinions through interviews.

- Dependencies—A link in a Bayesian network reflects a causal relationship. A→B means that A is one of the causes of B. As A and B are random variables, if the causal relationship A→B is true, then the probability distribution for B will differ for the various outcomes for A.

Inference

Once the Bayesian graph has been created and the probability distributions have been defined, specific software computes the overall distribution of the variables that are represented on the graph.

This process is based on inference, and in a Bayesian network, this means simply using Bayes' Theorem. After a new piece of evidence has been introduced, the distributions are computed again with that additional information. The probability distribution of the variables in the graph is "inferred" from this new piece of evidence.

Learning

A Bayesian network contains knowledge in two different forms:

- The causal structure of the graph
- The probability tables

This knowledge is usually obtained from two sources: empirical data and/or expert opinions. In practice, the experts will help build the causal structure of the model, and the probability distributions will be inferred from statistical data.

In theory, it is possible to derive causal structure directly from data; specific learning algorithms are used to this effect. In practice, however, it is not common because databases are often either unavailable or incomplete.

Building an entire model completely from data would require a global database in which all fields were simultaneously present. But even with the progress of business intelligence (BI) systems, no database will generally provide all the elements needed to be representative of all the variables in the graph.

Although building a learning structure from data may prove useful, such as for use in data mining, the Bayesian network learning process will prove more useful in most risk management applications because of the elements not normally found in BI systems.

Extension to Influence Diagrams

Bayesian networks represent a specific body of knowledge in a probabilistic graph. They are always applied to support or enlighten a decision-making process, especially in the risk management field.

Influence diagrams are extended Bayesian networks that can provide additional information for all types of decision making under uncertainty. Influence diagrams contain special nodes called decision nodes that are used to represent alternatives from among which the decision maker has to choose.

In general, influence diagrams are simply extended Bayesian networks including three types of nodes:

- Chance nodes (or random variables) that are represented using ellipses

- Decision nodes that are represented using rectangles
- Utility nodes (benefits or costs) that are represented using diamonds

The structure of an influence diagram is subject to some constraints concerning decision nodes: all decision nodes must be connected by a directed path, utility nodes have no children (they are just valuations), and utility nodes have no state and must be defined for all states of the parent node.

The concept of utility represented in influence diagrams by utility nodes is useful to introduce nonfinancial or qualitative criteria linked with ethical or social issues while retaining the elements of economic efficiency. If a model has to take into account risk to human beings, death and permanent disability may have consequences far beyond the direct cost. When taking into account risks to reputation, the long-term consequences are difficult to evaluate. To summarize, making decisions through the "utility optimization process" is a way to take into account the expectations and fears of all internal and external stakeholders, far beyond solely the short-term interests of stockholders.

The Continuum of Risk Modeling Methods and Model Limitations

Risk professionals can choose from among a broad spectrum of risk modeling methods when determining which one to apply to a given risk. Viewing the methods according to their placement along a continuum can assist the decision maker in choosing the best method to use. Some of the techniques on the continuum may be based on expert input, while others may rely on the input of historical data.

For example, methods that depend more on expert input include influence diagrams, the Delphi technique, and the preference among bets method. Over many decades, decision makers and risk analysts have successfully used these techniques to model operational risks in order to make management decisions in business niches as varied as energy, healthcare, and manufacturing.

Techniques located in the middle of the continuum rely on a blend of historical data as well as expert judgment to augment informational gaps. When using these techniques, the decision maker applies expert judgment to develop a model's methodology or approach, reflecting the interactions among important variables. Furthermore, expert judgment helps quantify cause/effect relationships based on experience and limited or peripheral data. For the task of quantifying strategic and operational risks, techniques such as system dynamics simulation and fuzzy logic are particularly well suited.

No one modeling method represents a magical solution for enabling organizations to quantitatively represent risk in an absolute sense. All of the methods have limitations related to quality of data inputs, type of data analyzed, and intended use of the model. To assemble a complete risk perspective, it may be necessary for an organization to use custom-designed models or multiple models.

Modeling Continuum

Historical Data Analysis	Hybrid Models	Expert Input
Empirical Distribution	System Dynamics Simulation	Preference Among Bets
Stochastic Differential Equations		Judgments of Relative Likelihood
	Fuzzy Logic	
Fit Parameters of Theoretical Probability Density Functions		Decomposition to Aid Probability Assessment
Extreme Value Theory	Bayesian Networks and Influence Diagrams	Delphi Technique
Regression		

Adapted from: Casualty Actuarial Society, Enterprise Risk Management Committee, "Overview of Enterprise Risk Management," 2003.

Semantic ambiguity and expert biases also present a challenge to modeling. How one frames a question can influence the answers it yields. For example, an imprecise question might be, "What is the likelihood of regulatory approval of a new drug?" A more effective query would be, "What is the likelihood of regulatory approval of a new cholesterol-lowering medication within the next twelve months?"

RISK QUANTIFICATION CASE STUDY— WOODWORKING WORKSHOP

Risk managers who perform ERM must be able to predict the probability of future losses using uncertainty modeling. This modeling enables the risk manager to provide more accurate recommendations to executive management regarding the selection of risk control measures. (Note that the values used in this case study are of a lower magnitude so as to clearly illustrate steps. Strategic decision making typically involves decision making using values of much higher magnitude.)

Applying uncertainty modeling to proposed enterprise-wise risk management (ERM) options requires several steps. The first is to determine which options the organization's stakeholders want to consider. Those options are then analyzed and compared using a variety of approaches:

- The expected average accident rate of each of the options is calculated, often by use of a tool such as a Bayesian network.

- The accident rates of the different options are compared.

- The economic and financial issues related to each option are considered. This process includes determining the cost of accidents, determining the costs of implementing each option, and developing an influence diagram.

- The expected value of **utility** is calculated so that it can be used to determine which option or options will optimize the organization's cost of risk.

Utility
An economic concept regarding the value established by an organization's decision-makers of nonfinancial or qualitative elements, such as ethics, social issues, and stakeholders' perception, that should be taken into account in the determination of which solution the organization should pursue.

Case Facts

Woodworking Workshop (W3) is a large woodworking company that operates three plants. The plants are equipped with a variety of equipment to manufacture wood products. Some of the equipment is complex and hazardous.

After an employee was seriously injured in an accident involving one of W3's machines, the workshop closed for the rest of the day and, as a result, lost revenues. Previously, other employees had been involved in minor accidents when using the same piece of equipment. The International Woodworkers Union (union) contends that the accident and others like it are the result of the organization's assigning inexperienced workers to the equipment and providing little or no training in how to operate it safely.

The risk manager must analyze the situation and offer options to reduce the risk associated with operation of this equipment. Following a brainstorming session with the stakeholders, three proposed options were drafted:

- Union representatives suggest that employees with little experience should be assigned to equipment that is the simplest to use.

- The Human Resources (HR) department recommends a training plan for employees in how to use the equipment safely.

- The plant managers support replacing the equipment. This proposal could be implemented at a reasonable cost because the current equipment is leased for five years; at the end of that period, W3 returns the equipment to the lessor and receives no salvage value.

W3's risk manager must apply uncertainty modeling to each of these three alternative options in order to develop a recommendation for W3's management team.

Case Analysis Tools and Information

W3 staff consists of 200 workers who are assigned to 200 pieces of equipment on the basis of planning constraints and needs. Although worker assignments may vary from day to day, at any given time, each worker has only one piece of equipment to operate, and each piece of equipment is operated by only one worker.

To help develop a reasonable assessment of the risks and to evaluate the impact of the three options considered, the risk manager will compile this information:

- Accident data by type of equipment and worker experience (source: W3's workers compensation insurer)
- Seniority of the workers (source: HR Department)
- Number and types of equipment (source: plant managers)
- Cost of training program (source: a training company)
- Cost of new equipment program (source: a potential supplier)

The data obtained from W3's workers compensation insurer reveal this information:

- The accident rate is higher for new employees.
- The accident rate is higher for complex pieces of equipment.

However, the risk manager realizes that the data provided by W3's workers compensation insurer do not provide sufficient detail. He decides to gather additional data from other sources and then compile a table of probabilities relating to when accidents do occur, as shown in the "Accident Conditional Probability Table" exhibit.

Accident Conditional Probability Table

Machine Type	Worker's Experience		
	New/Inexperienced	Some Experience	Experienced
Simple	10%	5%	1%
Medium	15%	10%	6%
Complex	20%	16%	11%

The values in the chart represent the percentage of accidents in relation to the workers' levels of experience and the complexity of machines. For example, an inexperienced worker assigned to a simple machine would have a 10 percent chance of having an accident over time.

Because the risk manager must base his recommendations on these estimated probabilities, he must make sure that all stakeholders involved in the decision-making process (for example, union representatives, the HR Department, and plant managers) agree with the probability values.

However, what if a consensus by all stakeholders on the values proves impossible to reach? A consensus is not necessary if all experts, who are representatives of stakeholders, are considered equivalent, because each expert's opinion may be given the same probability. Differences are resolved by relying on each stakeholder to provide input through its experts.

To apply the Accident Conditional Probability Table and determine the overall or average probability that an accident will occur to a worker, the risk manager needs two additional pieces of information:

- The percentage of staff in each of the three categories based on experience
- The percentage of equipment in each of the three levels based on complexity

The HR Department has provided this information relating to staff percentages:

- Seventy percent of the workers have less than two years' seniority and have never been properly trained; therefore, they are considered "new/inexperienced."
- Twenty percent are classified as having "some experience."
- Ten percent have been trained and have "substantial experience" (more than ten years).

The plant managers have provided this information relating to equipment complexity:

- Twenty percent of the machines are simple to operate.
- Sixty percent of the machines are of medium complexity to operate.
- Twenty percent of the machines are complex to operate.

The risk manager prepares the Workers Compensation Accident Probability Table and the accompanying calculations.

Workers' Compensation Accident Probability Table

	Machine Type	Workers' Experience			Total
		70% New/Inexperienced	20% Some Experience	10% Experienced	
20%	Simple	10% $70\% \times 20\% \times 10\% = 1.4\%$	5% $20\% \times 20\% \times 5\% = 0.2\%$	1% $10\% \times 20\% \times 1\% = 0.02\%$	1.62%
60%	Medium	15% $70\% \times 60\% \times 15\% = 6.3\%$	10% $20\% \times 60\% \times 10\% = 1.2\%$	6% $10\% \times 60\% \times 6\% = 0.36\%$	7.86%
20%	Complex	20% $70\% \times 20\% \times 20\% = 2.8\%$	16% $20\% \times 20\% \times 16\% = 0.64\%$	11% $10\% \times 20\% \times 11\% = 0.22\%$	3.66%
Total		10.5%	2.04%	0.6%	13.14%

For an example of the calculations, the first cell in the table indicates that new/inexperienced workers (70 percent of the worker population) who were assigned to simple machines (20 percent of the machines) accounted for 10 percent of all the accidents that occurred in a given period, usually a year. The probability that an accident will occur under the conditions represented in that cell in the current year is calculated by multiplying the three percentages: 70 percent, 20 percent, and 10 percent—a probability of 1.4 percent. The probability for each cell in the table is calculated similarly.

The probabilities calculated for each cell are added vertically and horizontally. The sums of probabilities along the bottom row are themselves added, as are the sums of the probabilities in the right column. The two totals should be identical. If they are not, a mistake in calculation has occurred.

In the table presented here, both totals equal 13.14 percent. This number is the average or overall probability that an accident will occur to a worker in a given period before any new risk control measures are implemented.

In using the data from the accident probability table, W3's risk manager must rely on a fundamental hypothesis: that worker experience and machine type are independent.

Case Analysis Steps

The proposed loss control options produced from the brainstorming session are analyzed and compared using several steps:

1. Each option is evaluated.
2. Based on that evaluation, the options are compared to one another.
3. Economic and financial issues are considered for each option.
4. The expected value of utility is calculated for each option.

Evaluation of Loss Control Options

As noted in the case facts, three proposed options are being considered: the union's, HR's, and the plant managers'. Before selecting which option or combination of options to recommend to senior management, the risk manager evaluates each one.

Union's Option

The union's option is to assign new workers to simple machines and experienced workers to complex machines to the greatest extent possible.

However, the respective numbers in the accident probability tables' cells showing experienced workers and machine complexity indicate that the union's proposal would not provide the optimal option for each individual worker. The "Workers' Assignment to Machines: Union's Option" exhibit shows the number of complex machines (40) far exceeds the number of experienced workers (20), and the number of inexperienced workers (140) far exceeds the number of simple machines (40). The proposal would have these results:

- The 20 experienced workers would be assigned to 20 of the complex machines.
- Forty of the 140 new or inexperienced workers would be assigned to the 40 simple machines.
- The others would be assigned according to availability.

Workers' Assignment to Machines: Union's Option

| Machine Type | Workers' Experience | | |
	New/Inexperienced (140)	Some Experience (40)	Experienced (20)
Simple (40)	40		
Medium (120)	100	20	
Complex (40)		20	20

The risk manager could use a probability table to calculate probabilities for the union's option. However, he chooses another method—the Bayesian network—that is particularly suited to quantifying risks of proposed options.

A Bayesian network is a graph representing the dependencies between random variables and decision variables. It allows the computation of conditional probabilities such as those computed manually (without software) in the previous table.

For example, the initial dependency that reflects the influence of a worker's experience and a machine's complexity on the probability of an accident can be represented simply, as depicted in the "Bayesian Network of Worker Experience and Machine Type" exhibit.

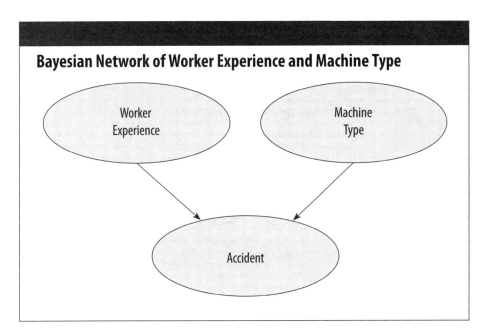

Bayesian Network of Worker Experience and Machine Type

A Bayesian network can be quantified with the introduction of appropriate probabilities, as represented in the "Bayesian Network Quantified With Probabilities" exhibit.

Bayesian Network Quantified With Probabilities

Experience Level of Workers	
New	70.0
Some	20.0
Experienced	10.0

Complexity of Machines	
Simple	20.0
Medium	60.0
Complex	20.0

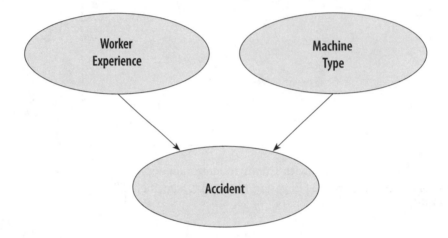

Workers' Experience Level and Machine Complexity Combined

Machine	Simple			Medium			Complex		
Experience	New	Some	Experienced	New	Some	Experienced	New	Some	Experienced
Yes	10.0	5.0	1.0	15.0	10.0	6.0	20.0	16.0	11.0
No	90.0	95.0	99.0	85.0	90.0	94.0	80.0	84.0	89.0

The "yes" row is the percentage of accidents that are expected to occur with each combination of level of experience and machine complexity. The "no" row is the percentage chance that the accidents that do occur will not be of that particular experience and complexity combination. The total of the "yes" and "no" percentages for any experience and complexity combination will be 100 percent.

Next, the risk manager prepares a Bayesian network to help him calculate the probabilities and compute the average or overall probability of an accident to a worker, as represented in the "Bayesian Network: To Compute Overall Probability of an Accident" exhibit.

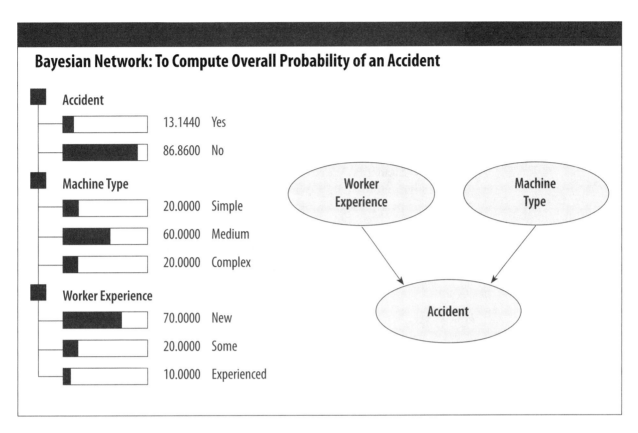

Bayesian Network: To Compute Overall Probability of an Accident

This image of a Bayesian network (including graph and overall accident probability), frequently produced by uncertainty modeling software, repeats in bar chart form what was previously expressed numerically. The 13.14 is the average or overall percentage that an accident will occur to a worker. Conversely, the 86.86 is the percentage that, on average, an accident will not occur to a worker. Adding 13.14 percent and 86.86 percent results in 100 percent, which means all possible outcomes have been accounted for. A worker either has or does not have an accident.

The risk manager can use an "influence" Bayesian diagram to calculate more complex conditional probabilities (for example, the expected probabilities that an accident will occur if the union's option is selected). It is called an influence diagram because it determines how a particular option, such as worker/machine assignments, influences another factor, such as accident rate. An influence diagram, as associated with the "Bayesian Network to Compute Overall Probability of Accident" exhibit, facilitates a quick assessment of a proposed option.

To accomplish this task, the risk manager must introduce two new elements in the network:

- A link between the worker's experience and the complexity of the machine
- A decision node that represents the choice between the current situation, in which workers are randomly assigned to the machines, and an "optimized" option, in which experience is taken into account

The influence diagram in the "Influence Diagram of Accident Probability With New Elements Added" exhibit indicates that the union's option would cause a slight increase in the overall rate of accidents, from 13.14 percent to 13.20 percent, thus worsening the current situation.

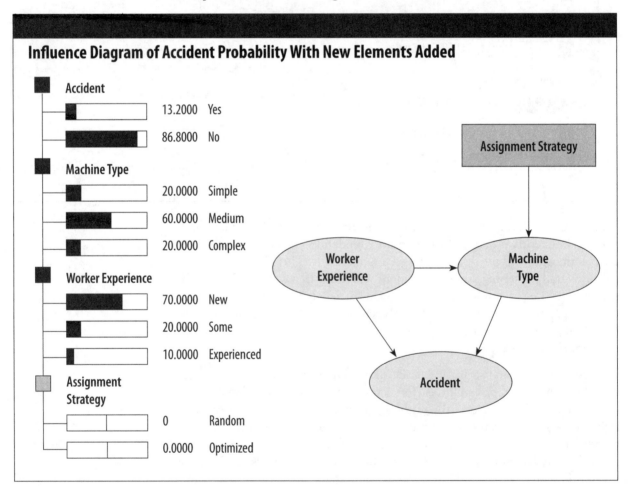

Influence Diagram of Accident Probability With New Elements Added

Accident

	13.2000	Yes
	86.8000	No

Machine Type

	20.0000	Simple
	60.0000	Medium
	20.0000	Complex

Worker Experience

	70.0000	New
	20.0000	Some
	10.0000	Experienced

Assignment Strategy

	0	Random
	0.0000	Optimized

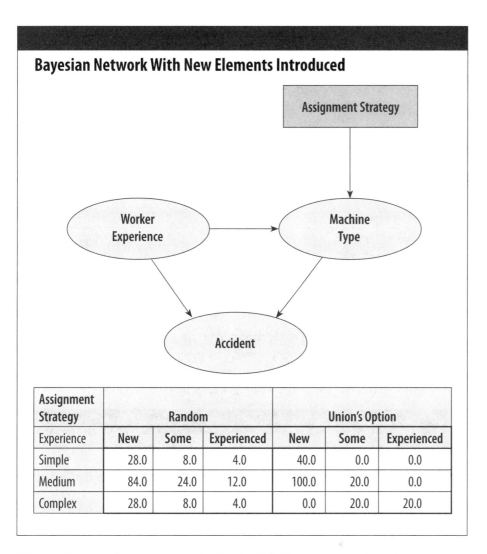

Bayesian Network With New Elements Introduced

Assignment Strategy	Random			Union's Option		
Experience	New	Some	Experienced	New	Some	Experienced
Simple	28.0	8.0	4.0	40.0	0.0	0.0
Medium	84.0	24.0	12.0	100.0	20.0	0.0
Complex	28.0	8.0	4.0	0.0	20.0	20.0

The result stems from a change in the "weight" or number of employees exposed to a given probability of an accident on a machine. For example, the probability of an accident for a worker with some experience is 16 percent, and the new plan assigns 12 more workers with some experience to complex machines, increasing to at least 6 percent the probability of accident for each of those workers. Although new or inexperienced workers are moved to simpler machines, the decrease of probability of an accident for each of those workers is only 5 percent.

HR's Option

To evaluate the option proposed by the HR Department, the risk manager needs additional information and analysis. The training program proposed by HR would apply to the 140 new workers and the 40 workers with some experience as shown in the "Probability Table for Training Program" exhibit. No training would be provided to the 20 experienced workers. The program would have these results:

- Of the 140 new workers, 20 would be expected to reach the "experienced" competency level, 100 would reach the "some experience" level, and 20 would remain in the "inexperienced" category.
- All of the 40 workers with "some experience" would be expected to reach the "experienced" level of competency.

Probability Table for Training Program

Workers' Experience	Training Program	
	Before	After
Inexperienced	140 (70%)	20 (10%)
Some Experience	40 (20%)	100 (50%)
Experienced	20 (10%)	80 (40%)

The risk manager prepares a probability table that takes training into account, as indicated by different percentages of workers classified as new/inexperienced, having some experience, or experienced. This table indicates that HR's option would lower the average accident rate to 9 percent.

Calculations for Determining Accident Probability Using HR's Option—The Training Program

	Machine Type	Workers' Experience			Total
		10% New/Inexperienced	50% Some Experience	40% Experienced	
20%	Simple	10% 10% × 20% × 10% = 0.2%	5% 50% × 20% × 5% = 0.5%	1% 40% × 20% × 1% = 0.08%	0.78%
60%	Medium	15% 10% × 60% × 15% = 0.9%	10% 50% × 60% × 10% = 3%	6% 40% × 60% × 6% = 1.44%	5.34%
20%	Complex	20% 10% × 20% × 20% = 0.4%	16% 50% × 20% × 16% = 1.6%	11% 40% × 20% × 11% = 0.88%	2.88%
Total		1.5%	4.1%	2.4%	9%

Plant Managers' Option

The plant managers' proposal to replace the equipment could be accomplished at a reasonable cost because the machines are leased and can be replaced as their leases come up for renewal. The managers believe some of the complex machines could be replaced with simpler machines, with the result that, within a year, 80 percent of the machines in use could be considered "simple." The risk manager prepares a probability chart (not shown) similar to the HR option probability chart for the plant managers' proposal. This chart indicates that this option, if exercised, would reduce the accident rate to 9.1 percent.

Probability Table of Effect of Leasing New Machines

Machine Type	Lease New Machines	
	No	Yes
Simple	20%	80%
Medium	60%	20%
Complex	20%	0%

A new influence diagram, depicted in the "Influence Diagram for Machine Choice Option" exhibit, is compiled to evaluate the situation.

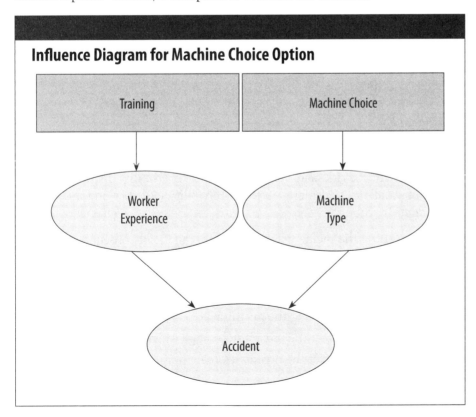

Influence Diagram for Machine Choice Option

Comparison of Accident Rates of Proposed Options

Having used the Bayesian network to calculate the accident probabilities under the three proposals offered, the risk manager can compare the results of the three proposals to one another as well as to the 13.14 percent accident probability the organization faces if no risk control measures or options are implemented:

- The union's option of reassigning workers would raise the average accident rate to 13.20 percent.
- HR's option of training the workers, while retaining the current machines, would lower the average accident rate to 9 percent.
- The plant managers' option of purchasing machines, without a training program, would lower the average accident rate to 9.1 percent.

However, the risk manager also determines that joint implementation of HR's option and the plant managers' option would lower the average accident rate to 4.9 percent.

Consideration of Economic and Financial Issues

To develop recommendations for senior management regarding the best option, the risk manager must take into account the economic and financial implications of various alternatives. For each option, these implications must be considered and compared:

- Costs of accidents
- Costs of HR's and plant managers' proposed option
- Financial implications of each option, as indicated in an influence diagram
- Value of utility

Costs of Accidents

Using W3's internal database, with additional information from external sources relating to the most severe accident possible (but not thus far experienced) for W3, the risk manager establishes the probability distribution for the cost of accidents, as depicted in the "Probability Distribution for the Cost of Accidents" exhibit:

- Ten percent of the incidents would have no financial consequences.
- Fifty-five percent could cost the organization approximately $10,000, including costs for healthcare, damages to the machines, and loss of revenues.
- Twenty percent would cost the organization approximately $20,000.
- Ten percent would cost the organization approximately $50,000.
- Five percent would cost the organization approximately $100,000.

These dollar amounts would vary based on the training and the types of machines selected.

Probability Distribution for the Cost of Accidents

Total Cost ($)	Probability
0	10%
10,000	55%
20,000	20%
50,000	10%
100,000	5%

Costs of HR's and Plant Managers' Proposed Options

The costs generated by each proposed option or loss control measure must also be accounted for. The union's proposed option of reassigning workers based on level of experience and complexity of machine would incur direct operating costs. However, the other two proposed options would require an initial outlay of capital.

HR estimates that the cost to train each worker would be $1,000.

The plant managers' proposal to replace the machines has become more complex. W3's chief financial officer (CFO) proposes that the replacement machines be leased for a five-year period, at the end of which they would be returned to the lessor with no salvage value. The CFO further proposes that the machines be leased at a reduced cost from a different supplier, Cheap & Complex. However, the new proposed supplier's machines would not help achieve loss control goals because they are less ergonomically sound than the existing ones.

After conducting a study and taking into account the specific needs of W3, the risk manager charts the division of the machines between the two suppliers, as depicted in the "Percentage of Machines for Each Proposed Supplier" exhibit.

Percentage of Machines for Each Proposed Supplier

| | Supplier | |
Machine Type	Simple & Expensive	Cheap & Complex
Simple	80%	0%
Medium	20%	20%
Complex	0%	80%

The chart indicates that the selection of a supplier will make a significant difference in terms of risk control. However, the CFO points out that the average cost per machine would drop to $1,500 for the new supplier, Cheap & Complex, half as much per machine for the original supplier, Simple & Expensive.

Influence Diagram With Financial Implications of Proposed Options

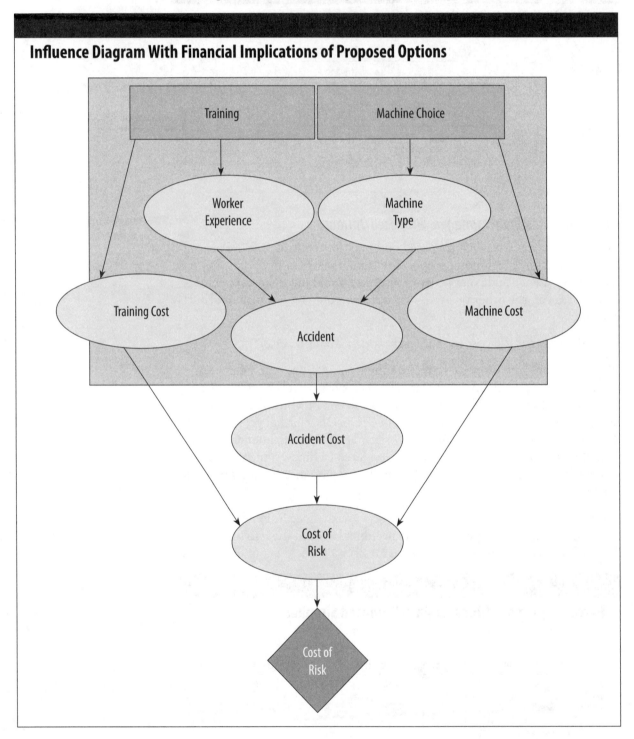

Development of an Influence Diagram

The risk manager prepares an influence diagram that takes into account the financial implications of the different proposed options.

The upper portion of the "Influence Diagram with Financial Implications of Options" exhibit includes the same elements (indicated by the square box) as the influence diagram used to determine that both the HR training option and the plant manager machines-replacement option, with Simple & Expensive as the supplier, led to practically identical options in terms of loss control efficiency. However, the new diagram contains additional elements to assess the financial consequences of both options.

The "Link Between Accident and Accident Cost" exhibit illustrates the probability distribution of accident costs. The decisions relating to type of machine and whether to implement training do not influence costs directly; rather, they indicate the probability of occurrence of an accident. The link can be assessed only by referencing the probability distribution between when an accident occurs and when an accident does not occur (see the corresponding table). In the case of "no accident," the cost remains zero because there is no possibility for the cost to be other than zero; therefore, a probability distribution with 100 percent is attached to the value "0."

Link Between Accident and Accident Cost

	Accident	
Cost	Yes	No
0	10%	100%
$10,000	55%	0%
$20,000	20%	0%
$50,000	10%	0%
$100,000	5%	0%

The "Link Between HR Training and Training Cost" exhibit shows that the HR training option, if implemented, would cost $1,000 for each worker trained. If the training is not implemented, then the cost would be zero.

Link Between HR Training and Training Cost

	Training	
Cost	Yes	No
0	0%	100%
$1,000	100%	0%

The "Link Between Supplier Choice and Machine Cost" exhibit shows the cost per machine depends on the supplier chosen.

Link Between Supplier Choice and Machine Cost

| | Proposed Supplier | |
Cost	Simple & Expensive	Complex & Cheap
$1,500	0%	100%
$3,000	100%	0%

The oval node labeled "Cost of Risk" in the previous "Influence Diagram With Financial Implications of Proposed Options" exhibit is the sum of three components: accident cost, training cost, and machine cost. This node indicates the total cost depending on which course of action—that is, which option regarding machine type and training is chosen.

In many cases, selecting an option is difficult because of the complexity of comparing two probability distributions with many variables. In this case, the decision is relatively simple because the probability distribution relating to leasing the machines from Simple & Expensive appears to be more favorable for all variables.

Calculation of Expected Value of Utility

Influence diagrams allow the introduction of an additional concept: utility. The "Comparison of Two Sequences of Decisions" exhibit compares the proposed options using utility and cost of risk calculations. This replaces the more limited concept of cost of risk and allows the organization to take into account other dimensions pertaining to ethics, social issues, and stakeholders' perceptions, among others. A "medium utility" or average utility is attached to a utility node depending on the situation considered. Here, the "situations" are linked to the cost of risk per worker in specific intervals (also referred to as categories):

- Between $0 and $1,000
- Between $1,001 and $5,000
- Between $5,001 and $50,000
- Between $50,001 and $100,000
- Between $100,001 and $150,000

These intervals, set by the CFO, are appropriate for W3 but may not be appropriate for another organization because each organization's situation is unique. A probability attached to a given situation results from prior decisions made and the propagation of the probabilities along the influence diagram. If a specific utility is attached to each of these situations, then the expected value of the utility may be computed for each of these situations.

Comparison of Two Sequences of Decisions

The table compares two sequences of decisions by combining the costs and probabilities to compute an expected value of the cost of each sequence. The solution on the left appears more advantageous because accidents would be less costly.

No Training and Leasing New Equipment
From Simple & Expensive

Accident Cost

Probability Percent	× Cost	= Expected Value
91.81	$0	$0.00
5.005	$10,000	$500.50
1.82	$20,000	$364.00
0.91	$50,000	$455.00
0.455	$100,000	$455.00
Totals		
100		$1,774.50

No Training and Leasing New Equipment
From Cheap & Complex

Accident Cost

Probability Percent	× Cost	= Expected Value
84.466	$0	$0
9.493	$10,000	$949.30
3.452	$20,000	$690.40
1.726	$50,000	$863.00
.863	$100,000	$863.00
Totals		
100		$3,365.70

Cost of Risk

Probability Percent	× Midpoint of Cost of Risk per Worker in Intervals	= Expected Value
0	$0 to $1,000 = $500	$0.00
91.81	$1,001 to $5,000 = $3,000	$2,754.30
6.825	$5,001 to $50,000 = $27,500	$1,876.88
.91	$50,001 to $100,000 = $75,000	$682.50
.455	$100,001 to $150,000 = $125,000	$568.75
Totals		
100		$5,882.43

Cost of Risk

Probability Percent	× Midpoint of Cost of Risk per Worker in Intervals	= Expected Value
0	$0 to $1,000 = $500	$0
84.466	$1,001 to $5,000 = $3,000	$2,533.98
12.945	$5,001 to $50,000 = $27,500	$3,559.88
1.726	$50,001 to $100,000 = $75,000	$1,294.50
.863	$100,001 to $150,000 = $125,000	$1,078.75
Totals		
100		$8,467.11

In this case, as long as the situation nodes are based on the cost of risk nodes, the utility can be computed at the expected value of the cost in each situation (or interval):

- Between $0 and $1,000—Utility = 500
- Between $1,001 and $5,000—Utility = 3,000
- Between $5,001 and $50,000—Utility = 27,500
- Between $50,001 and $100,000—Utility = 75,000
- Between $100,001 and $150,000—Utility = 125,000

A risk manager will seek the solution that optimizes the blend of utility and the cost of risk. However, utility and cost of risk are typically two independent variables, and there often is no correlation between them. A solution may have a very high utility as well as a very high cost of risk. For example, W3 could implement a repetitive and time-intensive training program that dramatically reduces injury to workers, creating a high utility value. However, such training could threaten to drive the company into bankruptcy because of its high cost and the reduction in productivity resulting from worker down time, creating, in turn, a high cost of risk.

The use of the concept of utility is particularly helpful when the decision to be made combines qualitative and quantitative criteria (for example ethical or social issues with economic efficiency). As mentioned, if the model must take into account not only financial consequences but also human risks or risks to reputation, then those nonfinancial elements can be considered in the decision-making process through the assessment of their utility by the decision makers (as well as stakeholder groups). If an organization wishes to limit bodily injury at all cost, then the utility attached to avoiding any type of bodily injury could be very high.

The benefit of using utility nodes is that it leads to a simple calculation of the expected value of a utility in a given situation linked to a sequence of decisions, and the decision criteria are based on the sum of the expected utilities for each situation, weighted by their respective probability. Some of the disadvantages of utility theory are that it assumes that all outcomes can be monetized and that all outcomes can be combined into a new outcome.

In this case, the risk manager presents the final analysis in the "Link Between Supplier Choice and Machine Cost While Accounting for Utility" table.

Link Between Supplier Choice and Machine Cost While Accounting for Utility

Situation	Utility	Supplier Simple & Expensive	Cheap & Complex
0–$1,000	500	0%	0%
$1,001–$5,000	3,000	91.8100%	84.4660%
$5,001–$50,000	27,500	6.8250%	12.9450%
$50,001–$100,000	75,000	0.9100%	1.7260%
$100,001–$150,000	125,000	0.4550%	0.8630%
Expected Utility		5,882.425	8,467.105

In this example, the original distribution of the value of the utility is at the midpoint of each of the expected value of cost intervals. However, given similar data, another organization might assign different utility weights to other factors, leading to a different distribution. In the "Additional Example of Link Between Supplier Choice and Machine Cost While Accounting for Utility" table, the cost of risk is the same as in the previous example, but the organization has distributed utility differently. As a result, the difference between the two utility values is much narrower, both in their total value and in the percentage difference between the two. This distribution demonstrates the critical need for organizations to carefully consider weights and values of utility.

Additional Example of Link Between Supplier Choice and Machine Cost While Accounting for Utility

Situation	Utility	Supplier Simple & Expensive	Cheap & Complex
0–$1,000	1000	0%	0%
$1,001–$5,000	3,000	91.81%	84.47%
$5,001–$50,000	7,000	6.83%	12.95%
$50,001–$100,000	20,000	0.91%	1.73%
$100,001–$150,000	10,000	0.46%	0.86%
Expected Utility		3459.55	3871.63

After completing the analysis of all three options, the risk manager is in a position to determine the course of action to recommend to senior management. In doing so, he acknowledges that HR's option and the plant managers' option, using the Simple & Expensive supplier, are not mutually exclusive. Based on earlier calculations, the risk manager determines that joint implementation of the two options would lower the average accident rate to 4.9 percent. Furthermore, both options are expected to be cost effective when taking into consideration the economic and financial implications of the two alternatives, such as the costs of accidents, the costs of HR's and the plant managers' proposed options, and the value of utility.

Correct Answers

The correct answers for this case study fall into these categories:

- Comparing the accident rates of three proposed options
- Comparing two sequences of decisions
- Determining the value of utility

1. Comparing the accident rates of three proposed options

   - The union's option of reassigning workers actually raised the average accident rate from 13.14 percent to 13.20 percent.

   - HR's option of training the workers, while retaining the current machines, would lower the average accident rate to 9 percent.

   - Plant managers' option of purchasing machines, without a training program, would lower the average accident rate to 9.1 percent.

   - The joint implementation of both HR's and the plant managers' options would lower the average accident rate to 4.9 percent.

2. Comparing two sequences of decisions

Leasing the equipment from Simple & Expensive (and implementing no training) would result in a lower accident frequency.

SUMMARY

In an organization that adopts an ERM approach, every department manager applies risk management techniques to each resource in his or her department's portfolio while also considering the risks and resources associated with other departments.

An organization can more effectively manage risk by creating risk centers, each with a risk owner, by performing these steps:

1. Subdivide the organization into smaller, more manageable components that each have risk owners.
2. Identify and assess the specific risks that each risk center faces.
3. Consolidate the individual risk assessments to assess and monitor the risks that the entire organization faces.

Risk practitioners have at their disposal a variety of methods for modeling uncertainty in their operating environments. Some of these techniques are heavily quantitative in terms of historical data inputs required. Others rely less on quantitative data and more on the judgments of experts. Other approaches are hybrids of historical and expert inputs. No single right or wrong technique exists. Rather than viewing these modeling techniques as mutually exclusive approaches, risk practitioners may regard them as a continuum of techniques to help assess uncertainty in the business environment.

The case study applying uncertainty modeling requires several steps. The first step is to establish in a brainstorming session the options the W3 stakeholders want to pursue. The second step requires extensive calculations using a Bayesian network to calculate the expected average accident rates of each of the three proposed options. The options are compared based on their respective accident rates. In the third step, the economic and financial issues of each option are considered, involving extensive calculations to determine the cost of accidents and the costs of implementing each option. Finally, the expected value of utility is calculated to determine which option minimizes the organization's cost of risk.

CHAPTER NOTE

1. Content portions were adapted from Casualty Actuarial Society, Enterprise Risk Management Committee, "Overview of Enterprise Risk Management," May 2003, www.casact.org/dare/index.cfm?abstrID=5297&fuseaction=view (accessed February 19, 2009).

Risk Treatment:
Reacting to Disruptions

Educational Objectives

After learning the content of this chapter and completing the corresponding course guide assignment, you should be able to:

▶ Determine the criteria used to define the levels of disruption.

▶ Explain the importance of managing risk to reputation.

▶ Describe activities that will prepare executives and managers to face disruptions.

▶ Explain how risk mitigation is achieved through business continuity planning.

▶ Describe the scope and stages of strategic risk redeployment planning.

Outline

Levels of Disruption

Managing Risk to Reputation

Activities to Prepare Executives and Managers to Face Disruptions

Mitigating Risk Through Business Continuity Planning

Scope of Strategic Redeployment Planning

Summary

Risk Treatment: Reacting to Disruptions

Chapters 7 and 8 discuss risk treatment in the context of risk reduction, beginning with an examination of the levels of disruption that may affect an organization's operations when events substantially deviate from expected levels and the management of reputation risk. Chapters 9 and 10 discuss risk treatment in the context of risk financing in enterprise-wide risk management (ERM).

After it has completed the risk assessment process, an organization must treat the risks it has identified, analyzed, and evaluated by selecting and implementing appropriate risk management techniques. This is the third step in the ERM process as depicted in the ERM process diagram on page 1.5:

1. Establish the internal and external contexts

2. Risk assessment—identification, analysis, and evaluation

3. Risk treatment—selecting and implementing appropriate risk management techniques

4. Monitor results and revise

5. Communicate and consult with all internal and external stakeholders

LEVELS OF DISRUPTION

An organization's expectations are not always met, and the volatility of the result (positive or negative) is the direct measure of "risk" in financial terms. However, some situations go beyond volatility, and organizations may experience disruptions. These range in impact from those that are routine, such as those that stem from fluctuations in normal business cycles, to those that are catastrophic, such as Hurricane Katrina. Organizations must effectively determine how to manage disruptions at all levels. Proper planning for disruptions helps ensure an organization's resiliency and, in many instances, its basic survival.

Organizations experience some type of disruption daily. Some disruptions, such as a customer complaint, are very basic and easily remedied. Other disruptions are more severe and interrupt normal business activities. The severity of some disruptions can reach a magnitude that causes an organization's normal operations to cease.

System Levels

Four system-level definitions are used to classify and resolve disruptions. The definitions are based on the disruption's degree of severity:[1]

- Simple state system—The disruption can be resolved through routine decisions.

- Complicated state system—The disruption is more difficult to resolve than a simple system's but is not unusual.

- Complex state system—The disruption is unusual, potentially critical to the organization.

- Chaotic state system—The disruption is a dramatic, unforeseen event that threatens the organization's survival.

The simple state system assumes that an organization's normal day-to-day activities have a range of volatility within normal parameters—information is known, and patterns are predictable and routine. Disruptions within this classification have easily recognizable causes and effects. Decisions about solving problems that arise within the simple system can be easily made based on experience and knowledge. Best practices are employed because the simple system usually contains highly regulated processes or procedures, and related communications are swift and easily understood.

The complicated state system encompasses disruptions that involve both known and unknown pieces of information. Best practices may not resolve the problem created by the disruption, because the solution may not be immediately apparent to the decision makers. Leaders will need to investigate their options to determine the best choice. Some expertise is needed. A need also exists for creativity and thinking "outside the box" in response to disruptions at this level. Therefore, communication should flow in both directions between decision makers and line workers, allowing for a flow of ideas and sharing of information.

The solutions to complex state system disruptions often are not easily discernible. There is a component of unpredictability, where imposed answers will not work. Here, time works to the leaders' advantage, because patterns will emerge that will provide additional details, enabling decision makers to implement the best choices. Communication must be free flowing, and management must be flexible to allow for experimentation in finding the best solutions.

In chaotic state system disruptions, cause and effect shift continuously. No patterns are discernible to the decision makers. Organizational leaders must quickly gain control and salvage as much as possible. Communication is from the top down only—commands are imposed with little dialogue. Disruptions at this level should be addressed through crisis management measures.

System Levels

System	Disruption	Information	Need	Communication
Simple	Normal	Readily available	Resolve known issue	Swift/one-way
Complicated	Volatile	Known and unknown	Investigate options; analyze	Two-way
Complex	Rupture	Known, unknown, shifting patterns, disruption of some activities	Use expertise, creativity, and flexibility for finding solutions	Free-flowing
Chaotic	Crisis	Known, unknown, shifting patterns, disruption of normal operations, survival threatened	Control a crisis	Top-down—direct

When an organization suffers any level of disruption, whether relatively minor such as a market downturn or a major catastrophic event, its leaders must act to restore the organization to its normal operational system—a new simple system. It accomplishes this by addressing the disruption in the context of each level that exists between the original level of the disruption and the simple level, in descending order ("working down").

A chaotic state system threatening the survival of the organization must be worked down to the complicated state system level as solutions are found. Then, working down to complex state system status allows the organization to regroup and, eventually, return to a new simple state system. This new simple state system and its accompanying organizational processes and strategy differ substantially from those that existed before the disruption.

Working down from the chaotic state system level to the simple state system level is a multiple-step process. The system must be worked all the way down, without skipping any level. Each interim system level allows the organization to re-examine its strategies and business opportunities.

Hurricane Katrina is a good example of a chaotic state system. Following the storm, life was catastrophically disrupted in New Orleans. Conditions included substantial loss of life, lack of essential services, and many businesses failing overnight. Over time, leaders brought the situation under control. From a chaotic state system, the city eventually returned to a new normal routine. New Orleans today, however, is totally different from what it was before Katrina. Its "new normal" (the simple state system) is very different from the pre-Katrina norm. The city, as with any organization returning from a chaotic state system, will never be the same. In a case like this, the organization must redefine its strategies for moving forward under new conditions.

Risk Management Responses

An organization can use risk management approaches to respond to the various levels of disruption and establish a new simple state system.

A solution to a disruption at the simple level is based on known information and on following the organization's best practices. Normal processes and procedures can repair any disruption at this level rather quickly.

Resolving a disruption at the complicated level requires an organization's leaders to analyze readily known information and newly developed information. This analysis will assist in developing several options. Ultimately, a single optimal solution will emerge from these options. Good management, operational practices, and daily oversight of situations are risk management approaches that will help the organization establish a new simple state system.

The complex system-level disruption may not be resolved as readily. At this system level, known information, new information, and shifting patterns create conflicting and confusing situations. The organization may need to reduce or suspend some activities. Leaders will rely on expert analysis, using both internal talent and external consultants. Creative approaches may be applied, and the organization will need to be flexible as it searches for the best solution. In some cases, trial and error may be employed to arrive at an appropriate solution. A business continuity plan may also be used as a guide for dealing with this level of disruption.

The chaotic system-level event threatens the organization's survival. Most activities will cease if the disruption is severe. The risk management approaches an organization should adopt in such situations include business continuity plans and strategic redeployment, which provide an orderly process that allows the organization to return to lower levels.

One common disruption an organization may face results from risk to reputation.

Risk Management Responses

System	Level of Disruption (by Increasing Severity)	Information	Need	Communication	Risk Management Response
Simple	Normal	Readily available	Resolve known issue	Swift/one way	Best practices will suffice
Complicated	Volatile	Known and unknown	Investigate options and analyze	Two way	Good practices and daily management
Complex	Rupture	Known, unknown, shifting patterns	Use expertise, creativity, and flexibility for finding solutions	Free flowing	Continuity planning
Chaotic	Crisis	Known, unknown, shifting patterns, survival is threatened	Control the crisis	Direct/top down	Strategic redeployment planning

MANAGING RISK TO REPUTATION

Managing an organization's tangible assets is one aspect of risk management; however, in an enterprise-wide approach to risk, intangible assets, which can often represent more than one-half to three-quarters of a company's total value, should also be managed.

Reputation is an intangible asset that relates to an organization's goals and values, results from the behaviors and opinions of its stakeholders (stakeholder perception), and grows over time. It is the comparison between stakeholders' experience and their expectations and is the pillar of the organization's legitimacy or social license to operate. An organization maintains a good reputation when it meets or exceeds stakeholder expectations.[2]

For an organization to maintain a good reputation, it must earn and retain the trust and confidence of its key stakeholders. Additionally, a good reputation can differentiate one organization from another, thus creating a competitive advantage, or, in the case of a government agency, greater effectiveness and efficiency of its service to the community. While a good reputation is built over time, good can turn to bad in an instant of poor decision making. An organization that fails to meet stakeholder expectations risks earning a bad reputation. A bad reputation can cost an organization its stakeholders and even risk the viability of the enterprise as a going concern.

Any event or scenario that could benefit or damage an organization's reputation presents risk to reputation. Successfully managing risk to reputation requires an understanding of these important concepts:

Reputation

An intangible asset that is a key determinant of future business prospects, resulting from a collection of perceptions and opinions, past and present, about an organization that resides in the consciousness of its stakeholders.

- Reputation as a key asset
- Reputation and a systemic approach
- Lessons learned from experience
- Implementing risk management for risk to reputation

Reputation as a Key Asset

Reputation is a key asset to an organization because of its intrinsic, intangible value (its goodwill reserve or reputational equity) and because of its potential to generate (or erode) future value. The value of some intangible assets, such as trademarks and licenses, is quantifiable. In comparison to quantifiable, tangible assets, reputation as an intangible asset is not quantified on a company's financial statements. Nonetheless, it is a key asset whose value is based on the beliefs of its stakeholders. For example, an organization's reputation might facilitate the recruitment of high-potential employees, who will, in turn, enhance the organization's value over time.

Managing risk to an organization's "reputation asset" involves managing stakeholder expectations and understanding that reputation is subject to both threats and opportunities. Identifying key sources of risks to reputation enables an organization to better protect that asset.

Stakeholders' Perspective

An organization should identify its key stakeholders and prioritize them in terms of relative importance because stakeholders' expectations and perceptions vary by enterprise. For example, a financial services organization might have government regulators as a key stakeholder, whereas a commercial builder might not. Conversely, a commercial builder might have its raw material suppliers (lumber, steel) as key stakeholders, whereas a financial services organization would not. As another example, a department of defense has many contractors and engineers as stakeholders, while a public health organization has many medical providers as stakeholders.

Additionally, the perspectives of each of these organizations' key stakeholders differ. For example, the builder's lumber supplier might have an expectation of a steady flow of product orders. A steady flow of product orders keeps the stakeholder satisfied and might minimize the need for a high level of communication as long as the stakeholder remains the lumber supplier of choice. Alternatively, the financial services company's government regulator stakeholders play a major role in daily business operations and might require frequent interactions to ensure their expectations are being met.

Stakeholders can be classified as internal—for example, an organization's management, executive board, and employees—and external, such as shareholders, customers, suppliers, regulators, governmental entities, and so forth.

A power/interest matrix such as the one depicted in the "Power/Interest Matrix for Prioritizing Shareholders" exhibit can be used to capture the broad range of an organization's stakeholders and prioritize their importance. For example, the exhibit's matrix may be applied to a scenario in which a garment maker has an exclusive contract with a major retailer as its sales arm (high power/high interest in the quality of the garment maker's reputation for quality and value). According to the matrix, the garment maker would want to expend maximum effort to maintain its reputation for quality and value with the major retailer. Conversely, the garment maker's zipper supplier may have no power and little interest in the garment maker's reputation. Thus, the garment maker may expend minimal efforts to maintain its reputation with the zipper manufacturer.

Power/Interest Matrix for Prioritizing Stakeholders

Interest		Low Power	High Power
	High	Keep Informed	Maximum Efforts
	Low	Minimum Efforts	Keep Satisfied
		Low	High

Power

Threat or Opportunity

Risks to an organization, such as legal and regulatory noncompliance, unethical behavior on the part of the board of directors or senior management, or the filing of major lawsuits, can threaten reputation as a key asset. However, when examining risk to reputation, organizations often consider only the downside, or threats that could adversely affect the company. The upside of risk—leveraging opportunities to enhance reputation—should also be considered. For example, shifts in the competitive marketplace or uncertainty surrounding environmental concerns could create opportunities for companies to focus on more profitable areas or to gain a competitive advantage by developing "green" technologies or alternatives.

In fact, leading companies search for ways to exploit risk and seek to maximize the positive consequences of risk and the respective probabilities of successfully achieving gains. Procter & Gamble (P&G), a well-known multinational company, established its five sustainability strategies in 2007 with specific, measurable goals in key areas.[3] As a direct result of this risk exploitation strategy, P&G has received numerous environmental awards that strengthen its brand reputation among its customers. Such recognition also contributes to product innovations that help to improve P&G's financial and reputational results.

Key Sources of Risks to Reputation

Key sources of risks to reputation must be identified in order for an organization to protect—or take advantage of—its reputation. A number of global business surveys have consistently identified key drivers of reputation that then become the sources of risk to reputation.

As illustrated in the "Key Drivers of Reputation and Sources of Risk" exhibit, an organization should consider how each of the key drivers interacts with its stakeholders. For example, if an organization identifies "the community" as one of its stakeholders, that stakeholder group would drive corporate social responsibility as a possible risk to reputation.

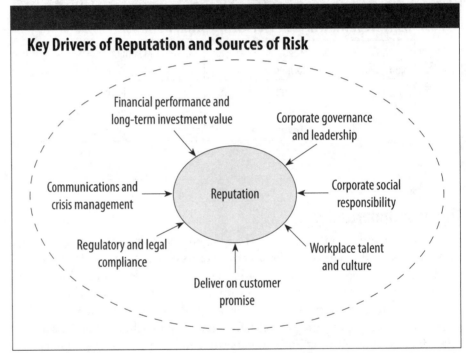

Source: Adapted from Galliard, Hindson, Louisot, and Rayner, "Managing Reputational Risk," an unpublished research article written in 2009.

Reputation and a Systemic Approach

An organization continually interacts with its stakeholders, its environment (internal and external), and its resources. All of these elements should be considered from a systemic, holistic perspective to determine, as they interact with the organization and with each other, what risk they present to reputation.

A systemic approach to risk to reputation can be examined by studying "The Essential Triangle," the mechanism of reputation, and potential negative impact on reputation.

The Essential Triangle

An organization is a dynamic combination of interactions between the organization itself, its message, and its stakeholders' expectations, known as "The Essential Triangle."[4] Reputation can be either enhanced or damaged as a consequence of these interactions.

In a systemic approach, the organization is considered within the context of a complex combination of available resources. Stakeholders have expectations regarding how these resources should be managed. The organization must work to gain the trust of stakeholders and assure them that resources are being integrated and optimized. Many organizations use transparent business practices and good governance to achieve this goal. For instance, a company could have a communication policy that includes periodic messages to shareholders about decision making, partnering, and acquisitions. The message that the organization transmits to its stakeholders is vitally important, especially concerning its business plans, its values, and its goals. The relationship between the communication and stakeholders' expectations can either enhance or damage reputation.

The Mechanism of Reputation

A systemic approach to risk to reputation also involves carefully managing the organization's interactions with the general public, its stakeholders, and its employees. The mechanism of reputation, or how the organization interacts with and communicates its message to its stakeholders on an everyday basis, can be expressed by grouping the key drivers of reputation around three ethical dimensions: goals and missions, rules (laws and regulations), and values (internal forces).

The organization should ask certain questions that apply to the driver/dimension intersects, such as "Are our daily business activities aligned with our corporate goals and mission?" "Are we compliant with (or do we exceed) current rules and regulations?" "Are our stated values or internal forces consistent with our strategic plan?" An organization's senior management is responsible for clearly setting the appropriate tone at the top.

By examining the mechanism of reputation through the key drivers of risk and several ethical dimensions, risks to reputation are revealed when the organization's message does not match expectations. For example, risk to reputation could occur as a result of discrepancies between the organization's employees or between its departments, between the organization's activities and its strategic plan, or between the organization's message and its stakeholders' expectations.

Mechanism of Reputation: Key Drivers and Dimensions

Dimensions

Goals and Missions	Rules (Laws and Regulations)	Values (Internal Forces)
Financial Performance and Long-Term Investment Value • Does the company have a consistent record of financial performance? • Does the company have good investment potential? • Which stakeholders are most linked to financial performance?	*Corporate Governance and Leadership* • Do the board of directors and senior management set an appropriate tone at the top? • Does the business plan include a compelling vision and mission? • Are the proper strategies in place, together with employees who are equipped with the competencies required to deliver on the business plan? *Corporate Social Responsibility* • Is the company viewed by its stakeholders as a good corporate citizen? • Do the company's actions reflect its stakeholders' long-term interests? • Does the company minimize the negative impact and maximize the positive impact of its business activities on the environment and society? *Regulatory and Legal Compliance* • Is the company viewed by its stakeholders and by the general public as law-abiding? • Does the company strive to comply with the spirit of laws and regulations rather than meet minimally acceptable requirements? • Is the company compliant with its internal policies and procedures?	*Delivering on Customer Promise* • Does the company have a consistent record of delivering high-quality, fairly priced products and services? • Is the company a market leader in innovation? • Is confidential customer information kept secure? • How responsive is the company's customer service department? *Workplace Talent and Culture* • Does the company recruit, hire, train, and develop high-quality employees? • How well does the company treat its employees? • Does the organization's corporate culture inspire employees to take pride in their work and in the business, and to give their maximum effort? *Communications and Crisis Management* • Does the company have a robust communications plan designed to manage stakeholder expectations? • Is the company transparent in its business activities, and does it clearly communicate decisions and implications of decisions to stakeholders? • Does the company not only have a crisis management plan but also engage in crisis scenario planning?

Key Drivers

Lessons Learned From Experience

The experiences that a number of organizations have had in recent years with reputation risk have been well documented by the business and news media. For example, as it was revealed that particular banks were burdened with a poor real-estate loan portfolio or had invested in mortgage-backed derivatives, those banks saw large numbers of customers withdraw their deposits. Some banks became insolvent as a result. When news broke that certain automobile manufacturers were in dire financial circumstances, those manufacturers saw their new-car sales virtually cease because potential buyers were not confident that new-car warranties would be honored or that other services would be available if the manufacturer became insolvent.

By considering two well-publicized cases of reputational risk management and the experiences of the companies involved, lessons learned are developed.[5] Three factors are common to both cases cited: the company quickly recognized that it had a risk to reputation, it rapidly made important decisions to manage the risk, and the companies' leadership and culture played key roles in successfully managing the risk. These factors are common not only to the companies discussed but also to the many other enterprises that have successfully managed risk to reputation during a crisis. Nor are risks to reputation confined to the for-profit realm. Following Hurricane Katrina, there were many governmental institutions whose reputation was enhanced by their response to the disaster and others whose reputations were sullied, resulting in leadership and legislated changes. Charitable organizations' reputations have been harmed by revelations of excessive executive compensation and by lack of transparency in the distribution of their benefits and services.

Manage Risk to Reputation: Cases

Johnson & Johnson		
Johnson & Johnson (J&J), founded more than 100 years ago, is a global leader in consumer healthcare, developing and manufacturing medical devices, consumer healthcare products, and pharmaceuticals. The company's credo, defining its core values, was developed in the 1940s by Robert Wood Johnson, chairman, a member of J&J's founding family. The credo challenges J&J to place the needs and well-being of the people it serves first.		
The Event: Tylenol product recall. Seven people died in September 1982 after consuming the painkilling drug.	Recognition	Authorities determined that certain bottles of Tylenol contained cyanide-laced capsules. The information caused a panic across the United States. At the time, Tylenol represented 17 percent of J&J's profits. Copycat cases of product tampering ensued, and hospitals admitted many patients who suspected they had been poisoned.
		Of 270 total cases of suspected product tampering, the Food and Drug Administration estimated only about thirty-six of the cases were a result of verifiable product tampering. J&J was not responsible for the product tampering (the criminals are still at large). Still, the company recognized that it needed to assume responsibility and act quickly to protect the public—turning to its credo.
	Decision Making	Guided by its credo, J&J decided to take an extremely proactive approach to the Tylenol poisonings. It implemented an immediate nationwide Tylenol product recall, ceased Tylenol product advertising, and subsequently revolutionized the product packaging industry and regained consumer confidence by reintroducing Tylenol with tamper-resistant packaging.
	Leadership and Culture	J&J's top management, leading by example and following the company credo, placed consumer safety first, ahead of any concerns about any effect on profit. Although J&J had crisis management plans, the extent of the Tylenol disaster far exceeded any existing plan. Instead, J&J and its CEO turned to the company's organizational culture and business philosophy, believing that if they remained true to their primary responsibility of protecting customers, the business would once again thrive.
The Outcome: J&J continues to be a global leader in its business segments.	J&J recognized the severity of the risk, immediately acted to respond to it, and successfully navigated the crisis because of the strength and values of its leadership and culture. Although its reputation was temporarily damaged as a consequence of the Tylenol poisonings, it used extensive marketing, promotional, and communications campaigns to regain consumer confidence. Additionally, the threat to reputation was turned into an opportunity as J&J innovated tamper-resistant packaging. J&J's holistic approach to crisis management preserved and even enhanced its reputation.	

Manage Risk to Reputation: Cases

Mattel		
Mattel, formed in the United States post-World War II, is today the largest manufacturer of children's toys in the world, with over 25,000 employees worldwide. Mattel has a formalized, highly structured approach to corporate responsibility and in the 1990s established its Global Manufacturing Principles (GMPs), which clearly state the desired product standards to which it aspires.		
The Event: Within the span of three weeks in the summer of 2007, Mattel suffered two major product recalls: one because of lead paint on toys, traced to vendors in China (lead paint has been banned in the U.S. in toys since the 1970s), and a second recall because of powerful magnets that could detach from toys and be deadly if swallowed.	Recognition	Lead paint, poisonous if swallowed, was discovered on more than eighty different Mattel product lines. Mattel immediately launched an investigation into the problem and at the same time initiated a product recall. As a result of the lead paint investigation, Mattel discovered a design flaw in various products using small, powerful magnets that could be extremely harmful if detached from the toys and swallowed. A recall was announced on those products as well.
		Mattel recognized that it needed to act immediately to retain parents' trust and confidence. The lead paint recall was global and affected more than 1.5 million total items. The company was able to trace the source of the lead paint to specific times, locations, and vendors. Because the company was unable to make the same determinations with toys containing the problem magnets, it recognized that it needed to take a stance that would respond to its stakeholders' concerns, and so it recalled all products with the defect dating back to 2002: over 17 million toys.
		Mattel also understood that, despite its GMPs, it had supply chain failure in China. Mattel recognized that it had to quickly remedy its magnet design flaw.
	Decision Making	Mattel took an extremely proactive approach to its multiple risks to reputation and business viability. Mattel has a global crisis management and communication strategy that it immediately implemented. Mattel's CEO assumed immediate, personal control over the crises, making clear to Mattel's management that they would do the "right thing." Mattel decided to be as transparent as possible, providing plentiful information about the recalls to concerned parents by holding press conferences and scheduling television appearances. Additionally, Mattel used the Internet, posting information on high-traffic sites designed to spread the word to key opinion leaders.
	Leadership and Culture	The message Mattel communicated to the public, its stakeholders, and especially parents was that the company assumed responsibility for the crisis, was committed to remedial actions and policies, would continue to communicate the status of changes, and would improve its products through better supply chain and product design controls. Mattel's CEO confronted the crisis directly, and the company did not attempt to hide the problem, blame others, or react slowly. Rather, it immediately dealt with the problem, made corrections to its GMPs, and strengthened its ethical standards.
The Outcome: Despite the cost of the product recalls and a depressed global economy reducing consumer spending, the Mattel brand rebounded from the crisis, and Mattel today retains its strong global position.	While Mattel terminated the contracts with some of its Chinese vendors as a result of the lead paint contamination, it implemented vigorous supply chain management using a GMP unit that grew to 500 employees after the crises. Vendors must now meet or exceed specific product specifications, and outputs are routinely audited to ensure compliance. Design changes were also made to Mattel products as a result of the magnet-related recall; magnets were subsequently encased in plastic to keep them attached to the products. Mattel's leadership reassured parents around the world with full-page newspaper advertisements outlining the critical steps it took to repair the damage done—part of an ongoing media campaign that focuses on GMP standards and corporate accountability.	

Implementing Risk Management for Risk to Reputation

Organizations can implement risk management for risk to reputation by following several risk management principles that must be viewed holistically, implemented actively, and monitored:[6]

1. Identify, evaluate, and prioritize reputational risks—Identify key drivers of risk to reputation, evaluate the tangible consequences of the increase or decrease in reputation as an asset, and prioritize accordingly. For example, poor corporate governance can lead to ethical breaches. Depending on the organization, the subsequent impact of the breach on reputation can cause a decrease in stock price, a wholesale withdrawal of bank deposits, criminal investigations, regulatory investigations, or a financial ratings downgrade.

2. Develop and implement risk responses—The appropriate response to a risk affecting reputation is contingent on the source of the risk (for example, sources could be a recently acquired company, supply chain practices, or revised regulatory requirements), whether the risk is a threat or an opportunity, the exposure relative to the organization's risk appetite (risk assessments regarding whether an exposure is acceptable or unacceptable differ among organizations), whether the risk is treatable, and the cost of treatment. Risk responses should be implemented in ways that address the gap between the message communicated by the organization and stakeholders' expectations.

3. Monitor and report—After risks to reputation have been identified, evaluated, and prioritized and risk responses designed and implemented, risks should be continually monitored by management, who should constantly be on guard for early risk detection so that immediate corrective action can be taken when required. Additionally, any changes in risk should be reported to the appropriate parties, whether internal or external to the organization, so that timely responses can be implemented.

When implementing risk management for risk to reputation, roles and responsibilities must be clearly defined. This begins with the importance of the CEO and board of directors in managing the organization's risk to reputation, but ultimately all of the organization's stakeholders play a role. For instance, the company's audit function can assure the board and senior management that the company's risk management program is effectively implemented.

Barriers to successfully managing risk to reputation are rooted in a lack of clarity, resources, or awareness. For example, some organizations place a low value on reputation as an asset, choosing to focus instead on tangible assets, while others are simply unaware of reputation's true value. However, a reputation carefully protected and built over time can provide the reputational equity required to help organizations navigate the inevitable gaps that will occur between stakeholders' experiences and expectations.

Organizations must also prepare managers at all operational levels to effectively respond to disruptions as they occur.

ACTIVITIES TO PREPARE EXECUTIVES AND MANAGERS TO FACE DISRUPTIONS

Disruptions are as much a state of mind as they are a situation. Therefore, preparing mentally and emotionally for disruptions is as critical as developing a process to deal with disruptions. The twenty-first century has redefined the way organizations behave and respond to disruptions. Political leaders, executives, and managers must understand that globalization and interdependencies between countries, industries, and organizations can cause minor disruptions to quickly develop into full-blown crises. The ability to react to such crises—and communicate the response—is critical to any entity's survival.

Globalization has created interdependencies between organizations that may not be immediately apparent. Therefore, even a small disruption within one organization can develop into a series of major global ruptures. Because an organization is accountable to its stakeholders, its executives must demonstrate expertise and flexibility when communicating about a disruption and outlining the organization's planned response. Enterprise-wide risk management (ERM) promotes the training of managers in crisis management, a skill that allows them to help restore stakeholder and overall confidence in the organization in a disruption's aftermath.

Stakeholder Concerns

When faced with a disruption—whether it is caused by, for example, natural or economic events—an organization must pay careful attention to the information it receives and the information it shares with its internal and external stakeholders, who scrutinize its decision making in times of crisis. Organizational responses to disruptions must address four basic stakeholder concerns:[7]

- Concern for safety and security
- Demands for transparency in executive decision making
- Need for clarity in communications
- Perceived lack of trust

Concern for Safety and Security

Organizational stakeholders, particularly regulators and consumers, have become increasingly concerned with safety and security issues. These issues arise from situations whose ramifications may cause widespread illness or environmental damage to a large geographic area. Examples of such scenarios include the medical use of contaminated blood, an explosion at a chemical storage facility, or food contamination that results in serious concerns regarding the safety of a nation's food supply.

Safety and security concerns also can arise from a loss of production that leads to shortages of critical goods. For example, disruption of production at oil refineries off the coast of Louisiana caused by Hurricane Katrina had the ripple effect of reduced gasoline supplies and sharply increased fuel prices throughout the country.

Another important source of security concerns is the increased size, responsibility, concentration, and interdependencies of businesses and institutions. A critical failure of one organization may affect others, resulting in a cascade of failures. For example, the potential economic failure of a large global insurance company can widen any economic rupture because it insures millions of businesses and households worldwide and its stock is held by several retirement and 401(k) plans. As organizations merge and grow into large international conglomerates, the potential for major or even systemic ruptures with far-reaching consequences also grows.

Demands for Transparency in Executive Decision Making

Stakeholders are increasingly demanding greater transparency in organizational decision making. Decision makers are held responsible not only for their final decisions, but also for the rationale and methodology they use to make those decisions. Government regulations impose additional layers of responsibility on decision makers.

For example, the Sarbanes-Oxley Act promotes accuracy of financial reporting and accountability by executives, who are subject to fines and imprisonment for any financial misreporting. Additionally, special interest groups (such as ethnic minority, environmental, and animal rights advocates) may pressure decision makers in times of crisis, often operating without complete data or a full understanding of the scope of the issues the organization faces. Organizations can counteract such pressure by providing accurate information and supporting documentation when communicating decisions to external stakeholders.

Need for Clarity in Communications

When responding to stakeholders in times of crisis, an organization must clearly communicate its message. The correct meaning and interpretation of information provided to stakeholders is affected by various filters:

- Media reports may describe emotions experienced during a disruption rather than objectively reporting facts.

- Emotional public outcries may spur political responses in the form of new regulatory constraints, preventing the development of a well-conceived plan to address the disruption and avoid a recurrence.

- Growing mistrust of executives, especially regarding their compensation packages, in light of reported organizational or industry mismanagement can lead to misinterpretation of information communicated to stakeholders.

Perceived Lack of Trust

When an organization responds poorly to a crisis, its stakeholders can lose trust and confidence in it and its industry. Reports of corporate mismanagement can further erode an organization's ability to effectively communicate with internal and external stakeholders. For example, when new drug trials are conducted by a university but are sponsored by the pharmaceutical industry without proper disclosure of the source, it is difficult to determine the accuracy of the study results. Upon learning of the funding source, stakeholders will call into question the value of the trial results and of the new medication.

The public also may lose confidence in political leaders when they are unable to protect citizens from systems ruptures. For example, the poor response of FEMA in the aftermath of Hurricane Katrina led to an increased demand for leaders to exhibit positive ethical, moral, and financial behaviors.

A New Approach to Crisis Management

Traditional crisis management is based on a framework of scenarios that are identified by the probability of their occurrence and on their potential severity.[8] The emphasis of traditional crisis management is on writing procedures, storing those procedures in manuals, and then periodically updating them to maintain a current state of readiness. These manuals are intended to provide directions for managers in the unlikely event that the exact scenarios addressed in the manual actually occur. In reality, manuals that are designed for specific events become quickly outdated and do not offer responses or solutions for events that are not outlined within them. In effect, traditional crisis management is not sustainable based on its design.

Enterprise crisis management begins well before any potential disruption. It addresses an organization's survival and resiliency and requires the involvement and understanding of top management. Managers should realize that crisis management is a process that continues before, during, and after a disruption. An essential component of enterprise crisis management is training management to expect challenges and to understand how to rebuild the confidence of all stakeholders following a crisis. This discussion concentrates specifically on training managers to deal with crises rather than on the overall crisis management process.

Training Managers to Deal With the Unexpected

Organizations continue to depend on traditional crisis management training, even though such exercises have not proved to adequately prepare managers to deal with the unexpected. Traditional training is most effective only for testing the functionality of equipment or response times to preserve critical business relationships.

Unless the scenarios chosen for traditional crisis management are relevant to the organization, training participants are unlikely to become engaged in the process. Unrealistic scenarios can also result in overall resistance to the training and undermine the participants' motivation. Such training often leads to the creation of a list of future improvements that are not acted upon after the training has been completed. Often, no further actions are taken until the next training session, which may not occur for several years. This lack of apparent results leads to complacency on the part of participants as well as a lack of organizational preparedness for emerging crises.

However, training continues to be an essential requirement for crisis management and is becoming more crucial as the number of crises and atypical risks increases. Simulations continue to be the best means of teaching managers to deal with the unexpected.

Enterprise crisis management training includes brainstorming sessions that stimulate creativity and provide opportunities to strengthen the organization. Working together as a crisis management team develops the abilities of many individual managers. Training participants must work in cross-functional teams and understand the nature of operating under stress. Enterprise crisis management can inspire resourcefulness in an organization, adding to its competitive advantage even during noncrisis times.

Top management must be involved in crisis management training, policy formulation, and exercises. These leaders must demonstrate to the organization the importance of preparation for eventual crises. Top management participation lends credibility to the exercise and assists in preparing the management team to handle any crisis that may arise.

Elements for preparing managers to deal with the unexpected include these:

- Team building
- Data room exercises or computer simulations
- Designation of a recovery team leader

A well-tested business continuity plan is a critical component of enterprise crisis management. The plan should involve all levels of management, particularly line managers. Line managers should be encouraged to participate in the development of the plan and be able to implement it when needed. Because line managers are most intimately involved with day-to-day procedures, they must have confidence that the plan will work. If they perceive potential flaws in the plan, they should report them up the chain of command.

Team building is an essential part of crisis management. It teaches managers how to work together without assigning blame or wasting time on recriminations. The ability to adapt to and work in a new environment is critical to an organization's resiliency.

Data room security and recovery are closely linked to an organization's business intelligence. As part of enterprise crisis management, the data room should be available to run various scenario exercises. In times of crisis, the data room often becomes the center of operations (or "war room"), where activities are coordinated.

The recovery team leader is in charge of crisis management during a disruption. He or she receives information from the field, filters it, and reports to top executives. The recovery team leader communicates the status of the condition of the organization. Typical reporting sometimes includes the use of a color key such as red, yellow, or green to signify the level of disruption. The "Crisis Management Mental Action Plan" exhibit outlines exercises that can be used to maintain a positive and productive mental attitude during time of crisis.

Crisis Management Mental Action Plan

1. **Reversing the polarity**—developing a positive polarity to crisis management; looking at the positive attributes that investment in crisis management training can yield

2. **Reversing the priorities**—getting chief executives and top managers involved

3. **Managing a continuous process**—avoiding unnecessary and undesirable planning rigidity

4. **Challenging accepted practices**—questioning existing crisis management initiatives or the absence of a credible crisis management response capability

5. **Changing the focus**—paying more attention to the beginning and end of crises, where crisis management can be most effective

6. **Lateral thinking**—paying greater attention to what might initially appear to be marginal or peripheral

7. **Addressing organizational taboos**—admitting the need for challenge and suggestion without recrimination

8. **Building/rebuilding confidence**—re-instilling confidence/trust in the organization—the core objective of crisis management

9. **Breaking inflexible mind-sets**—training oneself to deal with the unexpected

10. **Developing a fresh approach**—moving towards a new language and practice of crisis management

---

Source: Bertrand Robert and Christopher Lajtha, "A New Approach to Crisis Management," *Journal of Contingencies and Crisis Management*, December 2002.

MITIGATING RISK THROUGH BUSINESS CONTINUITY PLANNING

Over half of all businesses subjected to a catastrophic event fail immediately. Of those businesses that do continue operating, half fail within two years. An organization that adopts an ERM approach develops a detailed plan of action to mitigate risk and to maintain operations regardless of external and internal events that may otherwise prove disastrous. While a government agency may not fail immediately during a crisis, its effectiveness and mission may be reassessed or its leadership changed, leading to further disruption. In other instances, the agency's or department's mission may be folded into or reassigned to another department.

Business continuity management (BCM) involves establishing an operational plan that examines the many risks an organization faces and provides contingencies that allow its key operations and critical functions to continue in the event of a disruption, such as a natural disaster or major physical damage to a building. Many organizations call business continuity management "business resiliency" because continuity planning for risk helps organizations to withstand such events and, ultimately, to survive. This discussion is intended to provide an overview of business continuity issues, rather than an outline of a specific plan or process for business continuity planning.

The development of a business continuity plan (BCP) is an important component of BCM. A BCP allows an organization to analyze all possible eventualities to determine the critical functions that must continue during a disruption so that the organization survives, recovers, and resumes growth. The development and implementation of a BCP entails seven steps:

- Understanding the business
- Conducting a business impact analysis (BIA)
- Performing a risk assessment
- Developing the continuity plan
- Implementing the continuity plan
- Building a BCM/BCP culture
- Maintaining and updating the plan

While BCP and BCM contain the word "business," both terms refer to securing continuity of operations. Thus, applying the concept to other than for-profit entities can be accomplished by considering the "business of the agency" or the "business of the charity," for example. Thus, "business" considers the mission, vision, and strategy of the enterprise in addition to its survival.

Understanding the Business

To complete a business continuity plan, an organization must first understand all aspects of its business. This includes determining key objectives and how and when they will be met, as well as the internal and external parties involved in achieving them.

Once the organization determines its key objectives (for example, a key objective may be "continuing to manufacture and sell widgets"), it must examine how it uses its facilities, materials supply chain, human resources, communications, information systems, processes, distribution channels, and customers to achieve them. This allows the organization to identify the key processes that will constitute the basis for its BIA.

Conducting a Business Impact Analysis

An organization conducts a BIA to identify and assess the risks that may affect it. A BIA assesses what events may occur, when they may occur, and how they could affect achievement of key objectives. The BIA also measures the financial and nonfinancial effect of risks and explores organizational vulnerabilities, critical elements in developing strategies to protect organizational resources.

The analysis also distinguishes between critical and noncritical processes. This allows the organization to use the BIA to determine its recovery time objective, which is the time period within which a critical process must be recovered in order for the organization to resume operations after a disruption of operations.

Various international standards, such as ISO 31000:2009, take different approaches or use different terminology for the BIA. In some standards, the BIA and the risk assessment are combined. In other standards, the BIA goes beyond a more traditional risk assessment, which often focuses only on hazard risks and fails to assess the full impact of risk on all aspects of the operation.

Performing a Risk Assessment

An organization performs a risk assessment to identify and evaluate potential exposures and the probability that certain events will occur. It also indicates how susceptible the organization may be to particular disruptions. This helps the organization prioritize its BCM strategy and risk controls and assists management in making decisions regarding organizational risk appetite. A thorough risk assessment will reveal exposures and can assist in establishing methods for future risk mitigation efforts. Finally, the risk assessment helps the organization determine an action plan.

Assessments can be conducted at various levels. Convergys Corporation, for example, conducts three levels of assessment:[9]

- Enterprise assessment—a global assessment of risks that could affect the enterprise's overall business goals
- Site assessment—an assessment by risk owners at risk centers of risks associated with particular sites or locations or even specific geographies
- Program or project assessments—an assessment of a project's capabilities, resources, and limitations in relationship to a viable recovery strategy

Developing the Continuity Plan

After it has conducted the BIA and performed a risk assessment to establish recovery time objectives, an organization can begin to develop strategies to maintain critical functions during disruptions. Organizations may use one strategy or a combination of strategies to ensure resiliency:

- Active back-up model—This strategy entails the organization establishing a second site that includes all of the necessary production equipment housed at the primary site. Staff may be relocated to the second site if operations are disrupted at the primary site.
- Split operations model—In this model, an organization maintains two or more active sites that are geographically dispersed. Capacity at each site is sufficient to handle total output in the event of a disruption at either site.
- Alternative site model—An organization that uses this strategy maintains a production site and an active backup site that functions as the primary site as needed.
- Contingency model—This strategy involves the organization developing an alternate way to maintain production, perhaps using manual processes.

All of these strategies involve three levels of planning:[10]

- BCM organizational strategy
- BCM process level strategy
- BCM resource recovery strategy

These planning levels require the organization to examine its basic processes, determine potential points of failure, and create alternate operational methods.

Strategic choices for addressing a disruption of operations include these options:

- An insurance policy—This allows the organization to recover some of its financial losses if it suffers an insurable loss.
- Transfer processing—This entails the organization's entering reciprocal arrangements with another company or division to perform a necessary function in the event of a disruption of operations.

- Termination—With this strategy, an organization ceases production of the affected product or service.
- Loss mitigation—This entails implementation of risk controls and plans to reduce, minimize, or divert any loss.
- Do nothing—If an organization does nothing in the event of a disruption of operations, it absorbs the potential loss. This represents an increase of its risk appetite.

Implementing the Continuity Plan

Senior management must impress upon the organization that the BCP is integral to its survival and success. The business continuity coordinator (BCC) assists and directs each department in formulating a departmental plan. This ensures that the organization's component parts work effectively for the entire organization.

Each department's plan must include these elements:[11]

- Statement of acceptable level of functioning
- Recovery time objectives, resources needed, and potential failure points
- Tasks and activities required
- Procedures or processes
- Supporting documentation and information
- Structure to support the plan
- Description of division teams—purpose, team members, mission
- Explanation of interdependencies among the various division teams

The BCC presents the drafted BCP to senior management for approval. Once the BCP is approved, the BCC and senior management begin to influence the organization's culture to accept, practice, and maintain the BCP.

Building a BCM/BCP Culture

Senior management provides the vision statement and support for the BCP. It must also set expectations and objectives for middle management concerning maintenance of departmental plans.

Business Continuity Management (BCM) Encompasses All Divisions

Risk Management	Facilities Management	Human Capital Management	Technology Management
Intellectual Property Management	Reputation Management	Market Share Management	Supply and Distribution Management

Staff must be educated on the importance of maintaining the BCP. One way management can achieve this is to hold semiannual exercises in which staff members react to a hypothetical disaster scenario by using the plan to maintain operations. If successful, these exercises may find "holes" in the BCP that need to be addressed. Exercises also provide opportunities to amend the BCP as new processes are introduced and used.

External suppliers and customers should know that the organization has a BCP and be encouraged to provide their own contingency plans. When key suppliers and customers are prepared for a disruption of operations, their relationship with the organization is improved.

Maintaining and Updating the Plan

Organizational environments, processes, and products change rapidly in today's business environment, and so too should the BCP. A BCP is effective only if it is kept fresh and updated. The BCP should be reviewed in detail and amended as internal or external conditions warrant. Analyzing the written BCP is essential and should be done semiannually or when a significant change has occurred in product line, processes, or management. An organization must also determine how best to store its BCP. Companies often maintain electronic copies of the BCP on a secured server accessible from several locations, while written copies are also maintained by key members of the organization.

Business continuity planning may not be effective in all cases. When an organization's survival is threatened, strategic redeployment planning is required.

SCOPE OF STRATEGIC REDEPLOYMENT PLANNING

Small disruptions within an organization can develop into major ruptures that jeopardize its survival. During ruptures, business continuity plans are insufficient for fully restoring the organization and ensuring its survival. Once a rupture occurs, management must determine whether existing organizational strategies are still valid and, if they are not, make necessary strategic adjustments to ensure the organization's survival. When an analysis of the situation reveals that the disruption is due to a chaotic situation, the organization must reorganize its resources. In such cases, strategic redeployment becomes necessary for the organization to determine how to realign itself in order to survive, regain its position in the marketplace, and protect its reputation.

Strategic Redeployment Planning Stages

A strategic redeployment plan (SRP) is a comprehensive plan for resiliency after a severe disruption. It is designed to bring the organization back from the chaotic system to the simple system in four stages:

- Emergency stage
- Alternate marketing stage
- Contingency production stage
- Communication stage

Note that there is a specific communication stage in strategic redeployment planning that has a distinct meaning and context. All of the stages of strategic redeployment require effective, accurate, and timely communication both to internal and external stakeholders, not just the communication stage.

Emergency Stage

This stage, sometimes referred to as disaster recovery, starts at the moment of disruption and constitutes the organization's immediate response. This stage is designed to accomplish three objectives:

- Protect people—contact emergency authorities, evacuate the area, warn neighbors
- Protect physical assets—guard the site, organize salvage operations
- Protect reputation—communicate with all economic stakeholders, maintain control of all media releases

The emergency stage may include closing and cleaning the facility, recalling products, and meeting with employees and media to communicate status.

Alternate Marketing Stage

The second stage requires the organization to evaluate the disruption's impact on its reputation and market share. The organization must determine whether it needs a new marketing strategy. It must also consider consumer loyalty—will customers remain loyal during the crisis, or will they seek substitute products or services? Will suppliers and subcontractors work with the organization during this interval? Will competitors use the organization's disruption as an opportunity to increase their market share or capture the affected organization's current suppliers? In some cases, an organization will conduct an abbreviated SWOT (strengths, weaknesses, opportunities, and threats) analysis to answer some of these questions.

In this stage, no course of action to save the core business or resources should be ruled out, including pulling out of a market or a business. The organization's leadership may have to conduct a SWOT analysis to define a strategy compatible with the new levels of resources. One key is to set up a data room similar to one that would be established during the due diligence process. The business intelligence system will be the cornerstone for reliable data and information during a disruption.

Some organizations may use a color-coded approach at this stage, using "red," "yellow," or "green" to denote the level of disruption. Green indicates that the current strategy should be maintained and that there is no need to develop a new business model. Conversely, red might indicate the need for a radical alteration to the business model or even its complete replacement.

At a minimum, a new marketing strategy may determine whether the organization will maintain production of its traditional products and services. For instance, the organization may decide that a limited output of products or services should be continued for supplying certain customer segments.

Low-priority products or services may be discontinued. The organization must analyze the ultimate impact of the loss of the products or services and the impact on any synergies associated with those products or services. The organization must evaluate the impact of the loss of revenue from current as well as potential customers of these products or services. Such a situation would be indicated with a yellow color coding.

If the situation is in the red zone, the current strategy cannot be maintained and a new marketing strategy is needed. In this case, the organization will have to consider substitutions for the current products or services; what synergies may be created; what resources are needed; and, ultimately, how to restore desired goals and outcomes.

Contingency Production Stage

The third stage is based on the results of the analysis completed in the alternate marketing stage. This stage must minimize any downtime for the organization. The organization decides what products or services it will provide depending on the facilities available and whether its technology and machinery are adequate. It must also consider its supply chain with respect to the quality and cost of resources needed and determine whether the product packaging needs to be adapted for a new product. Other considerations during this stage include the availability of transportation and possible routes to distribute products and services.

Communication Stage

The sole objective of the communication stage is to preserve or enhance stakeholders' trust and confidence in the organization. This stage begins once a disruption occurs and is initially referred to as "crisis communication." When the organization's production and reputation have been restored, the crisis communication becomes "post-crisis communication." To meet the objectives of crisis and post-crisis communications, the concerns and expectations of all internal and external stakeholders must be identified and addressed. The organization must address four basic concerns:

- Safety and security of all stakeholders
- Transparency in all of management's decisions
- Clarity and consistency in communications
- Perceived lack of trust in management and the organization

The key to effective communication in a time of disruption is to establish a good relationship with the media prior to any crisis. The organization must maintain a permanent link with the media so that when a crisis occurs, it can leverage the goodwill created in normal times. To achieve clarity and consistency, information released to the media must echo the information provided to employees. The organization must keep channels of communication open with local authorities and industry associations open. Employees also need to have up-to-date information as soon as it is practical. Keeping employees, customers, suppliers, and other stakeholders well informed during a crisis will not only prevent defection to competitors, but will also strengthen loyalty and rebuild trust in the organization.

Conditions for Success

Strategic redeployment requires attention to the increasing concerns of internal and external stakeholders. If an organization fails to protect its reputation prior to a disruption, it may not survive the disruption. The manner in which the organization interacts with internal and external stakeholders determines its credibility in the marketplace. Successful redeployment is an organization-wide effort.

Depending on the nature of the crisis, the SRP may not involve major changes for an organization. In some dire circumstances, the plan may be drastic and involve major changes that take an organization in a new direction.

SUMMARY

Four system levels correspond to magnitudes of business disruptions—simple, complicated, complex, and chaotic. When confronted with a disruption at a particular level, an organization must "work down" through each level to return to a simple state system level.

Any event or scenario that could benefit or damage an organization's reputation presents risk to reputation. Successfully managing risk to reputation requires an understanding of these important concepts:

- Reputation as a key asset
- Reputation and a systemic approach
- Lessons learned from experience
- Implementing risk management for risk to reputation

Crisis management is an important, but emerging, field. Enterprise crisis management is used to prepare management to respond to major disruptions and to address stakeholder concerns. A well-prepared crisis management plan can be used to control crises as they emerge and, in some cases, to avoid major disruptions. Crisis management reinforces stakeholder confidence and helps organizations maintain competitive advantage.

BCM is a strategic and operational approach designed to maintain business operations in the event of a catastrophe. Its purpose is to analyze potential risks and determine the most effective solutions the organization may employ to mitigate the risk and resulting damage.

The BCP is an important component of the BCM process. The BCP is a detailed map for an organization to follow. It is a "living, breathing" document for the organization and must be reviewed and analyzed regularly to determine whether revisions are needed.

An SRP is a four-stage plan designed to reinforce an organization's resiliency and to allow it to survive and flourish following a crisis. Each stage is designed and developed to protect the organization, its stakeholders, its reputation, and its physical assets. As each stage is completed, the organization moves out of chaos and toward a new normal or "simple" system.

CHAPTER NOTES

1. David J. Snowden and Mary E. Boone, "A Leader's Framework for Decision Making," *Harvard Business Review*, November 2007, p. 72.

2. This discussion is adapted from "Managing Reputational Risk," an unpublished research article written in 2009 by Sophie Gaultier Gaillard, Alex Hindson, Jean-Paul Louisot, and Jenny Rayner.

3. "Procter & Gamble Deepens Corporate Commitment To Sustainability," March 26, 2009, www.pg.com/news/sustainability_goals.shtml (accessed July 30, 2009).

4. Adapted from Gaillard, Hindson, Louisot, and Rayner.

5. R. Knight and D. Pretty, *The Impact of Catastrophes on Shareholder Value*, Oxford Executive Research Briefings (Oxford: Templeton College, University of Oxford, 1997).

6. This three-step process, reflecting the process proposed in the ISO 31000:2009 standard, covers the six steps of risk management found in a traditional risk management approach.

7. The crisis management approach in this section is based in part on Bertrand Robert and Christopher Lajtha, "A New Approach to Crisis Management," Journal of Contingencies and Crisis Management, December 2002, pp. 181–191.

8. The crisis management approach in this section is based in part on Bertrand Robert and Christopher Lajtha, "Crisis Management Simulations: Flaws and Remedies," in International Handbook of Organizational Crisis Management, ed. Christophe Roux-Dufort, Christine M. Pearson, and Judith A. Clair (Thousand Oaks, CA: Sage Publications, 2007), pp. 315–326.

9. Adapted from an unpublished manuscript, Carol A. Fox and Michael S. Epstein, *Why Is Enterprise Risk Management (ERM) Important for Preparedness?* (Convergys Corporation, 2009).

10. PAS 56:2003, Guide to Business Continuity Management, The Business Continuity Institute, March 2003, p.14.

11. PAS 56:2003, Guide to Business Continuity Management, The Business Continuity Institute, March 2003, p.18.

Risk Treatment: The Supply Chain and Crisis Communication

Educational Objectives

After learning the content of this chapter and completing the corresponding course guide assignment, you should be able to:

▶ Explain how supply chain risk management is used to assess and mitigate risks that could disrupt an organization's flow of goods and services.

▶ Explain how risk mitigation is achieved through efficient communication in time of a crisis.

▶ Given a scenario involving a supply chain, recommend the risk-appropriate mitigation tools.

Outline

Supply Chain Risk Management

Crisis Communication

Recommending Appropriate Mitigation Tools— A Supply Chain Case Study

Summary

Risk Treatment: The Supply Chain and Crisis Communication

This chapter continues the discussion of risk treatment in the context of risk reduction. Traditional risk management entails the use of many risk treatment tools, including those that mitigate resulting losses. This chapter discusses the growing problem of supply chain risk. As organizations become more global and complex, more threats and opportunities related to supply chains have emerged. A change in the supply chain or the organization—whether from an actual event, threat, or opportunity—requires an organization to communicate efficiently with all of its stakeholders. The chapter concludes with a case study that examines these issues through a hypothetical supply chain risk mitigation problem that arises from a supply chain disturbance.

SUPPLY CHAIN RISK MANAGEMENT

Market globalization and outsourcing for economic efficiency have substantially increased interdependencies between events and the production of goods and services in different regions and industries. Supply chains may be viewed as branches of a tree connected to one another through a common trunk. A disruption in the availability of one good or service may have far-reaching effects on an organization, including, in the short-term, inability to deliver on contractual promises and, in the long-term, destruction of shareholder value.

Supply chain risk management entails assessing and mitigating all the threats that might interrupt the normal flow of goods and services from and to an organization's stakeholders. When applied to the production of goods, supply chain risk management encompasses managing the volatility related to producing, transporting, and storing goods, as well as managing the distribution channels from the initial raw materials to the final consumer product. Disruptions in an organization's production affect its immediate financial condition and may damage its brand reputation irreparably.

When applied to services, supply chain risk management encompasses managing the volatility associated with delivering the service to its end users, taking into consideration all the components of the value chain. Organizations must identify the risks and opportunities within supply chains and balance efficiency and best practices against vulnerability to disruptions. Supply chain risk management visibility has increased with the introduction of ISO 28000: *Supply Chain Security Management Requirements*.

Threats and Opportunities Inherent in Supply Chains

An organization must assess supply chain risk by examining both internal and external exposures and vulnerabilities. Internal exposures and vulnerabilities include these:

- Production location—Facilities may be vulnerable to natural disaster, manmade disaster, or terrorism.
- Production bottlenecks—Production may depend on a key machine or material; a malfunction or breakdown in the machine would slow or halt production.
- Information technology—The data center may be vulnerable, information backup may be unavailable, or staff may fail to follow restoration protocols.
- Infrastructure—Damage to infrastructure can impede or halt production altogether.
- Strikes or other employment issues—Production may cease, inventory cannot be moved, and orders are not filled.
- Machinery breakdown—Production may stall, or a critical backup in production may occur, while new parts (or new machines) are ordered and installed.

External exposures and vulnerabilities include these:

- Third-party suppliers—Disruption in production from the supplier could undermine an organization's ability to generate its product and to satisfy customer demand.
- Sole source suppliers—Disruption in supply when only one supplier of goods is available will reduce or potentially shut down an organization's ability to produce and satisfy customer demand.
- Single source supplier—Disruptions in supply can also occur when an organization chooses to rely on only one supplier, even when multiple suppliers are available.
- Change in demand level—Incremental or substantial changes in demand due to changes in customer taste or to competition can cause over- or under-production. If demand is not accurately forecasted, market reputation could be damaged.
- Financial risks—Increases in the cost of materials or transportation charges will cause costs to rise. Organizations may not be able to pass on increased costs due to consumer preferences, prior contracts, and competition. Exchange rate fluctuations may cause increases in materials costs and may also reduce the attractiveness of the product in overseas markets.
- Geopolitical environment—Imports and exports may be affected by government regulation or taxation. Unstable governments increase the chance of nationalization of an organization's overseas assets.

- Natural or manmade catastrophes—Storms, earthquakes, volcanic eruptions, and other natural disasters can damage an organization's facilities or interfere with its transportation routes. Pandemics may interrupt an organization's activities if too few employees are available to work. Terrorist activity can disrupt normal supply and distribution channels for extended periods.

- Merger of a key supplier with a competitor—Changes in ownership of key suppliers can affect the price of materials and the availability of supplies.

Organizations can also assess supply chains to uncover potential opportunities that may include these:

- Inventory and storage costs can be reduced by using the supply chain for just-in-time deliveries and work processes.

- Technology improvements can be leveraged to improve process efficiencies.

- Supplier relationships can be improved to build positive relationships that strengthen communication and minimize potential supply chain disruptions.

Balance Between Efficiency and Vulnerability to Disruptions

Once an organization assesses potential risks of disruption in its supply chain, it must determine how it will defend its production processes, distribution channels, and market reputation. It also should examine various options to maintain production efficiency. It also should test and consider its ability to accurately forecast demand for materials, labor, and sales. Flexibility in supply sources as well as product design can help balance efficiency against potential disruptions.

The business impact analysis of a supply chain disruption must take into account all the components of a potential loss, such as loss of net revenues, increased costs, and any mitigation costs. If the organization determines that a potential disruption would have little or no impact on the flow of revenues, it may choose not to consider such a disruption in its business continuity plan. To ensure continuity, the organization must thoroughly analyze the short-, medium-, and long-term consequences of any threat or disruption. Such consequences could include potential downgrades by a financial rating agency and/or legal requirements in foreign countries to ensure continuity for industries deemed vital in that jurisdiction.

Supply Chain Best Practices

The organization must periodically assess its supply chain and establish best practices for various disruption scenarios. This assessment requires a multidisciplinary team of managers to prioritize potential risks and determine disruption timing and recovery time. As it analyzes each type of disruption, the team should consider various responses. The response to each situation should depend on the likelihood and impact (the level and duration) of the potential disruption.

Based on this review, the team will establish best practices and then take action as needed. Such action includes the regular use of dry-running and updating the business continuity plan on a regular basis as conditions change.

Supply Chain Best Practices and Mitigation Techniques

Internal Disruption	Best Practices/Mitigation
Production location	Diversify locations
Production bottlenecks	Redesign product or production process to reduce or eliminate bottlenecks
IT and infrastructure failures	Maintain appropriate backup protocols, redundant systems, and maintenance
Strikes or employment issues	Maintain and educate staff on proper human resource management
Machinery breakdown	Maintain spare parts or establish changeover processes
External Disruption	**Best Practices/Mitigation**
Third-party/single suppliers	Diversify suppliers, contract carefully, maintain ongoing dialogue with suppliers
Sole source supplier	Consult with the supplier to mitigate some of the risks (expand to several production sites) and/or design technological innovations
Change in demand	Monitor and forecast changes in competition and environment
Financial risks	Legal contracts to provide protection for some risk, insurance contracts for others, and monitoring the environment to identify emerging financial trends that could affect costs
Geopolitical environment	Understand and monitor the political environments in which the organization operates
Natural or manmade catastrophes	Maintain and update the business continuity plan
Merger of a key supplier	Diversify suppliers, contract carefully, and maintain ongoing dialogue with suppliers

CRISIS COMMUNICATION

An organization's ability to communicate plans and activities to stakeholders during a crisis is critical to overcoming the situation and contributes to the success of any redeployment strategy.

For example, consider this scenario:

Smoke is billowing out of the fourth, fifth, and sixth floors of a building. Firefighters, police, and emergency medical technicians dart into the building and back to their rapid-response vehicles. Employees rush out of the building. Some are covered in soot, coughing, or screaming for co-workers, while several are brought out on stretchers. The media are on the scene, reporting live and questioning distraught employees. Executives' pagers and cell phones start beeping, the board of directors demands information, key clients and suppliers call, and the press wants a statement.

Clearly this situation has triggered reactions from many stakeholders, as well as the media. This is the moment for the organization to start managing the crisis and to protect its reputation. Crisis management, properly handled, will mitigate organizational risk on several levels. Communication is a key element in managing a crisis.

In a crisis situation such as this, the organization must conduct an alternative marketing strategic brainstorming session to determine whether a redeployment strategy is needed. Strategically redeploying assets—following proper analysis of available resources and market conditions—often enables an organization to quickly return to productivity.

Mitigating Risk Through Crisis Communication

Risk management is a complex system based on a web of relationships among internal and external stakeholders. Good risk management practices should be embedded within the organization and include all financial partners, suppliers, customers, and other stakeholders. This is particularly true in time of crisis.

When an organization implements its crisis management plan, its prime objective is to survive the crisis event. Survival depends on the organization's speedy return to normal operations—brought about by proper continuity, contingency, or disaster recovery planning—and the successful implementation of its strategic redeployment plan. Although crisis management includes several vital components, the quality of an organization's crisis communication is essential to its resiliency.

Stakeholder Communications

Crisis communication begins before any threats have materialized; it involves establishing a baseline of trust with all stakeholders. Every stakeholder must believe that management will competently handle and resolve any crisis. When a crisis occurs, the organization's message must be candid, address the prominent issues, and engage all stakeholders to be effective in restoring and maintaining stakeholders' trust. As part of its crisis communication plan, the organization should maintain an open dialogue with the media (press, television, and radio).

Additionally, effective communication conveying to various stakeholders that the organization has considered all risks promotes distinctiveness in the minds of those stakeholders. The messages should have a core theme that addresses corporate involvement in safety and security. Communications must also demonstrate that senior management is committed to maintaining an environment of transparency in its decision making. All crisis communications must be consistent, with each message tailored to its specific audience. To maintain stakeholders' trust in the organization and its management, the messages must embody corporate integrity and authenticity.

Communication with different stakeholder groups continues after the immediate crisis. The organization will operate differently and face both threats and opportunities differently after a crisis. It is important for the organization to examine and carefully select various communication tools for use with internal and external stakeholders in order to analyze the specific concerns of the stakeholders, provide the solution, and speak the stakeholders' language.

Internal Stakeholders

Internal stakeholders' individual needs must be acknowledged. Employees must be informed continuously, especially regarding how the crisis will affect their jobs and working conditions. New safety concerns may emerge and, if so, will need to be addressed. This can be done through meetings, displays of visual aids in the workplace, hands-on training, and the organization's intranet site.

Unit and operational managers must be made aware of ongoing risks. Their assistance in training and in maintaining attentiveness to potential risks is crucial to the plan's success. Because risk management is a key part of the responsibilities of line managers, they must be held accountable for specific aspects of the crisis management plan.

Stockholders must be informed of all steps taken to manage, mitigate, and even prevent future crises. Communicating organizational health in the annual report and during quarterly meetings is imperative. Senior management must report major trends and pending claims as well as demonstrate corporate resilience. The board of directors must also be informed regularly about strategic exposures, governance issues, and long-term resilience.

External Stakeholders

In addition to communicating with internal stakeholders, the organization must keep external stakeholders informed. Suppliers must be notified of procedures for scheduled deliveries during the period of disruption and of how the organization will make required payments. Maintaining goodwill with suppliers during a crisis will help them work with the post-crisis organization, which is a critical component of the organization's resilience.

Customers should be assured of the organization's continuity and safety. A sound communication plan can help to build trust and maintain consumer loyalty during the period of recovery.

Public officials and local authorities must be informed of the organization's efforts to ensure public safety and health and to demonstrate its commitment to the community. Statutory compliance must be monitored and reported. Other external stakeholders include local associations and special interest groups, which should be informed of the organization's recuperation efforts immediately after a crisis and as part of an ongoing effort to maintain strong relationships with these groups.

The media can be leveraged to transmit information to many internal and external stakeholders. Press releases and interviews on health, safety, and financial progress can help to restore and retain marketplace confidence.

Every communication from the organization must be truthful. Risk managers must speak clearly and honestly about current conditions, known risks, and potential risks. The organization must manage and monitor its communication with every stakeholder.

Benefits of Crisis Communication

Regular communication before and throughout a crisis will improve relationships between the organization and its internal and external stakeholders. Good communication will create an open and truthful environment that will encourage future investments in the organization and continue to provide it with favorable access to capital. As a long-term result of effective communication, the organization will be able to attract and retain the most talented employees because it has preserved its reputation post-crisis. Externally, this reputation will help the organization to continue to build relationships with new and existing suppliers and customers.

Protection of the organization's reputation through good crisis communications reduces barriers to the development of new markets. A successful and well-communicated crisis management plan will promote trust in the organization's products and services. As a result, the organization may be able to gain a competitive advantage based on its reputation and its stringent attention to managing past, current, and potential risks. Additionally, a well-communicated and well-executed crisis management plan may help to minimize litigation arising from the crisis event.

RECOMMENDING APPROPRIATE MITIGATION TOOLS—A SUPPLY CHAIN CASE STUDY

The twenty-first century consumer can choose goods and services provided by vendors throughout the global market. A breakdown in one link of the supply chain can have disastrous results for an organization. Every organization must prepare for a disruption in order to keep its goods and services flowing to its consumers.

When an organization analyzes its supply chain to determine and recommend risk mitigation tools, it is important to understand these concepts:

- Cascading disruption—seemingly unrelated events that can cause major disruptions
- Supply chain management—the development of sound relationships and diversity among suppliers
- Business resiliency planning—the development of plans that prepare the organization to respond to disruptions

To determine appropriate mitigation tools, an organization should analyze the companies with which it has a business relationship to identify potential dependencies. The purpose of this analysis is to determine apparent exposures and the impact of losses related to those exposures. The organization must then determine how to mitigate the immediate damage that would result from each exposure and select methods to reduce future risk.

Case Facts

Bakeries Inc. manufactures organic whole-grain sesame bread and crackers. The company purchases its ingredients—whole-grain flour, sugar, eggs, canola oil, and sesame seeds—from organic farms and processors. Bakeries' whole-grain flour is processed by Mille Company, which Bakeries uses exclusively. The products are sold to high-end retail stores specializing in organic foods.

Bakeries is the sole supplier of sesame bread and crackers to Health Foods, a regional high-end wholesome food specialty shop. Health Foods operates on a 3 percent margin, and Bakeries Inc. products constitute 35 percent of the shop's retail sales.

Originally privately owned, Mille Company has 300 employees. The company culture was built on the premise of providing organic alternatives to the public. Management actively solicited employee feedback on its products and processes and encouraged employee involvement. Three months ago, however, Mille Company was sold to a large food manufacturer. Rather than continue with the existing culture and corporate environment, new management began making production changes to increase the organization's bottom line. Several of the organic farms supplying wheat to Mille Company were unable to increase their production quickly enough to meet the levels demanded by the new corporate owners. Contracts were not renewed, and the new Mille organization began mixing nonorganic grain with organic grain to lower costs and increase supplies. A disgruntled employee reported Mille Company to the Food and Drug Administration (FDA).

The FDA investigated Mille Company, and the results of the investigation were made public. As a result of this investigation, Mille was required to cease branding its flour as "organic." Enraged consumer groups sued Mille Company for product fraud and fraudulent advertising.

Bakeries Inc. was unable to locate an immediate alternate source of whole-grain flour, and its production subsequently decreased by 60 percent. Canceling its contract with Mille Company required three months' notice, and cancellation within the contract period would result in a penalty. Bakeries Inc. also missed its production goals by 40 percent and was unable to fulfill its contract with Health Foods.

Health Foods lost profits and customers and sued Bakeries Inc. for breach of contract and false advertising. Bakeries, in turn, sued Mille Company, citing the same causes of action, along with an additional one: products liability.

Case Analysis Tools and Information

Determining appropriate risk mitigation tools for Bakeries Inc. requires this information:

- Supply chain elements
- Relationships between elements
- Existing contractual arrangements
- Available mitigation tools

Case Analysis Steps

Analyzing an organization and its supply chains to develop risk mitigation tools involves a series of steps. Following these steps will assist the organization in effectively uncovering potential solutions:

1. Identify the exposures and types of risk for each company independently.
2. Determine co-dependencies between each company.
3. Analyze the exposures and determine how each company can avoid or mitigate losses to these exposures.

Exposure Identification

The first step in developing supply chain risk mitigation tools is to identify exposures. An organization begins this process by examining the upstream and downstream flow of materials to identify the entities involved. A business continuity plan can be a valuable resource in this process. Based on this review, the exposures and types of risk for each entity can be individually identified.

The exclusive relationship Bakeries Inc. has with Mille Company to purchase all the organic flour it needs creates the potential for Bakeries' overdependence on a single supplier. Bakeries' contract with Mille Company specifies that Mille must deliver organically grown and processed flour. It also requires Bakeries to give Mille Company three months' notice if it wants to change the tonnage of flour purchased or, if it fails to give such notice, pay a monetary penalty to Mille Company.

When negotiating this contract, which is favorable to Mille Company, Bakeries Inc. failed to insist on inclusion of a renegotiation clause if ownership of Mille Company changed. Further, Bakeries Inc. had no contingency plan in place to address problems that could occur with production at Mille Company. Bakeries Inc. also neglected to monitor the organizational changes at Mille Company.

Bakeries supplies its products to only one company—Healthy Foods. Bakeries' failure to deliver contracted products to Healthy Foods jeopardizes not only Bakeries' future sales but also its survival. Because Healthy Foods can purchase similar products from other manufacturers, there is a good possibility that Bakeries will not recover its previous market share.

Defending the company in litigation will be costly, further straining Bakeries' shrinking profits. Failure to deliver its product and the resulting negative publicity can cause a major disruption for Bakeries Inc. With production and sales decreased by 60 percent, Bakeries may not survive.

Bakeries Inc.: Manufacturer of Whole-Grain Organic Products

Exposure	Type of Risk
One key supplier	Financial
Unbalanced customer base	Financial
Litigation—Mille Company and Healthy Foods	Financial/Reputation
Reputation	Financial/Reputation
Survival	Financial/Reputation

Mille Company, purchased by a large corporation, is undergoing internal cultural changes. Seeking to increase profits and production, the new management at Mille Company is improperly handling the need for an increased grain supply. It has no quality assurance program in place and may have purchased nonorganically grown wheat in order to produce the quantities required. Employees, who are already unhappy due to changes in the organization, noticed that the wheat purchased for processing had not been organically grown and made this fact public, creating a crisis.

FDA involvement will be costly to the organization because every shipment of wheat purchased must now be scrutinized. Flour production has decreased, and Mille Company is unable to adhere to its production and delivery schedules. Mille Company is receiving negative media coverage, and several consumer groups are launching independent investigations.

Wheat farms supplying Mille Company are coming under investigation regarding their farming methods. Many customers are canceling their orders to avoid being tainted by the negative publicity. Consumer trust is at an all-time low.

Breach of contract litigation is also expensive. The new corporate parent is forced to defend Mille Company but may ultimately decide to close the facility. The "Mille Company: Processes Whole-Grain Organic Flour and Sells It to Bakeries Inc." exhibit summarizes Mille's exposure.

Mille Company: Processes Whole-Grain Organic Flour and Sells It to Bakeries Inc.

Exposure	Type of Risk
New management and culture—employee risk	Social/Political/Legal
Broad number of questionable suppliers	Financial
FDA investigation	Legal/Reputation/Ethical
Small market	Financial
Reputation	Financial/Reputation/Social
Litigation	Financial/Reputation
Survival	Financial/Reputation

Healthy Foods has contracted with Bakeries Inc. as a supplier of sesame bread and crackers, which account for 35 percent of Healthy Foods' profits. Healthy Foods does not have another supplier for these products immediately available. Customers wishing to purchase these products are finding alternative sources, notably a large grocery chain. Sales of other products have also dropped due to decreased customers visits to Healthy Foods. Selling products reputed to be inorganic is tarnishing the company's reputation. Healthy Foods' management believes its only option is to sue Bakeries Inc. for breach of contract and faulty advertising. The "Healthy Foods: Retail Chain Selling Organic Baked Foods Supplied by Bakeries Inc." exhibit summarizes Healthy Foods' exposure.

Healthy Foods: Retail Chain Selling Organic Baked Foods Supplied by Bakeries Inc.

Exposure	Type of Risk
One key supplier	Financial
Customer loyalty	Reputation/Financial
Reputation	Financial/Reputation
Litigation	Financial/Reputation

Determine Co-Dependencies

Once the individual exposures have been identified and analyzed, the co-dependencies between the organizations have been determined, as shown in the "Organizational Co-Dependencies" exhibit.

Specific organic farmers are contractually bound to deliver organically grown wheat to Mille Company. Mille Company contracts for a certain tonnage and reserves the right to purchase additional wheat. The farmers agree to grow the wheat using only organic methods, and any violation of this agreement voids the contract.

Mille Company processes the wheat using no additives or preservatives. The company supplies flour to Bakeries Inc. based on a delivery schedule outlined in the contract. Mille Company is the exclusive supplier to Bakeries Inc, which must give Mille three months' notice if the contracted amount is to be changed. Bakeries Inc. is tied to Mille Company by contract and by reputation.

Using the flour it receives from Mille Company, Bakeries produces the whole-grain organic sesame bread and crackers sold at Healthy Foods' store. Based on the amount of product sold to Healthy Foods, it is Bakeries' principal customer. Failure to supply product on time to Healthy Foods constitutes a breach of contract that can drive Bakeries out of business.

Organizational Co-Dependencies

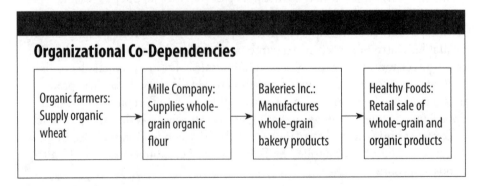

| Organic farmers: Supply organic wheat | → | Mille Company: Supplies whole-grain organic flour | → | Bakeries Inc.: Manufactures whole-grain bakery products | → | Healthy Foods: Retail sale of whole-grain and organic products |

Mitigation Plans

Mitigation plans are based on the analysis of the exposures and co-dependencies between the supply chain elements. Mitigation plans, which establish strategies in advance of a disruption, are an important part of any business continuity plan.

Bakeries Inc. is in crisis due to its broken supply chain. It needs to quickly find a substitute supplier of organic flour in order to resume baking operations. Concerns that other products it has sold may also have nonorganic components should be addressed with all stakeholders. Communication with customers is critical to the company's survival. Bakeries may need to increase production of other products to keep its operations going and to offset losses arising from its sesame bread and crackers line.

Mitigation plans for Bakeries Inc. include these:

- Find a new source of organic flour.
- Communicate to its business partners the steps it is taking to ensure that the products sold are truly organic.
- Communicate those same steps to customers.
- Use buffer inventory.
- Use hold-harmless agreements to their advantage.
- Review existing business continuity plan.

Mille Company must communicate with its business partners and the public. If the FDA's allegations are untrue, Mille Company must salvage—and may even rebuild—its reputation as quickly as possible. Cooperation with the FDA investigation will expedite the end of the crisis.

Mille Company may choose to increase its advertising when the FDA issues its report. Depending on the veracity of the allegation, Mille Company may need to redesign its business plan. The company is in crisis because of a failure to meld organizational cultures. Internal communication must be handled as carefully as external communication.

Mitigation plans for Mille Company include these:

- Cooperate with FDA investigation.
- Repair employee relations by improving communications.
- Communicate with customers.
- Redefine its business plan.

Healthy Foods lost valuable inventory items and needs to find an alternate supplier to lure customers back. Its reputation may be damaged, and it must find ways to communicate with the public to regain consumer trust.

Mitigation plans for Healthy Foods include these:

- Obtain new bakery product suppliers.
- Increase advertising.
- Regain customer trust.

The root cause of this disruption was the change of ownership of one company, Mille Company. The company's new management did not handle the change of culture well, incurring employee anger and ultimately a costly investigation and scandal.

Bakeries Inc. did not foresee that a change in its supplier's ownership and culture could affect its business. The disruption in its supply caused a loss in revenue, increased costs due to litigation, and a damaged reputation. Bakeries Inc. failed to maintain close ties with its business partners.

Healthy Foods is also damaged in this situation. It may find new suppliers of bakery products or be able to increase sales of other products. If not, it may not recover its customer base, and this may be the final circumstance that causes this boutique store to fall victim to a chain store operation.

Optimal Strategy

Bakeries Inc. did not evaluate its business plan thoroughly. When Mille Company was first purchased by a large corporation, it was in Bakeries' best interests to investigate the new organization to determine whether Mille Company would continue to supply the organic flour as contracted and whether the change in ownership posed a threat to Bakeries' supply chain.

Bakeries should develop secondary supply sources to avoid similar problems in the future. It may consider vertical integration, purchasing a milling operation, and contracting directly with organic farmers. Bakeries should also campaign aggressively in the marketplace to clear its name and should use marketing to its advantage.

Finally, Bakeries should use risk transfer to its advantage. It can do this by including a hold-harmless clause in agreements with both its suppliers and its customers. Should the company be unable to manufacture baked products due to circumstances that are defined as beyond its control, such clauses could minimize the financial repercussions.

Mille Company needs to communicate more effectively with its employees. It can do so by holding meetings and involving the original staff in the solutions. An alternative is to let the former employees leave the company, either voluntarily or not. Cooperation with the FDA is imperative, as the company must comply with all regulations. Depending on the outcome of the investigation, Mille Company may continue to process organic flour, or it may redefine its business plan and leave the organic market altogether.

Case Analysis and Solutions

Bakeries Inc.: Manufacturer of whole-grain/organic bakery products distributed to retail stores

Exposure	Type of Risk	Potential Solution
One key supplier	Financial	Diversify/Buffer inventory
Small customer base	Financial	Increase advertisement
Litigation—Mille Company and Healthy Foods	Financial/Reputation	Renegotiate contracts with hold-harmless clauses
Reputation	Financial/Reputation	Communication/Media
Survival	Financial/Reputation	Redefine strategy

Mille Company: Processes whole-grain organic flour, selling to Bakeries Inc.

Exposure	Type of Risk	Potential Solution
New management and culture—employee risk	Social/Political / Legal	Employee meetings/Training/ Change management
Broad number of questionable suppliers	Financial	Quality assurance program
FDA	Social/Reputation/Ethical	Adhere to all regulations
Small market	Financial	Increase consumer awareness/Advertise
Reputation	Financial / Reputation/Social	Communication—use media outlets/Community involvement
Litigation	Financial/Reputation	Resolve issues/Renegotiate contracts
Survival	Financial/Reputation	Return to a new simple state

Healthy Foods: Retailer of whole-grain organic foods supplied by Bakeries Inc.

Exposure	Type of Risk	Potential Solution
One key supplier	Financial	Diversify
Customer loyalty	Financial	Communication/Advertising
Reputation Risk	Financial/Reputation	Communication/Community involvement
Litigation	Financial/Reputation	Reevaluate business plan

These solutions may not be the only viable options. Other solutions could be exercised if justified by the analysis. In addition, specific circumstances and organizational needs or goals may enter into the evaluation, making an alternative action a better option.

Healthy Foods should find new product suppliers and advertise in order to better compete. It may redefine its business plan to incorporate a different mix of products or consider being acquired by its larger competition.

SUMMARY

Organizations must achieve a balance between operational efficiency, cost effectiveness, and vulnerability to potential disruptions. They must also accurately assess risk to their supply chain and predetermine measures and countermeasures to maintain production and market share. When the supply chain is affected, organizations must be able to adjust and adapt quickly. Failure to do so may result in loss of market share and brand recognition as well as a reduced capacity to raise capital.

Communicating in a truthful and transparent way throughout a crisis will mitigate organizational risk and benefit the organization in the short term and the long term. During a crisis, stakeholders must be continually engaged and informed so that their concerns are fully addressed. Providing information will increase trust in management and help to protect the organization's reputation, allowing for optimum access to capital, markets, talent, suppliers, and customers.

Developing risk mitigation tools involves a review of operations to identify exposures and risks as well as co-dependencies within the supply chain. This review will form the foundation of a risk mitigation plan.

Risk Treatment: Risk Financing

Educational Objectives

After learning the content of this chapter and completing the corresponding course guide assignment, you should be able to:

▶ Given capital budgeting data, evaluate the feasibility of a given investment proposal.

▶ Summarize the limitations of using cash flow analysis in financial decision making.

▶ Explain how the risk-return relationship affects an organization's financial decision making.

▶ Describe the elements that are considered in portfolio selection for an organization.

▶ Given a scenario, determine the cost of capital and optimal capital allocation.

Outline

Indigo Company Case—Evaluating an Investment Proposal

Limitations of Cash Flow Analysis in Decision Making

Importance of the Risk-Return Relationship

Portfolio Selection and Optimizing Risk Taking

Polytech Company Case—Cost of Capital and Optimal Capital Allocation

Summary

Risk Treatment: Risk Financing

When analyzing a potential investment, an organization should take into account the associated risks and expected returns and determine a financing strategy. Accomplishing this requires the use of a variety of tools and techniques, including cash flow analysis, portfolio analysis, and cost of capital calculations. A risk professional should understand how to apply each of these investment analysis methods.

INDIGO COMPANY CASE—EVALUATING AN INVESTMENT PROPOSAL

Investment proposals are opportunities for an organization to spend capital with the expectation that the expenditure will generate a sufficient return. A risk professional should understand the financial criteria organizations use to evaluate investment proposals in order to explain to management why, in financial terms, one proposal should be selected over another due to risk management considerations.

Understanding **cash flow analysis** and **net present value** is central to evaluating an investment proposal. With these techniques, the risk professional can evaluate a proposal in light of various risk management considerations, such as how the uncertainty associated with risk and the selection of loss control or risk financing techniques affect the proposal's profitability.

Underlying Concepts

To successfully complete the Indigo Company case, you should understand four capital budgeting concepts:

- Discount rate
- Present value
- Net present value
- Time-adjusted period of return

Discount Rate

The discount rate is the interest rate used to calculate, or discount, the value of a dollar (although any unit of currency could be used, this case uses the US dollar) that will be received in the future into current dollars. The term "discount" is used because a dollar received in the future is worth less than a

Cash flow analysis
The act of monitoring and estimating the movement of cash into and out of an organization.

Net present value
The present value of all future net cash flows (including salvage value) discounted at the cost of capital, minus the cost of the initial investment, also discounted at the cost of capital.

dollar received today, after accounting for the future dollar's opportunity cost, which is the interest that the dollar would have accumulated between today and the time it is actually received. Similarly, paying a dollar in the future is preferable to paying a dollar today because, by deferring payment, the dollar is available to earn interest.

Although the terms "discount rate" and "interest rate" are often used interchangeably, a discount rate is used to calculate a dollar's present value, while an interest rate is used to calculate a dollar's future value.

Present Value

Present value (PV) is the current value of cash that will be received or paid in the future. The present value is calculated using a discount rate.

Net Present Value

Net present value (NPV) is the present value of cash inflows, minus the present value of cash outflows, resulting from an investment. Knowing how to calculate the estimated NPV of an investment proposal is vital to understanding risk management. This calculation incorporates several elements:

- The amount of the investment at time zero.
- The number of years of the project's useful life.
- The estimated additional cash outflows, if any, that the project will require.
- The cash inflows that the project is expected to generate.
- The organization's required rate of return for the project—some organizations have a single required rate of return for all projects as a matter of strategy; however, it may be more accurate to consider the required rate of return relative to the project itself and its potential risk impact on the organization as a whole.
- The organization's depreciation method (for example, straight-line or accelerated) for capital projects.
- The organization's marginal tax rate on the project.

Time-Adjusted Period of Return

The time-adjusted period of return is the time required for the present value of the net cash flows (cash inflows minus cash outflows) generated from a project to equal the initial investment. That is, the time-adjusted period of return is the length of time required for the organization to recover its initial investment in present value terms. If the net cash flows are not discounted, the time required for them to equal the initial investment is known as the "payback period."

Case Facts

Indigo Company is considering the purchase of production equipment for $3,600,000. The equipment is expected to generate an annual income of $1,065,000 for its useful life of twelve years, but would require $73,000 in annual maintenance expenses. At the end of its useful life, the equipment would have no residual value. Indigo uses straight-line depreciation, has a marginal tax rate of 38 percent, and requires a 16 percent return on this investment.

This section of the case uses a present value discount factor (PVDF) of 5.197, which is the factor for an annual flow of $1 for twelve years at 16 percent interest. (The notation used throughout this case for this factor is $PVDF_{16\%, 12y}$ = 5.197.)

This case analyzes traditional risk management exposures based on the downside of risk. It was not designed to address the upside of risk. An example of a potential upside not included in the calculation is that prior to the purchase of the equipment, its manufacturer increases its durability, extending the useful life of the equipment to fifteen years. As another example, a more enthusiastic consumer response produces greater revenues than expected.

Case Analysis Steps

The Indigo Company case study applies capital budgeting methods to the selection of risk management techniques through several steps:

1. Conduct an initial NPV analysis.
2. Account for the cost of losses related to the equipment.
3. Analyze loss control measures.
4. Analyze a property insurance proposal for the equipment.
5. Account for "risk" as the volatility of earnings.
6. Summarize the results and make recommendations.
7. Evaluate the time-adjusted period of return.

After each step, a decision is made to accept or reject the equipment purchase using NPV analysis.

Step 1: Conduct an Initial NPV Analysis

To determine whether to accept or reject the proposed investment in production equipment, Indigo should calculate the investment's NPV. The decision rule is: if the NPV is greater than zero, then conditionally accept the project, pending any nonfinancial considerations. This calculation incorporates several variables:

- I_0 is the amount of the investment at time zero.
- N is the number of years of the project's useful life.
- NCF_{BT} is the net differential cash flow before taxes.
- NCF_{AT} is the net differential cash flow after taxes.
- NPV is the present value of cash flows.

Indigo Company Case
Conduct an Initial NPV Analysis

Data

$I_0 = \$3{,}600{,}000$

$N = 12$

Annual depreciation $= I_0/N = \$3{,}600{,}000/12 = \$300{,}000$

Required rate of return $= 16\%$

$PVDF_{16\%,12y} = 5.197$

Net Cash Flow Before Tax – NCF_{BT} (annual)

Annual income	$1,065,000
Annual maintenance	($73,000)
NCF_{BT} (annual)	$992,000

Taxes (annual)

NCF_{BT} (annual)	$992,000
Annual depreciation	($300,000)
Taxable income	$692,000
Annual tax (38%)	$262,960

Net Cash Flow After Tax – NCF_{AT} (annual)

Annual tax	($262,960)
NCF_{AT} (annual)	$729,040

Net Present Value (NPV)

$NPV = (NCF_{AT}\,(\text{annual}) \times PVDF_{16\%,\,12y}) - I_0$

NCF_{AT} (annual)	$729,040
$PVDF_{16\%,12y}$	5.197
$PV(NCF_{AT})$	$3,788,821
I_0	($3,600,000)
NPV	$188,821 Positive NPV

The NPV is positive; therefore, Indigo should accept the investment for further consideration. Indigo should review the model and its underlying assumptions to determine whether they produce realistic results. Models often do not consider all possible scenarios, such as a downturn in the economy. Also, nonfinancial considerations, such as social responsibilities or other ethical obligations, should be taken into account before making a final decision. In addition, this analysis does not account for the cost of any accidental losses related to the equipment.

Step 2: Account for the Cost of Losses Related to the Equipment

If the production equipment is damaged by fire or another peril, it will have to be repaired or replaced, resulting in lost production. Based on previous loss history with similar equipment, Indigo's risk professional devises a probability distribution of annual losses. Note that the loss probability distribution goes up to $10,000,000—well above the $3,600,000 cost to replace the equipment—to account for indirect losses, such as a loss of income (cash inflows) that could result if the equipment were damaged. A $10,000,000 annual loss amount may well exceed Indigo's risk appetite.

Indigo Company Case
Account for the Cost of Losses Related to the Equipment

Expected Losses (annual)

Probability (P)	Loss (L)	Expected Value ($P \times L$)
0.740	$0	$0
0.110	$100,000	$11,000
0.080	$500,000	$40,000
0.065	$1,000,000	$65,000
0.004	$4,000,000	$16,000
0.001	$10,000,000	$10,000
1.000		$142,000 Annual expected losses - $\Sigma\,(P_i \times L_i)$

Net Cash Flow Before Tax – NCF_{BT} (annual)

Annual income	$1,065,000
Annual maintenance	($73,000)
Annual expected losses	($142,000)
NCF_{BT} (annual)	$850,000

Taxes (annual)

NCF_{BT} (annual)	$850,000
Annual depreciation	($300,000)
Taxable income	$550,000
Annual tax (38%)	$209,000

Net Cash Flow After Tax – NCF_{AT} (annual)

Annual tax	($209,000)
NCF_{AT} (annual)	$641,000

Net Present Value (NPV)

$$NPV = (NCF_{AT}\ (\text{annual})\ \times PVDF_{16\%,\ 12y}) - I_0$$

NCF_{AT} (annual)	$641,000
$PVDF_{16\%,12y}$	5.197
$PV(NCF_{AT})$	$3,331,277
I_0	($3,600,000)
NPV	($268,723) Negative NPV

Because the NPV is negative when the expected value of losses related to the equipment is taken into account, Indigo should not purchase the equipment if it wishes to reach its target rate of return for the project of 16 percent. Again, scenarios may occur in which the organization's social license to operate is positively affected by implementing the project, a circumstance that may, in the long run, produce greater value to the institution than the negative NPV over the time horizon of the project.

Step 3: Analyze Loss Control Measures

The Indigo risk management team designs a loss control program that would reduce the annual expected value of losses to the equipment from $142,000 to $23,000, but would require implementing several loss control measures at an annual cost of $30,000. The implementation of the loss control measures would improve Indigo's return on its investment.

Indigo Company Case
Analyze Loss Control Measures

Net Cash Flow Before Tax – NCF_{BT} (annual)

		Taxes (annual)	
Annual income	$1,065,000	NCF_{BT} (annual)	$939,000
Annual maintenance	($73,000)	Annual depreciation	($300,000)
Annual loss control	($30,000)	Taxable income	$639,000
Annual expected losses	($23,000)	Annual tax (38%)	$242,820
NCF_{BT} (annual)	$939,000		

Net Cash Flow After Tax – NCF_{AT} (annual)

Annual tax	($242,820)
NCF_{AT} (annual)	$696,180

Net Present Value (NPV)

$$NPV = (NCF_{AT} \text{ (annual)} \times PVDF_{16\%,\,12y}) - I_0$$

NCF_{AT} (annual)	$696,180
$PVDF_{16\%,\,12y}$	5.197
$PV(NCF_{AT})$	$3,618,047
I_0	($3,600,000)
NPV	$18,047	Positive *NPV*

As a result of implementing the loss control measures, the NPV is positive, and Indigo would obtain its desired rate of return of 16 percent. However, Indigo faces uncertainty because it is retaining direct and indirect losses that could far exceed the expected annual amount of $23,000, and could even exceed its risk appetite. However, the level of uncertainty (risk) is likely to be lower than it was before Indigo implemented the loss control measures.

Step 4: Analyze a Property Insurance Proposal for the Equipment

In order to avoid unpleasant surprises, such as a major loss related to the equipment, Indigo could choose to transfer the financial consequences of any equipment losses to an insurer. Based on a quoted annual premium of $48,000 for property insurance coverage, Indigo uses NPV analysis to determine whether the investment in the equipment would still be profitable. (Note that the insurance quote assumes that Indigo would employ the proposed control measures.)

Indigo Company Case
Analyze a Property Insurance Proposal for the Equipment

Net Cash Flow Before Tax — NCF_{BT} (annual)

Annual income	$1,065,000
Annual maintenance	($73,000)
Annual loss control	($30,000)
Annual premium	($48,000)
NCF_{BT} (annual)	$914,000

Taxes (annual)

NCF_{BT} (annual)	$914,000
Annual depreciation	($300,000)
Taxable income	$614,000
Annual tax (38%)	$233,320

Net Cash Flow After Tax — NCF_{AT} (annual)

Annual tax	($233,320)
NCF_{AT} (annual)	$680,680

Net Present Value (NPV)

$NPV = (NCF_{AT} \text{ (annual)} \times PVDF_{16\%, 12y}) - I_0$

NCF_{AT} (annual)	$680,680
$PVDF_{16\%, 12y}$	5.197
$PV(NCF_{AT})$	$3,537,494
I_0	($3,600,000)
NPV	($62,506) Negative NPV

Because the NPV is negative when the cost of insurance is taken into account, Indigo should not purchase the equipment if it wishes to reach its target return of 16 percent for the project.

A Change in Tax Policy?

Assume Indigo decides not to purchase the equipment after taking into account the cost of insurance. If the proposed investment is desirable for society at large, the government might consider a reduction in Indigo's tax rate to provide an incentive for it to make the investment. By how much would the tax rate have to be reduced to make it worthwhile for Indigo to make the investment and still obtain its desired return of 16 percent?

If Indigo is to obtain its desired return, the NCF_{AT} (annual) must be at least equal to I_0 divided by the present value discount factor at 16 percent, or $3,600,000/5.197 = $692,707. The income tax amount must be reduced by at least the difference between the current NCF_{AT} ($680,680) and the required NCF_{AT} ($692,707) or −$12,027, which represents less than 2 percent of the taxable income. At a tax rate of 36 percent, taxes are calculated as $614,000 (taxable income) $\times$ 0.36 = $221,040, and the NCF_{AT} is $692,960 ($\geq$ $692,707), resulting in a slightly positive NPV. Therefore, the government would have to reduce the tax rate from 38 percent to 36 percent for Indigo to achieve its goal of a 16 percent return.

When the economy is weak or public policy focus is on "green" solutions to loss control challenges, the potential implications of tax policy should not be ignored.

Step 5: Account for "Risk" as the Volatility of Earnings

Having reviewed the available options (other than a possible change in tax policy), Indigo's management is willing to sacrifice return in order to avoid any unpleasant surprises due to an uninsured major equipment loss. Management would be willing to sacrifice up to two percentage points of its return (accept a 14 percent return) in exchange for reducing the volatility of its earnings through the purchase of insurance. Should Indigo purchase the equipment given this lower rate of return requirement? (This section uses present value discount factors of 5.421 and 5.660, which are the factors for an annual flow of $1 for twelve years at 15 percent and 14 percent interest, respectively.)

The NPV at a 14 percent discount rate is calculated as follows:

Account for Risk as the Volatility of Earnings—14% Discount Rate

$$NPV = (NCF_{AT} \text{ (annual)} \times PVDF_{14\%, 12y}) - I_0$$

NCF_{AT} (annual)	$680,680
$PVDF_{14\%,12y}$	5.660
$PV(NCF_{AT})$	$3,852,649
I_0	($3,600,000)
NPV	$252,649 Positive NPV

Because the NPV is positive, the investment is acceptable (before nonfinancial considerations). Even at a 15 percent discount rate, the NPV would be positive:

Account for Risk as the Volatility of Earnings—15% Discount Rate

$$NPV = (NCF_{AT}(\text{annual}) \times PVDF_{15\%, 12y}) - I_0$$

NCF_{AT} (annual)	\$680,680
$PVDF_{15\%, 12y}$	5.421
$PV(NCF_{AT})$	\$3,689,966
I_0	(\$3,600,000)
NPV	\$89,966 Positive *NPV*

The best solution for Indigo appears to be to purchase the insurance and accept a 15 percent rate of return.

Organizations vary in their attitude toward risk. Indigo has a risk-avoiding attitude because it has made an informed decision to sacrifice return to avoid uninsured equipment losses. An organization that has a risk-seeking or risk-optimizing attitude might accept the uncertainty of uninsured losses and invest only in those projects for which it receives a rate of return high enough to compensate it for retaining the risk.

Step 6: Summarize the Results and Make Recommendations

Based on the previous calculations, the implementation of the loss control measures causes the NPV of the equipment purchase to be positive at a 16 percent rate of return; however, without equipment insurance, the amount of retained losses is uncertain and may exceed Indigo's risk appetite. At a 15 percent rate of return (a rate Indigo's management is prepared to accept) and taking into account the cost of insurance, the NPV is also positive, and Indigo would reduce the volatility of its earnings. These are the final recommendations:

- Purchase the production equipment.
- Implement the loss control measures.
- Purchase the property insurance.

It is important to consider the nonfinancial aspects of an investment as well, such as the value of saving a life or other ethical considerations. Also, the model and its underlying assumptions should be reviewed to determine whether they produce realistic results.

Step 7: Evaluate the Time-Adjusted Period of Return

When evaluating a potential investment, some organizations also consider the period needed to recover cash invested in a project. When cash inflows occur over a period of time, the evaluation of an investment should take into account the time value of money. To evaluate its time-adjusted period of return, Indigo must determine how long it will take for the present value of its cash inflows to equal its initial investment, assuming a 14 percent return rate (the lowest rate Indigo's management is prepared to accept). The present value discount factor of the investment is the initial investment (I_0) divided by the net cash flow after tax (NCF_{AT}), which for Indigo is $3,600,000 divided by $680,680, or 5.289. The present value discount factor at 14 percent of an annual flow of $1 is 5.216 for 10 years and 5.453 for 11 years. Indigo's present value discount factor is between the present value discount factors for 10 and 11 years. Therefore, Indigo's time-adjusted period of return is between 10 and 11 years.

The time-adjusted period of return provides a check on the previous calculations. In Indigo's case, having a time-adjusted period of return (at a 14 percent discount rate) of a little over ten years for a twelve-year investment is consistent with its positive NPV.

Indigo Company Case: Summary of Recommendations

Step:	Answer:
Conduct an initial NPV analysis	The NPV is positive; therefore, Indigo should accept the project for further consideration.
Account for the cost of losses related to the equipment	The NPV is negative. Indigo should not purchase the equipment if it wishes to reach its target of a minimum return of 16 percent.
Analyze loss control measures	Because of the implementation of the loss reduction (loss control) measures, the NPV is positive. Indigo could invest in this new equipment and obtain its desired 16 percent return. However, Indigo faces the uncertainty of retained losses.
Analyze a property insurance proposal for the equipment	The NPV is negative. Indigo should not purchase the equipment; it could not obtain the 16 percent return required if management insists the equipment be insured.
Account for "risk" as the volatility of earnings	The best solution may be for Indigo to accept a slightly lower rate of return (15 percent).
Summarize the results and make recommendations	• Purchase the equipment • Implement the loss control measures. • Purchase the property insurance.
Evaluate the time-adjusted period of return	At 14 percent, the time-adjusted period of return is between ten and eleven years.

LIMITATIONS OF CASH FLOW ANALYSIS IN DECISION MAKING

Cash flow analysis based on the net present value (NPV) concept and the time value of money concept is a useful tool for evaluating alternative investment proposals. However, this approach does have limitations:

- It must be an ongoing process because the amounts and timing of cash flows change over the useful life of an investment.
- It does not formally factor in the effect of uncertainty (risk) with respect to future cash flows, losses, discount rates, or time horizons.
- It focuses on maximizing economic value and disregards an organization's nonfinancial goals and other stakeholders' interests.

Understanding these limitations allows a risk professional to make, or propose to executives, better-informed decisions.

Changing Values

While some threats or opportunities related to an investment may be of relatively limited duration, many capital investment proposals involve projects that span a number of years. The amounts and timing of differential (incremental) annual after-tax net cash flows associated with an investment can change over its useful life. For example, the launch of a new product may initially generate increased revenues for an organization. However, over time, as competitors sell the same or similar products with more features or a lower price, sales will decline. At some point, the product may no longer be viable from a cash flow analysis perspective. The same may be true of the services offered by a not-for-profit organization. Consequently, to be useful and informative, cash flow analysis must be conducted on an ongoing basis. As the internal and external contexts of an organization change, its risk profile also changes, and the original assumptions as to the amount and timing of cash flows should be reviewed.

Uncertainty (Risk)

Another limitation of using cash flow analysis to make risk management decisions is that the process considers expected cash flows and does not formally take into account the uncertainty as to whether the cash flows will be higher or lower than expected. By taking uncertainty into account, the organization might be more conservative in its forecast of future cash flows or its choice of discount rate.

The degree of uncertainty faced by an organization is difficult to predict and can be influenced by factors such as these:

- Managers, employees, customers, suppliers, and other stakeholders may perceive the organization as assuming more risk than is justified. This perception could adversely affect the organization's net differential cash flows through stakeholder demands to compensate for the higher risk, such as employees demanding higher wages or customers demanding lower prices.

- The organization may incur higher than expected legal costs if large losses prevent it from meeting contractual obligations.
- The organization's cost of raising funds may increase. (Associated with this is the possible loss of valuable investment opportunities.)
- The organization's income taxes may be higher than expected due to adverse tax rulings.

One approach organizations sometimes use when the degree of uncertainty is difficult to predict is to assign a "price tag" to the uncertainty, called the cost of uncertainty. This value, which is subjective, can then be treated like any other cost or cash outflow in the cash flow analysis of an investment. Another approach using cash flow analysis is to increase the required rate of return so that it includes a "risk premium" to reflect the uncertainty associated with an investment.

Adjusting cash flow analysis to account for uncertainty makes the cost of uncertainty explicit and reflects various factors such as senior management's risk attitudes or the effect of unexpected large losses on net cash flows. Although it is highly subjective, this approach appeals to many organizations.

In some organizations, more complex methods are used to adjust for the uncertainty regarding future outcomes. Many organizations use computer simulations based on stress models to evaluate the probability of bankruptcy under extreme conditions.

Nonfinancial Goals

Another limitation of cash flow analysis is that it focuses primarily on maximizing an organization's economic value and does not consider an organization's nonfinancial goals. For example, one important nonfinancial goal is to ensure that an organization meets its legal obligations with respect to the standard of care owed to others; contracts into which it enters; and compliance with federal, state, and local laws and regulations. Social responsibility is another important goal for many organizations. This includes the organization's ethical conduct, environmental responsibility, cultural sensitivity, and philanthropic commitments that it makes to the community or society.

Risk professionals should consider an organization's nonfinancial goals when developing its risk management program. Cash flow analysis is not an effective method for evaluating nonfinancial goals and should, therefore, be supplemented with other evaluation and decision-making tools.

IMPORTANCE OF THE RISK-RETURN RELATIONSHIP

When deciding whether to make an investment, an organization should consider its associated risk (uncertainty) and expected return. Higher-risk investments should yield higher expected returns to compensate for the associated volatility.

Managers responsible for organizational planning should understand the risk-return relationship associated with the organization's investments, including the importance of weighing risk against expected return. The organization should set a target return for each investment and determine whether it is likely to meet it, exceed it, or fall short.

In most organizations, investment decisions that involve higher levels of risk are often made by senior managers or executives. Day-to-day decisions involving lower levels of risk are generally made by operational or business-level managers.

Risk Appetite

An organization should also be aware of and stay within its risk appetite. Every organization has an overall risk appetite that reflects its level of comfort with varying degrees of risk. An organization that is more willing than most other organizations to accept higher-risk investments to increase its potential returns is considered to be a risk taker (risk-seeking attitude). An organization that is conservative with regard to risk and even willing to pay to avoid risk is considered to be risk averse (risk-avoiding attitude).

An organization's risk appetite depends on several factors:

- Its risk attitude
- Its perception of risk
- Its total assets
- Its financial condition and strength
- Its mission and strategic goals

In addition, the risk appetite of an organization's stakeholders may affect its own risk appetite. These stakeholders can include shareholders (if the organization is a publicly held company), employees, suppliers, the board of directors, and others.

An organization's risk appetite is not static. It varies over time depending on factors such as changes in the organization's strategy, perception of risk, and risk attitude. In addition, if the organization's risk profile turns out to be higher or lower than expected based on the current strategy, the organization may modify its risk appetite so as to accommodate the risk inherent in the current strategy.

Senior management must clearly communicate its risk appetite to decision makers at all levels of the organization. This will help foster consistency in the level of risk the organization assumes for its initiatives.

Risk Appetite—An Example

The creator of a popular series of children's animated movies has decided to sell several toys depicting the characters from these films. It has completed the design specifications for the toys and is in the process of finding a company to manufacture them.

The first company under consideration, Company Y, is an established toy company whose largest product line is a series of dressable dolls marketed to both children and adults. This line includes not only the dolls, but an extensive assortment of outfits, accessories, and other related items, many of which have quickly become collectors' items. The company has been in business for over fifty years and has been extremely successful for much of that time. It does not make many changes to its product lines and carefully considers each new doll it sells. Company Y only introduces three new dolls a year, using a well-designed and structured advertising campaign.

The second company under consideration, Company X, has been in business for fifteen years and sells battery-powered action figures that it markets mostly to children and teens. Several computer-based accessories are available where the children can track the figure's progress and play electronic games based on the character. Company X has developed cutting-edge technology to support these accessories and has a reputation in the industry as an innovative leader.

From a risk appetite standpoint, Company Y is less of a risk taker than Company X and would probably be hesitant to become involved in this new venture. The proposed line of toys is not compatible with its current business model, and the investment required for the new venture might not yield sufficient returns. Based on its conservative nature, Company Y would most likely not be a good fit for the product.

This new product would, however, be a good match for Company X, which is more receptive to risk, based on its reputation for innovation. Because this company already has advanced technology in place and is producing action-type figures, it could more easily adapt its processes to this new product line. The returns that Company X could expect to receive from this new product would most probably be sufficient to support the investment required.

Risk-Return in Financial Decision Making

The risk-return relationship should be a key consideration when an organization makes financial decisions. When deciding whether to make an investment, an organization should consider the expected cash flows and their timing. If an investment's cash flows are expected to be realized over a brief time horizon, management may view the investment favorably because it entails low risk with regard to the realization of its cash flows. In order for an organization's management to make investments that entail a high degree of risk, it must be assured that a significant potential exists for high returns. Conversely, the organization and its management should be satisfied with a relatively low return on investments that entail a low degree of risk.

ERM envisions the risk-return relationship within the context of risk-taking optimization. If an organization takes few risks relative to its risk appetite, it will not have optimized its portfolio of risk and return. The opposite is also true. The efficiency of an organization's risk portfolio should be assessed by analyzing individual sources of risk contained within the portfolio.

PORTFOLIO SELECTION AND OPTIMIZING RISK TAKING

Rarely will a risk professional analyze a single source of risk independent of all the organization's other risk sources. Understanding how adding risk from a particular source affects the organization's overall risk profile is vital to making risk management decisions that add value to the organization. The risk professional should view all the organization's risk sources together as a portfolio with an overall level of risk (volatility) and expected return. Several elements must be evaluated:

- Expected return from each source of risk in the portfolio
- Risk (volatility) of the return from each source of risk in the portfolio
- Expected return of the portfolio
- Risk (volatility) of the portfolio's return
- The effect of adding individual sources of risk on the portfolio's performance

This approach helps an organization determine which sources of risk to integrate with or eliminate from its risk portfolio. It can be applied to risk arising from both financial and nonfinancial assets. In addition, it involves the use of various metrics, such as standard deviation, correlation, and covariance.

Modern Portfolio Theory (MPT)

When finance professionals make decisions regarding an investment, they employ a portfolio approach, commonly referred to as Modern Portfolio Theory (MPT). MPT is the concept that investors, through diversification, can optimize their overall risk and return by carefully considering how the risks and returns of the various available investments interact when constructing a portfolio.

A portfolio's risk and return can be plotted on a graph that shows it in relation to an "efficient frontier," which is a line representing the set of available investment portfolios for which risk and return are optimized. Each point on the efficient frontier represents the highest expected return for a given level of risk or, conversely, the lowest risk for a given expected return. The slope of the line shows the optimal risk/return tradeoff available to the organization.

Adding an investment (a risk source) to a portfolio that moves it closer to the efficient frontier improves the organization's mix of risk and return. Once the efficient frontier is reached, no new risk sources can make the portfolio more efficient. Portfolios that reach the efficient frontier are optimized because they provide the maximum expected return for a given level of portfolio risk and the minimum portfolio risk for a given expected return. A higher return may be generated by changing the mix of risk sources in the portfolio so as to take on more risk. An organization that moves its portfolio up to its level of risk appetite on the efficient frontier reaches its optimal target portfolio.

The efficient frontier is stable in the short term. Over the long term it may shift because of factors such as technological innovation or changes in the organization's internal and external contexts, consumer tastes, or social and cultural values.

Modern Portfolio Theory Assumptions

There are four assumptions in the modern portfolio theory, which is derived from the initial model published in 1951 by Nobel Prize winner Harry M. Markowitz. These assumptions, which are not met in the real world, can create limitations in the implementation of the theory:

- Risk is heterogeneous: the risk computed with the Markowitz model (standard deviation as a measure of risk) cannot distinguish between the variation around the expected value and the risk linked to a significant loss (a fat tail) and the need to go beyond the model, to neutralize the positive performances and/or to develop a multi criteria evaluation of risk.

- Performance is homogenous (discrimination of the main factors of performance).

- Stability of the correlation coefficient matrix: many statistical tests have demonstrated that the correlation coefficient may be questioned. This is the most crucial weakness of the Markowitz model.

- Stability of the optimization (or optimal solution): with a high number of securities, the stability is questionable, as a small variation may induce important variations in the optimal proportion of each security in the portfolio.

Despite these assumptions, the model is reasonably robust and is a practical tool for creating efficient portfolios.

Efficient Frontier of Risk/Return

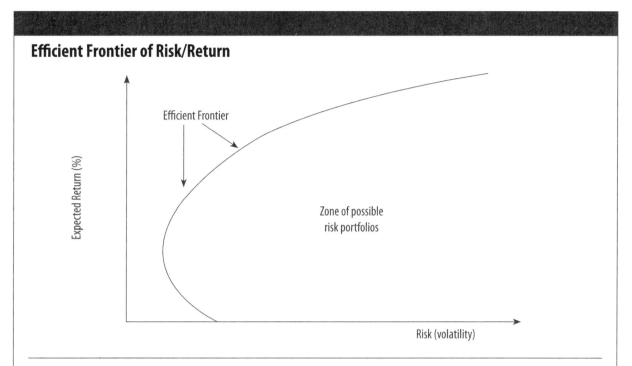

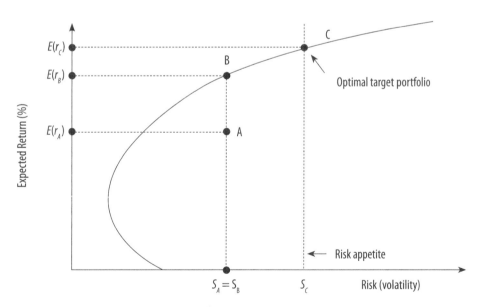

Assume an organization's portfolio today is at point A with a standard deviation of S_A (a measure of risk) and an expected return of $E(r_A)$. By changing the mix of risk sources in its portfolio, the organization could move up to point B on the efficient frontier. It retains the same portfolio risk ($S_A = S_B$) but the new portfolio's return of $E(r_B)$ is higher. The organization could also move to point C along the efficient frontier, whereby the portfolio risk is S_C (its risk appetite level) and the expected return is $E(r_C)$. Point C is the organization's optimal target portfolio. Note that as long as the organization is moving from point A closer to the efficient frontier, it is improving its mix of risk and return.

Applying the Modern Portfolio Theory to Nonfinancial Assets

MPT was originally developed for investments in financial assets, such as securities, but it can also be applied to investments in nonfinancial assets, such as real estate or new products. By taking into account all sources of risk his or her organization faces, a risk professional can construct an optimal risk portfolio.

Just as with financial risk sources (seen as stock investments), a risk professional should assess the risk and returns associated with nonfinancial risk sources and how the interactions among all of the organization's risk sources (both financial and nonfinancial) affect its overall risk profile. With this approach, the risk professional should select the combination of risk sources that moves the organization closest to its optimal target portfolio on its efficient frontier.

However, when MPT is used to optimize portfolios that contain nonfinancial assets, the limitations of using nonfinancial assets should be considered relative to financial assets:

- Financial assets are divisible into small units that allow for optimization. For example, a stock portfolio can be optimized by selecting individual stocks. If the portfolio is comprised of stocks of three companies, an optimal allocation might be 50 percent, 40 percent, and 10 percent, based on market value. Nonfinancial assets are not as easily divisible. For example, a single investment in real estate, software development, or product development may be difficult to divide into units. The indivisible nature of nonfinancial assets might limit the ability of an organization to develop an optimal solution.

- Financial assets can be purchased or sold in active markets in which the assets are continuously valued. For example, most stocks and bonds are traded daily. Nonfinancial assets are typically less liquid than financial assets. For example, months (or even longer) might pass before an organization is able to sell its factory. Or, if a new product development project is abandoned, the investment may have little or no salvage value.

- Many financial assets produce returns that can be approximated by a normal probability distribution (represented by a bell-shaped curve). That is, most financial assets do not produce fat-tail probability distributions. Nonfinancial assets are typically more likely than financial assets to have wide-ranging variations in returns and produce fat-tail probability distributions. For example, a biotech firm's investment in the development of a new drug has a relatively high probability of being either a total loss or a blockbuster success. Examples of normal and fat-tail distributions can be found in the "Probability Distributions" exhibit.

- Some metrics that are normally used for financial assets may not apply to nonfinancial assets, requiring extremely complex calculations to be performed.

Probability Distributions

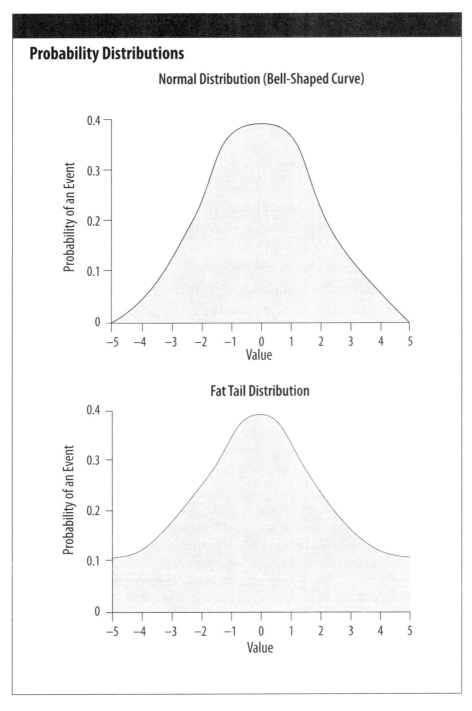

A major advantage of adding nonfinancial sources of risk to a portfolio is that they offer diversification because they are largely not correlated with financial risk sources. In order to precisely determine how adding a source of risk affects a portfolio, a risk professional can use the statistical measures of correlation and covariance.

Statistical Metrics—Correlation and Covariance

Correlation and covariance are key statistical metrics that are useful for selecting sources of risk for a portfolio. Both convey the direction of and strength of the association between two variables—that is, the extent to which the values of two variables change together. Correlation is a scaled version of covariance and is expressed as a number from –1 to +1, which is called the correlation coefficient.

Risk professionals use correlation and covariance measurements for several purposes, including:

- Identify and quantify relationships among various sources of risk
- Communicate throughout the organization the degree of uncertainty in a risk portfolio
- Prioritize investments in risk control
- Optimize financing for multiple sources of risk
- Evaluate risk management program effectiveness

Correlation and covariance can also be used to evaluate competitive risk. For example, assume surveys reveal a strong covariance between only two out of ten features in a new product's design and consumers' preferences. Using this information, the product is then redesigned to emphasize the features most important to consumers, improving its competitive position.

Correlation and covariance provide a common statistical language for describing the relationships among various sources of risk. The interaction among risk sources can have a significant impact on risk management decision making.

For example, consider ENR Consultants, a regional engineering consulting firm that operates a large fleet of autos. ENR incurs third-party liability costs stemming from at-fault auto accidents and accounts for them as a cost of doing business. Because its revenue is based on hourly consulting fees, ENR has a very low appetite for risk arising from employee injuries, particularly those that result in lost work time. ENR's risk manager noticed a significant increase in costs arising from third-party auto liabilities, but has been unable to convince senior management of the merits of a fleet safety program. The risk manager conducted a covariance and correlation analysis that showed a strong, positive relationship between two variables: third-party auto liability costs and employee injuries involving lost work time. Because these two sources of risk are strongly correlated, ENR's senior management agreed to invest in a fleet safety program, which significantly reduced ENR's risk arising from these two sources and improved its net income.

If two variables' values tend to move together, then their covariance (and correlation coefficient) is positive. For example, the covariance of the price of gasoline and the cost of operating a fleet of vehicles is usually positive. Conversely, if two variables' values tend to move in opposite directions, their covariance (and correlation coefficient) is negative. For example, the demand for hot chocolate will likely have a negative covariance with the demand for popsicles. Lastly, variables that are independent, or uncorrelated, will have a covariance (and correlation coefficient) of zero.

Correlation Coefficient Values

Correlation coefficient values range from perfectly negative (-1) to perfectly positive (+1):

−1 Perfectly negative correlation	If one variable's value goes up, the other variable's value goes down in a direct proportion. For example, if the demand for heating oil is perfectly negatively correlated with temperature, every time the temperature goes up, the demand for heating oil goes down by the same magnitude.
Between −1 and 0 Negative correlation	If one variable's value goes up, the other variable's value goes down, but less than with perfectly negative correlation. If the demand for heating oil is negatively correlated with temperature, every time the temperature goes up, the demand for heating oil goes down, but less than it would if there were perfectly negative correlation.
0 No correlation	There is no relationship between the variables. Variables with no correlation are independent. For example, the revenues of a restaurant in California and the likelihood of a tornado touching down in Kansas are not correlated. Because there is no relationship between the two, the restaurant sales and probability of a tornado in Kansas are independent variables.
Between 0 and +1 Positive correlation	If one variable goes up, the other goes up, but less than with perfectly positive correlation. For example, the probability of a fire at a warehouse increases if the warehouse next door is on fire. The probabilities of fire at the two warehouses are positively correlated, but less than they would be if there were perfectly positive correlation.
+1 Perfectly positive correlation	If one variable's value goes up, the other variable's value goes up in a direct proportion. For example, if an organization holds an investment portfolio that exactly mimics the S&P 500 index and the value of the S&P 500 index goes up by 2 percentage points, the value of the organization's investment portfolio also goes up by 2 percentage points.

When using correlation and covariance in risk probability analysis, it is important for risk professionals to alleviate any possible misperceptions about correlation, understand how correlation/covariance matrices are used, and be aware of the limitations of correlation and covariance analysis.

Common Misperceptions about Correlation

Correlation does not measure causality. Causality defines and measures cause and effect, that is, how one variable influences another. Correlation is purely a statistical relationship between the movements of two variables and is not a measure (or even an implication) of causality. Causality is often difficult to prove, and some situations call for the use of specialized tools, such as root-cause analysis.

Assume a student conducting research proposes there is a strong, positive correlation between an increase in the demand for popsicles and an increase in the demand for window air conditioners. Furthermore, the student states that an increase in the demand for popsicles *causes* an increase in the demand for window air conditioners. Both demand patterns are tied to an underlying condition: warm weather. However, the student misinterpreted the results and formed an illogical conclusion.

Common, underlying factors are frequent reasons for positive or negative correlations between two variables but do not indicate causality between the variables. Underlying factors can be obvious or, on occasion, difficult to identify. When analyzing correlations, risk professionals should confirm underlying factors because many risk control and financing applications are only effective when tied to an underlying factor.

As with any statistical measure, care must be used in interpreting the results of correlation analysis. Correlation results may be skewed by abnormal observations, inaccuracy of data, or an insufficient number of observations. Accordingly, a risk professional should not rely solely on correlation analysis.

Correlation/Covariance Matrices

When a risk professional considers how a source of risk interacts with other risk sources, correlation or covariance are typically reported in the form of a matrix, which shows the correlation or covariance for pairs of risk sources. A correlation matrix always has a value of "+1" along the diagonal, meaning that a risk source is always perfectly positively correlated with itself.

Correlation Matrix for the Return on Various Investments

	Symbol	FYY	TYY	$/Y	SIL	OIL
US Treasury Bill 5-Year Yield	FYY	1	0.907	−0.517	−0.344	−0.236
US Treasury Bill 10-Year Yield	TYY	0.907	1	−0.495	−0.286	−0.231
$/Yen	$/Y	−0.517	−0.495	1	0.409	0.273
Silver	SIL	−0.344	−0.286	0.409	1	0.39
Oil	OIL	−0.236	−0.231	0.273	0.39	1

Sources of risk that have a low positive correlation, no correlation, or a negative correlation with other risk sources in a portfolio are generally good risk sources to add to the portfolio (all factors that could influence the correlations being equal), and will tend to move the organization closer to its efficient frontier. This is because the portfolio will benefit from increased risk diversification, with the exposure to risk from individual risk sources reduced. Risk sources that have a high positive correlation with others in the portfolio, all else being equal, often will not move the organization closer to its efficient frontier because there is little or no risk diversification and the additional expected return may not be high enough to justify the additional risk to the portfolio.

Beyond Correlation and Covariance: Extreme Events and Copulas

While correlation and covariance are commonly used statistical measurements, both have significant limitations. Under some scenarios, neither is capable of fully describing the relationship between multiple variables. Two instances where this arises are extreme events and copulas. Extreme events are often referred to as "outliers" or "unusual observations" in statistics. The difference between normal distributions and long-tail distributions is that the latter focus more on extreme events. Copulas, which provide links between two statistical observations, express correlations among long-tailed probability distributions.

Outlier events, particularly those for which there is no historical data, may not be fully represented in a covariance matrix. For example, insurers selling workers compensation insurance in New York City did not have any historical data that indicated the scope of employee injuries resulting from the terrorist attacks of September 11, 2001.

At-Risk Metrics—Value at Risk (VaR) and Cash Flow at Risk (CFaR)

At-risk metrics, which are obtained from risk measures, are used to characterize the level of uncertainty (risk) present in a portfolio. Most at-risk metrics are used to measure the likelihood that the value of an asset will fall below a threshold level. A normal probability distribution is generally used to illustrate the potential variability in the value of an asset.

Two types of at-risk measures are value at risk (VaR) and cash flow at risk (CFaR). VaR is used primarily by financial firms, which depend on the value of financial investments. CFaR is used primarily by nonfinancial firms, which depend on the value of cash flows.

A major drawback of at-risk metrics is that they quantify the consequences of uncertainty in purely financial terms. They do not contemplate the influence of nonfinancial consequences, such as those arising from social responsibility or other ethical considerations.

Value at Risk (VaR)

VaR is used to measure the probability of an investment's value falling below a threshold level. It is defined as the threshold value expected to be exceeded over a certain time horizon with a certain probability. Often, the time horizon is very short and the probability is low. For example, a one-day, 5 percent VaR of $300,000 means there is a 5 percent probability of losing $300,000 or more over the next day.

VaR provides decision makers with three key benefits:

- The potential loss associated with a decision can be quantified.
- Complex positions are expressed as a single figure.
- Loss is expressed in monetary terms that are easily understood.

However, VaR is limited in that it does not accurately measure the extent to which a loss might exceed the VaR threshold.

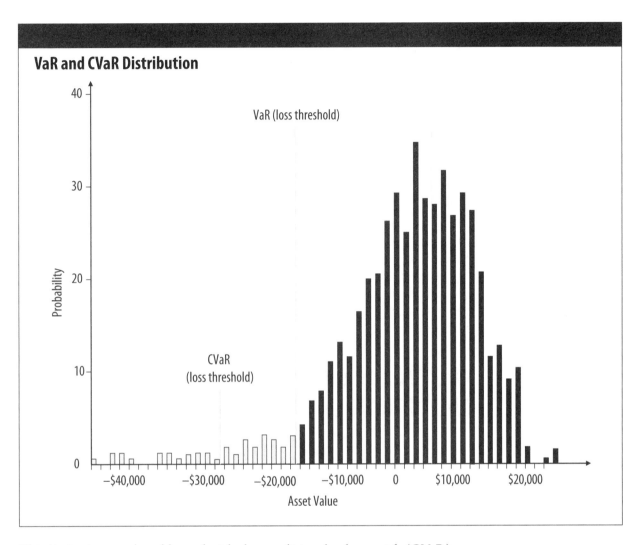

VaR and CVaR Distribution

VaR (loss threshold)

CVaR
(loss threshold)

Probability

Asset Value

This limitation can be addressed with the conditional value at risk (CVaR) metric. CVaR provides the same benefits as VaR but takes into account the extremely large losses that may occur, usually with very low probabilities, in the tail of a value distribution. CVaR is defined as a model to determine the likelihood of a loss given that the loss is greater than or equal to the VaR value.

Initially developed for the banking and finance industries, VaR and CVaR have been used as risk models by other industries such as the agricultural industry, which uses it for decisions regarding crop selection. It has also been used by utilities in deregulated markets to determine plant capacities. For an example of a VaR and CVaR distribution, see the "VaR and CVaR Distribution" exhibit.

Cash Flow at Risk (CFaR)

CFaR is analogous to VaR, but it uses as inputs account values taken from the income statement and the statement of cash flows instead of asset values from the balance sheet. CFaR assumes that cash flows are a random variable based on a normal probability distribution and measures whether cash flows will fall below a given threshold defined by the organization. It is therefore primarily concerned with liquidity risk.

The benefits and limitations of VaR also apply to CFaR. However, CFaR has the added benefit of measuring whether a business generates sufficient liquidity to survive as a going concern.

Extreme Events and Stress Scenarios

At-risk metrics are based on normal probability distributions and, therefore, do not accurately measure extreme loss scenarios. Therefore, a decision maker using at-risk metrics may not anticipate catastrophic scenarios. Consequently, it is essential to complement at-risk measures with stress scenarios that take into account extreme events. Capturing the risk of extreme events is precisely why Basel II for banks and, in the European Union, Solvency II for insurance companies, assess compliance using specific stress tests designed for that purpose.

Cost of debt
The rate of return required to compensate a company's debt holders for the use of their capital.

Cost of equity
The rate of return required to compensate a company's common shareholders for the use of their capital.

Weighted average cost of capital (WACC)
The average of the cost of equity and the cost of debt calculated according to the proportion that each represents of the whole invested capital.

Tax shield
The amount of income taxes saved because of the deductibility of interest expense.

POLYTECH COMPANY CASE—COST OF CAPITAL AND OPTIMAL CAPITAL ALLOCATION

Choosing the optimal financing strategy for a capital investment improves the chances that it will be profitable. To determine how to structure the financing (debt versus equity) for a capital investment, a risk professional should understand these concepts:

- Cost of debt
- Cost of equity
- Optimal capital structure
- Weighted average cost of capital (WACC)
- Financial leverage
- Tax shield
- Bankruptcy costs

Case Facts

Polytech, a publicly traded company, is considering the construction of a plant to manufacture a new product. It estimates that the plant would cost $30 million to build. Polytech's current capital structure consists of $10 million in debt and $100 million in equity (with market values of $10 million and $100 million, respectively).

Case Facts

Other case facts include these:

- Polytech's tax rate = 40%
- The risk-free rate of return (r_f) = 4%

For Polytech's debt:

- Polytech's current credit spread (risk premium) = 2.10 %

For Polytech's equity:

- The expected market return (r_m) = 10%
- The market risk premium (r_m-r_f) = 6%
- Polytech's current beta (β) = 1.20
- Polytech's last annual dividend (d) = $1.40
- Polytech's share price (P) = $35.00
- Polytech's annual dividend growth rate (g) = 5%

Polytech's finance department determines that there are four options for financing the $30 million capital investment in the plant:

	Option 1	Option 2	Option 3	Option 4
Debt	$0	$13,500,000	$22,500,000	$30,000,000
Equity	$30,000,000	$16,500,000	$7,500,000	$0

Which financing option presents Polytech with the optimal capital structure (balance between debt and equity) for this investment and why?

Case Analysis Steps

To determine Polytech's optimal capital structure, these steps may be followed:

1. Review the case facts and assumptions.
2. Understand the goals of Polytech's board of directors.
3. Determine Polytech's optimal capital structure by estimating its cost of debt and equity and by calculating its WACC for each of the four options.
4. Summarize the results.

Optimal Capital Structure—Organization-Specific Factors

An organization's optimal capital structure often depends on organization-specific factors. One such factor is its age, that is, its position in the life cycle. Start-ups and companies with strong growth usually have a low level of debt because of several factors:

- Fewer benefits
- Board members are often shareholders
- High bankruptcy costs
- Desire for financial flexibility
- Utilization of retained earnings or equity offerings for financing

An organization's debt level often increases as it matures because it tends to have higher free cash flows and more regular cash flows.

Optimal capital structure also may be determined by these factors:

- How well the organization is able to take advantage of the use of debt based on its income tax rate and degree of financial leverage
- An implied hierarchy in the financing due to the information asymmetry between board and shareholders. A board's preferences (in order) often are internal financing, issuing debt (borrowing from a bank or the capital market), and issuing equity.

Step 1: Review the Case Facts

Review the case facts previously presented. Note that some facts apply specifically to Polytech's debt and others to Polytech's equity.

Step 2: Understand the Goals of the Board of Directors

To determine an organization's optimal financing method, a risk professional must understand the financial goals of its board of directors. Polytech's board of directors has established these financial goals:

- Limit the use of debt to 40 percent or less of total capital to ensure that Polytech's capital structure remains similar to that of its competitors
- Maintain financial flexibility
- Ensure long-term survival
- Maintain a predictable source of funds
- Maintain the share price
- Maintain financial independence
- Maintain a high credit rating

Step 3: Determine the Optimal Capital Structure

There are five common methods of determining an organization's optimal capital structure (debt versus equity). The various methods often produce differing results.

Methods to Determine Optimal Capital Structure

There are five common methods of determining optimal capital structure:

- Maximize the difference between return on equity (ROE) and cost of equity

- Maximize the arbitrage between fiscal gains and bankruptcy costs

- Calculate the optimal debt to total assets ratio to keep the probability of bankruptcy below the level fixed by the board (the operational result approach)

- Compare with similar companies

- Minimize the cost of capital—choose the debt/equity (capital) ratio that minimizes the weighted average cost of capital (WACC)

Polytech chooses the minimum cost of capital method and must determine which of the four capital structure options results in the lowest WACC. To accomplish this, Polytech must determine its cost of both debt and equity for each option.

Estimate the Cost of Debt

The cost of debt consists of interest expense, which can be separated into two components—the risk-free rate of return (r_f) and the risk premium. The risk-free rate of return (r_f) is the market rate of return on a risk-free investment, such as US Treasury bills. The risk premium, also known as the "credit spread," is the amount of additional return an organization must pay investors in order for them to purchase the organization's debt. To estimate the cost of debt, the credit spread is added to the risk-free rate of return (r_f) and the sum is multiplied by one minus the tax rate (representing a "tax shield" because interest payments are generally tax deductible):

$$\text{Cost of debt } K_D = (\text{risk-free rate of return } r_f + \text{credit spread}) \times (1 - \text{tax rate})$$

The weight of the debt in an organization's capital structure (W_D) is equal to $D/(D + E)$, where D is the amount of the organization's outstanding debt, and E is the amount of its outstanding equity. As the weight of debt (W_D) increases, the probability of bankruptcy for the organization also increases. As its probability of bankruptcy increases, an organization's credit rating decreases, increasing its credit spread (risk premium) and cost of debt. Therefore, the cost of debt (K_D) increases as the weight of debt (W_D) in an organization's capital structure increases.

Polytech's risk-free rate of return (r_f) is 4 percent, its credit spread ranges from 2.00 percent to 5.70 percent, and its cost of debt (K_D) ranges from 3.60 to 5.82 percent, depending on the option considered.

Polytech's Weight of Debt (W_D) and Estimated Cost of Debt (K_D)

	Current	Option 1	Option 2	Option 3	Option 4
Debt (D)	$10,000,000	$10,000,000	$23,500,000	$32,500,000	$40,000,000
Equity (E)	$100,000,000	$130,000,000	$116,500,000	$107,500,000	$100,000,000
$W_D = D/(D+E)$	9.09%	7.14%	16.79%	23.21%	28.57%
Tax rate (t)	40.00%	40.00%	40.00%	40.00%	40.00%
Risk-free rate (r_f)	4.00%	4.00%	4.00%	4.00%	4.00%
Credit spread	2.10%	2.00%	2.80%	3.90%	5.70%
$KD = (r_f + \text{credit spread}) \times (1-t)$	3.66%	3.60%	4.08%	4.74%	5.82%

One might conclude that because the cost of debt rises with its use, minimizing the use of debt would be a rational decision for an organization. However, an organization's cost of debt needs to be considered in conjunction with its cost of equity.

Financial Leverage

Advantages of using debt

One advantage of using debt is its associated financial gain because interest payments generally are deductible. This manifests in two ways:

- Cost of the debt $= K_d \times (1-t)$, where K_d is the nominal rate and t is the corporate income tax rate. This implies that the higher the corporate income tax rate, the higher the value of using debt.

- The present value of the tax gains due to the deductibility of interest payments on debt, assuming that transactional costs are negligible.

Another advantage of using debt is that it provides discipline for choosing capital investments:

- Debt constitutes an implicit mechanism of discipline, especially when an organization generates rich free cash flows that otherwise could drive the board to a nonoptimal investment.

- Debt issuance obliges the board to undertake only capital investment proposals that generate enough cash inflows to cover themselves.

A third advantage of using debt is it deters hostile takeovers in the form of leveraged buyouts that may be attempted by corporate raiders.

Disadvantages of using debt

One of the disadvantages of using debt is the associated bankruptcy costs. The probability of bankruptcy is the probability that free cash flows will be insufficient to cover payment of interest on the debt. The probability of bankruptcy increases with the level of debt and depends on several factors:

- How much of the cash flow is needed to cover the payment of interest on the debt

- Variance of free cash flows

Two kinds of costs constitute the "perceived" bankruptcy cost—direct and indirect. Direct costs are legal and administrative costs. Indirect costs include these:

- Loss of clients who perceive financial difficulties

- Pressures on payment requirements from suppliers

- Difficulties to raise external cash to finance profitable projects

All else being equal, these statements generally are true:

- Companies that have uncertain cash flows are less likely to borrow.

- Adequate operational cash inflows allow an organization to borrow more.

- A government guarantee increases the use of debt.

Estimate the Cost of Equity

The cost of equity could be considered a projection or informed estimate of a reasonable rate of return on the shareholders' investment. It can be estimated by using one of several market-driven models, primarily the capital asset pricing model (CAPM) and the discounted cash flow (DCF) model.

The CAPM is a method of pricing securities based on the relationship between risk and return. Under the CAPM, to calculate the cost of equity (K_E), that is, the required rate of return on equity, use the formula:

$$K_E = r_f + \beta\,(r_m - r_f)$$

where r_f is the expected rate of return on a risk-free investment; β is the beta, a measurement of the relative risk of a specific share compared to the market as a whole; and r_m is the expected rate of return on the market as a whole over the period being analyzed.

The market risk premium for equity is calculated as $r_m - r_f$. Polytech's expected market rate of return (r_m) is 10 percent, its risk-free rate of return (r_f) is 4 percent, and its market risk premium ($r_m - r_f$) is 6 percent.

The CAPM takes into account the fact that the return demanded by investors (the required return) increases with the use of debt. As the weight of debt W_D increases, the beta (β) increases and, as a result, the cost of equity increases.

The DCF model can also be used to estimate Polytech's required rate of return on equity. It assumes that the required rate of return is a function of the present value of future cash flows from dividends in perpetuity. The dividends are assumed to grow at a constant rate. To calculate cost of equity (K_E) under the DCF method, use the formula:

$$K_E = (d/P) \times (1+g) + g$$

where d is the last annual dividend, P is the current share price, and g is the expected annual dividend growth rate in perpetuity. The last annual dividend (d) must be multiplied by a factor ($1+g$) to reflect the dividend growth rate for the current year.

By averaging the results of the two models, Polytech's estimated cost of equity (K_E) varies from 10.17 to 11.07 percent.

Polytech's Estimated Cost of Equity (K_E)

	Formula	Current	Option 1	Option 2	Option 3	Option 4
Beta		1.20	1.19	1.24	1.34	1.49
CAPM	$K_E = r_f + \beta\,(r_m - r_f)$	11.20%	11.14%	11.44%	12.04%	12.94%
DCF	$K_E = (d/P) \times (1+g) + g$	9.20%	9.20%	9.20%	9.20%	9.20%
Average (CAPM; DCF)		10.20%	10.17%	10.32%	10.62%	11.07%

Calculate the Weighted Average Cost of Capital (WACC)

Polytech's WACC is calculated based on its estimated cost of debt (K_D), its estimated cost of equity (K_E), and the weights of its debt and equity (W_D and W_E) :

$$\text{WACC} = (W_D \times K_D) + (W_E \times K_E)$$

WACC is calculated by applying the WACC formula to the value of the each of the components for each option.

Polytech's Weighted Average Cost of Capital (WACC)

	Current	Option 1	Option 2	Option 3	Option 4
W_D	9.09%	7.14%	16.79%	23.21%	28.57%
W_E	90.91%	92.86%	83.21%	76.79%	71.43%
K_D	3.66%	3.60%	4.08%	4.74%	5.82%
K_E	10.20%	10.17%	10.32%	10.62%	11.07%
$\text{WACC} = (W_D \times K_D) + (W_E \times K_E)$	9.61%	9.70%	9.27%	9.26%	9.57%

The optimal choice is the debt and equity mix that minimizes Polytech's WACC. On this basis, Polytech should choose Option 3, with Option 2 a close second. Note that the WACC amounts are estimates based on assumptions that may or may not be accurate. As a result, the fact that the WACC for Option 3 is slightly below that for Option 2 may have no significance in terms of choosing one over the other.

Step 4: Summarize the Results

Polytech, a publicly traded company, is considering a capital investment of $30 million to build a new plant. Its finance department has determined that Polytech has four options for financing the investment, each with a different amount of debt and equity. Of the five common methods for determining an organization's optimal capital structure (debt versus equity), Polytech chooses the minimum cost of capital method and must determine which of the four options results in the lowest weighted average cost of capital (WACC). Polytech estimates its cost of debt (K_D), which increases with the weight of debt (W_D) in its capital structure due to the increasing chance of bankruptcy. Polytech also estimates its cost of equity (K_E) using both the capital asset pricing model (CAPM) and the discounted cash flow (DCF) model and averaging the results. The CAPM takes into account the fact that the return demanded by equity investors increases with the use of debt. Option 3 produces the lowest WACC for Polytech followed closely by Option 2. Option 3 meets the goals of Polytech's board of directors by maintaining financial flexibility and limiting the use of debt to a weight of less than 40 percent of Polytech's total capital.

Polytech's decision should not be made solely based on its WACC because there are likely to be additional financial and strategic considerations. For example, taking on $22.5 million in debt (Option 3) may unexpectedly reduce Polytech's share price, making Option 1 or Option 2 more attractive.

SUMMARY

The NPV method for evaluating an investment uses cash flow analysis to estimate net cash flows, which are discounted to their present value using the organization's required rate of return. Investment proposals with a positive NPV may be conditionally accepted pending nonfinancial considerations. A proposal's NPV may change from positive to negative when the organization's cost of accidental losses and/or the earnings volatility they create is considered. Proposals with a negative NPV may become acceptable by applying one or more risk control or risk financing techniques, such as the purchase of insurance. Cash flow analysis does have limitations, which include possible weaknesses of the assumptions made and the difficulty of accurately estimating future cash flows.

The relationship between risk and return should be considered as part of an organization's strategic and financial decision making. In general, the higher the risk of an investment, the higher its expected return.

The portfolio approach, which uses Modern Portfolio Theory (MPT), is vital for optimizing an organization's risk and return. An organization should evaluate its financial and nonfinancial risk sources to determine its efficient frontier of risk and return. It should also consider its risk appetite in attempting to move to its optimal target portfolio. To determine which risk sources to include in a portfolio, risk professionals use a variety of statistical metrics, such as correlation, covariance, value at risk (VaR), and cash flow at risk (CFaR).

Organizations are often faced with decisions as to how to finance capital investments. Determining the optimal capital structure (debt versus equity) for financing an investment involves these activities:

- Understanding the financial goals of the board of directors
- Estimating the cost of debt
- Estimating the cost of equity
- Calculating the weighted average cost of capital (WACC)

Risk Treatment: Alternative Risk Transfer and Derivatives

Educational Objectives

After learning the content of this chapter and completing the corresponding course guide assignment, you should be able to:

▶ Evaluate the role of alternative risk transfer (ART) and derivatives in risk financing.

▶ Given a scenario, determine the rationale behind winding down a captive insurer.

Outline

Purpose and Functions of Derivatives and Alternative Risk Transfer (ART) In Risk Financing

Case Study: Winding Down a Captive Insurer

Summary

Risk Treatment: Alternative Risk Transfer and Derivatives

Organizations traditionally use insurance as a primary method of transferring the financing of risk to a third party. However, organizations can also take advantage of risk transfer techniques that do not involve insurance—alternative risk transfers (ART). As part of an enterprise-wide risk management (ERM) approach, organizations can optimize the effectiveness of their risk financing programs by combining risk retention techniques with ART techniques and traditional insurance solutions. They can also address a variety of risks and reduce the cost of their risk financing programs by using a combination of derivatives, both capital-based and insurance-based. The chapter concludes with a case study involving a hypothetical corporation that is considering winding down its captive insurer. Use of a captive insurer is one type of ART.

PURPOSE AND FUNCTIONS OF DERIVATIVES AND ALTERNATIVE RISK TRANSFER (ART) IN RISK FINANCING

An organization's risk manager should be familiar with the advantages and disadvantages of various forms of alternative risk transfer techniques and be able to evaluate the role that **derivatives** can play in its risk financing program.

Derivatives and alternative risk transfer (ART) techniques are playing an increasingly larger role in risk financing as alternatives to more traditional insurance-based risk financing options.

Key Features of Alternative Risk Transfer Techniques

ART uses risk financing techniques other than traditional insurance and reinsurance to provide protection against the organization's losses. Simply stated, ART is any risk financing technique that is an alternative to traditional insurance.

ART allows an organization to tailor solutions for its specific risk financing needs by financing loss exposures for which an insurance market has traditionally not been available. With ART, an organization can spread its financing over several years by tapping into capital markets that were once used only

Derivative
A financial instrument whose value is derived from the value of an underlying asset, which can be an index, an asset, yield on an asset, weather conditions, inflation, loans, bonds, an insurance risk, or other items.

to provide capital to insurers or reinsurers. The organization can then use its capital for its core business purposes rather than for insurance and, ultimately, may be able to realize a higher return on its investment or equity.

Major Benefits of ART

ART can offer an organization benefits that traditional insurance usually cannot offer:

- Diversification of its portfolio of risks over time
- Reduction of the cost of risk
- Additional underwriting capacity, profit, and investment income
- Direct access to reinsurers
- A stronger negotiating position with insurers because of the availability of alternatives to insurance
- Centralization of losses retained throughout an organization
- A smoothing out of losses and premium costs over time
- Greater flexibility and availability of insurance coverage for a more customized fit
- Greater transparency of coverage for stakeholders
- Obtain coverage pricing equity

Major Types of ART

Four major types of ART are used in risk financing:

- Derivatives
- Securitization of insurance risks
- Finite risk insurance plans
- Captive insurance companies

Another type of risk transfer that is not traditionally considered an alternative risk transfer—but still transfers all or part of the financial consequences of loss to another party—and that is not considered insurance is a hold-harmless agreement (also referred to as indemnity agreements). These agreements assign responsibility for losses arising out of a particular relationship or activity. One party to the agreement (the indemnitor) agrees to assume the liability of a second party (the indemnitee).

Counterparty risk
The risk that the other party to an agreement will default.

Regardless of which type of noninsurance alternative risk transfer is used, the transferor's protection is only as reliable as the transferee's ability and willingness to pay money when needed to restore the loss. This uncertainty over whether the other party will default on the agreement is referred to as **counterparty risk**. To reduce this uncertainty, the transferor may want to monitor the transferee's ability to pay this obligation if it were to become due.

The Role of Derivatives and ART in Risk Financing

ERM addresses all categories of risk. One method an ERM approach employs to address risks is to simultaneously use capital markets and insurance markets to reduce the cost of an organization's risk financing, such as through the use of derivatives. These instruments may be used to manage financial risks and the strategic risk of capital availability and can also fund losses.

Major Types of Risk Financing Derivatives

Two major types of derivatives are used in risk financing:

- Insurance derivatives
- Hedging

Insurance Derivatives

A derivative, in general, is a financial contract that derives its value from the value of another asset (such as a commodity), from the yields on another asset, or from the level of an index (such as the Standard & Poor's 500 stock index). An **insurance derivative** transfers its underlying underwriting risks to capital markets. It increases in value as specified insurable losses increase; therefore, the seller of the risk, who is the purchaser of the derivative, can use this gain to offset insurable losses. The purchaser of the derivative accepts underwriting risk and receives a commensurate return for doing so. The purchaser of a catastrophe derivative evaluates the likelihood that a particular catastrophic event, such as hurricane or earthquake, will occur within a specific period when pricing the derivative.

The value of an insurance derivative can be based on the level of insurable losses experienced by a single organization or on the level of an insurance industry index of insured losses. An example of the latter is a financial instrument whose value is determined by all insured hurricane losses that occur along the coast of a country in the third quarter of a particular year. If an insurer buys such a derivative and third-quarter hurricane losses, per a hurricane property loss index, exceed a predetermined target level of, for example, $100 million, the owner of the derivative could receive a cash payout of $10 million. This amount could be used to offset the insurer's claim payments to insureds who have incurred property losses from the same hurricanes.

Used originally because of the limited availability and affordability of certain types of reinsurance, insurance derivatives are becoming more prevalent as an alternative risk financing method for funding losses. Reinsurers also use insurance derivatives to hedge against high-risk perils such as earthquake and windstorm.

Insurance derivative
A financial contract whose value is based on the level of insurable losses that occur during a specific time period.

Derivatives can be traded in two ways: over-the-counter (OTC) or as exchange-traded derivatives (ETD). OTC derivatives are traded directly between two parties. ETDs are traded through an intermediary such as the Chicago Board of Trade (CBOT).

Two types of financial contracts that are based on the insurance derivative concept are swaps and insurance options.

A swap is an agreement between two parties to exchange payments. Insurers can spread their risks through swap arrangements. In such cases, the swap becomes an insurance derivative; the underlying asset is a portfolio of a specific class of insured risks for an individual insurer. For example, one insurer could exchange a portion of the cash flows (premium and losses) arising from its hurricane losses in a particular geographic area with a portion of the cash flows arising from another insurer's tornado losses in another geographic area.

An option is an agreement that gives its holder the right, but not the obligation, to buy (exercise a call option on) or sell (exercise a put option on) an asset at a specific price at a specified time. An insurance option derives its value from insurable losses—either an organization's actual insurable losses or an insurance industry index of losses. The value of an insurance option increases as the underlying insurable losses increase beyond the value of the strike price (the specific price at which the option holder can buy or sell the underlying asset). Therefore, an organization can use gains from an insurance option to offset its insurable losses. For example, an insurer can purchase an insurance option with a strike price of $50 million, which is based on the amount of covered fire losses in a restricted geographic area over a certain period of time. If the insurer's actual fire losses were $75 million, the option would likely be exercised.

Derivatives allow two parties to buy and sell the volatility associated with the value of underlying assets. Organizations can use them to mitigate losses. Additionally, because derivatives may have low transactions costs, are flexible in form and design, and are leveraged, they make excellent instruments for offsetting risk.

Hedging

Hedging
A financial transaction in which one asset is held to offset the risk associated with another asset.

Forward contract
A contract that obligates one party to buy and another party to sell a specific financial instrument or physical commodity at a specified future date and price.

An organization can use **hedging** to offset the volatility of assets to which it is naturally, voluntarily, or inevitably exposed. One type of hedge is a commodity hedge, of which these are some common examples:

- An airline may offset the volatility of jet fuel prices by entering a futures or **forward contract** to purchase a fixed quantity of jet fuel over a particular period for a predetermined price. If the market price for jet fuel increases over the term of the contract, the airline saves money (and increases its profits) by having purchased jet fuel below the prevailing price. If the price drops, the airline's risk is still reduced because it pays a known jet fuel cost.

- An insurance company may purchase lumber using a **futures contract** when a hurricane is anticipated, thereby offsetting (hedging) losses related to the rising price of the lumber in the storm's aftermath.

- If an organization wishes to hedge its interest rate risk (a financial risk) because of a planned divestiture, it may purchase a Treasury futures contract and secure a fixed future interest rate.

- Organizations that operate internationally may use derivatives to hedge their **foreign exchange rate risk**.

Securitization of Insurance Risks

Securitization of insurance risks is the process of creating a marketable investment security based on an insurance transaction's expected cash flows using a **special purpose vehicle (SPV)**. Any asset with cash flow can be securitized. With securitization, assets are combined into a pool and then split into shares and sold to investors.

Through the options contract market, these types of securities can be bought and sold as financial protection against natural catastrophes such as hurricanes or earthquakes. Insurance and reinsurance companies, investment banks, and unregulated funds actively engage in the trading of these types of securities. Investors find this allows them to participate only in the insurance portion, or loss volatility, of the risk without having to participate in the overall underwriting or investment risk of an insurance company. Investors do participate in a portion of the insurer's underwriting risk, but only to the extent covered by the investment security. The insurer is likely to either retain or reinsure the remaining underwriting risk. Further, investors usually do not participate in even a portion of the investment risk of the insurer.

One type of insurance securitization is a **catastrophe bond** (or cat bond). Catastrophe bonds were developed, in part, as a response to the limited availability and affordability of catastrophe reinsurance. They are typically structured to provide protection against events that occur infrequently (with probabilities of less than .01). This is because the issuers of the bonds want them to be triggered (and, consequently, priced) at a level commensurate with a highly infrequent event.

Balcony financing (or mezzanine financing) is a blending of debt and equity financing. The mezzanine lender does not require collateral and can offer the company the funds it needs for risk financing without having an active interest in the company. However, mezzanine lenders charge unusually high rates because the associated risk is so high. If the company is unable to repay the loan, the mezzanine lender can convert the loan to equity (ownership in the company). Consequently, the risk to the borrowing company is also high. This type of financing is typically used in leveraged buyouts to fill the gap between less expensive forms of financing and the purchase price. Real estate developers also use mezzanine loans to secure supplementary financing for their development projects.

Futures contract
An agreement to buy or sell a commodity or security at a future date at a price that is fixed at the time of the agreement.

Foreign exchange rate risk
The risk that a change in the relative value of a foreign currency as compared to the currency used for the entity's financial statements will adversely affect the business operations of the organization.

Special purpose vehicle (SPV)
A facility established for the purpose of purchasing income-producing assets from an organization, holding title to them and then using those assets to collateralize securities that will be sold to investors.

Catastrophe bond
A type of insurance-linked security that is specifically designed to transfer insurable catastrophe risk to investors.

Balcony financing
Debt capital financing that can be converted into equity by the lender as the loan goes into default (also known as mezzanine financing).

Finite Risk Insurance Plans

Finite risk insurance plan
A risk financing plan that transfers a limited (finite) amount of risk to an insurer.

Finite risk insurance plans transfer a limited (finite) amount of loss to an insurer for three to five—but sometimes as much as ten—years. A large percentage of the insured's premium is used to fund the insured's own losses. The plans usually include a profit-sharing arrangement between the insured and the insurer and are often characterized as hybrid plans because they combine the retention through self-insurance with the transfer of guaranteed-rate insurance. Finite risk solutions allow an organization to spread the cost of any large losses over time because aggregate limits apply for the entire duration of the insurance contract, not just one year at a time.

Margin
An amount paid to the insurer under a finite risk insurance plan to compensate it for each type of risk it incurs and for its administrative expenses.

The insurance contract in the finite risk insurance plan is often manuscript; that is, protection and insurance contract language are negotiated between the insurer and the insured. It is tailored to meet the insured's individual needs. The plan may not be canceled (except for breach of contract). In addition to the premium, the insured pays the insurer a **margin**.

The insured is allowed to commute the plan at a specified time. A commutation is an agreement to extinguish all liabilities between the parties to an insurance contract that usually involves payment from the insurer to the insured. The finite risk insurance plan can be written as insurance or reinsurance. When it is written as reinsurance, it can reinsure a captive insurer or a commercial insurer.

Finite risk insurance can be better understood if it is analyzed in terms of these various types of risk: investment risk, credit risk, and underwriting risk.

Investment risk is the risk that an insurer's investment income will be less than the insurer expects. Investment risk includes timing risk (that the insured's losses will be paid sooner or later than expected). Interest rate risk is the chance that interest rates will be below the expected rate during the term of the insurance contract. For example, an insurer's investment income will be lower than the insurer expects if losses are paid sooner than expected and/or interest rates are lower than expected.

Credit risk is the chance that an insurer will not collect premiums owed by its insured. For example, under some insurance plans, an insured pays a premium as the insurer pays losses. The insurer is contractually obligated to pay all covered losses under the insurance contract even when the insured fails to reimburse the insurer despite its contractual obligation to do so.

Underwriting risk is the chance that an insurer's losses and expenses will be greater than expected losses. For example, suppose an insurer receives $5 million in premiums for a finite risk plan and expects to earn $1 million in investment income on the deposit premium. Therefore, the insurer expects to have $6 million available to cover losses and expenses during the coverage term. Also suppose the limit of the finite risk insurance contract is $15 million, which is the maximum the insurer could be required to pay. Based on these values, the insurer is assuming $9 million of underwriting risk under the insurance contract.

Because the insurer assumes a carefully controlled, limited amount of risk, the underwriter of a finite risk insurance plan will usually agree to cover a broader range of exposures than it would cover under a traditional insurance plan. In addition to covering commonly insured property and liability exposures, it can be used for more difficult-to-insure exposures, such as product recall, warranties, environmental liability (including cleanup), and illiquid commodity price fluctuations.

Finite risk insurance plans can be either prospective or retroactive plans. A prospective plan is arranged to cover losses from events that have not yet occurred. A retroactive plan (sometimes called a retrospective plan) is arranged to cover losses from events that have already occurred. A loss portfolio transfer (LPT) is a type of retroactive plan that applies to an entire portfolio of losses. These losses usually have established reserves, but uncertainty exists as to the timing of the loss payments and the potential for further loss development. The self-insurer or captive insurance company can use an LPT to convert its unknown liabilities (retained losses) into a known quantity (premium).

For example, ABC Corp. is acquiring XYZ Co., but XYZ has retained product liability losses from prior years that ABC does not want to retain after the acquisition. ABC can transfer those losses (an unknown liability) to an insurance company for a premium (a known amount). This allows ABC to remove those losses from its books. However, ABC may have to pay an insurance company profit and administrative costs to absorb the losses. Also, the transaction may not be tax deductible to ABC if the IRS deems the transfer not to be a valid transfer of risk. (A valid transfer of risk is one in which a 10 percent chance exists that a 10 percent loss can occur.)

Captive Insurance (or Reinsurance) Companies

A captive insurance company is a subsidiary formed to finance the losses of its parent company (or companies) and affiliates. Usually, its primary purpose is to reduce the parent's cost of risk financing. The captive insurer's relationship with its parent is similar to that with insurers. The captive collects premiums, issues insurance contracts, and pays covered losses.

The "Relationship of a Captive to Its Parent(s) (Insured)" exhibit illustrates this relationship. The illustration indicates that the captive insurer may insure the parent for first- and third-party losses and obtain reinsurance directly from a reinsurer.

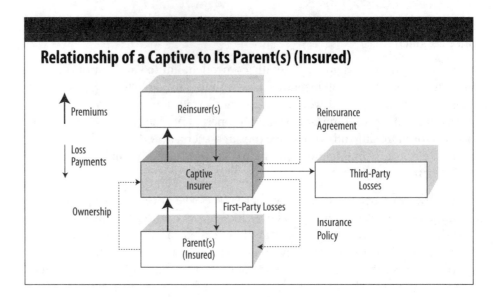

Relationship of a Captive to Its Parent(s) (Insured)

In the broadest sense, there are two types of captive insurance companies—single parent captives and group captives. Single parent captives are owned by one company and insure all or part of the loss exposures of the parent company. Group captives are owned by a group of companies, an association, or an insurance agency to insure the loss exposures of a group of insureds.

Group captives can be of several types:

- An association captive is sponsored by an association, such as a car dealers' association.

- An agency captive is owned by insurance agents or brokers to insure their clients rather than being owned by the insured organizations.

- A protected cell company (PCC) is a group captive in which each participant pays premiums and receives reimbursement for its losses from, as well as credit for, underwriting profits and investment income. With a PCC, each participant is assured that other participants will not be able to access its capital and surplus should the other participants become insolvent.

Two other types of captives are not technically group captives but perform similar functions:

- A rent-a-captive insures multiple companies that rent capital from a captive insurer, to which it pays a premium and receives reimbursement for its losses. A rent-a-captive also receives credit for underwriting profits and investment income.

- A risk retention group is formed under the requirements of the U.S. Liability Risk Retention Act of 1986 to provide liability coverage, except for personal insurance, employers' liability, and workers compensation.

In most states, regulations require a captive insurance company to use a **fronting company** for workers compensation or automobile liability insurance, among other types of insurance, if the captive is not licensed in the state.

Premiums are paid by the captive's parent to the fronting company, which issues an insurance contract. Insurance contracts are often referred to as policies. The fronting company deducts its fees and expenses and passes on the balance of the premium and the risk of loss to the captive insurer, which acts as a reinsurer of the fronting company. In some cases, the fronting company may retain a small quota share percentage of the loss. The captive insurer, in turn, can reinsure some of its risk to one or more reinsurers.

Captive insurers can decide not to use a fronting company and instead be a direct writer captive insurer that issues insurance contracts directly to its parent(s) and affiliates. For instance, a fronting company is not necessary in the U.S. for many types of property, marine, and liability coverages; therefore, a captive insurer can issue insurance contracts directly to its parent for these types of coverages. Instead of using a fronting company for coverages such as workers compensation, the captive can write a deductible reimbursement program with the parent. In this case, the parent company will have a high deductible program with a commercial insurance carrier and then insure the deductibles with the captive. One advantage to direct writing is that the parent organization can save the fees charged by the fronting company, which can range from 5 percent to 30 percent of the premium. This cost savings can make a direct writer captive insurance plan less expensive than commercial insurance and many other risk financing plans.

"The Operating a Captive as a Reinsurer" exhibit is similar to the "Relationship of a Captive to Its Parent(s) (Insured)" exhibit, except that it indicates how a fronting company is aligned with the captive insurer (which performs some of the same functions as a reinsurer of the fronting company), the parent(s), and third parties.

Fronting company
A licensed insurer that issues an insurance policy and reinsures the loss exposures back to a captive insurer owned by the insured organization.

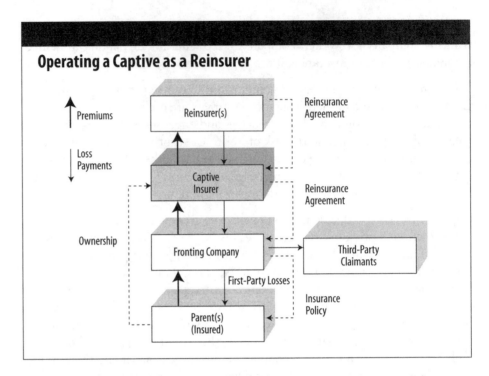

Operating a Captive as a Reinsurer

An organization may decide to form a captive insurance company if, for example, commercial insurers are not responsive to its availability, capacity, pricing, or pricing stability needs. An organization also may decide to form a captive insurance company if it is not deriving sufficient value from its traditional insurance transaction.

Sometimes captive insurance companies are formed to insure nontraditional loss exposures such as warranties, inventory shrinkage, patent infringement, or mortgage default. Captive insurance plans are also commonly used to cover losses that offer substantial cash flow advantages, such as those covered by workers compensation, general liability, and automobile liability insurance contracts. The captive can earn investment income on the cash flow generated by the loss reserves.

Advantages and Disadvantages of ART

Some types of ART transfer risks to the capital markets. Such transfers may be more cost-effective and require less time to implement than insurance risk bonds. They also can facilitate mergers and acquisitions with the use of loss portfolio transfers, thereby creating a competitive advantage and increased cash flow. ART also can be used to reduce the cost of risk, obtain insurance that is otherwise unobtainable, negotiate with insurers, and control losses. Hedging has been found to reduce inventory cost (and, as a consequence, earnings) volatility.

However, some ART solutions can be high-risk ventures that are complicated and difficult to understand. In addition, an organization must address certain financial accounting issues when considering ART. The Financial Accounting Standards Board (FASB) has issued statements and pronouncements that have limited opportunities to obtain favorable financial accounting treatment for some finite risk insurance plans. Financial Accounting Standards No. 113 (FAS 113) applies specifically to reinsurance, including finite risk reinsurance. The IRS also applies its principles to finite risk insurance.

Under FAS 113, a transaction must meet two conditions in order to qualify as reinsurance:

- The reinsurer must assume significant insurance risk under the reinsured portions of the underlying insurance contracts.
- It must be reasonably possible that the reinsurer may realize a significant loss from the transaction.[1]

If it is determined that a transaction meets the standards specified by FAS 113, then the annual premium is allowed as an expense on the insured's financial statements each year. If the transaction does not meet FAS 113's standards, then the insured must account for the premium payment as a deposit to fund its losses. The insurer cannot recognize the annual premium payments as an expense until the losses are incurred. Consequently, the company loses the tax advantage of deducting the premium as an expense and instead must wait until the loss has been paid to deduct the expense, which could be several years later.

CASE STUDY: WINDING DOWN A CAPTIVE INSURER

Organizations have been creating and using captive insurance companies for many years. Occasionally, a captive insurer must be closed as a result of a merger or an acquisition, an adverse IRS ruling on tax deductibility of premiums, or a relocation of the captive to another domicile that has more favorable regulations, or because the business reason for the captive no longer exists.

When a captive insurance company is no longer accomplishing the function it was created to perform, the parent company may decide to close it. This case study is based on the experience of a hypothetical company that is in the process of being acquired by another company. The company's chief financial officer (CFO) wants to close the captive to improve the strength of the company's balance sheet. From the information given in the case, the student is to evaluate the options and make a recommendation to the company's board of directors for further action.

Case Facts

The case facts are in two sets. The first set applies to the captive insurance company's owner—the Raponda Corporation (Raponda). The second set applies to the captive insurance company itself—Ageus Insurance Company, Limited (Ageus).

Raponda Corporation

Raponda, a U.S.-based, mid-sized company with international operations, manufactures cosmetics and personal hygiene products. The company's processes include transforming basic materials and mixing others, involving the use of solvents and other specialty chemicals. Raponda has been paying steadily increasing dividends to its shareholders.

Raponda's Exposures

After dealing with several serious occupational health claims, Raponda initiated a strenuous loss prevention program and as a result substantially reduced the frequency of employee injuries. Raponda's properties in the U.S. are mainly **highly protected risks (HPRs)**, but its foreign locations are not.

Because of the nature of its business, the company has a significant products liability exposure, which reinsurers are reluctant to cover. Consequently, there is a lack of capacity in the market. Raponda's chief risk officer believes the company needs $500 million of products liability coverage, but thus far he has been able to obtain only $300 million in coverage.

Raponda's International Operations

Raponda has two specialized manufacturing locations operating in Europe as well as several large sales hubs. International operations account for less than 25 percent of the sales but 40 percent of last year's profits.

Ageus Insurance Company

Raponda owns Ageus, a U.S.-owned captive that is domiciled offshore in Bermuda. The management of Ageus is provided by Raponda's main insurance broker.

Ageus' directors are a local Bermudian lawyer, a management company representative, Raponda's CRO, Raponda's assistant treasurer, and Raponda's corporate counsel representative. Audits are performed by the Bermuda office of Raponda's auditors.

Coverages Written by Ageus

Ageus writes insurance contracts directly for Raponda, its parent, covering property insurance and other lines. Ageus reinsures Frontage Insurance Company as the fronting company for general and products liability. Until recently, Ageus also used Frontage for reinsuring Raponda's U.S. workers compensation exposures. Last year, however, Raponda changed to a high deductible program with Frontage and purchased a deductible reimbursement insurance contract directly from its captive, Ageus.

Highly protected risk (HPR)
A large property whose construction meets high standards of risk mitigation and control characteristics and whose management maintains best practices loss control and risk mitigation techniques for the specific occupancy.

Of Ageus' premiums in the most recent year, 74 percent of gross written premiums are Raponda's business, and 26 percent are from unrelated business. Of Raponda premiums, 20 percent derive from property exposures, 50 percent from general and products liability exposures, and the remaining 30 percent from the company's workers compensation exposures.

Historically, Ageus purchased reinsurance protection, but as reinsurers began to raise rates while restricting coverage, Ageus sought other alternatives. Two years ago Ageus participated in a pool with other captives, in which they reinsured each others' portfolios. The results were initially satisfactory; however, they have recently begun to turn negative. Ageus also writes some commercial third-party insurance in hopes of improving its return on capital.

The "Raponda's Premium by Lines of Business" exhibit illustrates Raponda's income or premium by line of business.

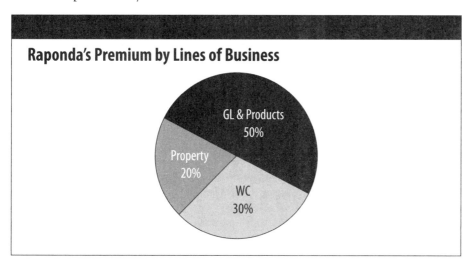

Raponda's Premium by Lines of Business

Case Analysis Tools and Information

For an accurate assessment of Raponda's financial and insurance situation, a spreadsheet that shows its revenues, profits, equity, insurance budget, and loss retention can provide essential information. This spreadsheet appears in the "Spreadsheet on Raponda's Financial and Insurance Program" exhibit (note that the exhibit's asterisks can refer to valuable information that should be used when interpreting the numbers in the spreadsheet).

The numbers from the spreadsheet can be graphed to indicate the trends in Raponda's revenues, profits, and equity over the last several years, as well as how the trends for each of three variables relate to those of the other variables.

Raponda's worldwide revenues have increased from $1 billion to $1.75 billion over the last five years, while profits have increased from $110 million to $145 million. Shareholder equity has increased from $1 billion to $1.5 billion. The jump in revenues and profits from 20X2 to 20X3 was due largely to Raponda's large international acquisition in 20X3.

A graph of these numbers can reveal trends in Raponda's insurance budget (what it charges its operating companies for insurance) over the last several years. The insurance budget is often trended by dividing it by the organization's revenues.

Raponda's insurance budget has decreased slightly as a percentage of revenues, from 0.95 percent to 0.80 percent. The decrease is probably due more to rising revenues than to a decrease in the insurance budget itself.

Spreadsheet on Raponda's Financial and Insurance Program

		20X1	20X2	20X3	20X4	20X5	
Corporate							
World-wide revenues		$ 1,000	$ 1,000	$ 1,500	$ 1,700	$ 1,750	*
Profits		$ 110	$ 100	$ 170	$ 200	$ 145	
Shareholder equity		$ 1,000	$ 1,050	$ 1,100	$ 1,200	$ 1,500	
	Millions of USD						
Insurance budget		$ 9.5	$ 8.5	$ 12.0	$ 14.5	$ 14.0	
As percentage of revenues		0.95%	0.85%	0.80%	0.85%	0.80%	
Risk retention history	Per loss	$ 1.0	$ 0.5	$ 1.5	$ 2.5	$ 5.0	**
	Annual aggregate	$ 5.0	$ 3.5	$ 7.5	$ 10.0	$ 15.0	***
Retention as percentage of profits (line 20 retention)		4.5%	3.5%	4.4%	5.0%	10.3%	

* Large acquisition in Europe in 20X3

** High deductible workers compensation instituted in 20X4

*** Note: Annual aggregate figures apply to Raponda's own business only.

20X5 is the last year of complete information.

The "Raponda Corporation Risk Retention History" exhibit illustrates how Raponda's level of retention has changed over the years. Retention should be viewed on both a per-loss and an annual aggregate basis.

Raponda's per-loss retention has increased from $1 million to $5 million over the last five years, while the annual aggregate has increased from $5 million to $15 million. The large increase in the annual aggregate retention in 20X4 was due to the implementation of the high deductible for workers compensation coverage. Annual aggregate applies to only Raponda's business and not to the third-party business that Ageus also writes.

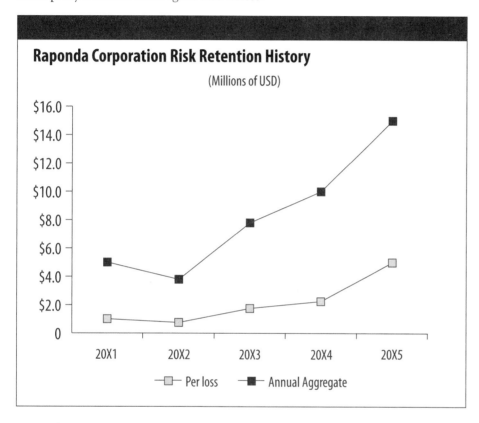

Raponda's retention as compared to profits has increased from 4.5 percent to 10.3 percent, as shown in the "Spreadsheet on Raponda's Financial and Insurance Program" exhibit.

The "Raponda Corporation Revenues, Profits, and Equity" and "Raponda Corporation Insurance Budget as Percentage of Revenues" exhibits illustrate the amounts and percentages depicted in the "Spreadsheet on Raponda's Financial and Insurance Program" exhibit.

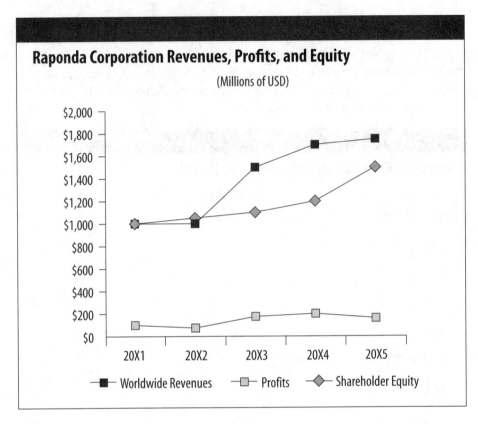

Ageus covers both U.S. and international exposures for Raponda. On the basis of gross premium written, its U.S. coverages were at a high of 90 percent of total in 20X1 and 20X2 and fell to 50 percent beginning in 20X4 and continuing into 20X5.

Ageus wrote $9.8 million of Raponda's insurance and another $3.5 million in third-party business. Ageus' reinsurance costs are $2.45 million. Expenses for the captive are $1.2 million, and other expenses (for fronting, U.S. federal excise tax, letters of credit [LOCs], onshore legal expenses, and other taxes) are $1.45 million.

Ageus started with initial capitalization of $2.5 million. It now has $15.5 million in retained earnings as well as loss reserves, including reserves for losses incurred but not reported (IBNR), of $45.0 million, making total assets $63.0 million. Of these assets, $50.0 million are managed by financial professionals. Ageus also made a loan to Raponda for $13.0 million. Ageus has guarantees to Frontage Insurance for $45.0 million.

Case Analysis Steps

Raponda's management recently issued a company-wide announcement that the company would be merging with a much larger company. The company's CFO wants to improve Raponda's balance sheet by extracting as much capital as possible from Ageus. In fact, the CFO prefers to close the captive and return all available capital to Raponda.

The chief risk officer and the captive managers maintain that the captive has no surplus capital because of the level of retentions and the expected hard insurance market. The chief risk officer also believes that the captive would be unable to close quickly because of the third-party commercial insurance it is currently writing, as illustrated in the "Ageus Coverage of Raponda's Business and Unrelated Business" exhibit.

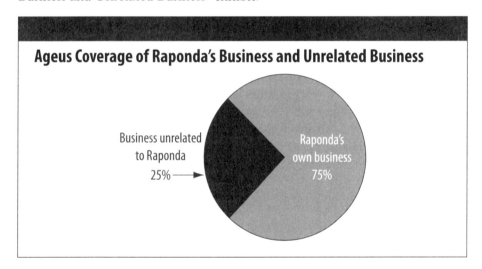

Ageus Coverage of Raponda's Business and Unrelated Business

Business unrelated to Raponda 25% →

Raponda's own business 75%

Also of concern to him, as well as to the insurance regulators in Bermuda, is how to handle the historical loss reserves that are still on Ageus' books, as well as any future claims. The Bermudian insurance regulators will refuse to allow the transfer of any money back to Raponda without first addressing these issues.

These steps provide a framework for analyzing the situation and determining the best course of action in relation to Ageus:

1. Analyze exposures
2. Develop a list of options and define possible outcomes of each
3. Determine impact on Raponda
4. Evaluate results and propose actions
5. Consider other issues
6. Make recommendations

Analyze Exposures

All available information about Ageus' exposures should be compiled and analyzed, and any additional information needed should be determined. If such information is not available, it may be necessary to make assumptions; if so, those assumptions should be clearly stated.

Develop a List of Options and Define Possible Outcomes of Each

With the exposure information gathered, a list of options can be developed and the outcomes of each option can be defined. Based on the facts of this case, here are some options:

The option preferred by Raponda's CFO is to close Ageus as quickly as possible and return the capital to the parent company. The CFO has cited low returns on capital as a reason for closing Ageus. However, if this option is chosen, the captive regulators in Bermuda require that Ageus' liabilities be totally extinguished before it is closed and that the capital be returned to Raponda. The regulators would be concerned about any future liabilities associated with the captive. All claims would have to be closed, and there could be no possibility that any future claims would be filed. Methods for extinguishing the liabilities must be addressed as part of this analysis. For example, as part of the process of closing down, it might be possible for Ageus to transfer its old losses to another insurance company—possibly even to the new owner's captive in Guernsey. If so, the methods for the transfer must be considered.

Another option would be to improve Ageus' situation by adding more third-party business and reducing expenses, thereby allowing the captive to remain active and separate from the new owners' risk financing program.

Yet another option would be to reduce Ageus' aggregate limits to previous levels and close down the captive's third-party insurance activities. Ageus would still be active and operating, but at a reduced level and capacity. This option would also free up capital for paying a dividend.

The final option introduced here is to "mothball" the captive, which is just short of closing it down. In this scenario, Ageus would become dormant and would no longer write new business. It would continue to handle the claims submitted on old insurance contracts unless it transferred the losses to another company. It would remain on Raponda's or the new owner's books as a captive and would probably continue to pay Bermuda's captive insurance regulatory fees. The advantage to this option would be that it would require less expense if Raponda or the new company decided to reactivate the captive at a future date.

Are there other, better options available to Raponda?

Determine the Impact of Each Option

Any decision regarding the closing of Ageus will have some impact on Raponda. The company's current situation (financial, marketing, strengths, weaknesses) should be considered, and the effect on those factors of implementing each option should be determined. Effects considered should include the more usual hazard risks, as well as financial, strategic, and operational risks. For each risk identified, a plan for addressing the risk should be stated.

Evaluate Results and Propose Actions

With the information compiled from the preceding steps, the pros and cons for each feasible option can be evaluated and compared with those of the other options as well as to the pros and cons of taking no action. This evaluation should result in the selection of one option for recommended action.

Consider Other Issues

Before a recommendation is made, it is important to step back and identify any other issues that have not been taken into account that could affect the outcome of the proposal, and what the effects would be. It should also be determined whether additional parties should be consulted and how their input could affect the outcome of the proposal.

As a proactive measure, the chief risk officer might find it advisable to make a list of the advantages and disadvantages of the two captives' domiciles, Bermuda and Guernsey. He could also investigate the possibility of moving one of the captives onshore, giving access to TRIA (terrorist coverage) for Raponda's property exposures. If the acquiring company is headquartered in a European country, it might benefit from moving one of the captives to Ireland, which offers tax advantages to such organizations.

The managers of Raponda's various business units are demanding a return of "their" premiums from the buildup of the retained earnings in Ageus before the merger is announced. Is this request feasible under any of the options? On what would it depend?

Steadfast Insurance Company was at one time the fronting insurance company for Ageus on workers compensation and products liability. There are still LOCs based on Steadfast's having held Ageus' assets. Steadfast is being liquidated, and there appears to be no way of easily getting through to anyone at the liquidator's office to get the LOCs released. How would it be possible to get these LOCs released?

Ageus currently uses Frontage Insurance Company as a fronting company for its general liability and products liability coverages. Frontage will not accept **commutation** of the loss reserves guaranteed by the captive because future products liability claims may arise under those fronted insurance contracts. What negotiating position could the CRO use to convince Frontage to commute?

Commutation
An agreement that specifies how to value, settle, and discharge all obligations between parties to a reinsurance agreement.

Loss portfolio transfer (LPT)
A type of retroactive plan that applies to an entire portfolio of losses.

Ageus could transfer its losses to another insurance company through a **loss portfolio transfer (LPT)**. An LPT would also alleviate Ageus' commutation problem with Frontage Insurance Company. Frontage would not have to commute the remaining losses, because they are being transferred to another insurance company through an LPT. The decision might be made to transfer the losses to the new owner's captive in Guernsey. If so, Ageus would probably have to hire an insurance consultant or attorney to get its LOCs released from Steadfast Insurance Company. Because the income associated with the captive had been consolidated back to the parent each year, there should be no U.S. federal income tax consequences associated with returning the remaining capital in Ageus back to Raponda.

Make Recommendations

The information generated by the previous steps should result in selection of a recommended option and the rationale to justify it.

Correct Answers for Raponda and Ageus

The options mentioned here are not the only viable options. Other options could be exercised if justified by the analysis. In addition, specific circumstances and organizational needs or goals may enter into the evaluation, making an alternative action a better option.

The first option is used if Raponda's CFO prevails. The decision would be to close Ageus and its operations. The company would have to get the permission of Bermuda's insurance regulators before closing the captive, and any capital would be returned to Raponda.

A second option is to keep Ageus open. In fact, the operations may be expanded to include a higher percentage of third-party business.

A third option would be to keep Ageus open but to close down the captive's third-party insurance activities and reduce its aggregate limits to previous levels.

A fourth option is to "mothball" Ageus, keeping it open but dormant on Raponda's books. No new business would be placed in the captive. Claims would either be allowed to run out or be transferred to another insurance company through an LPT. Regulatory fees would probably still be required by the Bermudian regulators.

SUMMARY

ART solutions have become a substitute for more traditional insurance-based risk financing options. Risk financing derivatives can be used in or with insurance derivatives, hedging, and securitization of insurance risks. Other risk transfer options such as finite risk insurance and captive insurance companies are also commonly used. Each of these types of ART has advantages and disadvantages that the risk manager should be aware of when choosing the appropriate risk financing technique.

A hypothetical case that examines the rationale behind winding down a captive insurer involves Raponda, a U.S.-based cosmetics and personal hygiene company. Raponda is merging with a larger company. It has a captive insurance company that the CFO wishes to close to improve Raponda's balance sheet before the merger. The CRO and managers of the captive do not believe that there is any capital available in the captive and want the captive to remain active. In essence, the options are to close the captive, keep the captive active but separate from the new company, keep the captive active at a reduced level, or to keep the captive open but inactive. A six-step process provides a framework for gathering and analyzing the information needed to determine the best course of action.

CHAPTER NOTE

1. Financial Accounting Standards Board, Statement of Financial Accounting Standards No. 113, "Accounting and Reporting for Reinsurance of Short-Duration and Long-Duration Contracts" (FASB, December 1992), p. 7. Available online at www.fasb.org/pdf/fas113.pdf, p. 6 (accessed January 27, 2006).

Monitor and Review: The Role of Governance and Compliance in ERM

Outline

Integrating Governance and Compliance With Enterprise Risk Management

Governance and Enterprise Risk Management

Compliance Issues in Enterprise Risk Management

Ethics and Social Responsibilities in Enterprise Risk Management

Summary

Educational Objectives

After learning the content of this chapter and completing the corresponding course guide assignment, you should be able to:

▸ Explain how integrating governance and compliance with risk management could enhance an organization's overall performance.

▸ Describe the role of good governance in enterprise risk management.

▸ Describe the compliance issues in enterprise-wide risk management.

▸ Describe an organization's ethical and social responsibilities to its stakeholders regarding risk.

Monitor and Review: The Role of Governance and Compliance in ERM

Chapters 11 and 12 discuss governance, compliance, and assurance, three concepts essential to the enterprise-wide risk management (ERM) process depicted on page 1.5.

1. Establish the internal and external contexts
2. Risk assessment—identification, analysis, and evaluation
3. Risk treatment—selecting and implementing appropriate risk management techniques
4. Monitor results and revise
5. Communicate and consult with all internal and external stakeholders

Corporate governance and compliance present organizational challenges that can best be met when the two disciplines are integrated with risk management. The resulting good governance helps the organization manage risk and achieve goals in a way that protects all stakeholder interests. An integrated approach also should include adherence to a sound ethical policy—including social responsibility issues—the cornerstone of ERM.

INTEGRATING GOVERNANCE AND COMPLIANCE WITH ENTERPRISE RISK MANAGEMENT

Organizations should use an integrated approach to addressing corporate responsibilities in the management of threats and opportunities while ensuring responsible corporate behavior and regulatory compliance. Such an approach drives an increase in the growth and overall performance of the organization.

This integration requires that the separate business disciplines of governance and compliance develop a common language, systems, and goals in conjunction with the risk management discipline. This constitutes a systematic approach to managing corporate responsibilities. Critical to this integration process is a clear understanding that the key role of ERM is to "lift the fog of future uncertainties" and to ensure that the organization appropriately allocates resources to achieving this goal.

Major institutions comprising many departments, disciplines, and locations in multiple regulatory jurisdictions may be under pressure to meet regulatory changes and adopt new standards while simultaneously improving performance and maintaining profitability. Under these circumstances, many organizations seek an integrated approach that addresses their corporate responsibilities for managing threats and opportunities while ensuring regulatory compliance and responsible corporate behavior throughout the organization. The chief risk officer should be prepared to demonstrate why risk management is the cornerstone of these efforts as part of making the case for ERM with board members and executives.

Integrating compliance and governance with risk management provides for a better understanding of threats and opportunities. It also allows the organization to exploit risks, enhance opportunities, and manage threats. The disciplines are not merged, but become highly interdependent. This interdependence permeates all business units or departments throughout the organization as a risk management culture becomes embedded within all processes, which enhances overall corporate performance while allowing the organization to operate within regulated environments. Risk management can be considered a key element in this process because it works to improve the development and execution of sound decision making that optimizes organizational risk taking. Because all departments have responsibility for the ERM process, governance and compliance should be integrated with and support risk management within the organization.

Risk management includes the processes and structure that allow for the identification, assessment, treatment, and management of potential threats and opportunities through its "monitor results and revise" step. This contributes to an organization's success by enabling it to anticipate changes in its internal and external contexts and react appropriately and rapidly.

Governance is the system by which an organization is directed and controlled. It establishes the structure; sets the policies, procedures, processes, and measurement standards; and determines the mission, values, and the culture of the organization. In this manner, rights and responsibilities are assigned throughout the organization.

The "establish internal and external contexts" and "communicate and consult" steps of the risk management process entail governance. Thus, governance is intertwined with the strategic goals of the organization.

Compliance is primarily concerned with adhering to applicable laws and regulations established by governmental entities, as well as following requirements the organization has developed through its own procedures, policies, and contracts. Compliance also involves documenting adherence to all applicable requirements throughout the organization.

Compliance does not constitute risk management, although the risks of noncompliance are myriad. If compliance constituted risk management, it would be the only requirement for an organization's social license to operate. An organization's social license to operate entails more than compliance with rules. Risk management, governance, and compliance contribute to an organization's social license to operate, because social license to operate involves obtaining and managing the approval from all stakeholders to continue the organization's endeavors and existence. Stakeholders include, but are not limited to, employees, regulators, customers, suppliers, shareholders, investors, the media, and the public in general. Approval of all stakeholders is a critical component that contributes to the overall success of the organization.

GOVERNANCE AND ENTERPRISE RISK MANAGEMENT

Governance determines an organization's direction and, therefore, defines the scope of potential risks to which it is exposed. Some risks stem directly from the governance framework and philosophy (structure, policies, practices, and their implementation), which might not support the organization in the pursuit of its goals. However, the governance framework can also serve as an effective risk management and compliance tool.

Each organization develops a framework to fit its purpose. Therefore, no two organizational frameworks are exactly alike. However, external factors such as regulation, market norms, and expectations must be considered for an organization's governance framework to be effective:

- Governance does not entail only regulation and legislation; it also involves doing what is right for the stakeholders.

- Governance is broader than boards and committees; it extends throughout both internal and external compliance controls and audits.

- Governance requires transparency of disclosure, effective communication, and proper measurement and accountability.

An organization's governance and compliance resources must be properly aligned and integrated with its risk management systems in order for it to effectively carry out and fulfill its long-term and short-term goals.

Good governance helps an organization manage risk by ensuring that its goals are achieved and its interests are served in ways that protect the interests of its stakeholders. Governance provides a framework within which an organization can manage certain types of risk. Without good governance, conflicts of interests could occur, stakeholder interests might not be adequately represented, and negative outcomes from management activities—whether inadvertent or intentional—could expose the organization to liability losses. Ideally, good governance integrates with enterprise risk management to manage uncertainties and risk.

These are some of the issues risk managers should consider regarding how an organization integrates its governance and its risk management process:

- Need for good governance
- Good governance in organizations
- Implementing governance plans

Need for Good Governance

Many medium-sized or large companies separate ownership (shareholders) from control (such as a board of directors, a president and an administrative body, or managers). In the United States, such companies are usually known as corporations or businesses that are incorporated (Inc.); in France, such a company is called an "SA" (Société Anonyme) or "SAS" (Société par Actions Simplifiées); in the United Kingdom, it is called a "PLC" (Public Limited Company). Because the vast majority of shareholders (the company's owners) are not actively involved in managing and controlling the company, good governance provides the mechanism to protect the interests of shareholders and other stakeholders.

Good governance plans benefit an organization by providing the social license to operate that links the organization to its stakeholders through social responsibility and allowing the organization to achieve its goals within acceptable risk parameters.

Benefits

Good governance plans offer many benefits to organizations in addition to compliance with legal and regulatory conditions. These include providing a business model of operations against which board of directors and management activities can be compared; ensuring that board of directors and shareholder goals are aligned; increasing shareholder value through the pursuit of business strategies that do not exceed the organization's appetite for risk; developing a culture of management accountability and corporate transparency; and developing an organizational reporting structure that clearly designates responsibilities for governance to the most practicable, effective parties.

For example, in order to adequately represent shareholder interests, a company may include on its board of directors industry experts who are independent of the company and only a limited number of directors who are the company's officers. The board is responsible for designing the overall governance process, which the organization's executives and managers then implement.

Social License to Operate

Good governance plans also address a holistic, focused perspective regarding an organization's higher, more altruistic reasons for existence and the role it plays in the community in which it operates. Additionally, an organization's governance practices should focus on whether the organization contributes in positive ways to its stakeholders, including those who hold environmental or community interests, in order to obtain and maintain its social license to operate. In effect, such an organization would seek to be considered a "good corporate citizen," operating in partnership with its stakeholders.

Governance goals related to an organization's purpose or social license to operate include fair treatment of employees; compliance with internal, industry, or legal guidelines; limited impact on the environment (pollution issues); support of the community—both locally and more broadly in support of global concerns such as sustainable design (the reduction in use of nonrenewable resources in the course of business operations); and socially responsible strategic decision making.

For example, to reduce its impact on the environment as well as its exposure to risk, a coal processing facility could install additional scrubbers in its manufacturing units to reduce emissions that lower air quality. In another example, a community would have a vested interest in a local chemical manufacturing plant's retaining employment levels while also acting in a socially responsible, environmentally safe manner.

Goals

The primary goal of governance is to build measurable value through a framework of ethical behavior, fairness, transparency, fiscal accountability, and social responsibility. Other goals of governance include helping organizations manage uncertainty in an ever-changing competitive environment, achieving strategic goals, and providing broad direction and oversight of management for the organization's stakeholders.

An organization's board of directors develops the governance strategies that are subsequently implemented by senior management. For example, a board can ensure ethical, fair, and transparent executive compensation practices by considering whether executive compensation is based on risky deal-making and whether it rewards poor financial or unethical performance. A proper executive compensation and performance scheme takes a long-term view of performance and results, versus an environment in which managers pursue new business for short-term financial gain without an enterprise-wide view of risk and how the business will adversely affect the organization.

Good Governance in Organizations

An organization's shareholders generally want managers to make risk management and other decisions that increase the value of their shares. In the public sector, improving the value proposition can include achieving service gains as well as budget containment. Good governance practices are one important way this goal can be achieved. The organization's chief executive officer (CEO), chairman of the board, or managing partner should lead the way in establishing the governance framework. This is so that the process is led from the top and no stakeholder is overlooked by the governance process—many corporate failures are as a result of those at the top not following the governance processes that they created. Stakeholders, in addition to shareholders, benefit from good governance, such as understandable, transparent corporate communications, and active representation of their interests. A good governance process clearly defines strategies, states who has ownership of the process, and indicates who it affects or influences.

Ownership of Governance

Those who are typically responsible for and accountable for managing the organization's risk are the organization's board of directors, senior executives, and auditors (both internal and external). While the CEO and board of directors have ownership of the governance process, the daily implementation of the process is the responsibility of senior executives and management. This ensures that day-to-day business decisions align with strategies at the corporate and operational levels.

For example, a board of directors will design governance strategies for the organization, such as identifying and understanding risks to the organization, designating the structure and composition of the board of directors, safeguarding the accuracy and integrity of financial reporting, and making timely and transparent disclosures regarding decision making.

Impact of Governance

After an organization's board has developed a framework for the type of governance strategies it desires, top management is responsible for crafting the details and communicating the strategies. In order for the organization to gain employees' and other stakeholders' support for good governance, the details of the governance strategies are developed in consultation with those who are affected by it.

For example, to create an enterprise-wide risk management process, senior management could consult with the organization's employees, investors, customers, suppliers, and creditors.

Implementing Governance Plans

Implementing good governance plans benefits from the endorsement of the organization's stakeholders at the corporate and operational levels. This helps to ensure that resistance to the new plan is minimized, that support is properly aligned, and that governance-related risks are appropriately managed.

Corporate

Because of the variation in business structures around the world, as well as in legal and regulatory conditions, the type of governance strategies an organization establishes at the corporate level will vary by region and according to the organization's requirements. However, most good corporate governance strategies capture issues relating to shareholder values, transparency, accountability, and planning and decision making.

For example, implementing a governance strategy related to transparency could involve establishing formal policies and procedures for publicly announcing decisions and ensuring the announcements are reviewed and approved by senior management, are issued in a timely fashion, include all relevant information, are factual, and clearly state the anticipated impact of the decision.

Operational

At the operational level, governance goals relate to the ways organizations design, implement, and maintain the specific elements of good governance practices. Implementation of good governance includes not only aligning an organization's operational structure to match its strategic goals, defining specific roles, and assigning responsibilities, but also establishing a working plan that can be modified and adapted according to shareholder and competitive requirements.

For example, a technology company based in the U.S. might purchase a business located overseas, intending to operate it as a wholly-owned subsidiary. However, employment practices in the region in which the acquired company is located might not only differ with the U.S. company's, but be in violation of U.S. labor law. The U.S. company will have to modify its governance plans applying to employee treatment in a way that integrates with the new environment while simultaneously serving the interests of its existing stakeholders.

COMPLIANCE ISSUES IN ENTERPRISE RISK MANAGEMENT

Companies are increasingly required to ensure that their risk management programs have adequately complied with various rules, regulations, standards, and codes of conduct.

Most organizations must comply with a variety of laws, regulations, reporting standards, and specific voluntary obligations (as a result of contracts or internal policies) in order to maintain their business operations. Depending on an organization's type of business structure, market environment, stakeholders, and risk management program, compliance issues can vary. To optimally recognize and respond to compliance issues, an organization should understand its own specific compliance environment and prioritize compliance based on the organization's goals and legal obligations.

When assessing the various compliance issues related to risk management, risk management professionals should familiarize themselves with a working definition of compliance, understand the drivers of compliance, and recognize that some required compliances could conflict.

Compliance Defined

Compliance is the process of adhering to—and the ability to provide evidence (including proper documentation) of adherence to—both compulsory requirements defined by laws and regulations and voluntary requirements resulting from selected standards, contractual obligations, and internal policies or procedures.

Compliance requirements can apply to an entire organization or to a part of an organization. Issues related to a failure to comply vary. For example, in the U.S., a publicly held company or a company filing for an initial public offering (IPO) is required to comply with the Sarbanes-Oxley Act of 2002 in areas of governance, financial management, and reporting. An organization's failure to comply with SOX can result in legal action and/ or sanctions from government regulators against the board of directors. Large fines may be levied against the company, and top executives may face imprisonment.

Additionally, an organization could voluntarily commit to having frequent, transparent communications with its key stakeholders as part of its overall governance strategy. For example, the organization could hold monthly stakeholder roundtable meetings to discuss key business decisions and their implications. Failure to hold such meetings would not expose the organization to legal action. However, loss of stakeholder confidence and damage to reputation could occur.

Drivers of Compliance

Drivers of compliance include risk appetite and risk tolerance as well as the levels of compliance to which a company aspires or adheres. The underlying reasons for the drivers of compliance vary from company to company based on company profile and business objectives.

Risk Appetite and Risk Tolerance

An organization's risk appetite is the amount of risk (including threats and opportunities) on a broad level that it is willing to assume to generate value. The amount of risk an organization assumes varies according to internal and external contexts, type of business, business intelligence systems, goals, and governance. For example, the manner in which the organization wishes to be viewed by its key stakeholders (such as employees, customers, and regulators) is a function of risk appetite. Thus, an emerging, entrepreneurial business might have a greater risk appetite in relation to its customers and prospects than would a long-established, mature company. Consider, however, that the impression the organization makes or wants to make on stakeholders in relationship to its risk appetite also presents to the world a vision of what the organization sees as its social license to operate. Compliance and social license to operate should always remain linked.

An organization's risk appetite and risk tolerance measures the degree of losses that management has determined to be acceptable. For example, an organization should be able to reasonably quantify its tolerance for losses or for positive and negative events. Thus, a risk tolerance of 10 percent customer turnover in a time of economic growth might be acceptable, whereas a 20 percent customer turnover in the same environment would not be tolerated. Management throughout the organization should understand the tradeoffs between the risks and rewards, the opportunities and threats faced. Leadership should be accountable for their risk-reward decision making.

Risk tolerance, social license to operate, and compliance have become inextricably linked. For example, in the past, manufacturers frequently considered associated levels of personal injury and even potential associated deaths acceptable when developing a product. Today, manufacturers must do more than simply comply with their risk tolerance objectives and compliance obligations, because product-related personal injuries and deaths can deflate a manufacturer's social license to operate and potentially damage its reputation and that of its stakeholders.

Level of Compliance

An organization tailors a level of compliance appropriate for its specific operations. For example, a publicly held multi-national manufacturer and distributor based in the U.S. would have to comply with Sarbanes-Oxley and would have the option of adopting the ISO 31000:2009 or the COSO framework for risk management. Additionally, based on the type of operations, an organization might opt to comply with corporate social responsibility and environmental standards.

Alternatively, an entrepreneurial sole proprietor or partnership might have very few mandatory internal or external compliance requirements. These types of businesses could voluntarily elect to comply with selected standards at a certain level, such as insurance requirements and health and safety standards.

Level of Compliance Examples

Compliance levels can be either voluntary or mandatory, internal or external.

Compliance	Internal	External	Voluntary	Mandatory
COSO	X	X	X	
SOX	X	X		X*
ISO 31000:2009	X	X	X	
BS31100	X	X	X	
AS/NZS 4360	X	X	X**	
Credit rating organizations	X	X	X	
Stock market regulators		X		X
Public sector governance		X		X
COMAH (Control of Major Accident Hazards)		X		X
Return on investment	X		X	
Corporate social responsibility	X		X	
Health and safety	X		X	
Environment	X		X*	X*
Insurer-required	X		X*	X*

* Dependent on location and type of business

** Mandatory in Australia and New Zealand

Conflicting Compliances

Because of the variety of organizations represented in the global marketplace, as well as the variation in rules, regulations, standards, and codes of conduct, conflict among compliances can occur. These conflicts may relate to the organization's type of business operation, geographic location, and organizational goals. To address these conflicts, risk managers must understand how compliances develop, recognize and resolve conflicts, and communicate responses to the conflicts to employees and other stakeholders.

How Compliances Develop

Contemporary business compliances have developed and evolved for a variety of reasons. Senior managers and boards of directors are increasingly being held to higher standards of accountability. The functional and operational business environment has become increasingly complex, requiring a framework of laws, regulations, rules, and standards to manage and govern them.

Additionally, because various stakeholders have heightened expectations of the organizations in which they are invested, they are making more demands on management and requiring increased transparency. Risk, whether a threat or an opportunity, must be assumed in order to return value to the organization, yet stakeholders typically associate risk with lack of compliance. Lastly, compliance programs help organizations address their business risks and the events or actions that present risk that are multiplying at an ever-accelerating rate. Compliance helps manage and pace that change.

Organizations must balance mandatory or voluntary compliances with risk appetite. For example, a journalist under pressure to meet a story deadline might write her article on a laptop computer in a cramped airplane seat. The journalist's employer could be in breach of health and safety rules applying to computer keyboard and screen use. If the journalist sustains an upper limb disorder as a result of working on the plane, the employer may incur a workers compensation claim. However, the journalist's working under such adverse conditions might be the only way for the employer to publish the story quickly. Thus, the employer's risk appetite has determined that getting the story completed is more critical than risking the health of the journalist.

Recognizing Conflicts

There are several different ways to recognize conflicts between an organization and its compliance requirements. Two frequently used ways to address conflicts are through either informal or formal approaches.

The informal approach, used by most organizations, involves waiting for conflicts to emerge. Once a conflict emerges and is identified, the organization addresses it. For example, a change in "greenhouse gases" legislation might require an industrial facility to comply with new emissions standards based on the level of its CO_2 emissions.

In contrast, organizations using the formal approach do not merely recognize conflicts when they occur; they recognize in advance conflicts that could occur. Organizations that use this approach first examine their goals. Both broad goals for the entire organization and goals for its component parts or operational units should be considered, with a particular focus on what the goals are designed to achieve. For example, a finance department executive should prepare in advance to comply with auditing and reporting standards.

Once goals and their related purposes are determined, senior management should drill down into the compliance environment of the goals and the compliance issues related to the activities needed to achieve those goals. Senior management ultimately can compile a list that is a "living" document of business activities cross-referenced with compliance issues.

Compliance issues are tracked to each aspect of the business, and a hierarchy of compliance issues is developed to include possible threats (possible sanctions) and opportunities (possible market expansion) applicable to each. This process is, in effect, a risk assessment of potential compliance conflicts. This is an example of items that could be listed in a compliance hierarchy:

- Corporate-wide compliance issues with serious sanctions
- Corporate-wide compliance issues with less serious sanctions
- Corporate-wide compliance issues with few or no sanctions
- Operational unit compliance issues with serious sanctions affecting the corporate level
- Operational unit compliance issues with moderate sanctions affecting the corporate level
- Operational unit compliance issues with serious sanctions but not affecting the corporate level
- Operational unit compliance issues not affecting the corporate level but with serious sanctions for operational management

The likelihood of the potential conflict and the impact of the conflict on the organization's goals can then be evaluated to provide a better perspective of how and when compliance conflicts might occur.

Resolving Conflicts

Once potential conflicts are recognized and the link is made between goals and compliance issues, an organization should work to resolve the conflicts. Several actions can be undertaken to resolve compliance conflicts:

- Terminate one or more of the activities that produce the conflict
- Tolerate the compliance conflict
- Treat the compliance conflict
- Transfer the activity that produces the conflict elsewhere; for example externalize the given activity (downstream to a subcontractor or a supplier or, occasionally, upstream to the customer)

If an organization decides to treat the compliance conflict, there are several options it can consider. Senior management could opt to stop the activities that contribute to the compliance conflict (a directive control), limit or eliminate the conflicts as they become apparent (a detective control), take action to reduce the impact or likelihood of the conflict when it occurs (a preventive control), or respond to the conflict after it occurs (a corrective control).

As with the compliance hierarchy items, these compliance conflict actions should be prioritized and linked with an action plan that includes activities, due dates, and role accountabilities.

Communicating the Responses

Once compliance conflicts have been recognized and an action plan devised to resolve them, the response to compliance issues must be clearly communicated to all parties involved in the action or event. Care should be taken when communicating the responses internally to ensure the appropriate individuals and units are involved, identify any areas of responsibility that might overlap (such as information technology and finance), and emphasize the level of importance associated with any action items so that staff understand that failure to meet compliance requirements can affect company operations and jobs.

The organization's key external stakeholders should also be involved in any compliance issue communication. Often, external stakeholders will have either responsibility or accountability for the outcome or the control, and there may be other parties who should be consulted and informed throughout the process. For example, a change in public health regulations could require a manufacturer to change the type of manufacturing components used and the companies that supply those component materials.

ETHICS AND SOCIAL RESPONSIBILITIES IN ENTERPRISE RISK MANAGEMENT

Organizations have ethical and social responsibilities to many internal and external stakeholders. These responsibilities go far beyond providing a return on shareholder investments. The risk management decision-making process must consider how all of an organization's stakeholders will be affected.

The ethical and social responsibilities an organization wishes to embrace or identify itself with must be built by organizational consensus in order to become part of its culture. To begin building this consensus, an organization should develop or review its **code of ethics**. This code must be more than a list of do's and don'ts, and should be dynamic, because today's business environment changes rapidly. The ethical culture of an organization is the basis for its direction regarding social responsibility and provides the foundation for its ERM. This ethical component is the linchpin of an organization's social license to operate and should be considered in an individual context and in the context of its relationship to ERM.

Code of ethics
The minimum standards of expected behavior for those to whom the code applies.

Social Responsibilities Toward Internal and External Stakeholders

Almost every decision an organization makes has consequences for its internal and external stakeholders. These stakeholders may include shareholders (in the case of for-profit companies) and customers, board members, and employees (in the case of both for-profit and not-for-profit organizations). Other examples of stakeholders include suppliers, contractors, government organizations, regulators, and the community.

Most organizational decisions have consequences beyond the organization's walls. Therefore, in making decisions, an organization must adopt a broad outlook that encompasses all stakeholders. This outlook is referred to as

Social responsibility
An organization's responsibility to its stakeholders and society to consider the consequences of its actions on all stakeholders and to protect the welfare of society overall.

social responsibility. For example, suppose an organization used a subcontractor on a construction project that performed substandard electrical work. Rather than pursue resolution with that subcontractor, the organization hires another contractor to repair the faulty work. The organization may believe it is the only party affected by this decision. However, others may be affected because the organization's shareholders may earn reduced dividends as a result of the faulty work, and the work could continue to pose a hazard to employees and members of the public. Before having decided not to work with the initial subcontractor, the organization might instead have considered several questions:

- Is this decision fair to all the stakeholders involved?
- Will the administrative and legal time spent to pursue the original contractor exceed the cost to correct the substandard work provided?
- Can other steps be taken to resolve this matter fairly for all stakeholders?

Social responsibilities go beyond adhering to laws and regulations; they can include decisions such as resisting employee layoffs that improve profits. Other social responsibilities involve issues such as outsourcing, pollution, and the level of corporate commitment to the local community.

Social Responsibilities Contrasted With Governance

While social responsibilities are based on organizational beliefs, governance is a set of parameters within which governments and organizations operate. Governance varies widely from organization to organization and certainly from nation to nation. Organizations are guided by governance, which is institutionalized and often tradition-bound. Such governance is both internal and external.

An example of internal governance that upholds tradition is an organization's adherence to a strict dress code, even when other organizations have relaxed their dress codes to "business casual." As another example, to enable a win-win relationship, the customer points out language in a proposed contract that could be detrimental to the supplier.

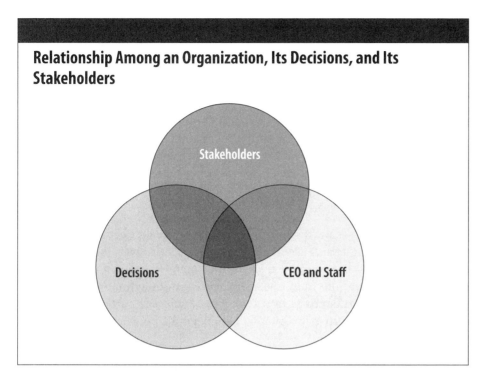

Relationship Among an Organization, Its Decisions, and Its Stakeholders

More stringent internal governance consists of an organization's audit committee, which provides standards related to risk management, financial controls, and change management.

Organizations are also subject to external governance—standards and rules set by governing bodies, regulators, and special interest organizations. Organizations may have different philosophies in their approach to compliance with external rules and regulations. Some organizations may attempt to meet minimum standards, while others may exceed requirements. Some organizations may ignore external standards entirely. For example, following a 2008 fatal crane collapse in New York City, the operation at the collapse site was cited by the New York Environmental Control Board for thirty-eight violations, thirty-six of which were classified as the most serious types of violations. Despite having received many complaints from the public about this specific worksite, government regulators did nothing, and in fact, the city's head crane inspector was later arrested on bribery charges.[1]

Risk managers may encounter ethical situations in their organizations that require them to make decisions that do not comply with best practices or that barely comply with local regulations. If this occurs in an organization that has a sound code of ethics, the organization has a foundation from which to rethink its policies or procedures. One of the most important roles of the risk manager is guiding the organization through such decisions.

Organizations may also choose to operate according to higher standards than those set by laws and regulations, even when such an approach is more costly, because to do so supports the culture of the organization. This approach sets a high ethical example for employees by indicating that their employer is prepared to go beyond government regulation to ensure the health and safety of its employees and members of the public. Organizations that base decisions on long-term sustainability as opposed to profit may benefit, as well, by using these decisions as marketing tools.

An example of corporate governance that incorporates social responsibility appeared in Berkshire Hathaway Chairman and Chief Executive Officer Warren Buffett's 2006 annual report to shareholders. Buffett's partner, Charles Munger, stated that it takes more energy to produce the fuel additive ethanol than it does to produce the power it delivers; therefore, the company would not be investing in ethanol.[2]

This type of decision is an example of the inherent conflict between short-term profits and long-term, sustainable growth. As global warming experts increasingly predict dire consequences for the planet if carbon emissions are not reduced, organizations must consider their environmental impact. Failure to do so could allow them to be targeted by outside interest groups—another source of external governance—that will apply public pressure for change.

Practical Considerations for Social and Ethical Responsibilities

Management develops and administers policy; operations put policy into action. There is extensive interplay between the two, however, because operationally, policy may not work as drafted. For example, suppose how to respond to a report of inappropriate client/staff sexual conduct in a group home is covered by a written policy. However, the policy says that if an incident is not documented by proof, such as videos or witnesses, the complaint will be classified as "unfounded." This creates a dilemma for staff members and management who may believe the complaint is valid despite the absence of such proof and who are concerned about the possibility of future inappropriate behavior.

ERM sets the framework for correcting such a situation by establishing a strong communication process to support its resolution. When an organization has a sound ERM framework in place, feedback is not only acceptable; it is solicited to bring about better management controls, reduce risk, and find solutions to problems that may affect profits, create liabilities, and damage its reputation if left unaddressed.

In Practice—Human Resources, Operational, and Sustainable Practices

Social and ethical responsibilities and attendant threats and opportunities exist throughout the organization in areas such as these:

- Human resources practices
- Operational practices
- Sustainable practices

Human Resources Practices

Human resources play an important role in defining and carrying out an organization's ethical and social responsibilities. The organization has important social responsibilities in recruiting new employees and in encouraging diversity. Once hired, new employees should be properly oriented. Organizations must also map employee knowledge so that, over time, this intellectual capital is preserved and passed to a younger generation of incoming employees.

The organization's internal communication process is also an important component in establishing the culture of the organization. This process should adopt the most effective available communication channels to assure that stakeholders have access to required information. Newer technology, such as wikis or instant messaging, rather than outdated methods such as memos and other forms of written communication, may be most effective for today's workforce.

Human resources are also responsible for encouraging management to involve the organization in its community and to support employees who volunteer for local charities. Other areas of social responsibility include offering adequate health care coverage and an employee assistance program to help employees with emotional or personal issues. If downsizing becomes necessary, the organization should establish procedures that give employees appropriate notice, severance, and job placement assistance.

Social and ethical responsibility issues often arise in the administration of employee pension funds. The Associated Press reported that Missouri pension fund administrators were making personal use of company cars; inappropriately charging dining and other expenses to their business credit cards; and routinely accepting gifts, travel, and meals from investment companies they monitored.[3] A culture that encourages transparency in conjunction with having a strong ethics code can help discourage such behavior.

Senior management and human resources staff play a key role in risk management by shaping and applying consistent standards of conduct to all members of the organization. Management must also ensure that practices that support these policies are in place.

Operational Practices

Operational practices can include technology, marketing, and other related organizational functions.

An important component of any organization is knowledge transfer from one area to another or from one person to another. An organization's information technology resources are one of the operational practices that help employees obtain needed information to perform their jobs more safely and efficiently.

As telecommuting has become more prevalent, organizations have developed sophisticated policies that cover many operational aspects. For example, employees' eligibility, rules for working at home, the furnishing of equipment, and reporting of workplace injuries may all be covered in a policy. However, many organizations may not have policies relating to organizing knowledge so that an employee who might benefit from a more senior coworker's experience can access this information electronically from home.

To remain competitive, organizations must invest in technological practices, even when they may reap no apparent or immediate return on investment. How an organization uses its information is equally as important as the technology systems the organization has available. Podcasts, wikis, blogs, and open-source applications are just a few of the technologies organizations can use to transfer and share information. Use of such applications will, however, create dilemmas because a balance must be achieved between proprietary information and data that can be shared with other, perhaps competing, organizations. Risk managers must develop intellectual property policies to protect the organization against improper use of proprietary information.

Operational practices also extend to the organization's marketing activities. An organization's advertising influences public perception and can sway consumers both positively and negatively. Businesses must balance their advertising content against public and ethical standards. Often, decisions related to advertising are difficult and may cause unforeseen problems.

In recent years, many companies have been accused of various advertising indiscretions. For example, manufacturers of sugar-laden breakfast cereals were criticized for targeting children with their advertising. Tobacco manufacturers were accused of targeting minority groups and third-world countries with advertising, even as the U.S. government took an active role in mitigating cigarette smoking. Many business leaders believe an organization's reputation is its most valuable asset, so an organization should consider its reputation before launching an advertising campaign.

Sustainable Practices

Sustainable practices are activities directed toward mitigating an organization's negative impact on the natural environment. An organization's sustainable practices affect its external stakeholders, both upstream and downstream. For example, organizations may embrace sustainable procurement practices, which may cost more but are better for the environment. Such choices, however, can have implications. Therefore, sound ERM requires that risk managers be involved in decisions to change procurement partners.

More specifically, some food outlets have begun to use biodegradable food containers made from corn or sugar cane. When exposed to hot water, the containers disintegrate. Manufacturers of such containers must clearly communicate how the products work and warn customers of the hazards of serving hot liquids if the containers are reused. For an organization deciding to use such containers, following an ERM approach involves considering the concerns of all stakeholders. The organization may be willing to use this new commodity because it is less damaging to the environment than the previous containers used. Corporate shareholders, however, may not share management's enthusiasm if the added expense of these products decreases the company's share value.

Another area in which an organization can support sustainable practices is waste disposal. A large manufacturing plant can generate large amounts of waste products from its processes, packaging, and shipping practices. When considering sustainable practices, an organization can seek methods of disposal that reduce the potential for pollution of waterways and streams, as well as find available ways to recycle some of its waste.

Issues in Corporate Culture and Ethics

Many ethical lapses have occurred in recent years—Enron, Société Générale's rogue trader, banks collapsing, the meltdown of Fannie Mae and Freddie Mac—the list is lengthy. How can ERM shape corporate culture and ensure that an organization complies with its own ethical standards?

Organizations can begin by embracing transparency in their operations, procurement, and relationships with governing and regulatory bodies. Transparency may not be possible in all cases, because many organizations develop and manage intensely private and proprietary information. Transparency can, however, be a consideration in each decision the organization makes.

Senior management, guided by its board of directors, must develop and embrace a corporate model of ethical behavior, because that model sets the tone for the rest of the organization. Balancing transparency with profits is never easy, but it must be a goal an organization strives for in all its operations. This is a sound ERM foundation.

SUMMARY

The integration of risk management with the business disciplines of governance and compliance is required to drive an increase in overall operational performance. As a risk management culture is embedded in all processes, the three disciplines become highly interdependent, but remain separate, which contributes to improved performance through information consistency and efficient resource utilization.

Good governance helps organizations manage risk by ensuring that their goals are achieved and interests are served in a way that protects all stakeholders. Issues that should be considered regarding how an organization's governance integrates with its risk management include the need for good governance, establishing good governance in organizations, and implementing governance plans.

Organizations of all types, both private and public, frequently must comply with a variety of complex rules, regulations, standards, and codes of conduct that can at times be inconsistent. In order to understand the many risk management compliance issues, risk managers must be familiar with a working definition of compliance, understand compliance drivers, and recognize that conflicts could occur among required compliances.

ERM requires strong adherence to a sound ethical policy. Organizations face many challenges in today's global and often volatile business climate. Sound business ethics are the cornerstone of ERM. Often, making ethical decisions means making what some stakeholders may consider a "wrong" decision. Making decisions related to ethical and social responsibility requires a dynamic organizational process that considers all stakeholders.

CHAPTER NOTES

1. Micah Kellner, "Latest Crane Accident Reveals Need for Buildings Reforms," June 12, 2008, www.micahkellner.net/tag/crane-collapse (accessed March 11, 2009).
2. "How to Invest Like Warren Buffett," June 1, 2006, www.moneyweek.com/investment-advice/how-to-invest/how-to-invest-like-warren-buffett.aspx (accessed March 11, 2009).
3. Judy L. Thomas, "Apple for the teacher, but luxury for execs," *Kansas City Star*, October 18, 2008, www.kansascity.com/perksandpensions/story/847240.html, (accessed March 12, 2008).

Monitor and Review: Assurance in ERM

Educational Objectives

After learning the content of this chapter and completing the corresponding course guide assignment, you should be able to:

▸ Explain why review and monitoring are necessary in enterprise-wide risk management (ERM) to achieve continuous improvement.

▸ Explain what activities are required to ensure adequate assurance of the effectiveness of risk management activities.

▸ Summarize the financial rating agency expectations in ERM.

Outline

Review and Monitoring for Continuous Improvement

Assurance and Risk Management

ERM to Meet Financial Rating Agencies' Expectations

Summary

Monitor and Review: Assurance in ERM

Risk management's purpose is to identify, quantify, and manage an organization's risks and exposures. An organization must monitor and review its enterprise-wide risk management (ERM) program to ensure its effectiveness, especially when rating agencies include an evaluation of the ERM process in their methodologies. An effective ERM program can help an organization to lower its cost of capital or even gain access to capital in a tight market situation.

REVIEW AND MONITORING FOR CONTINUOUS IMPROVEMENT

The pace of change in today's business environment is rapid and new developments emerge on an almost daily basis. Changes in the business environment require an organization to review and monitor its risk management plan. Routine monitoring is also required to detect emerging trends and identify both threats and opportunities for continuous improvement of the process.

An organization must review and monitor its risk management process to verify that its ERM program is working as planned and continues to support its goals. When organizational changes occur (such as the introduction of a new product or acquisition of a major new customer), the risk management program should be reviewed and changed if necessary. Such a review also should occur when the organization's internal or external contexts evolve.

Review and Monitor

The review and monitor step is outlined in many international standards and ERM processes. When establishing an ERM program, it is important that the organization builds in monitoring opportunities to assess the program's effectiveness. Within the ERM framework, the organization must periodically measure performance against established goals and key performance indicators. Is the program working as planned? Are the goals still appropriate based on the current internal and external organizational environment? What information can be extracted from the results of performance measurements?

Key performance indicators can include these:[1]

- Reductions in total risk costs
- Status of specific goals

- Implementation of risk treatment recommendations

The purpose of the review is to identify deficiencies and to establish a plan to correct problem areas. To ensure that corrections will be made, the plan should also summarize which parties will be responsible for individual areas of the plan. Continuous improvements result from incremental changes to the plan.

Unexpected events, such as losses, can also trigger a review of the process between previously scheduled periodic reviews. The organization should conduct a review after a loss occurs to determine not only what lessons can be learned from the event, but also whether the risk management program requires changes. Significant successes or failures within the ERM process also may lead to a review. Such a review would assist the organization in building for future success or in avoiding similar failures.

Review and monitoring of the process can occur at various levels:

- Self-assessments—Self-assessments, also known as feedback loops, are lower-level assessments.
- Audits—Internal audits are lower-level assessments; financial audits are higher-level assessments.
- Compliance reviews—External compliance reviews are higher-level assessments and can involve fines, restitution, loss of license, or other administrative proceedings.
- Legal proceedings—The adjudication process is the highest-level assessment, whether through administrative law courts, tort law, or criminal law.

Self-Assessments

Organizational self-assessments occur as part of the overall course of business operations. Monitoring mechanisms should be built into the ERM process to provide for review and documentation of all processes. Once they have identified risks, organizations use a risk register to describe and prioritize organizational risks. The risk register can also be used to establish a monitoring process and the frequency with which activities will be monitored. Frequency could be weekly, monthly, quarterly, or some other designated interval, based on the level of the risk or the process that is being monitored. Some systems or processes have self-auditing components that look for variation beyond optimal levels and flag those beyond optimal levels for operator and management treatment.

Each risk owner should periodically review and update the risk register to validate the effectiveness of risk treatment/exploitation mechanisms. Operational or line managers are often in the best position to undertake a review of activities within their departments. Based on this review, the manager can determine how these activities affect risk management goals and also uncover potential problems or opportunities. These reviews can sometimes identify significant deficiencies that require changes to the process. Managers can detect patterns of repeated failures within the system that could potentially prevent the organization from meeting strategic goals. As part of the ERM process, managers interact with each other as well as with risk managers not only to meet periodic review requirements but to raise issues as they arise. Such a process results in continuous improvement for the entire organization.

A risk owner must quickly detect emerging trends that could trigger a disruption or crisis or offer a new opportunity for the organization. Such an event cannot wait until the next scheduled review; it must be promptly revealed and thoroughly evaluated to determine how it will affect the organization and its risk management process.

Audits

Both internal and external audits present an opportunity to review and monitor an organization's risk management activities. Review of the organization's risk management activities is part of the internal audit department's assurance responsibilities. Internal audits, however, cannot be relied on to monitor the plans to the extent that self-assessments at various organizational levels accomplish. Internal audit reviews occur less frequently than other assessments and entail a less detailed assessment of processes and operations. Internal audits work more effectively to test underlying assumptions than to identify required changes or emerging conditions. An internal audit will verify that the risk management process appropriately supports the organization's strategy and goals and that controls are in place. As such, the internal audit function supports the monitoring efforts at other levels within the organization.

An external audit takes an objective view of the organization from an outside perspective. Most of the focus of external audit is on providing assurance on financial statements. This review can identify potential weaknesses in the stability of the organization that would require changes in the ERM program and the risk management process. In addition to performing a financial audit, some organizations have hired consulting firms to conduct an external audit of quality practices, manufacturing efficiency, salesperson effectiveness, and other organizational processes.

Not-for-profit and government organizations are all subject to external performance audits that review more than financial statements. These audits review the operation of a program to determine if objectives are being met. A performance audit can provide an additional level of monitoring for an organization's risk management process.

Compliance Reviews

The process of complying with external legal and regulatory requirements provides further assessment of the organization's risk management process. Much of the documentation that is collected within the organization to demonstrate compliance with requirements provides an additional level of assessment for the risk management process. As with the audit function, such documentation provides an additional layer of review but cannot replace the primary assessment and monitoring performed by individual risk owners through self-assessments.

Internal governance strategies also provide for a review of the organization's strategies and the alignment of external and internal stakeholder goals. Because a purpose of internal governance is to assist the organization in dealing with uncertainty in the business environment, internal governance provides additional monitoring for the organization's risk management process.

Legal Proceedings

If the other levels of monitoring and review fail and stakeholders suffer losses as a result, the audit of last resort is the judge assigned to the case if those stakeholders file a legal claim for compensation. Therefore, an organization should envision the level of documentation required to prove the attention and care it has exercised in optimizing its risk taking while also taking into account the consequences, real or perceived, for its internal and external stakeholders.

ASSURANCE AND RISK MANAGEMENT

Organizations use audits to measure and encourage results as well as to accomplish goals for various processes, including the risk management process. Specific procedures are required to link activities to results for dependable measurements.

For purposes of the audit and risk management discussion, the assurance process provides information essential to the decision making process of an organization's stakeholders. These stakeholders can include major customers, regulators, and public interest groups. A structured and systematic audit procedure provides assurance to management on risk control effectiveness throughout an organization and provides for the monitoring of an organization's ERM process.

Organizational Assurance Strategy

Senior management needs assurance that organizational processes are performed at a defined level and within established parameters so that planned goals are achieved. This assurance is obtained through the findings and recommendations of assurance process reviews. Generally, an organization undertakes three types of assurance process reviews, which may overlap and/or even contradict one another:[2]

- Continuous reviews—regular measuring and monitoring of activities
- Management reviews—periodic reviews of each manager's area of responsibility
- Independent reviews—internal and external audits that validate the systems and processes for output and compliance

A best practice is to have one audit unit report organizational assurance issues directly to senior management and the board. The internal audit function is usually responsible for coordinating an organization's assurance program. While this approach does not replace any existing review or audit processes, it does minimize overlap and duplication while providing the forum for resolving differences in findings.

Risk Management and Assurance

The purpose of risk management is to identify, quantify, and manage an organization's risks and exposures. Organizational audits focused on risk exposure and controls provide valuable information to an organization's board and to its managers. Verifiable risk information provides assurance that the risk management program is functioning effectively. This assurance is required by the board and management to make quality business decisions. Risk management and assurance audits are linked and complementary processes.

Assurance audits are designed to verify that the risk management process supports an organization's strategy and identifies all significant risks. The assurance process also reviews critical controls to determine whether they are properly designed and implemented. Responsibility for the design and implementation of an ERM program, however, rests within the risk management department and is not the function of the auditors. Internal auditors are responsible for monitoring the ERM program to assess the effectiveness of controls and to identify potential compliance issues.

Assurance of the Risk Management Process

Reviewing and evaluating the effectiveness of an organization's risk management processes are important aspects of assurance. The purpose of a review is to provide assurance that the risk management processes are aligned with an organization's goals, that risks have been identified, and that effective risk controls are being implemented.

Management and the assurance audit unit must implement credible and reliable audit and review processes. When the internal assurance auditor has a reporting connection (direct or indirect) to the risk management function, or relies significantly on risk management's assessments and expertise, an external auditor should be incorporated into the process.

The format for the review of the risk management process varies based on the individual characteristics and needs of the organization. Three formats are used most often:[3]

- Process element format
- Key principles format
- Maturity model format

Process Element Format

The process element format reviews each element in an organization's risk management process to verify that these elements are considered. For example, such a review would examine how well the risk management plan had been communicated to key stakeholders. Such a review could also determine whether the external and internal contexts of an organization had been appropriately investigated using a strengths, weaknesses, opportunities, and threats (SWOT) analysis.

Other important elements examined include risk identification, analysis, and evaluation, which are critical to establishing a risk treatment plan. An audit of the risk management process using this format would also verify that a procedure is in place for continued monitoring so that changes to the process can be made based on emerging trends.

Key Principles Format

The key principles format is based on the idea that an effective program must meet a specified set of principles that are often outlined within various international standards and guidelines. Key principles also include ethical considerations that may not fit into any framework or guideline but that are critical to the organization's social license to operate in relationship to its stakeholders.

Important risk management process principles include the use of systematic approaches to provide consistent results; integration of the risk management process into organizational decision making; and the use of a process responsive to change. The risk management process should also be based on an organization's characteristics and internal and external contexts.

An audit based on key principles determines the degree to which an organization adheres to those principles. Auditors select key principles of the risk management process that apply to an organization and then review and test each one for proper utilization and results.

Maturity Model Format

The Risk and Insurance Management Society's (RIMS) Risk Maturity Model (RMM) is one of the formats used within this category. It is based on the premise that the risk management process develops over time and may only become fully implemented within an organization after several years. Progress is tracked by correlating the results of the organization's risk management process to a predetermined set of performance measurements. This format can be used to review the risk management process and then communicate the degree of an organization's progress to its senior management and board of directors. For example, a baseline audit may indicate that an organization's risk management process does not meet established standards, but a subsequent audit could reveal that the organization has made a limited amount of progress with recommendations for improvements in specific areas. The "Maturity Measurement" exhibit presents the range of compliance, from none to complete.

Maturity Measurement

Measure	None	Very little	Some	Good	Complete
Meaning	Very little or no compliance with the requirement.	Limited compliance with the requirement. Management supports the intent, but compliance is poor.	Limited compliance with element statement. Management agrees with the intent, but there is little compliance in practice.	Management completely subscribes to the intent, but there is only partial compliance in practice.	Absolute compliance with the element statement—in intent and in practice—at all times and in all places.

ERM TO MEET FINANCIAL RATING AGENCIES' EXPECTATIONS

Risks that an organization faces have always been important to rating agencies. Rating agencies also are concerned about how an organization manages those risks.

An ERM approach provides organizations with a framework for a global and integrated approach to risks, both opportunities and threats. Instituting ERM is also a signal to the market—investors, rating agencies, and so on—about an organization's concern for risk. These groups may consider an organization that does not use an ERM approach to address risks to be at a competitive disadvantage to organizations that use an ERM approach and that are consequently expected to be more motivated to optimize risk taking.

Understanding how rating agencies incorporate into their ratings their assessment of how an organization has implemented ERM entails examination of five topics:

- Role of rating agencies
- Examples of external requirements
- Criteria behind ERM rating levels
- Addressing gaps in compliance
- Monitoring and reporting progress

Role of Rating Agencies

Three major rating agencies publish ratings of organizations: Fitch Ratings, Moody's Investors Service, and Standard & Poor's (S&P). Each agency has the same purpose in assigning a rating: to provide an opinion of an organization's financial strength and ability to meet ongoing obligations to its stakeholders. Standard & Poor's was the first such agency to incorporate risk management practices of both financial and nonfinancial organizations into its rating.

An agency's credit rating of an organization has a direct bearing on the organization's cost of capital. An organization with a low credit rating is considered by creditors to be a bad risk to loan capital to and, as a result, will be charged a higher interest rate. The reverse is also true; an organization with a high credit rating is considered a good risk to loan capital to and will be charged a lower, more competitive interest rate. The significant reduction in the cost of capital resulting from lower interest rates may motivate an organization to find ways to earn a higher credit rating from a rating agency. One such method is to effectively implement ERM. Thus, one of the drivers for implementing ERM is an organization's desire to lower its cost of capital, or in the case of a public institution, optimize the value of its available resources.

When incorporating an assessment of an organization's ERM approach into the organization's rating, several rating agencies consider the organization's scope of operations and the complexity of its business. For example, an organization that participates in global markets for experimental pharmaceutical products and wants to receive an excellent ERM rating must have a more extensive ERM approach than an organization that focuses on a domestic, less potentially harmful line of business such as selling paper products.

Examples of External Requirements

Standard & Poor's focuses on two widely accepted aspects of ERM when assessing an organization's efforts to implement an ERM approach: risk management culture and strategic risk management. The analysis involved in rating those two aspects includes multiple subparts.

Risk Management Culture

The analysis involved in rating risk management culture includes these subparts:[4]

- Risk management frameworks or structures currently in use—How is risk currently identified, measured, and managed?
- The roles of staff responsible for risk management and reporting lines— Is a chief risk officer on staff, and, if so, how long has he or she held the position?
- Internal and external risk management communications—Has the organization communicated frequently and effectively with each of its stakeholder groups (such as its employees) regarding risk?

- Broad risk management policies and metrics for successful risk management—What is the organization's track record for handling risk? What benchmarks are available for the organization or the industry sector it is in?

- The influence of risk management on budgeting and management compensation—Do the decision makers of the organization have an economic incentive to ensure that ERM is implemented successfully?

Strategic Risk Management

The analysis involved in rating strategic risk management includes these subparts:[5]

- Management's view of the most consequential risks the firm faces, their likelihood, and their potential effect on credit—Is there a formal statement by the organization's management regarding which risks the organization can tolerate and which it cannot?

- The frequency and nature of updating the identification of these top risks—How well do the organization's executives understand how ERM will determine which risks are currently most critical in terms of financial impact on the organization?

- The influence of risk sensitivity on liability management and financial decisions—Do executive management understand the litigation trends affecting their lines of business, and do they seek appropriate risk treatment, such as purchase of adequate insurance coverage?

- The role of risk management in decision making—Are risk management considerations consistently taken into account in all organization-wide decisions?

Criteria Behind ERM Rating Levels

Standard & Poor's has outlined in general terms the criteria it uses to assign an ERM rating level to an organization. An ERM rating may be "excellent," "strong," "adequate," or "weak."

Excellent Rating

An organization that is rated as excellent can consistently identify, measure, and manage risks within management's preset tolerance levels. The organization must be able to demonstrate that it can consistently optimize **risk-adjusted returns**, and it makes risk management an important consideration in all of its organization-wide decisions.

Risk-adjusted return
A measure of an asset's financial value that considers the volatility incurred in producing the result.

Strong Rating

An organization that is rated as strong has a vision of its overall (organization-wide) risk profile and its overall risk appetite and tolerance. It can also demonstrate that it has a process for developing risk thresholds, from its overall risk tolerance, that are correlated to risk-adjusted returns for various management options.

Adequate Rating

An organization that is rated as adequate has a fully functioning risk control system in place for all major risks. Its risk management efforts probably are silo-based as opposed to ERM-based. Most organizations are currently assigned this grade. "Adequate" organizations typically cannot demonstrate a clear vision of their overall risk profile or overall risk appetite and tolerance. Their risk limits are usually established without coordination between silos or departments. Because there is no clear vision of an overall risk tolerance, there is no optimization of risk-adjusted returns.

Weak Rating

An organization is rated as weak if it is unable to demonstrate that it can consistently identify, measure, and manage risk across the company and thereby limit its losses. A "weak" organization's risk management efforts are sporadic, and its losses cannot be expected to be limited by management's risk tolerance. It only sometimes considers risk management when making organization-wide decisions.

Addressing Gaps in Compliance

To achieve a higher ERM rating, an organization must address the gaps in its ERM program. For example, Standard & Poor's may determine that a compliance gap exists if an organization displays characteristics that indicate it should receive less than an excellent ERM rating. Such characteristics include inconsistently identifying, measuring, and managing risk and inconsistently considering risk management when making organization-wide decisions. These characteristics may lead to situations in which losses occur that are not limited by management's risk tolerance.

Addressing the gaps primarily involves removing the inconsistencies. Hiring a chief risk officer who will assume responsibility for doing so can help in this effort. Also helpful toward this end is a formal statement by an organization's management regarding which risks it finds acceptable and which it does not. Regular communication regarding risk to and from each of the organization's stakeholders will also assist in removing inconsistencies.

The management of some organizations may incorrectly believe that if it complies with Section 404 of the Sarbanes-Oxley Act, which requires testing of internal controls over financial reporting, the organization should receive a high ERM rating. However, Standard & Poor's recognizes that financial reporting constitutes only a minor percentage of the business risks of an organization. A more robust process of identifying, measuring, and managing risk is required. Therefore, risk management is not limited to adhering to government laws and regulations.

Monitoring and Reporting Progress

Rating agencies typically formulate and report their ratings annually, when organizations publish their financial statements. The agencies then continually monitor an organization and periodically review its rating, usually quarterly. Mergers, acquisitions, catastrophe losses, or other unusual events, discovered through the monitoring process, might necessitate more frequent reviews of a particular organization's rating.

Adding analysis of an organization's ERM program to its rating may improve the rating process. A rating analyst who is familiar with an organization's ERM program may be able to provide more predictive and less reactive reports. The rating process has typically been effective at reacting to recent events. For example, when an organization incurs two consecutive quarters of performance below expectations, its credit rating will likely be lowered sharply. However, an analyst who is familiar with an organization's ERM program may be able to predict whether the organization will be able to recover from those two quarters. The analyst may still report a lower credit rating for the organization but may lower it less severely.

SUMMARY

Because organizations exist in a rapidly changing environment, they must establish a process to review and monitor their ERM program. Monitoring can take place through self-assessments, internal and external audits, and compliance reviews. If this monitoring fails, the organization may have to prove in court the level of care it has developed for managing risks.

The purpose of risk management is to identify, manage and quantify an organization's risks. Assurance audits focused on risk exposures and controls provide management with verified data on which to base business decisions.

By incorporating ERM into its rating criteria, rating agencies such as Standard & Poor's have created an incentive for organizations to implement an ERM program. Organizations expect to lower their cost of capital, or even gain access to capital in a tight market situation, if they successfully implement an ERM program. Risk management culture and strategic risk management are the two widely accepted aspects of ERM that Standard & Poor's examines to assess whether an organization's ERM program has been successfully implemented.

CHAPTER NOTES

1. Standards Australia and Standards New Zealand, Risk Management Guidelines: Companion to AS/NZS 4360 (Sydney, Australia: Standards Australia and Standards New Zealand, 2004), p. 92.
2. Standards Australia, Delivering Assurance Based on AS/NZS 4360, Risk Management (Sydney, Australia: 2004), pp. 21–22.

3. Standards Australia, Delivering Assurance Based on AS/NZS 4360:2004, Risk Management (Sydney, Australia: 2004), pp. 57-58.

4. Amra Balic, Keith Bevan, Richard Cortright, Evan Gunter, Laurence Hazell, Terry Pratt, Trevor Pritchard, Raam Ratnam, Ivana Recalde, Jayne Ross, Lisa Wang, Jeanette Ward, and Arthur Wong; Standard & Poor's, *To Apply Enterprise Risk Analysis to Corporate Ratings*, Standard & Poor's, May 7, 2008, p. 3.

5. Amra Balic, Keith Bevan, Richard Cortright, Evan Gunter, Laurence Hazell, Terry Pratt, Trevor Pritchard, Raam Ratnam, Ivana Recalde, Jayne Ross, Lisa Wang, Jeanette Ward, and Arthur Wong; Standard & Poor's, *To Apply Enterprise Risk Analysis to Corporate Ratings*, Standard & Poor's, May 7, 2008, p. 3.

Communicate and Consult: Risk Ownership and Communication With Stakeholders

Educational Objectives

After learning the content of this chapter and completing the corresponding course guide assignment, you should be able to:

▶ Explain why risk ownership by internal stakeholders is critical to increase the chances of success for an enterprise-wide risk management (ERM) program.

▶ Describe the need and methods for communication with stakeholders.

▶ Explain why risk ownership by external stakeholders is essential to the success of an ERM program.

▶ Identify the questions that an ERM business case needs to answer and the methods for developing responses to them.

▶ Summarize the process for establishing a set of measurable risk criteria for a given organization.

Outline

The Importance of Risk Ownership by Internal Stakeholders

Communication With Stakeholders

The Importance of Risk Ownership by External Stakeholders

Developing an ERM Business Case

Determining an Organization's Risk Criteria

Summary

Communicate and Consult: Risk Ownership and Communication With Stakeholders

Chapters 13 and 14 discuss making the business case for enterprise-wide risk management (ERM). Chapter 15 applies project management techniques in the implementation of ERM and change management in general.

Because ERM is successful only when it permeates an entire organization, effective communication is one of its vital components. This is the basis of the final step of the ERM process depicted on page 1.5:

1. Establish the internal and external contexts
2. Risk assessment—identification, analysis, and evaluation
3. Risk treatment—selecting and implementing appropriate risk management techniques
4. Monitor results and revise
5. Communicate and consult with all internal and external stakeholders

Risk ownership is essential to the successful implementation of an ERM program because it places the responsibility, accountability, and authority for volatile situations on those stakeholders directly affected by risks. To operate efficiently, ERM requires an organization to clearly communicate with all of its stakeholders. Communication about risk should be an ongoing process that strives to engage all stakeholders in a constant "dialogue" with the organization. It is important for an organization to establish risk ownership not only by its internal stakeholders, but also by its external stakeholders. Because an organization is affected by external stakeholders' performance, and vice versa, both must have reasonable assurance that all involved in an economic network identify and manage their own risks.

THE IMPORTANCE OF RISK OWNERSHIP BY INTERNAL STAKEHOLDERS

Risk ownership is an essential and a necessary component of an ERM program. Internal stakeholders and/or partners who are affected by volatile situations (risks) are often in the best position to understand and manage that volatility as risk owners.

Risk ownership is indispensable to an ERM program because it places the responsibility for risk taking on the stakeholders directly affected by the risks. When risks are effectively managed by risk owners, the variations from expectations are often within the organization's risk tolerance. When risk ownership is not established, the situations are more likely to be ineffectively managed and the outcomes may fall outside the organization's desired range, or risk appetite.

Various groups of internal stakeholders are responsible for different types of risks, but always in a transversal approach. Each owner's risks differ in scope and impact from board-level risks, which differ from risks faced by management, which are different from risks faced by other employees. The chief risk officer is responsible for coordinating these internal stakeholders' risk management activities and providing leadership, training, and communication venues.

In order to appreciate the value of good stakeholder communication management, consider the high turnover rate of employees, customers, and even investors. In *The Loyalty Effect*, Frederick Reichheld reports that, on average, U.S. companies lose half of their employees every four years, half of their customers every five years, and half of their investors every year.[1] This turnover may be caused by the failure to understand or appreciate the level of risk perception by each stakeholder or their lack of a sense of risk ownership.

Why Risk Ownership Is Essential to Increasing an ERM Program's Chances of Success

Risk ownership is the concept that responsibility for each activity that creates a risk for an organization is assigned to one party. Each risk owner then has the authority to manage that risk, is responsible for the outcomes of his or her actions, and is accountable for management of that risk.

Risk ownership for a specific risk should be assigned to the stakeholder who either creates the risk or is primarily affected by its volatility, because he or she is often best positioned and motivated to manage the risk. For example, a project manager charged with outsourcing a construction project must evaluate each risk involved, identify the relative importance of each risk, and then determine suitable risk management actions. Then, with guidance from internal policy and, when needed, from the chief risk officer or senior management and the board, the project manager determines how to manage the risk, reports on the success of his or her management actions, and is rewarded for successful efforts.

For this model to succeed, no "risk orphans" can exist. Each risk must be assigned to a risk owner. The failure to assign each risk to an owner may have catastrophic loss consequences or cause significant gains to be missed.

How to Motivate Ownership of Risk

Assigning risk ownership to individuals should be a thoughtful process. Individuals to whom risk ownership is assigned must have the competency to manage the risk. Competency is achieved when the organization provides the appropriate training, incentives, and tools to manage the risks. For example, a line worker handling a hazardous machine may be assigned the responsibility of managing the risk associated with the machine's use. That worker should be thoroughly trained in the operation of the machine, receive rewards for achieving production goals, and have the authority and resources to take necessary actions to create the desired level of risk.

Risk owners must stay within the organization's risk appetite and follow the established rules regarding the management of risk. Their responsibilities are to understand the organization's goals and values and to measure and manage risks involved in their operations. They must also promote safety and risk awareness, juggle priorities according to risk analyses, and report their risk activities to others.[2]

Proper motivational techniques help implement risk management and risk ownership. While many theories of motivation exist, a simple definition of motivation is "a need or desire that causes a person to act."[3] The greater a person's motivation, the harder he or she will strive to reach his or her objectives.

A motivated employee can support an organization's goals, fail to influence the goals, or actively work against an organization's goals. Ideally, employees should be motivated to act in support of an organization's goals and accept responsibility for the risks that are assigned to them. These are examples of assertions that managers can use to motivate risk owners:

- Accepting risk ownership and behaving in a positive manner are good for the organization and are also good for the worker. Doing so could increase pay, job security, and job safety, or provide recognition.
- Failing to accept risk ownership is a negative behavior and could create accidents or injuries, produce a poor performance review, generate coworker ridicule, or even result in job loss.

There are many practical ways to motivate an employee to accept risk ownership through positive, rather than negative, reinforcement:

- Explain the risk and the possible outcomes—both positive and negative
- Make sure the risk owner knows why he or she is in the best position to manage the assigned risk
- Define an acceptable performance and how it would support the organization's goals
- Provide the risk owner with the appropriate training and resources to manage his or her risks
- Measure the risk owner's performance against the disseminated standard
- Evaluate an above-standard performance to determine how to apply the positive results throughout the organization or adjust below-standard behavior to achieve the best results
- Provide sufficient incentives, such as rewards and penalties, for managing the risk

Positive Illustration of Risk Ownership

Edward is a middle manager in a large manufacturing company. He is responsible for the production of a certain number of widgets every day. Because the manufacturing process involves machinery and labor, and both are sensitive to variation from the expected outcomes, Edward must manage each effectively in order to achieve production goals. As the production risk owner, Edward feels responsible for having procedures in place to appropriately respond to the possibilities of broken machines and ill workers. This enables Edward to take prompt action in response to these situations and ensures that production continues and goals are achieved despite these threats.

Similarly, if an employee discovers a way to produce widgets faster or of higher quality, Edward may want to investigate the opportunity to increase value and evaluate the impact on his objectives. If the other employees have the same skills, and the machines can tolerate the increased output, he may wish to generalize the new procedures for his entire crew.

For example, assume a worker tells Edward that if she could rotate between two different machines several times during her shift, she could avoid fatiguing the same muscles and thereby increase her production. The worker also claims that the rotation would reduce boredom, increase alertness, and result in fewer accidental injuries. Edward likes the idea and implements it for all his workers. As a result, production rises 20 percent and workers compensation losses fall 10 percent. Worker morale is higher, and senior management is impressed. When formally recognized for the improved results, Edward defers credit to the worker who originally thought of the plan. He credits her ownership of the risks to the production line's performance. They are both subsequently promoted.

Negative Illustration of Risk Ownership

In contrast, consider Michelle, a service manager for a medium-sized city. She, too, uses machinery and labor to process paperwork in providing a certain service. However, Michelle has not been motivated to accept ownership for the risks in her job. Instead, she believes that if one of the machines breaks down, her only responsibility is to call a repair service and wait for the machine to be repaired. Similarly, if one of her workers is injured, Michelle thinks her only response is to call human resources (HR) and report the injury. Service grinds to a halt as Michelle waits for others to fix problems that she should have managed. Additionally, if she is approached by one of her subordinates about improving a process whose outcome is uncertain, she is likely to consider the opportunity an unnecessary burden and not investigate its potential gains.

For example, assume a worker approaches Michelle and suggests the organization could avoid interruption in servicing incoming customer calls during equipment failures if it rerouted calls to another call center. Michelle resists the idea and refuses to investigate its potential because she is concerned the other call centers are located in catastrophe-prone areas along the coast. The organization does not implement the plan. When a fire destroys Michelle's office building, her team's customer service performance deteriorates drastically as a result of insufficient access to operable phones and relevant computer records. Shortly thereafter, sales for the entire organization fall 40 percent, while sales in Michelle's region fall 80 percent. Management decides to save costs by not reopening Michelle's call center. Michelle and her workers are laid off.

Defining Internal Stakeholders as Risk Owners

The stakeholder model shown in the "Stakeholders of an Organization" exhibit applies to every organization; there are internal and external stakeholders who have an interest in an organization's success. Internal stakeholders, those who are directly employed by or involved with an organization, include the organization's owners, board of directors, managers, and labor. Stakeholders in governmental entities include cabinet officer positions, presidents, prime ministers, governors, mayors, and employees. The boxes in the stakeholder model shown in the "Stakeholders of an Organization" exhibit that represent each of these internal stakeholders are more lightly shaded than those representing the external stakeholders.

Risk Ownership by an Organization's Owners

An organization can be owned by one of several legal structures. Common ownership structures include sole proprietorships, partnerships, corporations, and government entities. If the organization is a government, its owners are the citizens it serves. In such a case, the public must take ownership of the risks created by the government entity. This responsibility includes oversight duties and voting for representatives to act in the public's interests. The public's failure to accept risk ownership for its government can result in abusive or wasteful government programs.

If an organization is a corporation, the owners are shareholders, and each has a duty to monitor the corporation. Common shareholders have the responsibility to vote for a board of directors to guide the corporation's employees in achieving the shareholders' goals. These goals may include a level of economic performance (profit or growth), a level of social justice (employee or public relations), or a level of environmental stewardship. The variability in achieving these goals must ultimately be borne by the shareholder. They should vote for board members who will pursue the shareholders' goals. The shareholders own the corporation, and they own the risks associated with that corporation.

Stakeholders of an Organization

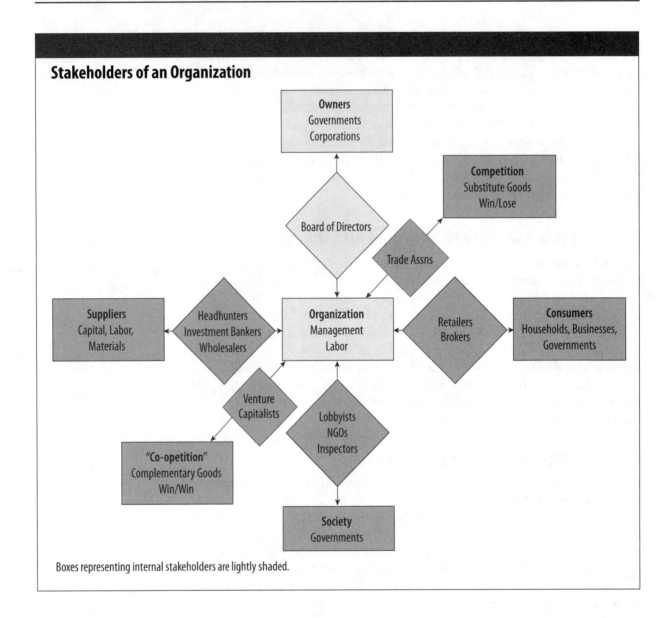

Boxes representing internal stakeholders are lightly shaded.

Shareholders are people and organizations, such as trusts and financial management firms that have an interest in an organization's profits and losses. Communication usually includes an annual report and, when necessary, a profit warning statement, which is a statement released prior to an earnings release that warns that losses will be greater than previously estimated. This statement covers four areas of concern:

- Societal and business trends that may affect the profitability of the company
- An overview of major pending claims
- Reputation-related issues that the company may face
- An update on the company's resilience in the face of obstacles and its likelihood of continued growth

Risk Ownership by the Board

Depending on an organization's structure, the public or shareholders vote for representatives to achieve established goals. Public entities and governments have boards of governors, boards of regents, city managers, committee directors, and elected officials. These stakeholders are intermediaries that act in the interests of the owners—the public. Likewise, the intermediary for corporations, the board of directors, should represent the interests of the shareholders. These boards must accept the responsibility of being owners of certain risks.

Typically, boards manage strategic goals. In most instances, strategic goals are accomplished over two years or more. For example, the board directives for a retail grocery company may instruct employees to begin searching for acquisition targets among smaller, competing grocers. The strategic goal, growing the company, may be a long-term goal such as increasing gross sales five percent per year by acquiring competing stores. But the board must also recognize the possible consequences for any variation from its goals, which includes preparing contingency plans for this volatility. In the grocery chain example, the growth may exceed five percent. The board should have plans in place to manage this positive risk and could comply with this risk ownership duty by working closely with the firm's executive team, including the chief risk officer. The team would be charged by the board with allocating and managing the resources necessary to accommodate the increased sales and corresponding work load. Boards also must set performance standards and remuneration for executives and plan for variations from these standards.

Board members' focus may vary from nation to nation. In the United States, return on investment and mitigation of financial and reputational risk are a board's primary focus. In European countries, directors may believe that they have an additional role to protect employees.[4] The number of directors on a given board may vary from three or four to fifteen or sixteen. Members are elected for a specific term. It is their responsibility to choose the company's chief executive officer (CEO), determine and distribute dividends, determine the feasibility of mergers and acquisitions, and audit and approve the organization's financial statement.

Boards that accept responsibility and ownership for their risks proactively create plans for their organizations to survive volatile economic conditions. The failure to proactively manage board-level risks creates situations in which the organization is unable to take advantage of speculative opportunities, fails to meet desired goals, and may suffer catastrophic economic outcomes.

Risk Ownership by Management

Management must understand the organization's communication model and deliver clear and consistent messages to employees. Each management layer must implement risk management in his or her area through risk owners and keep senior managers apprised of risks and the potential impacts of business decisions on that area.

Senior management must ensure that an organization's medium-term plans and actions follow the board's strategies. The risks the CEO and other senior executives take and own are strategic risks. The senior executives communicate their goals and budgets to middle management, who are the operational risk takers and owners. These events mature within one operating period, which is typically one year. Middle managers then convey their plans to line managers, who are tactical risk takers and owners.

In an organization using an enterprise risk model, each manager, regardless of his or her position, is responsible for risk management. At each management level, managers are responsible for setting the appropriate risk objectives. Once objectives are set, performance standards must be enacted to ensure they are carried out effectively and with accountability.

While senior managers are responsible for the organization's successful management of threats and opportunities, they cannot monitor and manage every risk; they can only integrate risk management with the existing culture Authority on matters that encompass risk management must be vested at all levels of management—and by labor, too.

Middle management (also referred to as operational management) must have the authority to manage the risks it is responsible and accountable for at the operational level. It must ensure the appropriate level of risk is achieved through the control of specific functions, processes, and people. Providing suggestions for improvement to senior management establishes a clear line of responsibility. If problems occur, senior management can then assist in addressing the internal threats and opportunities.

Line management consists of department heads or functional managers who operate as risk managers within their specialized area. Because they are in the best position to understand and manage their risks, risk ownership at this level is essential in an ERM program. Line managers must understand the organization's risk appetite, develop policies and procedures within that range, and work with middle and senior managers to achieve optimal results.

Risk Ownership by Employees

All employees must be made aware of their role as risk owners. Employees must also understand the culture of an organization to fully implement ERM. Employees must be educated to understand how their actions may affect the organization as a whole. While owners, board members, and managers own certain types of risks, labor is responsible for managing volatile situations that arise in the course of its work. An effective way to ensure that labor's risk ownership is understood and accepted is to clearly define the risks associated with each role in its job description. The risks, and the employee's ownership of them, should be unambiguously presented in each employee's recruitment and training.

For example, Hector is hired to operate a saw in a lumber mill. Various managers are responsible for providing Hector with a safe work environment, safe tools, and adequate training in the operation of the saw, but Hector also bears some risk ownership as well. Hector must learn about the hazards associated with his job. He must also bear responsibility for being physically fit enough to operate the saw and for not being mentally or physically impaired. He also is required to report any unusual conditions or damage observed. When these conditions are made part of the job description and clearly presented to Hector, he will be empowered to manage the risks he owns.

The Risk Professional's Responsibility to Internal Stakeholders as Risk Owners

A chief risk officer's role is to make certain that risk ownership is properly managed. These duties may include assisting in apportioning risk ownership to the appropriate parties, coordinating risk ownership actions, training risk owners in executing their risk ownership jobs, and helping to prepare risk reports. In an ERM setting, the chief risk officer is a senior member of the organization who interacts with the CEO and the board so that other managers and the board can access the chief risk officer's knowledge and expertise. The chief risk officer may act as a coach, ensuring that management understands ERM and accepts ownership of its risks.

A key role for the chief risk officer is to coordinate activities by the risk owners to ensure consistency throughout the organization. The principal method for achieving coordinated actions is to ensure that an effective and efficient communication network exists. The chief risk officer must work closely with the information technology (IT) department to provide training and tools for sharing ideas, observations, and recommendations. With organizations becoming reliant on technology to drive growth and manage processes, IT holds tremendous responsibility for the volatility of information and assets. Not only must physical assets be protected from fire and other threats, a security program must be in place to monitor threats to information. IT personnel, with their specialized knowledge, are in the best position to take ownership of those risks, to design risk management plans, and to provide reports on their activities.

Chief risk officers must also work closely with the HR department, which performs the recruiting, training, and continuing education programs and can also be involved in remuneration and incentive program design. As such, HR plays a critical role in establishing or communicating the risk ownership for each job. This requires a close relationship with the chief risk officer to ensure that each position's risk ownership role is clearly articulated.

Finally, the chief risk officer must also work closely with the internal audit team to ensure that risk ownership is independently monitored. The audit team must have a broad understanding and acceptance of ERM and risk ownership to ensure it is viewing issues holistically. While it is not responsible for the organization's ERM implementation or management, the audit team owns its own risks, which include gathering and disseminating information.

Its role is to monitor and evaluate the organization's operations, and to make recommendations to the board and senior management designed to improve the management of risks.

The chief risk officer observes how risk owners interact and perform their risk management duties to ensure that all volatile events are appropriately managed by the proper risk owner. In many past instances, most notably those involving the American corporations Enron, Fannie Mae, and Freddie Mac, the traditional model of managing risk failed. When risk ownership is present only at the senior level (and often only with the chief financial officer), risks are managed in silos, with less than a holistic approach.

COMMUNICATION WITH STAKEHOLDERS

Business communication, especially in an ERM context, requires knowledge and judgment. An organization that successfully communicates with its stakeholders is more likely to achieve its goals.

To be efficient, ERM requires an organization to clearly communicate with all of its stakeholders to ensure that risks are understood by all. Ignoring the needs of some stakeholders can have disastrous results. There is often too much emphasis on communication in time of a crisis. Instead, communication about risk should be an ongoing process that strives to engage all stakeholders in a constant "dialogue" with the organization. The goodwill generated by transparent communication in quieter times will create a cushion of trust and credibility that is beneficial should turbulent times lead to a crisis.

A successful risk management (RM) communication system requires an understanding of several key concepts:

- Foundations of ERM communications
- RM communication channels
- RM communications with stakeholders

Foundations of ERM Communications

Communicating with stakeholders is essential to every aspect of the ERM process, including understanding goals, risk appetites, and values; hiring and retaining employees; vendor and customer relations; public relations; describing risks; implementing change; and reporting ERM program success to others. Effective and efficient communication is of paramount importance to success.

The foundations of an effective ERM communication system are typically built on an understanding of management style, communication ethics, communication problems, and practical guidelines for effective communication.

Management Style

An organization's culture indicates its particular management style of leadership and communication. That style influences communication with all of the organization's stakeholders. Management may exhibit a delegating, directive, or supportive style. In a delegating style, management provides broad, strategic direction but lets stakeholders create their own methods of attaining goals. In contrast, managers who use the directive style make most decisions and tell others exactly what to do to achieve goals. Management limits the flow of information in the interest of efficiency. Finally, in a supportive style, management explains the rationale for goals and decisions and encourages stakeholders to pursue related endeavors. Management is open to feedback from others, and stakeholders may establish their own communication networks.

Communication Ethics

The cornerstone of insurance contracts is the concept of utmost good faith. This notion means that parties to a contract have neither concealed nor misrepresented a material fact. Instead, all important information is disclosed that is needed in underwriting the insurance contract.

Doing the "right thing" is not as easy as it sounds, especially when dealing with confidential information and external stakeholders. For example, assume a CEO expects to have to lay off some employees soon but currently needs those employees to complete a project. At what point should this information be disclosed to the board of directors, to the employees, and to the shareholders?

There are usually no easy answers to ethics questions, but at a minimum, organizations must comply with legal requirements. For example, sometimes an employment contract specifies disclosure of certain job attributes. However, if an organization knows the job requires the employee to handle hazardous materials, should this also be disclosed, even when doing so is not required by law? The guideline may be that everyone should use morally informed judgment in resolving ethical challenges and that in all cases the decision must be based on the values held by the organization. Guiding principles may be found in the organization's culture or value statement. Ethical relations among stakeholders, including ethical communications, enhance the organization's reputation.

Communication Problems

One of the key communication problems in risk management is the use, and misuse, of technical jargon. Risk management involves technical areas such as risk description, statistics, finance, and engineering. The communication challenge is to translate the terms of art used in these disciplines into simple vernacular language. A classic example is the multiple interpretations of the word "risk." Ask twenty businesspeople to define risk, and twenty different definitions may be offered. Some may define it as volatility; others, as the possibility of losses; and still others, as the possibility of unexpected losses or gains. Until each of the organization's stakeholders has a common or shared understanding of such a fundamental risk management term, communication of RM information will be problematic.

A related problem in communication exists when the audience is unfamiliar with risk management concepts. The person(s) receiving the message may not appreciate how a single piece of information fits into a portfolio approach to risk. For example, it may not be clear to a stakeholder how a fire at an organization's manufacturing plant could result in the loss of the design plans needed to defend a patent infringement lawsuit. Correlations between significant losses need to be explained.

Another communication problem is that many risk management issues have emotional effects. In communicating about risks, perception on the part of the intended target may prove to be more important than facts. Reporting on catastrophic outcomes may trigger anger, embarrassment, or fear, and the message may result in an unintended action.

There is also the challenge and difficulty related to expressing ideas. This is a common problem when oral presentations are required. Often a person delivering a message who is challenged to explain risk in his or her own area of expertise assumes that the audience understands all of the associated technical, legal, or financial concepts—such as, for example, when an IT manager tries to explain to a marketing team the technical reasons why a computer system fails to provide desired client information.

Finally, an additional challenge is to avoid pre-judging another's risk appetite—especially that of an external stakeholder. External stakeholders have their own individual management styles and communication ethics. Learning what the other's risk appetite is before communicating the organization's RM information will help in tailoring the information to the audience.

Practical Guidelines for Effective Communication

The basics of effective communication include several practical guidelines. Understanding is best achieved when the communicator takes responsibility for learning these guidelines:

- Understand the purpose—Is the message one of information or persuasion?
- Know the audience—Be aware of the receiver's current position and potential response.
- Use concrete, specific language—Avoid jargon.
- Keep it simple—Stick to the point, and be concise.

- Link new information to existing ideas—Provide a reference point.
- Repeat the message—State the main idea in the introduction, again in the body, and again in the conclusion.
- Provide for feedback—Involve the audience with open, as opposed to closed, questions.
- Plan for crises—Every crisis is an opportunity to build stakeholder relations through effective communication.
- Introduce a timeline for review—Monitor and improve communication efforts.

RM Communication Channels

Communicating RM ideas with people both inside and outside the organization is a routine task that requires careful thought, preparation, and execution. Expressing ideas with stakeholders is done via one of two communication channels, depending on whether the audience is internal or external.

Internal Stakeholder Communication Channels

Formal and informal communication channels enable information to spread throughout the organization. The organization's official structure is a guide to understanding formal communication channels. For example, when a line and staff structure is adopted, the lines of communication are quite clear. One reports up and down along the lines. Managers direct messages down the lines to control subordinates' activities. Messages directed upward provide managers with information to be used in making decisions.

The advantage of this formal system is that everyone knows to whom to report. The major disadvantages are that employees do not have direct access to each other and that the message may be distorted as it passes through the lines or may take a long time to reach the audience. Informal communication channels overcome both of these problems. These channels are an important source of information in most organizations. But they need to be monitored and controlled to mitigate the chances of information becoming invalid or distorted. A common blend of channels is the risk committee, which brings internal stakeholders together from various organizational levels. Risk committees permit the exchange of ideas that can subsequently be distributed through formal channels.

External Stakeholder Communication Channels

To achieve optimal understanding with external stakeholders, the organization must have well-defined external communication channels and procedures. For example, when dealing with vendors, the chief risk officer should know exactly with whom to discuss risks in the capital, labor, and commodity markets. Likewise, detailed instructions should exist so that after a loss, information can be properly related to customers, regulators, and insurers. These instructions must also specify what can and cannot be discussed with others. A practical example concerns how to prepare a request for proposal (RFP) for insurance coverages. Protocols should be established regarding what information can be released and what should remain confidential. The organization's ERM standard operating procedures (SOP) should provide instructions and templates concerning appropriate external stakeholder communication channels. It is important to keep in mind that communication is a two-way street; the organization must not only communicate its message on risks but also listen to external stakeholders' perception of those same risks. This is the reason why the ISO 31000 framework insists on "communicating and consulting."[5]

RM Communications With Stakeholders

Risk management concepts and processes require a consistently applied communication system to ensure proper understanding and implementation by all involved. This requirement is exemplified when the chief risk officer presents the allocation of the cost of risk to other managers. The method of communication should be familiar to all managers so they can focus on the message rather than a novel presentation approach. Formal RM communication systems include verbal and nonverbal communications, business presentations, business e-mails, visual displays, and RM reports.

Verbal Communications

Effective speaking requires skills in expressing facts, emotions, and suggestions for acting on risks. A key component of effective speaking is good listening skills. To enhance verbal communications, a good speaker spends more time listening than speaking. Doing so increases the likelihood that the message has been received and understood, which is especially important when discussing risky events. Verbal communication also includes making presentations to groups. For example, when the chief risk officer presents the annual ERM report to the board of directors, speaking and listening skills are often thoroughly tested.

Nonverbal Communications

Written reports, memos, and body language play an important role in effective communication. Drafting written reports is an essential skill for ensuring understanding of the organization's risks. The chief risk officer prepares an annual ERM report and interim reports when needed. A well-written report is much more likely to be read and understood. Producing good reports requires planning, composition, and revision. Start with an outline that details the main points. Then compose the body to flesh out the skeleton. Be sure the information is accurate and, when required, use citations to substantiate the main points. Finally, set the document aside for a while and look at it later with fresh eyes. If possible, ask another person who is not familiar with the details and jargon of risk management to read the document to be sure the message is clear.

Business Presentations

A risk owner is sometimes required to make a formal presentation to others regarding their risks and how he or she is managing them. The approach for the business presentation is a critical factor in successfully disclosing this information. The group's characteristics help define the appropriate presentation techniques. A large group requires a more formal speech, whereas a small group requires a more interactive approach. People often judge the substance of an oral presentation by the speaker's presentation style. Developing a professional style helps ensure that the audience will focus on the importance of managing risks. Practical pointers in public speaking include dressing appropriately for the occasion, matching nonverbal signals to the words, focusing on the audience by looking directly at it, watching and listening for feedback, speaking more slowly than necessary, and remembering to breathe.

Often a presentation is accompanied by visual displays, which can clarify, simplify, emphasize, and summarize ideas. But they should be used sparingly and designed carefully. Risk professionals often must evaluate tremendous amounts of data, such as with loss runs or simulation analyses. But it is important to share only the main points—such as the summary statistics—rather than the entire data set. This underscores the fact that visual displays should use a font large enough to enable people in the back rows to clearly see the message being presented. Graphs, pie charts, and tables should be designed using only basic information so that the message is obvious. Finally, providing sources for the information in the visual displays adds credibility.

Business E-Mails

Like other managers, the risk manager sends and receives dozens, if not hundreds, of e-mails daily. In many cases, vital messages are buried in extraneous material. Some scan the "from" and "subject" boxes and decide whether to delete the message without reading it. A message from the risk manager may not be received in the most positive light, so its subject line should be compelling. The subject box and first paragraph must convey the urgency of the message. Practical suggestions for the subject box are to type a fresh topic line rather than forwarding someone else's wording. Make sure the subject line is interesting or provokes an emotional response. If the e-mail passes this hurdle, the receiver may scan the preview box. In turn, the message may be opened and read. The first paragraph of the message should be an executive summary of the main points. This summary may be all that people read, so it should be done well. Use bullet points to emphasize the highlights or requested action.

RM Reports

With the increasing importance of ERM to organizations comes the requirement for them to prepare formal reports for stakeholders. For example, the annual statements of publicly held organizations include a risk management report to their stockholders.

Government regulators are increasing their scrutiny of risk reports from banks, investment bankers, insurers, and other entities in the capital markets.

A key requirement of risk management is to produce timely and relevant risk reports for internal and external stakeholders. In an ERM framework, the chief risk officer must be sure that the reports are holistic, rather than silo reports. The level of an RM report's comprehensiveness and transparency is increasingly a major concern for senior managers, boards, shareholders, rating agencies, and regulators.

As is true for other communication methods, an RM report should be thoughtfully planned and artfully presented. The structure should follow a standard format as described in the ERM SOP. This format should be consistent with other internal reports or in compliance with leading practices or government rules. Generally, the RM report should consist of a concise executive summary with the main points; a brief introduction; a sufficient (but not excessive) body to support the main points; and appropriate attachments, references, and supporting evidence.

THE IMPORTANCE OF RISK OWNERSHIP BY EXTERNAL STAKEHOLDERS

Within the context of ERM, all stakeholders, including those outside the organization, must take ownership of their risks. External stakeholders must be able to understand and manage their own risks as well as those of the organization.

Risk ownership is essential to the success of an ERM program because it places the responsibility, accountability, and authority for risk on those stakeholders affected by risks. It is especially important for an organization to establish risk ownership by its external stakeholders because, as independent agents, they may need to be convinced of the importance of their part in the overall risk management process.

Because an organization is affected by external stakeholders' performance, it must have reasonable assurance that external stakeholders identify and manage their own risks. Equally important is the alignment of external stakeholders' risk appetite with those of the organization. When appropriate, external stakeholders must operate within the organization's defined risk appetite, which can be accomplished through contractual clauses, if necessary. An external stakeholder's failure to control risk can have devastating consequences to an organization, particularly if the stakeholder is a key part of the organization's essential supply network.

Methods to Establish Risk Ownership

Risk ownership is not clearly defined in some organizations. Even in organizations that define and assign ownership, stakeholders, when made aware of their risks, may attempt to transfer ownership to others so that they can focus on other activities. A successful ERM program requires the organization to establish risk ownership and develop a program to help owners manage their risks.

Establishing Risk Ownership

Establishing risk ownership requires effective communication. An organization that embraces ERM must ensure that external risk owners understand its goals and expectations and that they implement and explain the processes they follow to manage their risks. For example, an importer of children's toys must clearly explain to the exporter the need for safe, lead-free products. The exporter, as an external risk owner, must accept responsibility for producing products that meet or exceed the importer's expectations. To achieve this end, the exporter should explain the manufacturing processes it has implemented to ensure the safety of its products.

Organizations frequently make the error of delaying the assessment and management of risk associated with a project and its external stakeholders until long after the project has begun. Risk management must be embedded in any project at the onset and in any relationship with a partner from the beginning of the relationship. Establishing the optimal level of risk ownership by external stakeholders is one of the first steps in the ownership management process. For example, when preparing the schedule of external stakeholders, the chief risk officer should articulate each stakeholder's expected level of risk ownership.

When external stakeholders are associated with "free resources" (air and water, for example) and have no contractual relationship with the organization, assigning risk ownership may be challenging. In such cases, consultation and communication can help develop shared visions based on common interests. For example, if a chemical plant is located upstream from a reservoir (a type of free resource), the plant must take care not to contaminate the reservoir, even if it has no direct relationship with the municipality that has rights to the water.

Developing a Program to Manage External Stakeholder Risk Ownership

The chief risk officer must have a system to continually establish, monitor, and update risk ownership by the organization's external stakeholders. This program is especially important in relationships with suppliers, business partners, regulators, and customers. Before entering into a business relationship, the organization should assess the external stakeholder's values, culture, and risk appetite to ascertain whether the relationship is a good fit. Finding the right business partner can ensure a long-term, profitable relationship. Choosing an inappropriate partner decreases an organization's chances of success.

In developing a program to manage external stakeholder risk ownership, a chief risk officer should answer five basic questions:

- Are the two organizations' goals compatible?
- Do the organizations have similar cultures and business practices?
- Do they have complementary skills and resources?
- Are both organizations dealing from positions of strength?
- Can effective communications be achieved between partners?

Of the criteria contained in the questions, effective communication may be the most important. Nowhere are barriers to ERM communication more evident than with external stakeholders. These barriers include preexisting paradigms that consumer groups or individuals may hold, distrust of the organization or the broader arena in which the organization operates, and decision-making based on limited information. Can the parties trust each other and honestly disclose the extent of risk that each owns? Before entering into any business alliance, the organization should assess its willingness to share information with the prospective partner. Both parties must agree to be transparent and disclose all material risks they own, and mutual monitoring of the performance of each party relating to this disclosure should continue throughout the relationship. This issue is addressed in the International Organization for Standardization (ISO) 31000 reference to communication/consultation with stakeholders.[6]

After the organization enacts the action plan to manage external risk ownership, it should assess the chances for the plan's success. Does the plan provide a mechanism for external stakeholders to reveal any events that weren't anticipated, such as contract problems, supplier inadequacies, or regulatory issues? Does the plan include a system to evaluate the steps taken to manage the unexpected events or variation from the expected (that is, volatility)?

The metrics of performance presented in a dashboard view (a visual representation of the performance metrics, often graphical) can be useful when monitoring the success of the risk ownership plan. Claim data, quality control, and employee turnover are a few of the performance metrics organizations can use to monitor success.

The importance of monitoring the risk ownership plan can be illustrated by this example: A contractor fails to notice that a subcontractor neglected to obtain the specified limits of insurance required in the contractor's request for proposal (RFP) specifications. An employee of the subcontractor is subsequently injured, and the contractor's insurance pays a significant portion of the loss. In this example, a work plan had been developed that required that subcontractors be qualified and fully insured; however, the subcontractor failed to discharge its responsibility in the relationship. This was not a failure of the risk ownership plan; it was a failure to monitor and enforce the plan.

Defining External Stakeholders as Risk Owners

The stakeholder model shown in the "External Stakeholders of an Organization" exhibit applies to the internal and external stakeholders of every organization. External stakeholders, those who are indirectly involved with an organization and who are essential to optimizing the success of an organization's ERM program, include these parties:

- Suppliers
- Customers
- Society, including local government and nongovernmental organizations (NGOs)
- Competitive organizations
- **"Co-opetition"**
- Intermediaries

The boxes in the stakeholder model shown in the "External Stakeholders of an Organization" exhibit that represent each of the external stakeholders are more lightly shaded than the boxes representing internal stakeholders.

Co-opetition
An arrangement whereby two or more organizations agree to work together for their mutual benefit in a certain area, such as sharing common costs, while remaining competitors in the market.

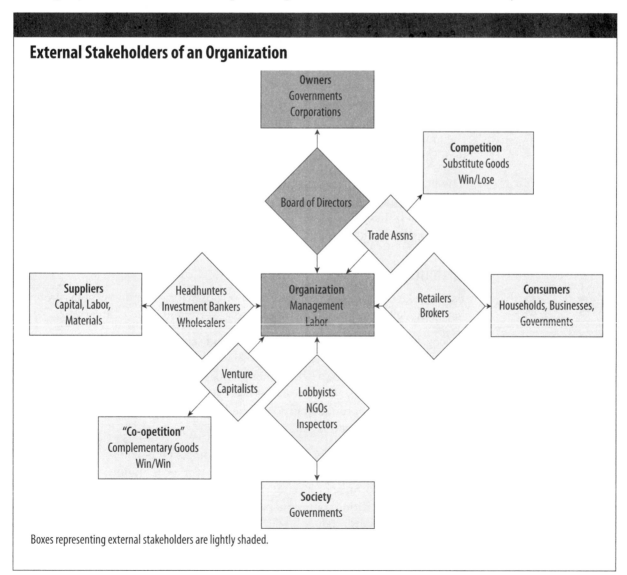

External Stakeholders of an Organization

Boxes representing external stakeholders are lightly shaded.

Suppliers

In 1982, poisonings connected with the pain relief medication Tylenol ultimately cost its manufacturer, Johnson & Johnson, more than $100 million. Stores that stocked Tylenol expected their supplier, Johnson & Johnson, to accept ownership for this risk. Johnson & Johnson accepted responsibility and took immediate action—even though it was subsequently found to have no legal liability. If a major drug manufacturer is associated with a flawed product, not only are its customers (the stores) likely to become outraged, but the general public may become vocal opponents of the company. However, in this case, Johnson & Johnson actually enhanced its reputation because of the strong risk ownership position and actions it took.

As production becomes increasingly global, it is critical that suppliers properly manage their risk. Consumers will reject an organization's attempts to blame an upstream provider for a crisis, as, for example, Mattel attempted to do after toys it had imported from China were found to contain lead. Organizations must thoroughly evaluate and screen suppliers by insisting that they accept risk ownership and practice ERM.

Suppliers include those that provide capital, labor, or commodities. Significant failures in the capital markets highlight the necessity of establishing risk ownership and responsibility for managing variability. For example, the failure of banks to anticipate and manage volatile money supply was a factor in the economic recession of 2008–2009.

The management of risk for the supply chain—often called procurement risk management—is developing into a new field of risk management. Procurement risk management is essential for all organizations involved in global business and substantial outsourcing.

Customers

Another key external stakeholder is an organization's customers. This group may include households, businesses, and governments.

As consumers of the organization's goods and services, customers must also acknowledge a certain degree of risk ownership. Although the U.S. court system appears to favor the consumer and pass risk ownership to the organization, the courts also recognize that the consumer has certain duties to use products for their intended purpose. The law expects reasonable persons to be informed about the goods they consume.

For example, homeowners are discouraged from using lawn mowers as hedge trimmers or wearing a necktie while leaning over a car engine with a moving fan belt. What is the appropriate level of risk ownership by consumers, and how can organizations communicate that risk ownership to consumers? The answer lies partly in product labeling and advertising.

In today's fast-paced world of instant and often subjective communication, a single organizational blunder that generates adverse publicity can damage a company irreparably. Therefore, customer relationship management should be embedded in an organization's ERM strategy. A critical consumer concern is the ability to both question and obtain quick answers from company executives. Only if an organization understands the consumer's frustrations or experiences can it effectively counter any criticism. Each communication with the public demonstrates the organization's credibility, its corporate culture, and its intentions.

Society

The external stakeholder class referred to as "society" includes the public at large, NGOs, and governments. The public is a risk owner inasmuch as it is responsible for monitoring the capitalistic system and ensuring the efficient and cost-effective flow of goods and services from suppliers to consumers. When inefficiencies and variability (risk) occur in quality, service, or cost, the public in many societies or countries has the right to protest, boycott, blog, or otherwise make its discontent known.

In response to some issues, members of the public band together to form public action groups called NGOs. NGOs can pressure organizations to modify their behavior or production. Alternatively, they can lobby governments to impose new regulations and rules. Not only do NGOs have a stake in an organization's actions and activities, they also are responsible for monitoring variations from expected outcomes.

For example, coal-burning plants face increasingly strict regulation as a result of concerted campaigns by consumer groups to limit carbon emissions. South Dakota's Big Stone II coal-fired power plant faced significant opposition from environmental groups. The Sierra Club and the Minnesota-based organization Fresh Energy opposed the plant and delayed its Environmental Protection Agency approval.[7] National public advocacy groups in many cases have the funding and media connections to dramatically affect business. Therefore, organizations should bring interested external groups into the planning process as early as possible to seek consensus in order to avoid the failure of key organizational agendas and projects.

Regulators, officials, and agency personnel empowered to protect the public interest are important external stakeholders of an organization. These government organizations also fall into this category when they act as regulators rather than customers. As such, they are responsible for monitoring variability in the economic and legal systems and for taking action to establish equilibrium. Their degree of risk ownership varies with political administrations. For example, in the 1980s, the U.S. experienced a shift away from government regulation. In the decades since that time, regulatory control of organizations decreased in many respects.[8] Economic occurrences, such as bank failures and investment banker bailouts, and crises in financial organizations have encouraged regulators to shift again toward an environment that supports governmental risk ownership and responsibility for managing volatile economic conditions.

In another example of society's risk ownership, after the September 11, 2001, terrorist attacks, insurance coverage for losses resulting from terrorist acts became critical but generally unavailable. The increased demand for such coverage caused the federal government to take action to create a more stable economic system. The result was passage of the Terrorism Risk Insurance Act (TRIA), which provided governmental support that allowed commercial insurers to underwrite the terrorism peril and required insurers to provide terrorism coverage for commercial policyholders.

Competition

The U.S. economic system depends on sufficient competition to spur innovation and produce optimal levels of goods and services at fair prices. Each competitor bears a responsibility to accept ownership of the risks in this economic system. While some firms' preference might be for the bankruptcy of competitive organizations, the lack of competition can lead to governmental antitrust actions to eliminate oligopolies and monopolies. As a result, firms do act to maintain a reasonable amount of competition and to ensure that their competitors' trade practices are fair.

Co-opetition

Many organizations, both public and private, enter into strategic alliances with other organizations. For example, a manufacturer may enter into a joint venture with another manufacturer to supply goods to a consumer. These two organizations are considered to be in "co-opetition." As in the relationship between an organization and its suppliers, organizations in co-opetition also must accept risk ownership and establish a formal system of communication and monitoring of the partner's risk management practices. One partner's failure to manage volatility in its operations may indirectly cause significant losses for the other. For example, organizations depend on financial rating agencies to assess suppliers of capital and customers. The failure of a rating agency to accept responsibility and ownership of the volatility of its analyses leaves the organization without the tools it needs to assess credit worthiness and ensure financial stability.

Intermediaries

Risk ownership must also be established for the various intermediaries between the principal stakeholders. Intermediaries are parties that facilitate transactions between internal stakeholders and other external stakeholders. For example, an organization may access the capital markets through an investment banker or insurance broker. The organization may obtain key personnel through an executive search firm or workers through a labor union. Likewise, the organization may find it more cost- and time-effective to use a wholesaler to acquire raw materials from the commodity markets.

In all these cases, the intermediaries shoulder significant responsibility and ownership of risks. Economic conditions have demonstrated the volatility of intermediary operations. For example, the financial failure of Bear Stearns and Lehman Brothers revealed the uncertainty and risk inherent in dealing with supply intermediaries. However, distribution intermediaries between business organizations and consumers must also accept risk ownership. A record number of retailers have gone bankrupt, leaving some organizations without distribution networks.

The organization must carefully assess the strength of all of its intermediaries and ensure that they acknowledge and manage their risks.

The Risk Professional's Responsibility to External Stakeholders as Risk Owners

The chief risk officer plays a critical role in managing relationships with external stakeholders. The chief risk officer's duties include helping assess each stakeholder's degree of risk ownership and method of managing its owned risks and making sure that appropriate channels of communication have been established and are consistently used.

A chief risk officer should maintain an up-to-date schedule of all external stakeholders, with contact names and information, along with a list of possible volatile concerns in each stakeholder relationship. The chief risk officer reports all external stakeholder risks to the organization's board and other senior managers. The chief risk officer also should work closely with stakeholders' chief risk officers to monitor any changes in these risks.

In addition, the chief risk officer should monitor each external stakeholder's risk management activities. Any changes in a stakeholder's processes that create new risks should be quickly noted and discussed. For example, a large pet supply store that purchases cat and dog food from a firm in China faces risk of loss if the processing plant in China fails to deliver the quantity and quality desired on the expected delivery date. The chief risk officer is responsible for monitoring the supplier's production processes and ensuring that they are managed within the organization's risk appetite.

The chief risk officer may encounter some resistance to these measures from external stakeholders, especially international stakeholders, who may object to disclosing certain information or to following U.S. risk management procedures. The failure to maintain full transparency in these business relationships may be sufficient reason to terminate the affiliation.

DEVELOPING AN ERM BUSINESS CASE

Justifying the value created by an ERM program is a critical step in gaining organizational acceptance for the program. A business case for ERM can provide an organization's executives and stakeholders with compelling information to justify the resources required to implement an ERM program.

A business case (sometimes called a feasibility study) is an argument supporting an investment or an action. A business case should address what resources an organization must commit and what it can expect to receive in return for that investment. This is particularly difficult to accomplish when making a business case for ERM. Though the resources required to implement an ERM program might be relatively easy to determine, the return on the investment is more difficult to quantify. Rather than constructing standards of ERM value that can be different for various industries and subject to change, a series of practical questions and the methods of resolving those questions can guide the development of an ERM business case.

Before making the investment required for an ERM program, an organization's executives will require answers to questions that might be asked of any proposed program. The business case for ERM should therefore answer these questions:

- Why does the organization need ERM?
- What resources must be committed to ERM?
- How will the success of the ERM program be measured?
- Who will be in charge of the ERM program?
- What could "go wrong with" or derail the ERM program?
- Why might an organization not want to implement an ERM program?

Why Does the Organization Need ERM?

ERM will help an organization meet oversight challenges, as well as control and drive improvement. However, these overarching values can appear vague and may not convince executives to invest in ERM. Identifying quantifiable data to support the implementation of an ERM program is difficult because it is an emerging discipline, but guiding questions can help to more specifically define the value of ERM for an organization.

What Benefits Have Other Organizations in the Industry Experienced?

Financial institutions that have implemented ERM programs have reported improved performance management, better risk-based pricing, and reduced capital allocation and credit losses. Similarly, publicly held companies have reported stock price improvements, debt-rating upgrades, early warning of risks, loss reduction, and regulatory capital relief. ERM's increasing strategic value is attributable to these benefits gained by early adopters.

An organization with a well-integrated ERM program can enjoy these advantages:

- Highly efficient and effective management
- Discovery of new opportunities
- An increased probability of achieving goals

Including evidence of ERM as a competitive advantage can be persuasive evidence in a business case.

What Compliance Models Are Other Organizations in the Industry Adopting?

Although ERM has not been mandated by reporting and governing organizations, emerging compliance models focus on an organization's adoption and integration of ERM. Therefore, compliance with accepted models is becoming a driver of ERM, which is a compelling reason for organizations to view ERM as a strategic priority. Organizations can convert the significant costs they have incurred to comply with the Sarbanes-Oxley Act of 2002 into a business benefit by implementing an ERM program, which provides more benefits than simple compliance. Implementing ERM may also help organizations avoid potential rating agency downgrades and risks to their reputation.

What Strategies Should Be Driven From the Board Level Through the Organization?

An organization can use ERM to implement and monitor a consistent cross-functional program to more effectively address threats and opportunities. Implementing such a program can ensure that decisions throughout the organization are consistent with the stakeholders' risk tolerance. This can be a compelling argument in a business case if the organization has previously failed to address stakeholder concerns. Board members and executives can defend against potential regulatory investigations by demonstrating their organization's ERM effectiveness in compliance oversight issues.

How Can ERM Help to Maintain Consistency in a Changing Environment?

Consistency in risk monitoring is an important organizational capability, especially in a changing environment. Having a clear process to make informed decisions improves an organization's resilience. An ERM program with risk monitoring systems is clearly valuable if impending changes in the organization's environment are obvious and the potential for gains or losses based on knowledge of the shifts in risk can be demonstrated. Evidence of situations in which the organization failed to take adequate action and quantifying the value of that failure can be compelling additions to a business case. For example, if a steel forming company did not recognize that the cost of raw materials would rise and failed to secure prices at the lower rate, the difference between the anticipated and actual costs can be calculated as a loss that could have been avoided were an ERM program in effect.

What Resources Must Be Committed to ERM?

The investment required for an ERM program depends on the organization's current risk management program.

The extent of an ERM program depends on the organization's size, goals, values, industry, risk profile, competitive environment, and financial resources. Some risks are apt to be a key concern for any organization and should therefore be prioritized for action. ERM methods for addressing these prioritized risks can then be drafted and the required investment estimated.

The resources committed to the existing risk management program, as it addresses the prioritized risks, are then compared to the investment required in the proposed ERM program. The difference is the resources required. The estimate of resources should include four types of costs:

- Infrastructure improvements
- Capital expenses
- Change issues in processes
- Oversight, facilitation, and training

How Will the Success of the ERM Program Be Measured?

Measures of success are important because they provide a way to determine whether an ERM program is making a difference. In a business plan, the measures are the target goals against which actual results can be compared. There are two broad and closely related approaches to measuring ERM success:

- Results-based—Success of the ERM program in addressing the organization's risks
- Activity-based—Success in the implementation of the ERM program

Success of the ERM Program in Addressing the Organization's Risks

Obvious goals for an organization implementing ERM are to effectively address risks, especially those identified as high priority for action, and to be able to measure the effectiveness of the actions taken compared to the resources committed. Executives need to be able to respond to the question, "Was implementing ERM a good decision, and would we have had different results if ERM had not been implemented?" Management can use this "results-based" method to evaluate the ERM program's success. Measurements of this type of success can fall into a number of categories, depending on the risks that the organization is attempting to address.

To be effective, measurements of success proposed in an ERM business case should be practical and logical and embody these characteristics:

- Quantifiable in terms of currency, percentage, number, or as compared to internal or external benchmarks
- Consistent and traceable over time using standards that are readily identifiable
- Related to the probability or severity of the organization's key risks
- Representative of predictive and historical indicators
- Useful in supporting management decisions
- Timely and cost effective
- Simplified, but not overly simplistic, monitoring process

Success in Implementation of the ERM Program

The success of an ERM program's implementation can also be evaluated based on the ERM program's activities. This method of evaluation relies heavily on the engagement of senior executives and the board members; establishment of policies, systems, and processes; defined risk appetites; development of communications and an ERM dashboard; and integration of ERM in strategic planning, business processes, and performance management.

The "ERM Measurements of Success—Examples" exhibit illustrates some of the measurements that could be used to assess the success of the ERM program in a given organization.

ERM Measurements of Success—Examples

ERM Actions	Possible Measurements	Example
Integrate risk assessment into strategic planning	• Number of risks identified and assessed that challenge the organization's strategies • Number of key risk indicators (KRIs) identified and tracked periodically • Number of instances in which tracking KRIs showed improved results	A textile manufacturer identified four risks associated with procuring raw materials that would jeopardize its ability to meet its profitability strategic goal. One KRI for each risk was identified as an indicator of a future increase in the cost of raw materials. The KRIs were monitored weekly. When one was triggered, the manufacturer purchased raw materials in advance of price increases.
Improve internal risk identification	• Increase in the levels the organization included in the risk-mapping process • Increase in the number of tools available to identify risks more effectively	A hospital involved its staff nurses in the risk identification process by training them in the risk-mapping process. To make reporting and communication effective for the nurses, it created a communication system that allowed the nurses to easily determine those risks already identified, or to report risks not yet identified, and provide suggestions for their treatment.
Implement more effective methods of identifying and treating external threats	• Number of external threats and opportunities identified • Number of predictive techniques and KRIs monitored for external threats	A pest control service company faces external threats in the form of the regulation of chemicals, liability class action suits regarding the use of chemicals, and rising competition. Three senior executives were each assigned one significant external threat and charged with determining predictive techniques and identifying KRIs to provide warnings of activity that might threaten the organization's strategic plans. Two additional senior executives were charged with identifying emerging threats not yet identified.
Reduce or avoid loss incidents	• Identification of key loss incidents • Use of the number of key loss incidents in prior years as benchmarks • Implementation of loss reduction activity • Change in loss incidents compared to benchmarks	An apartment complex linked an increase in trespassing to a series of robberies. The number of past trespasses was calculated using security cameras. After the implementation of security gates, electronic pass cards for the doors, and nighttime security patrols, the number of trespasses recorded was compared to the benchmark.

The Risk and Insurance Management Society's (RIMS) Risk Maturity Model (RMM)[9] provides an effective set of attributes for measuring the degree of ERM competency within an organization. The RMM framework distills elements of ERM by category and then into assumed best practice factors and indicators within each category. This approach provides a model for ERM benchmarking as an organization progresses in several areas of implementation:

- Adoption of ERM-based approach
- ERM process management
- Risk appetite/tolerance management
- Root cause discipline
- Uncovering risks
- Performance management
- Business resiliency and sustainability

Who Will Be in Charge of the ERM Program?

The effectiveness of ERM depends on the effectiveness of the organization's information and communication. Information and communication about risk should be integrated for the organization as a whole, by business unit, by functional unit, for product units, and by geographic units. To make this possible, one or more senior executives should be in charge of ERM. Small organizations may distribute ERM responsibilities across several executive managers, depending on the degree to which ERM has been actualized within the organization.

What Could "Go Wrong With" or Derail the ERM Program?

Naturally, an organization's stakeholders will want to understand the positive aspects associated with implementing ERM. However, an ERM implementation also can fail. An ERM business plan should inform stakeholders about possible events that could derail the program. A well-informed organization can avoid repeating errors encountered by early adopters. Mistakes and negative drivers can be broadly categorized:

- Failure to secure strong board and executive management support and/ or align risk appetite with strategic plans can derail an ERM program. If the organization's leaders cannot agree about the value of the program or define acceptable risk limits, any further ERM program plans could come under constant question, stunting confidence in the program.

- Lack of communication, realistic goals, or common vocabulary can cause misunderstandings and potentially narrow the focus of the ERM program. This could lead to potential risks being overlooked. The extent of the ERM program, its purpose, definition of terms, and the desired impact of the program should be communicated throughout the organization.
- Failure to clearly define the roles and responsibilities for ERM and accountability for implementation of the program can degrade the importance of implementation.
- Failure to acknowledge current risk management programs or individuals with developed risk management skills and abilities can create dissension.
- Having a false sense of security because an ERM program is implemented can result in the organization's failing to collect risk information from all processes and effectively identify actual risks.
- Allowing regulations and compliance to define the conditions for an ERM program's success limits activity and does not allow the organization to effectively recognize the benefits of the ERM program.
- Overcomplicated data and reports can overwhelm the monitoring process and cause essential indications of risk to be overlooked. An ERM dashboard should simplify the monitoring process and provide dynamic access to information.

Why Might an Organization Not Want to Implement an ERM Program?

Despite the many advantages ERM can provide, ERM programs have not been fully embraced by all business sectors. For example, the financial services industry has been quick to recognize the benefits of ERM because of compliance issues and quantifiable, economic benefits. Conversely, for other businesses, the qualitative costs related to risk to reputation, social responsibility, risk culture, and sustainable development are only just emerging and being recognized.

Additionally, organizations in the public and local government sector remain compartmentalized. Silos still exist in these organizations—a scenario that does not support the development of ERM. A public risk manager often is not an organizational decision maker, and continuity of service—essential to the success of an ERM program—is often absent from the public and local government sectors.

An organization might not want to implement an ERM program for these reasons:

- Difficulty blending ERM with the current corporate culture
- Board does not support the ERM concept
- Board does not discern quantifiable benefits
- Stakeholders do not want the organization to pursue certain ERM initiatives
- ERM program is perceived as being a costly investment
- Existing organization infrastructure does not facilitate required information flow

A final reason why an organization might not want to adopt an ERM program is because an organization's senior management might feel overwhelmed with the perceived amount of information required to support ERM and the information technology infrastructure with business intelligence applications required to collect and interpret it. For ERM to be effective, all segments of an organization must communicate with each other; data must be exchanged and the information gathered must be analyzed, prioritized, and integrated into the organization's overall strategic plan.

DETERMINING AN ORGANIZATION'S RISK CRITERIA

The risk criteria that an organization adopts establish the boundaries for its risk appetite. These are the thresholds that it will monitor and act on. By initiating a formal process for setting these thresholds that involves stakeholders, an organization's senior management ensures that the most effective criteria are selected and that they will be monitored in the most efficient way.

To deploy an ERM program, an organization's senior management determines which risks are within the tolerance limits of the organization's risk appetite. Accomplishing this requires determining the risk criteria it will apply to define its risk appetite and the thresholds it will use to establish limits. The risk criteria selected may depend on an organization's internal policies, mission statement and goals, and the interests of stakeholders. Broad risk criteria and thresholds may be developed initially as part of the organization's strategic planning and then refined as particular risks are identified and risk analysis techniques chosen.

Based on the nature of the risk criteria and thresholds, measurements are identified for collection, monitoring, and response.

Because risk criteria and thresholds for each organization are unique, the process for determining them and establishing the organization's measurable risk criteria can most easily be completed by answering several questions:

- What risk criteria should we measure?
- What threshold should we apply to each risk criterion?
- How can we validate the risk criteria and thresholds selected?
- How will we measure the thresholds selected?
- How will we organize, score, and evaluate the measurements gathered to prioritize the risks?

What Risk Criteria Should We Measure?

Senior management's first step in determining an organization's risk criteria is to consider the areas of potential impact that could significantly affect the organization's ability to meet its mission and goals within the parameters of its internal policies. Several such areas exist:[10]

- Direct damages to assets
- Market capitalization (in a for-profit environment)
- Market penetration
- Earnings before interest and taxes (EBIT)
- Key performance indicators (KPIs)
- Value of company to potential buyer
- Value at risk
- Legal and statutory requirements
- Community priorities
- Humanitarian concerns

Based on the areas of potential impact, risk criteria are then drafted that define the ways in which the significant risks to each area can be assessed. The risk criteria must correspond to the nature of the areas of potential impact and the way in which the risk criteria can be measured.

What Threshold Should We Apply to Each Risk Criterion?

In the second step, senior management drafts thresholds for each risk criterion that are acceptable to the organization. Collectively, the thresholds constitute the organization's risk tolerance. Thresholds define the boundaries between risks that require treatment and risks that do not.

Thresholds might be assigned to a risk criterion as a finite limit. For example, a KPI for a hospital monitoring the instances of staphylococci infections incurred by patients in its care might set the limit of a single instance as the threshold before investigation and remedial action are required.

Risk Criteria Examples

Areas of Potential Impact	Measurable Risk Criteria Examples
Direct damages to assets	• Number of losses • Average dollar value per loss
Market capitalization	• Number of shares outstanding • Current price per share
Market penetration	• Percentage of market by product line • Geographic spread by product line
Earnings before interest and taxes (EBIT)	• EBIT margin
Key performance indicators (KPIs)	• Error rate • Cost of raw materials • Units of output • Injury rate
Value of company to potential buyer	• Finite dollar value
Value at risk	• Change in market prices • Change in interest rates • Change in exchange rates
Legal and statutory requirements	• Increased environmental-impact reporting • Decreased restrictions to market barriers
Community priorities	• Political obligations • Compliance pressures
Humanitarian concerns	• Requests for contributions • Increased requests for voluntary performance

Another common approach is to divide thresholds into three categories. A private school with a KPI of number of student injuries is used as an example:

- An upper category defines thresholds that are intolerable regardless of the benefits the activity may bring and for which risk control measures are essential whatever the cost. For a private school, any injuries occurring on school buses are intolerable, and risk control measures will be applied in whatever manner possible. These potential losses are beyond the risk tolerance of the school.

- A middle category defines thresholds at which costs and benefits are taken into account and opportunities balanced against potential adverse consequences. Again using the example of the private school, physical education and sports teams have costs and benefits. The costs stem from potential injuries to students and from compensating the trained staff required to ensure the proper degree of safety. The benefits are gained from maintaining or increasing enrollment due to being able to offer a well-rounded educational program. Some minimal level of student injuries is expected and tolerable in the physical education and sports program.

- A lower category defines thresholds at which positive or negative risks are negligible or so small that no risk treatment measures are needed. If the private school accepts the fact that some students will drive themselves to school, the institution can require a signed release from students and parents absolving it of any liability for students' operation of their own vehicles and damage that might occur to vehicles while on school property. The risks to the school are negligible; therefore, the threshold of loss frequency and severity can be relatively high before treatment in addition to the signed releases is necessary.

How Can We Validate the Risk Criteria and Thresholds Selected?

The third step in the process is ensuring that the most important risk criteria and appropriate thresholds have been selected for the organization. Stakeholders who understand the organization's external and internal risks are in a key position to review the risk criteria and thresholds drafted by senior management. When choosing stakeholders to perform this review, senior management should select persons based on certain characteristics:

- Individuals who understand the risks that the organization may be facing
- Individuals from a variety of functional areas
- Individuals with a wide knowledge base
- Individuals with knowledge of the external environment and of the internal functions of the organization

To uniformly gather information from the individuals selected to validate the risk criteria and thresholds, senior management might conduct interviews or a survey, hold a workshop, or use a combination of approaches.

Following the collection of data from these individuals, senior management must determine how to score the data to make a final decision regarding the risk criteria and thresholds to implement. The data might be scored by popular vote, severity of impact, frequency of instances reported, possibility of occurrence, time to develop measurement capability, or a combination of factors.

How Will We Measure the Thresholds Selected?

In the fourth step, after the thresholds have been selected, senior management must determine the type and frequency of measurements to be used. Some measurements can be collected from various existing reports:

- Annual reports
- Audit reports
- Management reports
- Operational reports
- Loss reports
- Regulatory reports

Measurements that are not readily available must be collected. Certain questions can help senior management define the measurement process:

- Who has information about the data that must be collected?
- Is the information limited to a single business segment or spread over multiple functional areas?
- Are industry benchmarks needed against which to compare data? If so, where can these benchmarks be located, or what available data can reliably serve as benchmarks?
- Who should be responsible for gathering the data?
- What is the frequency at which data should be collected?
- How should the data be reported?

How Will We Organize, Score, and Evaluate the Measurements Gathered to Prioritize the Risks?

At the fifth step, senior management must determine how the data reported regarding the thresholds can be used to prioritize risks for treatment. Dashboards are useful in organizing large quantities of information for fast scoring. However, any dashboard should also recognize measurements that are unusual and outside the thresholds that might have been considered.

For example, an insurer might be monitoring the number and average loss size of property claims. The numbers reports might be within the thresholds considered below the point at which action is required to address unacceptable results. However, if the individual reporting the losses recognizes that most of them are occurring within one geographic area and should have been preventable by the property owners, a dashboard or reporting system should allow the individual reporting the data to issue red flags for immediate attention.

A combination of data reported through a dashboard or another system as well as red-flagged items can then be prioritized for treatment as risks that threaten the organization's results. These data are incorporated in the overall business intelligence systems.

SUMMARY

Risk ownership at all levels of an organization is critical to its chances of success because risk ownership assigns the task of managing volatile events to personnel close to where they may occur. A formal plan to assign risk ownership must be in place so that no risk goes unmanaged. Allocating risk ownership allows each internal stakeholder to focus on his or her area of expertise and achieve his or her goals. The chief risk officer acts as an internal consultant, assisting both in the development of risk ownership and coordinating efforts among all risk owners.

Communication on risk within the ERM framework is critical to ERM efficiency. The foundations of ERM communication include understanding management style, communication ethics, common communication problems, and practical guidelines for effective communication. Effective communication requires setting up internal and external stakeholder communication channels and developing professional communication skills. Specific RM communication skills are applied to business presentations, business e-mails, visual displays, and RM reports. Good communication skills help to ensure consistency of information across media and stakeholder groups as well as the effectiveness of ERM programs.

An organization's goals are best achieved if both the organization and its stakeholders clearly understand the risks each stakeholder faces. As risk owners, external stakeholders must control the risks they own and report their risk management processes to the organization. Within the ERM model, the organization must have reasonable assurance that all external stakeholders, suppliers, customers, society, competition, co-opetition, and intermediaries are responsible and accountable for managing the risks they own. This can be achieved only through constant communication/consultation on risk established with all stakeholders in order to reach a shared understanding on how to optimize risk taking throughout the network of partnerships and common interests.

A business case should address what an organization would have to commit to a project and what it can expect to receive in return for its investment. Because this is difficult to accomplish for ERM, a business case for ERM should answer specific questions:

* Why does the organization need ERM?
* What resources must be committed to ERM?

- How will the success of the ERM program be measured?
- Who will be in charge of the ERM program?
- What can "go wrong with" or derail the ERM program?
- Why might an organization not want to implement an ERM program?

To deploy an ERM program, an organization's senior management determines which risks are within the tolerance limits of its risk appetite. Risk criteria and thresholds selected should correspond with the type of risk and the way in which risk levels are expressed. Questions can guide senior management through this process:

- What risk criteria should we measure?
- What threshold should we apply to each risk criterion?
- How can we validate the risk criteria and thresholds selected?
- How will we measure the thresholds selected?
- How will we organize, score, and evaluate the measurements gathered to prioritize the risks?

CHAPTER NOTES

1. Frederick F. Reichheld, *The Loyalty Effect* (Boston: Harvard Business School Press, 1996), p. 4.

2. Deloitte, "Nine Principles for Building the Risk Intelligent Enterprise," www.deloitte.com/dtt/cda/doc/content/dtt_NinePrinciples.pdf (accessed March 26, 2009).

3. www. dictionary.reference.com/browse/motive (accessed March 26, 2009).

4. Joshua Kennon, "The Board of Directors: Responsibility, Role and Structure," www.beginnersinvest.about.com/cs/a/aa2203a.htm (accessed June 17, 2007).

5. International Organization for Standardization, ISO/FDIS 31000:2009(E): *Risk Management—Principles and Guidelines on Implementation* (Geneva, Switzerland: International Organization for Standardization, 2009).

6. International Organization for Standardization, ISO/FDIS 31000:2009(E): *Risk Management—Principles and Guidelines on Implementation* (Geneva, Switzerland: International Organization for Standardization, 2009).

7. WCCO-TV, "EPA Files Objections to Coal-Fired Power Plant," wcco.com/energy/coal.power.plant.2.916456.html (accessed April 27, 2009).

8. Inner City Public Interest Law Center, "A Brief and Selective History of U.S. Regulation," www.innercitypress.org/reghist.html (accessed April 27, 2009).

9. Steven Minsky, RIMS State of ERM Report 2008 (New York: Risk and Insurance Management Society, Inc., 2008), pp. 10–22.

10. Adapted from Risk and Insurance Management Society, Inc, *ERM Planning Template* (New York: RIMS, 2007), p. 5.

Communicate and Consult: Project Management

Educational Objectives

After learning the content of this chapter and completing the corresponding course guide assignment, you should be able to:

▶ Describe how to develop and implement a project management plan.

▶ Describe the activities required to manage risk in a project.

▶ Outline the steps to manage change in an organization.

▶ Describe enterprise-wide risk management project implementation planning and methods of incorporating continuous change.

Outline

Project Management Plan Development and Implementation

Managing Risks in a Project

Organizational Change Management Steps

Implementing ERM—Continuous Change

Summary

Communicate and Consult: Project Management

Project and change management planning provide a framework through which an organization can undertake a new ambition or alter current processes in a deliberate, controlled manner. A project manager or change agent must understand the scope and nature of their responsibilities, identify the disciplines necessary to achieve his or her goals, and use scheduling tools to effectively facilitate planning and completion or integration of the project or change. Although enterprise-wide risk management (ERM) is not a project, but a process embedded in an organization, a project-structured framework can be used during the initial phases of ERM implementation to more fully engage the organization in the ERM process. Project management can also be used in association with the ERM process when it requires project management techniques to produce the desired results or change.

PROJECT MANAGEMENT PLAN DEVELOPMENT AND IMPLEMENTATION

Effectively planned projects and project management provide a systematic method of reaching goals when organizations must achieve results that are not possible through routine processes.

Project management plans outline the activity and steps required to achieve a stated goal. The purpose of project management is to anticipate risks associated with meeting the project's objectives and to organize and control activities so that the project is completed successfully.

To develop a project management plan, a project manager must understand the scope and nature of the project, apply the disciplines necessary to achieve the project goals, and use scheduling tools to effectively facilitate the planning and completion of the project.

Project Scope

A project is a unique undertaking with established goals that is outside of routine processes and requires people, materials, and financial resources. Projects can have a wide array of magnitudes, durations, and complexities. Because projects are unique undertakings, there may be no established routines for the process. Therefore, a plan must be developed to ensure that issues and contingencies, such as the loss of key personnel or delays in receiving raw materials, are considered so the project goals can be achieved.

A project management plan defines who will work on the project, what materials will be needed, when work will begin and be expected to end, where the work will take place, and how the project will be conducted. Project management disciplines and scheduling tools can increase the effectiveness of planning the project and tracking the results.

A project goal is a final result desired by the project sponsor. The project sponsor defines the goal in a project charter, which documents the existence of the project and provides the authority to undertake the actions required to achieve the desired results.

Project constraints are quantifiable criteria that must be met for the project to be successful and are often documented in a project scope statement. In general, there are four types of project constraints:

- Quality—standards of quality against which the outputs will be measured
- Timeliness—timeframes within which the work must be accomplished
- Budget—resource inputs allocated to the accomplishment of the project
- Boundaries—factors, such as ethical or legal issues, that limit the project team's options in accomplishing the project

Project Management Disciplines

Depending on the nature and complexity of the project goal, the project management plan could encompass many disciplines, including projecting and controlling integration with existing systems or communities, communication, time management, human resources management, quality management, cost control, procurement, risk management, technology, and environmental issues management. All project management plans should include two disciplines:

- Managing the project team
- Communicating project information and progress

Managing the Project Team

A crucial resource allocated to the achievement of any project is the people who will take the actions necessary to complete the work. Because a project is outside of the scope of routine processes and unanticipated problems may be encountered, the project team must understand its goals and have members who are able to deal with unexpected situations or find the resources that can. Though a project operates out of routine processes, the organization that is implementing or has implemented ERM must include the ERM process in the project as a project risk management tool.

Whether the skills required to accomplish project goals are available among current employee resources or must be attained, either temporarily or permanently, will influence the mix of employees and external contractors or consultants selected to work on a project. If skills that will not be required within the organization in the future are required to complete the project, contractors with those skills may be hired. If skills must be developed in team members or other employees, consultants may be hired to impart knowledge to accomplish the project.

Team Communication Checklist

☐	Project overview	• Project goals and objectives
		• Project scope statement
		• Project outcomes
☐	Team members' roles and responsibilities	• Expectations regarding behaviors
		• Responsibilities of each team member and how the work of each is linked together
☐	Results orientation	• Commitment required by members to achieve the project outcome
		• Protocols in balancing team requirements and ongoing job duties
☐	Communication expectations	• Forum that will be used for collaboration and communications
		• Expectations regarding the sharing of information and ideas
		• Information resources available and the expectation that team members serve as information resources for each other
☐	Team cooperation expectations	• Acceptance of and respect for the contributions of each member
		• Expectations regarding constructive feedback and positive contributions
		• Protocols for conflict resolution

Effective team interaction requires a group development process for members to become accustomed to the concepts of the project, adjust to one another, and agree on how to coordinate their efforts to accomplish the project goals. Project managers should allow time for team members to work through the phases and guide them so that they do not regress or become stuck in one stage.

As a project team comes together, the project manager informs team members about the scope of the project and the level of participation expected. There are five stages of project planning:[1]

1. Forming—Team members transition into being part of a working group by expressing expectations and establishing a team identity.
2. Storming—Team members offer different ideas that address the tasks to be accomplished.
3. Norming—Team members collectively decide how the group will function.
4. Performing—Team members collectively meet their objectives.
5. Adjourning—Team members collectively bring closure to the project and disband.

One way in which ERM differs from a traditional project is that it has no conclusion. Because of the nature of change within and outside of an organization, the ERM process is constantly focused on emerging, changing, or disappearing risks. Thus, it has no final deliverable.

Communicating Project Information and Progress

Communication is crucial to a project's success. Information must be collected, exchanged, and adequately stored for accountability and reference. For this reason, a communication plan is part of project management. Communication activities take place internal to or external to the project team.

Internal to the project team, communication can be broken into three phases:

1. Defining and implementing the project—The goals, objectives and constraints for the project are communicated, the role of each team member is clarified, and initial tasks are assigned. The project manager communicates deadlines for tasks.
2. Interacting to achieve objectives—Team members interact to resolve questions and work through issues that arise.
3. Evaluating and closing the project—The team's achievements are compared to the project goals, an important step in judging the success of the endeavor. In addition, many organizations ask team members to evaluate the effectiveness of the team's interaction so improvements can be made in future teamwork. Closing the project often involves a group debriefing to formulate recommendations regarding actionable follow-up activities and to improve similar projects.

As the project progresses, oral, electronic, and written communication have important roles in ensuring that team members are informed.

- Oral communication is a significant part of problem-solving between project team members. Oral communication is effective in brainstorming and consensus-building and when there is no immediate need for written records.

- Informal electronic communication is effective for making assignments and expediting responses to questions. Team members should be coached regarding the appropriate distribution of electronic communication; often, there is a tendency to include team members in exchanges when only those involved in the decision-making process or information exchange are necessary.

- Formal written communication is required when a record of actions or decisions might be needed afterward. Project status reports, legal requirements, and changes to the project scope should all be communicated to team members in writing.

External to the project team, communication to organizational employees and stakeholders is generally formal and written. Stakeholders for a project may include the head of the organization, senior management, current or potential customers, shareholders, line or functional managers, and communities. Written statements regarding the achievement of milestones and project updates are carefully crafted for external communication to ensure that the tone is appropriate.

Applying Scheduling Tools

The **Gantt chart** and **PERT (program or project evaluation and review technique)** diagram are widely used project management scheduling tools. Each of these can be used for scheduling and tracking a project; however, due to the unique nature of the tools, project managers often use them together.

Developing and applying scheduling tools involves a sequence of steps.

Defining and Ordering Activities

The first step in developing a Gantt chart or PERT diagram is defining the activities or tasks to be completed in the project, determining which activities must be completed before others can be accomplished (called predecessor activities), and assigning time estimates for each activity. This information can be displayed in a table and is the key information required by software used to generate the Gantt charts or PERT diagrams. The "Project Activities" exhibit provides both time estimates and items that must follow others in the process. Note that activities in this project beyond B do not have B as a predecessor. Thus, B may be completed independently from the other activities.

Gantt chart
A bar chart displaying the amount of time required for each activity in a project, the sequence of activities to be performed, and the current schedule status of the activities.

Program evaluation and review technique (PERT)
A technique that identifies a project's necessary accomplishments (called events), defines when the events must be finished for the project to be on schedule, and identifies those events that are most time-sensitive.

Project Activities

Activity	Predecessor	Time Estimate
A	—	4.00 weeks
B	—	5.33 weeks
C	A	5.25 weeks
D	A	6.33 weeks
E	C, D	5.40 weeks
F	C, D	4.50 weeks
G	E, F	2.00 weeks

Critical path

The sequence of activities in a project that take the longest time to complete and determine the overall time length of the project.

The next step is to determine the **critical path**, which consists of activities that must be completed on time. Activities that allow slack time can be delayed without changing the project's completion schedule.

Gantt Chart

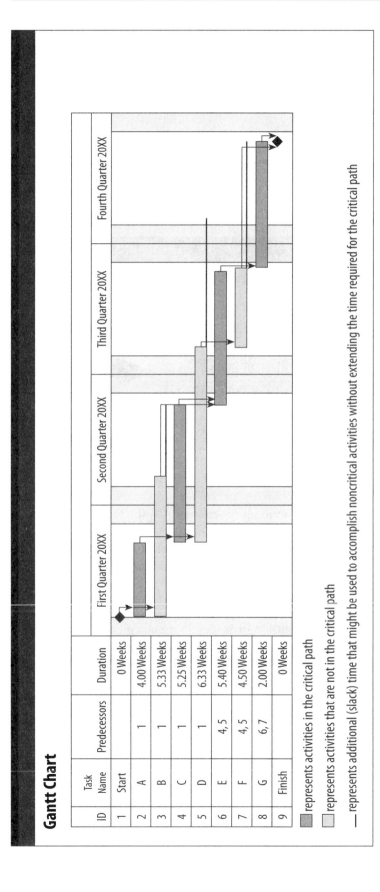

ID	Task Name	Predecessors	Duration
1	Start		0 Weeks
2	A	1	4.00 Weeks
3	B	1	5.33 Weeks
4	C	1	5.25 Weeks
5	D	1	6.33 Weeks
6	E	4, 5	5.40 Weeks
7	F	4, 5	4.50 Weeks
8	G	6, 7	2.00 Weeks
9	Finish		0 Weeks

represents activities in the critical path

represents activities that are not in the critical path

— represents additional (slack) time that might be used to accomplish noncritical activities without extending the time required for the critical path

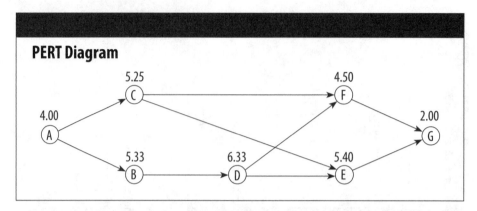

PERT Diagram

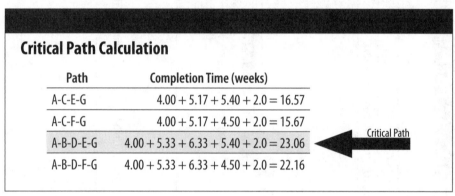

Critical Path Calculation

Path	Completion Time (weeks)
A-C-E-G	$4.00 + 5.17 + 5.40 + 2.0 = 16.57$
A-C-F-G	$4.00 + 5.17 + 4.50 + 2.0 = 15.67$
A-B-D-E-G	$4.00 + 5.33 + 6.33 + 5.40 + 2.0 = 23.06$
A-B-D-F-G	$4.00 + 5.33 + 6.33 + 4.50 + 2.0 = 22.16$

← Critical Path

The critical path can be determined by adding the task durations for all paths that appear in the PERT diagram. The critical path is the sequence of activities that add up to the longest overall duration. The "Critical Path Calculation" exhibit shows a 23.06 week completion time. While the "Project Activities" exhibit shows B as an independent activity, the time to complete B must be included in the critical path. Alternatively, project management software applications can be used to visually identify the critical path in a project by color-coding the Gantt chart or PERT diagram.

Monitoring Progress and Managing Change

As a project progresses, the Gantt chart is useful for managing a project's progress and any changes to it. The completion of activities can be plotted on the Gantt chart, providing a visual snapshot of progress made toward the project goal.

Changes to a project and its activities are inevitable. If monitoring the project's progress reveals that activities on the critical path have begun to lag, resources from other activities may have to be diverted to critical-path activities, or additional resources beyond the team may have to be obtained to ensure the project is completed on time.

Controlling Scope Creep

Scope creep can occur when the scope of a project is not properly defined, documented, or controlled. It is generally considered a negative occurrence that is to be avoided. Even so, scope creep, to some degree, occurs in virtually every project.

Typically, scope increases when new facets or features are added to existing product designs without corresponding increases in resources, schedule, or budget. As the scope of a project grows, the project team overruns its original budget and schedule as defined by the critical path.

If the budget and schedule are increased along with the scope, the change is usually considered an acceptable addition to the project and is not considered to be scope creep.

Scope creep can be controlled through various activities during the planning phase of the project:

- Clearly identifying the project in the scope statement before the project begins—A clear definition of the deliverables, resources, and project duration is essential in determining those activities that are in excess of the scope statement.

- Estimating the complexity of the project as completely as possible— Underestimation of a project's complexity often leads to unanticipated additional activities.

- Defining management's expectations—Management's failure to define end users of the products and services often leads to the expansion of a project's activities beyond the scope statement. The expansion may become necessary to make the product or outcome of value to the users.

- Involving all end users early in the project development—Involving end users only in later stages of the **project life cycle** can result in unanticipated activities as additional requirements are added.

MANAGING RISKS IN A PROJECT

A project manager must master a number of disciplines to achieve a project goal within quality, time, budget, and boundary constraints. The disciplines vary according to the nature of the project and its complexity. Risk management is one discipline that is necessary for successfully completing projects.

Managing risks in a project is one of many disciplines a successful project manager needs to have mastered. Many projects, especially those of large scope or long duration, include the risk of failure from losses. Some losses are similar to those that all organizations face, while others are common only to projects. Managing risks in a project is similar to managing risks for an organization, but it requires an increased focus on the time and budget allocated. Project risk management involves three primary activities:

Scope creep
A project management phenomenon that occurs when unplanned activities are added or existing activities are increased, resulting in a project that exceeds its original budget or time schedule.

Project life cycle
A model of how a project is planned, executed, and monitored from its inception to its completion.

- Applying the risk management process within the context of the project
- Addressing common project losses
- Monitoring risks on the project's critical path

Risk Management Process Within the Context of a Project

There is always risk associated with a project. The purpose of project risk management is to ensure that the levels of risk are optimized so that the project's goal is achieved. The project risk management process is a structured way for the project manager to identify and assess risk and respond appropriately.

The team assigned to a project might consider the project risk management plan informally, or it might develop a formal project risk management plan at the beginning of a project and apply it throughout a project's life cycle to ensure that changing circumstances are tracked and managed. The effort required depends on the scope of the project, with larger projects requiring more formal and detailed risk management considerations than smaller projects. When project risk management is done formally, the project team follows the same steps in applying the risk management process to a project that would be followed for an organization practicing ERM.

The Risk Management Process

1. Establish the internal and external contexts—the context of the project in relation to the strategic goals of the organization and its relationship to its stakeholders

2. Risk assessment—identification, analysis, and evaluation

3. Risk treatment—selecting and implementing appropriate risk management techniques

4. Monitor results and revise

5. Communicate and consult with all internal and external stakeholders

---

Projects are intended to introduce change within an organization. This can include the development of a new product, process, procedure, or formation of a new operating division. By applying ERM process techniques to a project, the organization synchronizes its strategy and risk management with the strategic goals and operational objectives of the project. A project is likely also to alter the risk portfolio of the organization. The impact of this change in risk profile must be considered, addressed, and communicated to the board (where applicable), executives, and risk owners.

Establishing the Internal and External Contexts

A project necessarily will affect the organization and its stakeholders. In some cases, the board will have approved the project plan. In other cases, senior management will have done so. The first step in the ERM process is to ensure that the project plan and charter are associated with the mission, vision, and goals of the organization. If a project represents a change in strategy, the communication and consult component of ERM to all stakeholders likely will be more extensive relative to a project that introduces an internal procedural change.

Risk Assessment

Risk assessment involves identifying and analyzing risks by considering the range of possible project outcomes. In this activity, the primary concern is determining which potential risks will require treatment.

One method of assessing project risks is to review each of the project activities with—if the activities are complex—a breakdown of the tasks that need to be accomplished for each. The parameters for each activity, such as time estimates, costs, quality measurements, staff requirements, and predecessor activities, are reviewed to determine acceptable variances between what was planned and what is acceptable while still achieving the project's goals. In this assessment, the time estimates for activities on the critical path are scrutinized because any risk that extends the critical path will also extend the final completion date of the project identified in the **project constraints**.

Project constraint
Any limitation to the solutions that can be applied in achieving a project goal.

Acceptable variances for each activity become the basis for analyzing foreseeable risks that can cause results to fall outside the acceptable parameters. For each activity and associated task, the project team judges the likelihood and the severity of the impact to the project in a risk analysis matrix.

Using the risk analysis matrix, the project team can prioritize the risks according to their potential to negatively affect project results. This prioritization can be accomplished in a number of ways, such as rating the risks by order of concern or grouping risks by urgency of action required. Any risk to activities on the critical path deemed likely to extend the project beyond its completion date receives a higher priority for treatment.

Risk Treatment

Once the risks are prioritized, the project team considers the appropriate risk management techniques for addressing the threats to the project and implements the technique or combination of techniques most feasible for each risk.

Sample Risk Analysis Matrix

Activity: 4.2.1—Obtain steel for product components to be roll formed.

Risks	Likelihood (frequency)			Project Impact (severity)		
	Low	Medium	High	Low	Medium	High
Increased steel prices (external)			X		X	
Availability of steel of required quality (external)			X			X
Loss of company's purchasing officer (internal)		X		X		

The most effective technique or techniques for managing a risk is determined by considering how the risk might affect the project's successful completion. The techniques selected should treat the risk in a manner that will create an outcome that is within acceptable variances. The threats that appear in the "Sample Risk Analysis Matrix" exhibit are used as examples:

- The risk of increased steel prices might jeopardize the budget constraints for the project. To address this, the project team might use the risk financing technique of a noninsurance risk transfer through a hedging arrangement by entering into a futures contract to buy steel at a future date at a fixed price.

- The risk of availability of steel of the required quality might jeopardize timeliness of project completion as activities are delayed while the required steel is located or produced. The risk control technique of separation might be employed, using multiple purchasing channels to obtain the steel.

The project team should not overlook the opportunities that accompany risk. For example, during the duration of the project, a new steel roll forming machine is introduced whose energy efficiency offsets the cost of modest steel price increases. Competitors who have invested in older technology may be loath to invest in the newer technology, giving this project team and the organization an advantage that did not exist at the beginning of the project.

In addition to using risk management techniques, project teams address risks through contingency planning, which involves planning for a possible event through alternative procedures. The alternative procedures are established in advance and should be within the variance requirement of each activity. Project team members should be empowered to activate contingency plans in response to triggering events. Contingency planning facilitates keeping the entire project on track within the project constraints. For example, the risk in the sample risk analysis matrix of the loss of the company's purchasing officer can be addressed through a contingency plan; if the officer is no longer available to perform his or her responsibilities, a team member can assume the task and work through the project sponsor to obtain the information and authority needed to perform that role.

The project team should recognize that there are limits to the available resources for risk management and that it is not practical to apply risk management techniques to every identified threat. Planning should apply to highly likely losses that would significantly affect the project's outcome. Some resources should be held in reserve to deal with circumstances that change as the project progresses.

Monitor Results and Revise

As the project progresses, the project manager compares the quality, time, budget, and other constraints established in the project's **scope statement** to the project status. The variances established for each activity are useful in determining whether individual activities are progressing within acceptable parameters.

Scope statement
A clarifying project document that details the objectives to be accomplished, products or deliverables, potential costs and gains, and success measurements.

The project manager must also monitor the progression of the entire project to estimate whether the project's goal will be achieved. For example, each activity might be at the maximum variance from its budget allocation. Any significant additional expense could push the entire project outside its budget constraints. If a project is marginally within budget, the project manager might reallocate resources from less critical activities to activities with greater resource requirements.

Communication and Consultation

Project teams must recognize that while they have resolved many of the conflicts and issues that arose as they progressed through project phases, their stakeholders will have unresolved questions and concerns that often require the same kinds of discussions that occurred in previous project sessions. Therefore, the project team must consider when it should consult with and communicate with each stakeholder that can or will be affected by the project's outcome. While this can often mean allowing stakeholders to participate in some of the project team's discussions, they may still need additional information. Thus, an extensive communication period and process may be associated with the testing and delivery phases of a project's plan.

Common Project Risks

Some risks are common to projects. By anticipating these common risks, a project manager can treat them.

There are risks inherent to projects that the project team can control or influence. There are several sources of common internal risks and methods of treating them:

- Project scope—The lack of a clearly defined project scope can be the starting point of design flaws that can plague a project at any point in its life cycle. The farther the project progresses, the more it costs to correct a design problem and bring activities back on track with intended goals. For example, information technology projects are subject to changes and scope creep if the project scope is not sufficiently defined. Therefore, it is economical to clearly define the project's goals, mission, and constraints in a detailed scope statement before any activities begin. Team members should ask the project sponsor to clarify any vague details, and answers should be appended to the scope statement as documentation.

- Human resources—Team members and project participants are important resources in accomplishing a project. The loss of key team members can derail a project at a critical project phase. Bringing new team members up to speed in the middle of a project can take time. If the success of a project depends on specific skills, the human resource risk can be mitigated by combining internal and external resources. For example, software programming might be outsourced to contractors for the duration of a project.

- Operational risk—Operational risks arise from a company's business functions and inadequate or failed internal processes, people, and systems. Examples of operational risks include failures of or disruption in employment practices, workplace safety, systems, workmanship, and management. If the project team depends on any organizational operations for project completion, it should consider the ways in which failures in those operations could jeopardize the project and then prepare contingency plans to mitigate the potential loss. For example, a project activity requiring data entry by internal personnel faces an operational risk in the form of errors that might be entered as a result of poor execution and unavailable resources because of staffing shortages. A contingency plan to outsource data entry with sufficient quality controls would mitigate this operational risk.

Some external risks are beyond the control of the project team. There are several sources of common external risks and methods of treating them:

- Natural perils—Natural perils are events outside human control, such as floods, windstorms, volcanic eruptions, and earthquakes. Physical property or data sources can be damaged or employees can be injured. Depending on the nature of the property, loss prevention and control techniques can be applied to reduce the chances or the severity of loss. Transfer through insurance might be appropriate so that damaged property can be replaced. For example, the risk management technique of duplication can be applied to data so that backups are available if the primary source is damaged.

- Political risks—Political risk refers to complications that result from decisions made by political or regulatory bodies that alter expected outcomes or the value of an outcome by changing the probability of achieving business goals. Political risks can be at a macro level, affecting all participants in a country equally, such as the declaration of war or currency actions. Political risks at a micro level can affect an industry or the local economy, such as appropriation of funds for local projects, regulation changes, or shifts in political power. A project team should consider how political or regulatory changes might change the feasibility of its assigned project and mitigate the risks, if possible. Mitigation against macro-level risks can include intellectual property safeguards, risk diversification, **political risk insurance**, and exit planning. Mitigation on a micro level can include contingency planning, hedging, and building local political leverage through community activities and lobbying.

- Commercial and social expectations—Projects that involve product or service development are launched to meet a need. Failure to meet the commercial or social need, or a need that changes during the project, is a threat. The project team can mitigate failing to meet a need by conducting adequate surveys before the project design and repeating the surveys throughout the project duration to ensure that the resulting products and services meet customers' expectations.

- Technology evolution or obsolescence—For long-term projects, the possibility of technological changes creates of the possibility of developing products or services that are obsolete before they are completed. To mitigate the loss, the project team should scan the technology horizon to determine what is in development that might render current hardware, software, and systems obsolete. For especially long-term projects, the project design should include plans for transferring the product to new platforms by choosing portable technology.

Political risk insurance
Insurance whose coverage is triggered by a macro-economic or government action. A type of financing to pay for resulting losses.

Monitoring Risks on the Project's Critical Path

Protecting the value of a project includes dealing with the uncertainty associated with its timely delivery. The project manager is responsible for turning uncertain events into certain outcomes. Management of risks associated with activities on the critical path is essential to ensuring that a project is completed by its target date.

The project manager can take specific actions to manage the timeliness of activities on the critical path:

- Manage the buffer in the critical path
- Manage risks for critical path activities
- Monitor completion of activities on the critical path

Manage the Buffer in the Critical Path

Slack time
The difference between either the latest start time and the earliest start time, or the latest finish time and the earliest finish time for activities in a project's critical path.

Time estimates for project activities are not exact. Start and finish times for any activity might be early or late. The result is **slack time** for an activity, which is the amount of time by which an activity can be delayed without affecting the overall completion time of the project. The sum of all of the slack times for activities on a critical path is the buffer available in the critical path.

Project Activities Showing Slack Time

Activity	Predecessor	Time Estimate	Latest Start - Earliest Start (day count from project inception)	Slack Time
A	—	4.00 weeks	0 - 0	0
B	—	5.33 weeks	30-28	2
C	A	5.25 weeks	70 - 63	7
D	A	6.33 weeks	102 - 99	3
E	C, D	5.40 weeks	150 - 145	5
F	C, D	4.50 weeks	185 - 182	3
G	E, F	2.00 weeks	198 - 195	3
				23 days total

The "Project Activities Showing Slack Time" exhibit calculates that there are twenty-three days of slack time or "buffer" in this project. As this is a long-term project, this may be considered a relatively brief time span. In a short-term project, the team may want to consider reducing slack time. At the beginning of the project, the duration of the buffer is known. As time progresses and some activities take longer than anticipated, buffer days are used. Throughout the project, the project manager monitors the days remaining in the buffer. If the buffer becomes critically low, resources can be added to critical path activities to ensure that the entire project is accomplished by the target deadline.

Manage Risks for Critical Path Activities

The derailment of activities on the critical path is a key concern for the project manager. Therefore, these activities are given additional attention and higher prioritization for treatment. The project manager monitors the availability of people, expertise, funding, materials, and data for these activities to reduce the controllable internal loss exposures.

Monitor Completion of Activities on the Critical Path

As activities are completed on the critical path, the project manager collects data from the team members to monitor the progress of the project. In regularly scheduled meetings, progress and problems with activities are discussed.

Project Risk Management Planning Template

Activities/Tasks	Risks	Risk Management Treatments to Address Risks	Contingency Plans	Priority for Treatment (High/Medium/Low)	Critical Path Activity (Yes/No)	Treatments Implemented	Dates Implemented
1.							
2.							
3.							
4.							
5.							
6.							
7.							
8.							
9.							
10.							
11.							
12.							
13.							
14							
15.							
16.							
17.							
18.							
19.							
20.							
21.							
22.							
23.							
24.							

Resources are identified that can resolve bottlenecks. If necessary, the project's sponsor may be asked to assist in resolving organizational issues that inhibit progress.

Just as there are steps for planning a project, there are also several steps that should be followed when implementing changes in the way an organization operates.

ORGANIZATIONAL CHANGE MANAGEMENT STEPS

Although it is not always possible to anticipate when an organizational change may be necessary, organizations can expect change and should plan for it. In fact, in today's fast-paced environment, the rate of change in competitive industries is ever increasing. When properly managed, change can present opportunities for reinventing the organization and its culture.

Major organizational change is a complex process. Steps in the change management process might appear simple relative to the effort required to accomplish each step without undermining or derailing the process. Therefore, discussion of the steps in the change management process encompasses not only actions required to complete each step, but also cautions regarding fundamental errors to be avoided. There are seven change management steps:

1. Articulate the need for change
2. Appoint a leadership team
3. Develop a written statement of the **vision** and **strategies**
4. Communicate the vision and strategies
5. Eliminate barriers to change
6. Recognize incremental successes
7. Entrench the change

Vision
An idea of what an organization wants to become.

Strategies
Large-scale action plans for interacting with the business environment in order to achieve long-term goals.

Articulate the Need for Change

When an organization recognizes that change is needed, it first has to articulate the need for the change. For example, these organizational threats could lead to the articulation of the need for change:

- Projections indicate that net income losses will occur within five years if current actions continue.
- High customer satisfaction standards and **cycle-time** targets cannot be achieved using current processes.
- A change in the legal or regulatory environment causes an industry-wide crisis.
- The organization's weaknesses have been publicly disclosed, and competitors are exploiting them.

Cycle-time
The total duration of a process from start to finish.

How the need for organizational change is articulated affects how a proposed change is received. Even at executive levels, individuals may exhibit complacency that leads to resistance to any departure from current methods of operation. To counter this resistance, the articulation of need should convey a sense of urgency. A sense of urgency helps persuade key individuals to invest in the change and creates the momentum required to spur the organization to action. Reasons for urgency must be supportable; if people perceive the urgency as false or exaggerated, they may withhold support for change.

Actions

Conveying a sense of urgency requires bold actions by a leader, referred to as a change agent, to reduce complacency and demonstrate the disparity between the status quo and a desirable future. To convey this sense of urgency, the change agent must convincingly demonstrate how the proposed change will affect results, using supportable evidence to motivate the organization's decision-makers to support change.

Cautions

The need for change should be articulated clearly and succinctly, with supporting data appended or available. Convoluted messages lose the power to persuade an audience.

If the articulation of need conveys insufficient urgency or if urgency is confused with anxiety, it may not generate support for change. If it provokes anxiety, decision-makers may lose confidence in the corporate leaders' ability to effectively guide the organization.

Appoint a Leadership Team

Major transformations are usually associated with one highly visible change agent and a collaborative team of sponsors of the change, referred to as the leadership team. The change agent and leadership team should have the credibility and authority to take action, obtain resources, and direct others' actions. The leadership team is made up of carefully selected individuals who recognize the need for the change and provide solid and broad-based support for accomplishing it.

Actions

Assembling a leadership team involves selecting individuals based on the scope of the proposed change. A leadership team for a transformation that encompasses the entire organization would involve its president, division general managers, and department heads. If the target of the change is a particular plant, department, or functional area, the team may include "key players" from middle or lower-level management in charge of those areas. They are responsible for creating the vision of the change and "selling" it to others.

Members of the leadership team should have the power to eliminate any obstacles to progress, expertise relevant to the change, credibility that allows the need for change to be taken seriously by other employees, and leadership to drive the change process.

Cautions

An organization may underestimate the difficulty of implementing change and the importance of building a strong leadership team. A change in one department may be doomed to fail if it requires support from other departments that are not directly involved in making the change. A change agent must have sufficient autonomy and authority to drive the actions of all departments involved. One way to ensure this is to include champions from the executive ranks on the leadership team, even for changes that do not involve the entire organization.

Successful change leaders must have a deep conviction that the change will fundamentally improve the organization or its results, and they must be able to articulate their vision in a credible and compelling way. They must also have the people and organizational skills to implement their vision. Control and responsibility must be placed in the units undergoing change, and the change must be led by individuals with knowledge of those areas. Some organizations make the error of putting human resources or staff personnel, who may not understand the operations process, in charge of a change project.

An effective coalition is essential to building an effective leadership team. A team with the wrong combination of individuals can fail to develop the essential level of teamwork required. For example, team members who discourage the healthy exchange of ideas or who foster mistrust among team members can undermine a team's progress.

Develop a Written Statement of Vision and Strategies

The change agent and leadership team create a vision and the strategies that will direct the effort for achieving that vision. The vision articulates the conception of the future that would result from the change, with some commentary on why employees should strive to create that future. Strategies are then derived from the vision.

Actions

The change agent and leadership team craft an effective vision statement that is realistic, desirable, feasible, motivational, and focused enough to guide decision making and that can be communicated readily. An effective transformational vision provides a general direction for improving the organization's products, services, cost control, and/or relationships with customers and stakeholders. It has these additional qualities:

- It may be clearly described in five minutes or less.
- It considers trends in technology and the market.
- It is stated in positive terms.

Following the crafting of the vision, the change agent and leadership team develop strategic statements that support the vision and demonstrate its feasibility. The strategies provide the logic and detail to show how the vision can be accomplished.

Sample Vision Statement

We will be the world leader in our industry within five years. Our leadership will be reflected in profit generation, innovation, and work environment. Achieving this goal will require an aggressive annual revenue growth that expands internationally. We will use innovation to reduce our costs by at least 30 percent to improve our profitability. We will improve our leadership and management skills to create a positive work environment with a turnover of 5 percent or less annually.

Cautions

Without a clearly articulated vision, transformation can dissolve into a tangle of confusing, incompatible, and time-consuming projects that go in the wrong direction or into a dead end. A common error is to mistake plans and programs for an appropriate vision. For example, some organizations assume that actions focused on training, team creation, and other activities that should produce positive results constitute a vision. However, a vision should succinctly align, direct, and inspire collective action toward a common end point that improves the organization's measurable results.

Change agents sometimes have a sense of direction that is too complicated or undefined to be useful. The vision statement should be clear, simple, focused, and jargon-free.

Communicate the Vision and Strategies

The change agent, with the support of the organization's decision makers, then communicates the change vision and supporting strategies to all employees, using multiple forums to ensure that all members of the organization see and hear the message repeatedly and consistently over an extended period of time. Credible communication involves verbal communication as well as behavior by the leadership team that is consistent with the communication.

Actions

The change agent develops and implements a plan for communicating the message for change that reaches all employees multiple times. Most employees will make short-term sacrifices if they believe that transformation is possible.

If a vision is not communicated sufficiently, employees may prefer the status quo. For employees to buy into a vision, they must understand the message intellectually and emotionally. Employees must be able to conceive how the vision will positively affect their working environment, options, or rewards.

Cautions

Organizational forces that encourage the status quo can be substantial. Communicating the vision with an appropriate level of urgency may require removing sources of complacency or reducing their impact. Those tasks can be as simple as effectively countering expected arguments or as complicated as eliminating signals that are contrary to the message. For example, a company that must reduce excessive spending cannot expect employees to adopt a sense of urgency regarding spending if corporate executives have a fleet of luxury vehicles and regularly participate in company-sponsored excursions. Elimination of those "perks," however, would demonstrate the organization's sense of urgency and commitment to change.

Eliminate Barriers to Change

Organizational transformation involves many people from all levels. Employees must be empowered to become a part of the process and to understand the relevance of the change. However, employees cannot effect change if barriers prohibit them from action. They may embrace the vision but feel disempowered by real or perceived obstacles.

Actions

To eliminate barriers to change, the leadership team should use the momentum of the change process to change the systems, structures, and policies that are inconsistent with the vision and strategies. Such barriers can appear in forms such as these:

- Organizational structures that limit change, such as reporting systems that discourage interaction among departments

- Lack of skills required for the new environment, such as team-building and creative-thinking skills

- Inadequate information and human resources systems, such as performance-compensation systems that reward the status quo and fail to reward innovation and risk-taking

- Obstructive supervisors who fail to support employee empowerment, such as those who impose traditional bureaucratic leadership and fail to tap employees as sources of power, information, and ideas

Cautions

Resistance is likely in any step in the change management process, but it may first become apparent when changes in practices are implemented. Staff who are entrenched in the status quo may resist needed changes. If such staff members are influential among their peers, changes may be only nominally implemented.

Understanding Resistance to Change

Resistance is a signal to management to determine and address the causes of employees' attitudes toward proposed change.

People resist change when they believe:	People support change when they believe:
It is unnecessary or will make the situation worse.	The change will result in some personal gain.
Upper-level managers do not understand the real issues.	They expect a new challenge.
They will experience personal loss.	The change makes sense and is the appropriate action.
They had no input into the decision.	They were given an opportunity to provide input into the decisions.
They are not confident that the change will succeed.	The person leading the change is capable.
The changes were a surprise or kept a secret.	It is the right time for the change.
Resources are inadequate to implement the change.	Resources are adequate to implement the change.

These methods are effective in identifying and working with employees who resist change:

- Express empathy and support—Learn how employees are experiencing the change by actively listening in order to establish a base for joint problem-solving.

- Communicate—Dispel rumors, speculation, and fear through constant communication using many channels.

- Encourage participation and involvement—Involve employees directly in planning and implementing the changes.

Recognize Incremental Successes

The leadership team initiates goals, projects, and tasks that move the organization toward the vision and identifies the roles employees will play in reaching the vision. When a proposed change will take multiple years to implement, milestones are identified throughout the life of the project. The milestones are incremental goals with specific completion dates that ensure the project stays on track.

Actions

The leadership team clearly communicates the required actions through published goals and team charters. When goals must be broken down into smaller actions that are assigned to units throughout the organization, the team communicates the relationship and relevance of the assigned actions to the overarching goal.

The milestones represent visible improvements or short-term accomplishments, as well as progress toward the project goal. The leadership team celebrates the achievement of each milestone and rewards the people responsible for the success.

Rather than initiating a single, sweeping change throughout the organization, management may initiate changes on a smaller scale, such as in one department or division, and announce successes to the entire organization. Using one department or division as a pilot reduces uncertainty, and success in one unit builds confidence in the change that can carry over to other units.

Cautions

Failure to create short-term wins by establishing and celebrating incremental accomplishments makes the implementation of a significant change seem interminable. Complex change efforts can lose momentum if there are no short-term goals or sense of achievement. People may become complacent, leading to failure to achieve objectives. Continuous encouragement to achieve incremental steps ensures that employees are engaged in the change process.

Entrench the Change

As milestones are achieved, steps are required to entrench hard-earned gains and to prevent regression. New behaviors must be sustained, and gains should be consolidated and anchored in the organization's culture through formal policies and structures.

Actions

Managers throughout the organization must examine all the organization's activities and structures to ensure they align with the change. Systems, processes, and structures should be revamped to eliminate any opportunity for reverting to prior norms.

The organization's culture—the shared attitudes, values, goals, and persistent norms of behavior—must be aligned with the change. Shared values based on the vision should persist throughout the systems, processes, and structures created.

Individuals may not be able to see the broader perspective or effect of the change process while it is taking place. Once the change is completed, the leadership team must articulate the connection between new behaviors and processes and organizational success so that employees understand the scope of what has transpired and the positive outcome. New approaches will become part of the culture of the organization only when it is clear that they work and are superior to prior methods. Continuing communication about the significance of the change and support for the new practices are important, particularly if employees are reluctant to admit the validity of new practices.

Cautions

Resistance to change never fully dissipates. Even when stages of the process are successful, some employees may still crave the relationships, positions, or status that they had before change occurred. These people may seize any opportunity to regress to prior behaviors or ridicule the post-change organization, creating dissension.

A change is permanent only when everyone adopts it. Declaring victory too soon, before the new behaviors are fully entrenched, can undo change efforts. Until changes become a part of the culture, which can take years, new approaches are tentative. If performance-reward systems are incompatible with new responsibilities or the change has not fully permeated the entire organization, employees may return to more comfortable methods and familiar work processes.

IMPLEMENTING ERM—CONTINUOUS CHANGE

The goal of ERM is to embed risk recognition into every business decision. The effort required to accomplish this goal is substantial. Project management techniques and a project-structured framework can be used during the initial phases of ERM implementation. Project management techniques are valuable to the organization, as processes are developed and employees are empowered to take action in response to changing risks.

Too often, organizations have a static approach to risk management that deteriorates into a narrow compliance-based effort that leads to underperformance. However, organizations that effectively implement an ERM project can establish more reliable decision making and foster innovation to sustain performance.

An effectively implemented ERM project that responds to continuous change is essential to integrating ERM into the fiber of an organization. Opinions vary regarding the appropriate elements of an effective ERM implementation plan. Common among them is the need for organizational engagement that builds commitment to ERM from the organization's executives to every level of the organization. Project techniques can help to organize this engagement.

Developing and Implementing an ERM Implementation Plan

ERM should be embedded into all of an organization's strategic planning, business decisions, and performance management. Without this integration, ERM may be perceived as imposing an additional layer of bureaucracy rather than as being integral to how the business is run.

Developing and implementing ERM requires a systematic approach with enough flexibility to accommodate changes in the internal and external environments of the organization. The extent of the need to use project **frameworks** or project management tools depends on the company's size and its openness to embracing ERM principles.

Inception

It is often helpful in the inception phase for an organization's board and senior executives to define the scope of ERM by initiating a project. This project's charter should answer these questions:

- Why do we need ERM?
- What resources do we need to commit to the project?
- How do we measure success for ERM?
- Whom should we put in charge of the project and ERM for the organization?
- What can go wrong with the project and with ERM (variation from expected)?

It is essential that the board and senior executives drive the implementation of the ERM project because ERM involves the commitment of the entire organization. A common error in initiating an ERM project is failing to get complete buy-in from all key stakeholders. This executive group should ensure that all stakeholders understand the impact and scope of ERM and visibly work to support the required changes so that ERM becomes the standard.

A chief risk officer should be appointed (or an executive may perform that role in addition to other responsibilities). The chief risk officer and executives should determine and document various important aspects of the ERM project plan:

- The risk appetites of stakeholders and how they align with the organization's strategic goals
- The organization's risk management philosophy, goals, and policies

Framework
An approach to project planning and execution in which portions of the project are divided by requirements or problem statements and addressed separately, but in a way that will integrate.

- The ERM project charter, project goals, and scope statement, addressing quality, timeliness, budget, and boundaries

Planning

The planning phase of an ERM implementation is the point at which the project may be delegated to a team with close interaction with or under the leadership of the CRO. In this phase, the team defines the criteria for the successful completion of each deliverable in the project, which involves answering several questions:

- How will the process for accomplishing the implementation be documented and communicated?
- Which stakeholders should be involved in planning and executing the implementation?
- How should ERM be incorporated throughout the organization to support proactive business decisions at all levels?
- What information do employees need to make risk-aware decisions, and how can that information be presented effectively?
- What information do external stakeholders, customers, and regulators need, and how can that information best be communicated?
- What policies and procedures are needed to make ERM operationally integrated?

Projects inevitably will be spawned by an ERM implementation. These projects will require sound project management techniques.

Structuring systems to respond to the questions developed during the planning phase is often done using frameworks. Here are some examples of types of ERM frameworks:

- Risk identification framework—Employees should have information that supports the identification and tracking of changes to key performance indicators (KPI) as well as external factors and trends. KPIs and external factors tracked should relate to shifts in risk that can guide decision making. For example, a steel fabrication company tracks its past expenses for steel and labor. In addition, key risk indicators (KRIs) should be tracked to determine shifts in risks that might have future implications. Continuing the steel fabrication example, KRIs should be tracked to facilitate monitoring of external factors that affect the cost of steel, such as changes in labor and hiring at steel mills, regulations that affect the importation of steel, and purchasing shifts by competitors.
- Risk assessment and treatment framework—Employees should be able to share information about current risks, prioritization of risks, and risk treatments. For example, a framework should be in place that will allow an employee in the purchasing department who has noticed an increase in shipping prices to share that information with employees in the marketing

department who are responsible for pricing products and services for customers.

- Communications framework—Appropriate communication should ensure that stakeholders have timely information that builds confidence in the organization as well as information in times of crisis. Reporting to comply with legal, regulatory, and governance requirements is also included in a communications framework.

After defining required frameworks for project deliverables, the project team creates planning pieces (such as PERT diagrams and Gantt charts) that document required activities, the sequence of activities, and timeframes. The Gantt chart also tracks the execution of the project.

Execution

The most important tasks in the execution phase are to ensure that activities are properly implemented and controlled. In this phase, several activities take place:

- Systems are designed and developed.
- Prototypes are created, tested, and reviewed.
- Groups across the organization become more deeply involved in testing, production, and support.

Everyone in the organization should be responsible for managing some aspect of risk. Therefore, employees must be trained in risk management skills, and frameworks must be adapted to the organization's needs and employees' applications.

Monitoring

In the monitoring phase, the project team ensures that the ERM project deliverables will continue to be assessed. The CRO should be involved to emphasize the importance of the project. The project team should review and revise content in the frameworks established to ensure that it remains relevant.

The results of the project, including its effectiveness and costs, should be reported to the organization's board, senior executives, and stakeholders.

Most implementations have a final phase, which is the completion or closure of the project. This phase is characterized by the project manager's writing a formal project review report that contains critical results, rewards the team, lists lessons learned, releases the project resources, and informs senior management of the project closure.

An ERM implementation differs from other projects because there is no closure; it is not finite. The monitoring phase never ends. Because ERM involves a systemic grafting of risk management onto the culture and its integration with the strategic goals of the organization, the implementation of an ERM project is perpetual in nature and ever-changing. The ERM program must be formally reviewed at regular intervals to ensure that the established frameworks continue to provide the needed ongoing information in the most appropriate format. Any significant changes in the organization or environment, or shifts in the organization's risk appetite, can generate a revision to the ERM program.

Incorporating Continuous Change

Development of an ERM program might appear to be a sweeping **discontinuous change** as the momentum of the organization shifts in a more promising direction. But the benefits of a successful single fix do not last. As the environment, market, competition, risks, and consumers' needs change, **continuous change** becomes essential. Because the concept of continuous change is central to the ERM process, just as it is in the traditional risk management process, additional information is useful in ensuring that the philosophy is woven throughout the decisions made in implementing ERM in an organization.

Discontinuous change
A single abrupt shift from the past.

Continuous change
The process of constant evaluation and improvement to increase efficiency, effectiveness, and flexibility.

Continuous improvement is an ongoing effort to improve products, services, or processes. These efforts aim for incremental improvement rather than breakthrough improvement all at once. Continuous change is marked by a series of small, incremental change initiatives that have several advantages over large changes:

- They are easier to manage.
- They have a greater probability of success.
- Disruption is confined to small units at any given time.
- Employees are in a constant state of change-readiness.
- The organization adjusts more frequently to gain competitive advantages.

Operating in a state of continuous change requires continual external and internal monitoring. Externally, the organization should perform these activities:

- Identify the signals of significant change and continually search for those signals, such as KPIs and external factors and trends.
- Assume that the signals are based on substance, and identify possible consequences of the signals.
- Determine which aspects of the environment should be observed and measured to verify the speed and direction of the change.

Internally, the organization should develop and improve methods of sharing change information in a timely and concise manner.

In an ERM implementation plan, some tools that can be applied to promote continuous change are effective in visually conveying large amounts of information. These tools include dashboards and heat maps.

Sample ERM Implementation Plan

Inception

Establish an ongoing risk committee, with an executive-level sponsor, to review and revise the frameworks established.

Obtain board or CEO-level support.

- Train the board and upper management in ERM and why it is important. Articulate the expected benefits and costs.
- Establish responsibilities for all supporters, including a "chief risk officer" for the organization.
- Develop a charter for the ERM project and team.
- Support for the project should be made highly visible.

Develop a risk management policy.

- Understand the risk appetites of key supporters and stakeholders.
- Align risk appetites of all stakeholder groups with the organization's strategic objectives and strategies. Express risk appetite boundaries for the project in the project scope statement, where possible.
- Articulate and communicate risk management policy of the organization in the project scope statement.

Articulate goals for the ERM project.

- Develop goals that address the traditional risk management loss exposure categories of property, liability, net income, and personnel.
- Develop goals that address ERM issues of strategic risks, effectiveness, accountability, business processes, compliance, employee empowerment, cultural identity, reputation, and competitive advantage.
- Include all project goals in the project scope statement.
- Include all project constraints regarding quality, timeliness, budget, and boundaries in the project scope statement.

Planning

- Design frameworks for identifying, assessing, and managing risks.
- Design frameworks for internal and external communication.
- Determine how accountability, resources, communication, and reporting (internal and external) will be managed.
- Establish clear organization-wide risk management strategies for achieving the project goals.
- At functional levels of the organization, establish risk management objectives to the extent that they have a substantive effect on the organization's results and should be integrated into processes.

Execution

- Develop an organization-wide ERM vocabulary.
- Develop and enforce the use of a communications framework to support identification of changes to changing KPIs.
- Identify KPIs and external indicators of changes in risks that are to be monitored continuously.
- Identify measurement issues associated with key event indicators and methodologies or technical issues in reporting them.
- Determine the best technological methods of disseminating information about changes in KPIs.
- Create and deploy a risk "nervous system" for communication, reporting, and monitoring progress of the information collected in the communications framework.

Sample ERM Implementation Plan (continued)

- Determine persons responsible for monitoring key event indicators and how action will be taken based on the changes.

- Develop and enforce the use of risk assessment and risk treatment frameworks that are responsive to information disseminated in the communications framework.

- Inventory current risk management processes and then build on them.

- Develop tools to identify and evaluate risks and ensure that all business units use the same tools and terminology.

- Ensure that risk assessment focuses on enterprise-wide risks as well as traditional loss exposures.

- Create a matrix or another tool to prioritize each risk in terms of its likelihood (frequency) and potential impact to the organization (impact). Focus treatment on the most serious risks.

- Establish methods for continuously and incrementally treating internal and external prioritized risks throughout the organization based on information distributed through the communications framework.

- Record risk treatments.

- Create a risk management culture.

- Train all employees on what ERM is and why it is important.

- Continually communicate the importance of risk management throughout the organization.

- Design human resources policies and practices to support identification and reporting of risk-related information at all levels.

- Emphasize employee commitment to the risk management culture, and include performance measures and incentives to promote that commitment.

Monitoring

- Document and communicate ERM effectiveness and costs.

- Conduct periodic reviews of the KPIs and external factors and make required changes.

- Empower the committee to revise the substance and details of the communications and risk assessment and treatment frameworks in response to sweeping changes in the internal and external environments.

- Because the ERM process is iterative and recursive, an ERM implementation must become part of the ongoing and continuous organizational strategy.

Dashboards are management information systems that provide information in a way that is designed to be easy to read. For example, the dashboard in the "Sample Dashboard" exhibit could be used by a steel fabrication company to display information about changes in the price of steel, changes in production by leading mills, and competitors' purchasing changes. Dashboards give managers a graphical overview of information and allow them to access lower levels of data.

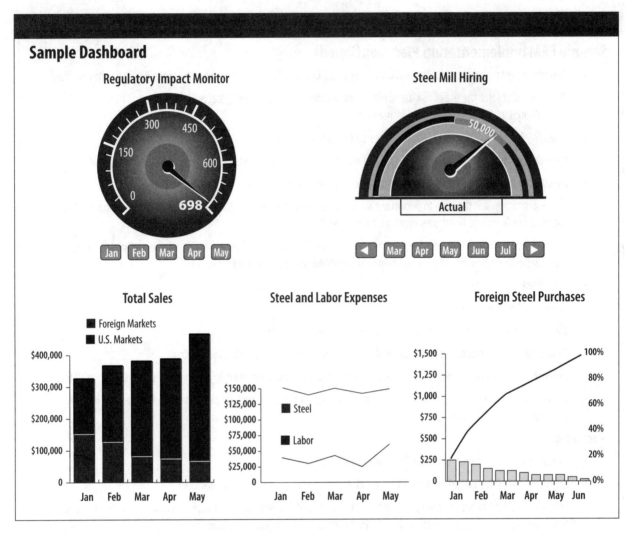

A heat map is a graphic representation of data in which the loss values taken by a variable in a two-dimensional map are represented as colors. Heat maps effectively represent large numbers of data points in ways that would be unwieldy and hard to interpret using traditional tables or charts. Many different types of heat maps exist that use various visualization techniques. Heat maps have ERM applications such as displaying information regarding close-call loss events and triggering automatic notifications of appropriate personnel for assessment and treatment.

Heat maps can be refined to display data categorized into three or more data groups—such as losses occurring by region and by product—when it is important to understand the correlation among these groupings. Refined heat maps display many different data items and can represent the value for each item using colors. While most heat maps address potential losses, the chief risk officer should also consider the impact of positive risk and opportunities that may arise. Thus, an ERM heat map displays grids and levels of positive impact and likely consequence.

Sample Heat Map

Severity of Impact		Very unlikely in next 5 years	Up to 1 time per year	Up to 5 times per year	Up to 20 times per year	> 20 times per year
	Up to $500k	1	2	3	4	5
	$500k to $5m	2	4	6	8	10
	$5m to $15m	3	6	9	12	15
	$15m to $25m	4	8	12	16	20
	< $25m	5	10	15	20	25

Likelihood of Consequence Occurring

SUMMARY

A project is a unique undertaking, outside of routine work processes, with established goals that requires people, materials, and financial resources.

To develop a project management plan, a project manager must understand the scope and nature of the project, identify the disciplines necessary to achieve the project goals, and use scheduling tools to effectively facilitate the planning and completion of the project.

Managing risks in a project is one of many disciplines a project manager needs to have mastered to successfully lead a project. Managing risks in a project requires three primary activities:

- Applying the risk management process within the context of the project
- Addressing common project loss exposures
- Monitoring risks on the project's critical path

The change management process is initiated by a change agent and developed by leadership team. The process involves all employees in an organization by building commitment in a common vision that fundamentally alters the way the organization operates. These are the change management steps:

1. Articulate the need for change
2. Appoint a leadership team

3. Develop a written statement of the vision and strategies

4. Communicate the vision and strategies

5. Eliminate barriers to change

6. Recognize incremental successes

7. Entrench the change

The initial implementation of ERM can entail using a project-structured framework to introduce the concept first to the board of directors and executives, and then to the entire staff. Therefore, project teams may be required for certain other phases of an implementation. Opinions vary regarding the appropriate elements of an effective ERM implementation. Common among them is the need for a process that builds commitment to ERM from the organization's executives at every level of the organization and ensures feedback from all levels to the executives.

CHAPTER NOTE

1. Adapted from Bruce W. Tuckman and Mary C. Jensen, "Stages of Small Group Development Revisited," *Group and Organization Management*, 1977, vol. 2, no. 4, pp. 419–427.

CHAPTER

Comprehensive ERM Business Case Study

Outline

Amiable Footwear, Inc., Case Study

Summary

Educational Objectives

After learning the content of this chapter and completing the corresponding course guide assignment, you should be able to:

▶ Given a case study, apply enterprise-wide risk management (ERM) strategies and tools to develop an ERM plan.

Comprehensive ERM Business Case Study

Enterprise-wide risk management (ERM) is a process. It involves engaging the enterprise at all stakeholder levels and its vision becomes integrated with business strategy. A case approach is used to develop the basic tenets of ERM in a simulated setting of a company engaging in an ERM project.

To make an ERM plan practical, a process is required that applies underlying knowledge in a series of strategies with tools that can be used to address a wide range of business types and sizes. The strategies and tools form a structure that can be embellished and tailored to a particular organization's unique characteristics and risks.

AMIABLE FOOTWEAR, INC., CASE STUDY

To demonstrate how ERM can be implemented in a wide range of organizations, this case study applies a series of strategies to a hypothetical organization using tools that structure thought processes and underlying ERM knowledge. The case study consists of three parts:

- Case facts
- An overview of the strategies and tools
- Application of the strategies and tools to the case facts

Case Facts—Amiable Footwear, Inc.

Overview	Amiable Footwear, Inc. (Amiable) is a manufacturer of high-performance athletic shoes. Amiable is a publicly traded corporate entity that has been in business for over thirty-five years. The organization was founded by an entrepreneur and amateur athlete in the basement of his house as he sought to create superior performance footwear. He expanded his business by hiring his friends, organizing them in teams to produce the footwear, and challenging the teams to compete with the incentive of securing management positions within the company as it continued to grow. That competitive spirit among the now-senior executives still exists. Amiable athletic shoes are unique in the sports world because they are made of 99-percent recycled materials, making them popular with athletes and celebrities who support "green" initiatives. The shoes are known for embodying cutting-edge innovations and research and through their endorsements from elite-athlete customers.
Mission statement	Amiable Footwear helps elite athletes excel within their sport by providing the finest equipment available while assuring them that the materials and processes used in their manufacture are safe for the planet and for those who produce and use them. Amiable Footwear is dedicated to providing consistently attractive returns to its business owners.
Organizational goals	• Increase profits by 5 percent per year • Exceed customers' expectations of the organization as a provider of athletic equipment that enhances performance and is ecologically friendly • Comply with all legal requirements in product development • Operate as a community member by supporting local organizations

Business strategies	1. Fiscal Focus—Safeguard Amiable as a financially prudent organization.
	
	   • Establish an annual operating budget that allows for not less than a 3 percent return to investors per year.
	
	   • Price products in accordance with expenses and market tolerance, considering the unique nature of the elite product.
	
	   • Invest prudently for capital expenditures.
	
	2. Customer Focus—Exceed customers' demands in cutting-edge sports technology. To accomplish this, we will:
	
	   • Maintain a staff of certified medical and engineering specialists to ensure that products continually outperform the competition.
	
	   • Design products that exceed customer expectations in style, design, sport-injury protection, and technology as established through an annual survey.
	
	3. Product Focus— Meet customers' demands by developing a high-quality and ecologically friendly product in a timely fashion. To accomplish this, we will:
	
	   • Establish protocols for outsourcing component-part manufacturing to ensure that components meet quality standards and are received within production timelines.
	
	   • Maintain trained assembly-work staff who meet demand requirements for production.

Manufacturing	Amiable shoes are assembled in the United States from components that are made throughout the world. Component manufacturing according to Amiable's specifications is awarded to the lowest bidder, with all associated costs considered. Therefore, the locations and companies used in the supply chain vary by product and over time. The final assembly consists of stitching, gluing, and heating around plastic shoe lasts (molds shaped like feet in various shoe sizes). A complex and flexible information system is in place to keep track of the multiple supply chains required for the many component manufacturers for each shoe type produced. Data related to the timing of delivery, quantity, and warehouse location of the components is crucial to the assembly process. All engineering and design for the shoes are performed in the U.S. by teams that include podiatrists and scientists. Shoe designs are based on software created by Amiable that focuses on anatomy and the effect of impact exerted under high-performance situations. Prototype designs are then tested by professional athletes and perfected until final designs are ready for mass production.
Materials used	These materials are currently used in Amiable shoes: • Upper shoe covering—Woven mesh cloth of plastic with rigid plastic inserts for supporting the shape. • Insole—Thin layers of cotton and plastic mesh. • Midsole—Rubber supporting plastic capsules of compressed air for shock absorption. • Outsole—Carbon rubber. • Adhesives—Vegetable glue and casein (milk product) combined under an exclusive patent held by Amiable in a formula that resists moisture and mold, which is otherwise uncommon for these types of adhesives. The adhesives are set by solvent evaporation, which is toxic and flammable. • Microchips—Electronic sensors are imbedded in the shoes so that information about physical characteristics and stresses can be later uploaded to a computer. The information is used to improve a user's performance and collectively compiled to improve Amiable's shoe designs. Amiable will release this innovation this year in its Premier line of shoes.
Quality control	Amiable tests its materials using procedures developed by the Shoe and Allied Trades Research Association (SATRA), which provides devices designed to test each element of the shoe. An inspector at the assembly factory checks for defects, shock absorption properties, and functionality of the microchips.
Marketing	Amiable shoes sell at price that is four times higher than other athletic shoes due to their unique nature. The shoes that contain microchips will produce diagnostic reports that will be available online. The shoes are sold throughout the world through sports clubs and authorized trainers and dealers and to athletic teams. Customers include professional athletes and serious amateur athletes who are runners, basketball players, and golfers. Top athletes from each sports affiliation act as spokespersons for advertising campaigns to promote Amiable's footwear.

Continued on next page

Corporate facility and distribution	Amiable's headquarters, engineering, design, and assembly facility, with an average of 1,000 employees, are located in Savannah, Georgia. All buildings at the Savannah facility are steel and concrete construction (Class 5 fire resistive) with sprinkler systems. This construction has load-bearing members that can withstand damage by fire for at least two hours. The strength of the structures provides superior resistance to causes of loss such as windstorm, earthquake, and flood. The buildings in Savannah have a replacement value of $50 million. The machinery and contents in Savannah have an actual value of $30 million. Warehouse inventory in Savannah averages $20 million, with no seasonal fluctuations.
	Amiable owns no trucks for transportation of components to or from the assembly operations. All components and finished products are shipped by common carrier trucks, shipped by air, or delivered by a railroad spur line that runs directly to the assembly plant from the international container ships that arrive at the Savannah Port Authority docks. All shipments are received FOB (free on board) at Amiable's warehouse. The plant has material-moving vehicles on site, such as forklifts, cranes, and specially designed vehicles used only on the premises to unload items from railroad cars and carry components to the warehouse or assembly area.
	Amiable owns some private passenger automobiles for use by executives and vans used to transport employees as needed. Security and maintenance have utility trucks used to patrol the premises.
	The facility and surrounding areas are fenced and security controlled. Employees must show photo identification cards to enter the parking lots surrounding the buildings. Vehicles must also be registered and bear a sticker to enter the surrounding lots. Security guards check all identification and vehicles. Security guards also spot-check vehicle trunks and interiors. Visitors, other than those there for business-related reasons, are not allowed to enter the facilities.
Financial data	Annual sales (mil.) $55,391
	1-year sales growth 12.8%
	Net income (mil.) $7,829
	1-year net income growth 15.2%
	Rankings/Stock indexes • S&P 1000 • Dow Jones Industrials
Risk management status	Amiable currently applies a traditional risk management process with a full-time chief risk officer and the following goals: **Pre-loss** • Economy—Amiable is a publicly traded stock company. In the interests of the stockholders, all decisions are made with consideration for the return on the investment. Risk management decisions are guided by the trade-off of expense with savings. • Externally imposed goals—Workers compensation and automobile insurance is required in all U.S. states in which Amiable does business unless a company can prove that it has financial resources dedicated to paying for losses. All corporate buildings have mortgages, which require insurance or proof of financial resources to compensate the mortgage company in the event of a loss of the secured property.

	- Tolerable uncertainty—Amiable executives are willing to tolerate a moderately high degree of uncertainty. - Social responsibility—Dedication is placed on creating a return to investors and providing quality with service to customers. Employee layoffs in the past indicate that Amiable is willing to make difficult decisions when necessary. **Post-loss** - Profitability—Continuity of operations, generation of profit, and achievement of financial goals for a sustained number of years are Amiable's primary goals.
Corporate activities	Amiable donates funds annually to sponsor a daycare center owned and operated by the Savannah area YMCA (Young Men's Christian Association). The daycare center is three miles from the Amiable facility. Amiable employees have preference in the placement of their children for daycare services, and membership is provided to Amiable employees at a significant discount.

Organizational Chart

- President and Chief Executive Officer
  - Chief Risk Officer
    - Vice President, Sales and Marketing
      - Market Researcher
      - Manager, U.S. Sales
        - Sales Team
      - Manager, Asian Sales
        - Sales Team
      - Manager, European Sales
        - Sales Team
    - Vice President, Finance
      - Manager, Accounting
        - Accounting Department
      - Manager, Finance
        - Finance and Investment Department
    - Vice President, Production
      - Procurement Officer
        - Purchasing Department
      - Manager, Operations
        - Production Department
        - Warehousing and Shipping
    - Vice President, Research and Design
      - Research and Design Team

Continued on next page

Three-Year Loss Run			
Year	Type	Number of Occurrences	Average Financial Loss Per Occurrence
Current year	Employees injured while using forklifts in warehouse—general back and shoulder injuries and broken limbs	3	$45,000
Current year	Injuries/illnesses related to glue used in manufacturing	14	$10,000
Current year	Loss of limb/serious injury associated with railroad delivery on spur line	1	$210,000
Current year	Liability lawsuits for injury resulting from material failure in shoe	42	$125,000
Current year	Back strains and lifting injuries on assembly floor and loading docks	18	$8,000
Current year	Eye injuries from use of machines used to trim excess materials in shoe assembly	4	$12,000
Current year	Hearing loss from noise in manufacturing area	5	$7,000
Current year	Repetitive motion injuries—office workers	12	$6,000
Current year	Repetitive motion injuries—manufacturing workers	15	$9,000
Prior year	Hand/arm injuries from use of manufacturing equipment	11	$9,000
Prior year	Auto accident involving two employees using company van	1	$63,000
Prior year	Back strains and lifting injuries on assembly floor and loading docks	14	$7,000
Prior year	Eye injuries from use of machines used to trim excess materials in shoe assembly	1	$5,000
Prior year	Hearing loss from noise in the manufacturing area	3	$6,000
Prior year	Liability lawsuits for injury resulting from material failure in shoe	21	$113,000
Prior year	Repetitive motion injuries—office workers	14	$8,000
Prior year	Repetitive motion injuries—manufacturing workers	18	$10,000
2 years ago	Employee falls from scaffolding while painting—general back and shoulder injuries and broken limbs	1	$58,000
2 years ago	Fire on assembly line from ignition of glue created by friction-generated heat and indirect loss from shutdown of assembly line	1	$1,623,500
2 years ago	Hand/arm injuries from use of manufacturing equipment	10	$13,000
2 years ago	Back strains and lifting injuries on assembly floor and loading docks	14	$9,000
2 years ago	Liability lawsuits from injury resulting from material failure in shoe	11	$92,000
2 years ago	Eye injuries from use of machines used to trim excess materials in shoe assembly	5	$11,000
2 years ago	Hearing loss from noise in the manufacturing area	3	$8,000
2 years ago	Repetitive motion injuries—office workers	11	$8,000
2 years ago	Repetitive motion injuries—manufacturing workers	13	$10,000

Strategies and Tools Overview

A process that consists of a series of strategies and associated tools is used to gather information that, in turn, will be used to develop an ERM plan for the organization. This process begins by addressing essential questions:

- How can an ERM plan be tailored to the unique attributes of the organization?
- What risks will be most detrimental to the organization or provide the greatest opportunity for the organization to achieve its strategies?
- How can the risks be prioritized for treatment?
- What are effective methods for monitoring the identified risks and emerging risks that affect the organization's strategies?
- How can the benefits of ERM be most effectively communicated to the organization's senior managers and board of directors?

Application of the Strategies and Tools

An organization's change from traditional risk management to ERM may require senior executives to change some important viewpoints:

- The internal and external contexts of the enterprise must be initially established.
- Communication with all stakeholders is essential in all phases of plan development and execution of the program.
- Risks reflect opportunities for loss as well as gain, making risk appetite and risk tolerance essential factors to determine and monitor.

To help senior executives adapt to these changes in perspective, the organization's chief risk officer, a senior executive, a consultant, or a team might be charged with the responsibility of developing the ERM plan. For simplicity, this case study refers to the person responsible as the chief risk officer.

The strategies provide guides for determining requirements to develop an ERM plan. The chief risk officer can complete some strategies by accessing corporate documents. Accomplishing other strategies requires responses that the chief risk officer must compile through interviews, surveys, and investigation.

Strategy 1: Establish the Internal and External Contexts

The first ERM strategy for the chief risk officer to complete is to assess aspects of the organization's internal cultural beliefs as well as its internal and external environments. These aspects are then compared to the organization's strategies to determine risks that create opportunities or threaten the strategies with failure. Steps are applied to complete this strategy:

- Determine the attributes of the organization's culture to assess stakeholders' appetite for risk.
- Conduct a SWOT analysis to examine the organization's internal and external contexts.
- Determine the feasibility of the organization's strategies by comparing them to the SWOT analysis, and refine the strategies if necessary.

Overview of Case Analysis Strategies and Tools

Strategy	Tools
1. Establish the internal and external contexts	
• Determine the attributes of the organization's culture to assess stakeholders' appetite for risk.	Attributes of the Organization's Culture questionnaire
• Conduct a SWOT analysis of the organization's internal and external environments.	SWOT analysis table
• Refine the organization's strategies by comparing them to the SWOT analysis to determine feasibility of strategies.	Strategic plan drafting and refining questions
2. Assess the risks	
• For each risk, determine the essential organizational resources at risk and related events that could affect the organization.	Exposure spaces model
• Consolidate the risks identified at the corporate level for treatment and monitoring.	Risk register
3. Treat the risks	
• Prioritize risks for treatment according to the level of disturbance that would result or the opportunity for capital optimization, and identify appropriate treatments.	Risk prioritization and treatment/ optimization table
4. Monitor and review risks and treatments	
• Determine what, how, and when risk criteria (including ethical responsibilities, social responsibilities, and external requirements) will be monitored and reviewed.	Risk monitoring and reviewing table
5. Communicate and consult	
• Develop communication suitable for a board presentation by responding to questions that create a case for adopting ERM.	Questions to develop an ERM business case

Attributes of the Organization's Culture

The organization's culture defines shared values, beliefs, and accepted behaviors of those within the organization. By determining the attributes of the organization's culture, a chief risk officer can identify risks the organization has been willing to take, change that might have to be implemented to enable risk taking to achieve the organization's strategies, and the organization's appetite for risks that must be managed.

Determining attributes of the organization's culture requires candid responses to frank questions asked of the organization's senior-level executives. Some questions are also asked of mid-level executives to determine whether consistency exists between actions that are intended and outcomes that are perceived. These questions determine the current state of risk management, risk appetite, and management's willingness to recognize the need for change.

From the responses to the questionnaire and the discussion they generate, the chief risk officer gleans senior- and mid-level management's attitude toward innovation associated with risk and willingness to change. Drivers, which can be recognized in the responses, provide the chief risk officer both an indication of senior executives' risk appetite and their willingness to embrace change.

As Amiable's chief risk officer examines the Attributes of the Organization's Culture Questionnaire using the Risk Appetite and Change Willingness Indicators as a guide, a mismatch between senior- and mid-level managers' perspectives becomes apparent. Also, the organization appears to exhibit a mix of positive and negative drivers:

- Senior-level managers believe that they are sharing decision-making and risk decisions (at least in some regards). However, mid-level managers perceive that they are being excluded from decision making and that communication is flowing only from the top of the organization down.

- Structures are in place that create a business silo around the engineering unit.

- Positive drivers are exhibited in the momentum to innovate and create cutting-edge product.

- Negative drivers are apparent in the lack of open communication, lack of rewards for risk-taking, and the development of silos.

Risk Appetite and Change Willingness Indicators

Areas for Review	Questions	Responses From Amiable's Senior- and Mid-Level Managers
Planning	Are managers at all levels encouraged to participate in risk identification, quantification, and management? If not, will managers at all levels be included in the process in the future?	Senior-level managers—We invite feedback from managers at all levels of the organization. Mid-level managers—We are handed our goals and told when to report. We have too much to do to investigate risks. Isn't that what senior managers should be doing?
Organizing	Is the current risk management process applied throughout the organization through effective allocation of resources, communication, and accountability? If not, will a process be established to effectively distribute risk management resources, communication, and accountability in the future?	Senior-level managers—Yes. We ask the corporate chief risk officer to submit an annual report indicating how risks are addressed, how much insurance costs, and what capital allocations are requested for budgeting purposes. Mid-level managers—We haven't heard anything about risk management.
Leading	Does the organization's chief risk officer have a leadership role within the organization evidenced by communicating the risk management process through words and actions, gaining cooperation needed for successful ERM? If not, will the organization's chief risk officer have this role in the future?	Senior-level managers—The chief risk officer submits a monthly report to the senior-level managers including losses, expenses, and progress on projects.
Controlling	Does the organization's chief risk officer have the authority to evaluate the timeliness and effectiveness of ERM activities and take corrective action? If not, will the organization's chief risk officer be granted this authority in the future?	Senior-level managers—Yes. The chief risk officer has a budget and limited expense authority. The chief risk officer is evaluated on compliance with budget and completion of projects.
Values and Behaviors	What evidence has the organization exhibited in the past indicating its tolerance for risk?	Senior-level managers—We took a considerable risk when we decided to implement microchip technology in our elite footwear. A significant capital investment was required for software development in order to get the innovation out there ahead of the competition.
	What parameters of acceptable risk have been defined by organizational decisions?	Senior-level managers—Annual investments in engineering are important, and we are willing to increase that budget as needed. The microchip technology is an example of an acceptable risk that Amiable has invested in. We would be willing to make capital investments in similar types of technology that promise a return and keep us ahead of the competition.

Continued on next page

Areas for Review	Questions	Responses From Amiable's Senior- and Mid-Level Managers
	Do some cultural units within the organization accept more risk than others? If so, which units better reflect the pattern of risk values that the organization would like to exhibit in the future?	Senior-level managers—By far, the engineering department has accepted more risks than any other unit. It creates new designs and technology. Other units should emulate this behavior. Mid-level managers—The engineering department gets all the funding for innovation. The rest of us are just expected to meet deadlines.
	What has the organization's reaction been when a working team accepts more risk than has normally been accepted in the past? Should this behavior continue?	Senior-level managers—We try to get teams to accept more risk by giving them greater latitude. However, team members are generally reluctant to venture out of their comfort zones. We would like to see more innovation in ownership by our teams. Mid-level managers—Team charters are written so strictly that there is little room to do anything outside the definition of what the team is to accomplish. Teams that have ventured beyond their charters have not been given good performance reviews.
Beliefs	What internal drivers (such as resource allocation, employee performance, and risk appetite) will influence the need for the organization to change its tolerance for risk in the future? Is the organization taking appropriate actions to address these changes now?	Senior-level managers—We currently have mechanisms for resource allocation and employee performance in place. At this time, any significant changes in risks taken are handled at the senior level of management. Mid-level managers—Things are run here the same way they have been since the company was founded: New products are given all the priority, and existing products are produced any way we can with what's left.
	What external drivers (such as political, social, economic, technological, and competitive environments) will influence the need for the organization to change its tolerance for risk? Is the organization taking appropriate actions to address these changes now?	Senior-level managers—Amiable is the leader in athletic footwear technology, and this keeps us in front of the competition. We have steadily increased sales regardless of turns in the economy. We are the industry leader and on the right path. We contribute to the YMCA to support the community. Mid-level managers—There are issues we would like to communicate to senior-level managers, but they discount our concerns. For example, there are holes in the software that will allow the microchips we are using in the shoes that are going to market soon to be tracked by GPS (global positioning system) software. It has not happened yet, but it is only a matter of time before someone figures it out. The company lays off workers when there is a temporary slowdown in orders, which creates conditions favorable for an information leak.

Risk Tolerance and Change Willingness Indicators

Positive drivers:

- Awareness about the future.

- Willingness to allow yesterday's successful products and services to erode in favor of future products/services.

- Embracing of risk by increasing the risk appetite and modifying the risk tolerance accordingly.

- Rewarding of employees for risk taking; successful or not, the lessons learned are important.

- Teamwork and collaboration.

- Open communication.

Negative drivers:

- Satisfaction with the status quo—If it is good enough today, it will be good enough for tomorrow.

- Attitude of complacency and invulnerability to future changes.

- Protection of current products/services.

- Avoidance of risks associated with innovation.

- Maintenance of current levels of risk appetite and risk tolerance.

- Rewarding of employees only for being successful.

- Creation of silos within the work environment.

- Limited communication.

Overall, the company supports innovation but does not distribute risk-taking throughout the organization. As a result, at least one risk is apparent that mid-level managers are unable to communicate or are ineffectively communicating to senior-level managers. Communication and information-sharing across the organization is ineffective.

SWOT Analysis Table

To understand the environments in which the organization is operating, the chief risk officer performs an internal analysis of the organization's strengths and weaknesses and an external analysis of opportunities and threats.

In evaluating the SWOT Analysis Table, the chief risk officer must determine whether the organization's current strategies will support its long-term goals. Adjustments to existing strategies or additional strategies may be required to achieve Amiable's goals.

SWOT Analysis Table

	Strengths	Weaknesses
Internal	• Reputation for an elite and a superior product. • Innovation and product leadership in microchip/sports technology. • Success in creating a high quality green product. • Positive and consistent growth. • World-wide market recognition.	• The organization's success is based on a single product line. • Reputation and image are the key selling factors for the product and are subject to attack that could cripple the organization. • The organization is dependent on other manufacturers to create component parts.

	Opportunities	Threats
External	• Expansion into other lines of footwear underserved by the industry. • Diversification into other types of sportswear based on existing reputation. • Increased market share resulting from expansion into new geographic markets. • Buyout of a competitor that is failing financially to create affordable footwear with Amiable's brand recognition. • Sale of patented glue, shoe designs, and microchip technology to other manufacturers.	• Other manufacturers can quickly duplicate Amiable's shoe designs at a lower price. • The potential for knock-offs or similar products from competitors is an increasingly important issue. • Innovation is cycled into product designs faster in order to stay ahead of the knock-offs, introducing chances for errors. • Industrial spying is a significant problem, making it possible for knock-offs to hit the market before Amiable's own products do.

Strengths can be paired with opportunities as areas of competitive advantage. The organization can build on its current reputation and growth to expand products and sales.	Weaknesses can be paired with threats as risks to be avoided. Loss of reputation could undermine Amiable in a highly competitive market. The speed at which new models must be introduced to stay ahead of the competition reduces design and research windows before production.

Because business strategies can be extensive, it is helpful to narrow the focus of the evaluation to particular strategies that place the organization's goals at risk. Amiable has a significant risk to its reputation, which is one of its key strengths. As Amiable strives to stay ahead of the competition and product knock-offs by implementing faster design cycles, less time is available for product research and design to maintain its reputation. In addition, the Attributes of the Organization's Culture Questionnaire includes comments from mid-level managers indicating that they are already aware of pending problems involving the microchip technology that will affect Amiable's reputation, but they have no effective method of communicating the problem to senior-level management to have the issues addressed. Additional possible evidence of speed-to-production problems is the increasing frequency and severity of liability lawsuits resulting from material failure in shoes over the last several years.

Amiable's business strategies are effective as far as they have been developed, but it appears that safeguards to product quality are inadequate if Amiable is to continue to meet its organizational goal of "exceeding customers' expectations of the organization as a provider of athletic equipment that enhances performance and is ecologically friendly." This additional product focus strategy could be drafted as "Establish and maintain uncompromising quality standards in product components and assembly."

The "Strategic Plan Drafting and Refining Questions" exhibit can be used to examine this additional proposed strategy.

Strategic Plan Drafting and Refining Questions

Considering the results of the SWOT analysis as well as information gained in the Attributes of the Organization's Culture Questionnaire, the chief risk officer must determine whether the organization's strategies are aligned with the organization's goals.

At this point, an organization's existing ERM goals should also be considered to determine whether they support the accomplishment of the organization's strategic goals. However, Amiable does not currently have an ERM program in place.

Overall, the strategy is financially supportable and appears necessary to avoid detrimental results to the organization's reputation. Amiable also has the opportunity to demonstrate the superiority of its product quality over the competition and prevent or mitigate some lawsuits by building the documentation that proves the steps it has taken to ensure the quality of its products.

Strategic Plan Drafting and Refining Questions

The development of an organization's strategic plan by senior management is important because it directs the activity of the organization for one year or multiple years. When drafting and redrafting a strategic plan, executives may include some or all of these analyses.

Questions	Responses to Questions for Amiable in Examining Drafted Strategy: "Establish and maintain uncompromising quality standards in product components and assembly"
Suitability of the Plan	
Analysis of the suitability of the strategic plan questions how it will work for the organization and in the current and future marketplaces.	
Can the strategic plan be accomplished? Can the needed changes in processes, products, knowledge, and personnel be successfully implemented and managed?	This strategy can be accomplished, but it will require the development of standards and parameters for those standards for components and finished products. Trained staff members will be required to set standards and perform quality checks. Performance standards should be identified for the new staff members.
Will the entire organization support the strategy?	Rather than isolate the development of standards and quality checks, the tasks should be disbursed to those departments most knowledgeable regarding the quality required. For example, the component quality standards should be stated in the purchasing orders, checked by the receiving department, and verified during assembly. Problems could be detected at several points, so the entire organization must be involved to support the strategy.
Is the strategy appropriate for the marketplace?	Our goals and sales have been successfully supported by our reputation for quality. The strategy is appropriate for our marketplace.
Are there environmental factors that would render the strategy ineffective?	Environmental factors at issue include the delay of components for assembly if they are found to be below standards. We must build penalties into our work orders for subcontractors whose materials delay production.
Will the strategy create a product or service sufficiently different from those of competitors that customers will purchase the organization's products or services instead of competitors'?	Yes. We already have the edge in developing a high-quality product. This strategy will help us ensure that we can back our high-quality claim with documentation that no competitor matches. We can use this documentation in marketing.
Feasibility of the Plan	
Analysis of the feasibility of the strategic plan examines resource allocation, cost, and impact. Resources include personnel, knowledge, property, money, and time.	
Cash flow issues—What initial investment is needed? Is the cash available? If not, what will it cost to obtain it?	Considering the additional staff, research, training, processes, and information systems required, an additional $20 million will be required annually to support this strategy. That can be supported through our current budgeting process without compromising the 3 percent annual return to investors established in our strategies.

Resource allocation—What additional resources are needed? Can they be easily obtained from outside sources, or must they be internally developed? What is the time frame for becoming productive?	Additional trained staff is needed for these tasks: • Establishment of standards • Verification of the inclusion of standards in contracts and work orders • Verification of compliance to standards in receiving and production • Quality control during product assembly • Quality control at product completion • Development of performance measures for employees (Fifty percent of these requirements can be accomplished using existing employees.) Training and information systems: • All employees should be trained in methods for detecting quality control problems. • An information systems should be available to all employees to identify quality control standards and tolerances and for reporting suspected problems.
Break-even point—How much time will pass between the point of initial investment and when the product/service produces enough profit to recover the initial investment? Is it acceptable? What is the net present value (NPV) of the investment in projects proposed in the strategic plan, and is it acceptable? How do the NPVs of proposed projects compare, and do they indicate that some projects should be included while others are eliminated?	If an extreme loss were to occur to an athlete or a sports figure that could be attributed to our products, the loss to our reputation would create such a loss of revenue that a break-even point or NPV is not calculable. If we consider only the liability lawsuits (the number of which doubled last year) from product failures for which the documentation that we will develop will provide a substantial defense, we can support the annual additional cost in the projected savings from liability lawsuits alone.

Continued on next page

Acceptability of the Plan	
The strategic plan should produce anticipated results or returns for the organization's stakeholders (shareholders, employees, and customers).	
Returns—For shareholders, will the strategy result in an increase in stock prices? How will employees individually benefit from implementing the strategy (such as better pay, career advancement, enhanced job functions, increased knowledge base)? For customers, will the product/service be improved while it remains at an acceptable price?	The more important issue is that this strategy will not result in a stock price decrease. If we continue to have liability losses at the current increasing rate, or if we have a significant event that receives media attention, we may not be able to sustain sales and price structure, which would result in falling stock prices and falling returns to investors. Employees can benefit individually with the career opportunities that will open for the new staff positions and training. Customers will benefit by having a more consistently superior product at a price that, while high compared to competitors, proves to be within market tolerances for the quality promised.
Risk—What are the risks inherent in the strategies? What happens if the strategy does not work as well as planned or even fails? How much risk is the organization willing to take? What risks does it want to avoid? If the product or service proposed is more successful than anticipated, can the organization meet the increase in demand?	The opportunities for gain from this strategy are increased documentation to uphold our reputation and possibly counter some of the competition's claims for having similar products. If the strategy does not work, we will maintain our status quo. The risk involves the expenses required to implement the strategy and the potential that it is inadequate to effectively support our quality claims. The risk to avoid is the possibility of damage to our reputation, from which we may not be able to recover. If the results are more successful than we anticipate, it is possible to add production shifts and increase orders for components to meet increased demand.
Reactions—How will each group of stakeholders react to the changes created by the strategy? What will be the impact of the reaction?	The board is likely to support the strategy because the integrity of Amiable's products has always been a primary board concern. Employees are likely to have mixed reactions. Some employees have been raising the concern of declining quality for several years, and they will accept the new standards. Other employees might see the standards as an additional layer of bureaucracy.

Strategy 2: Assess the Risks

After the internal and external contexts of the organization are examined, the chief risk officer identifies and assesses the risks to the organization and its strategies. Continuing the focus on the issues that Amiable's chief risk officer identified in the internal and external contexts, which are the risks the organization faces in striving to stay ahead of the competition with product design and the speed with which it brings products to market, the chief risk officer applies the exposure spaces model to those issues.

Exposure Spaces Model

The exposure spaces model is a concept for describing the attributes of a risk, including the resources that may change in value, the events that cause a change in a resource's value, and the impacts of the change.

As Amiable speeds its products to market in an attempt to outpace the competition that is creating knock-off or similar products at a substantially reduced price, what are the dimensions of the risks that result?

Risk Register

A risk register (or risk log) consolidates the individual risks identified in the exposure spaces model and through other assessment tools and establishes a means to treat and monitor those risks. While many risks are managed at the risk center level, financial risks and certain other critical risks are managed at the corporate level. The risk register rolls up all identified risks to the chief risk officer for monitoring and review by senior executives.

Considering the attributes of Amiable's "speed to market" risks, how can the chief risk officer apply the risk center register to those identified risks?

Amiable's "speed to market" risks examined through the exposure spaces model and consolidated in the risk register indicate that strengths can emerge from Amiable's need to speed products to market if the company can control the quality of the research underlying its designs and maintain its strength in quality production. The speed of creating innovative designs can outpace the competition, especially if elements of the designs are difficult to replicate. Excess patented designs can lead to sale/lease income or diversification of products. Amiable has the potential to build on its existing reputation to an even greater degree.

However, failure to maintain quality in the essential areas of research, design, and production can generate negative consequences and loss of reputation from multiple aspects.

Strategy 3: Treat or Exploit the Risks

After risks are assessed, they must be prioritized for treatment according to the degree of disturbance that they will potentially cause an organization or the degree to which capital can be optimized for a positive return. Risks are then reduced or financed.

Exposure Spaces Model—The Complete Model

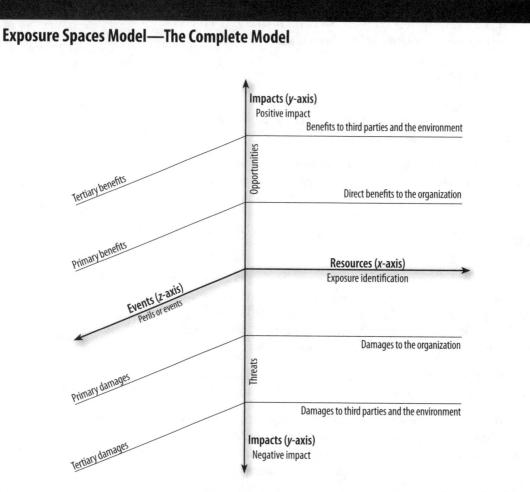

Exposure Spaces Symbol Key

Resources (*x*-axis)

H—Human resources, internal stakeholders

T—Technology resources, property, or assets

Inf—Information resources, intellectual capital

P—Partner resources, external stakeholders

Fin—Financial resources

Free—Free resources, resources not connected directly to economic transactions

Events (*z*-axis)

E—Economic events

N—Natural events

Ind—Industrial events caused by human construction

Hinv—Involuntary human events caused by mistakes

Hv ("Smart Alec")—Voluntary human events caused by intentional acts/ modification

Hv (criminal)—Voluntary human events caused by criminal actions

Impacts (*y*-axis)

Primary damages—Loss in direct and indirect value to the organization's resources

Tertiary damages—Losses to third parties and the environment

Primary benefits—Direct gains in values to the organization's resources

Tertiary benefits—Gains to third parties and the environment

Reputation—Represents other non-monetary impacts, including social justice and environmental stewardship values

Exposure Spaces Model Applied to Amiable's "Speed-to-Market" Risks

Resources at Risk	Events That Can Change the Value of the Resource	Impacts (positive or negative)
	• Economic • Natural • Industrial (human construction) • Human 　• Involuntary (human mistakes) 　• Voluntary (intentional acts) 　　• "Smart Alec" 　　• Criminal	• Primary damages • Tertiary damages • Primary benefits • Tertiary benefits • Reputation
Human/internal stakeholders • Designers and engineers • Assembly workers	A. Innovation Economically positive results can be achieved if designers and engineers with adequate resources are encouraged to seek product innovations that cannot be easily duplicated by competitors. Mistakes are likely to increase if more pressure is placed on the same number of designers, engineers, and workers.	Primary benefits will result if Amiable can achieve product innovations that are difficult to duplicate. Primary damages will result if mistakes in design result in inferior products that cause injuries. Amiable's reputation can improve or diminish based on the quality of the designs and engineering.
Property • Inventory, finished products • Technology	B. Unfinished Products/Inventory Economic changes to inventory and finished products will increase as the speed of moving products to market increases. Unused components may have to be scrapped if the models change and warehoused components are no longer required.	Tertiary damages can result from scrapping unusable inventory of components if Amiable employs supply chain delivery processes that require suppliers to deliver components just in time for production.
Information • Designs, patents, trade secrets	C. Proprietary Information Loss of propriety information could occur through voluntary or criminal acts. Alternatively, in its speed to market, Amiable could become very efficient at designing and patenting innovations in footwear and related products. These patents could present an opportunity to sell or license the rights to designs as well as to diversify through related products.	Primary damages can result from the loss of proprietary information. Primary benefits can result from the sale/lease of patented designs or the development of diversified products.

Continued on next page

Partner/external stakeholders • Suppliers, stockholders • Spokespersons • Customers • Distributors	**D. Stakeholders' Support** Stockholders, spokespersons, customers, and distributors can turn against or support Amiable's product based on changes in its perceived quality	Amiable will reap primary benefits if products are perceived as improved and cutting edge as it increases speed to market. Amiable will experience primary damages if the speed to market results in products that are inferior or are perceived to be. Amiable's reputation will be changed based on market perceptions.
Financial • Revenue based on product value • Short-term income • Long-term capital	**E. Design/Workmanship** Revenue as well as short-term income will be reduced if mistakes are made in the effort to speed products to market. If mistakes are severe, long-term capital might be reduced. However, cutting-edge products that are successfully brought to market will create positive economic results to revenue, to short-term income, and potentially to long-term capital.	If Amiable brings products to market hastily, errors will result in primary damages. If Amiable brings products to market effectively, it can result in primary benefits. Amiable's reputation will be changed based on the sustained quality of its products.
Free • Client endorsements • Positive product Internet rating by independent reviewers	**F. Product Endorsements** Amiable currently benefits from unsolicited client endorsements and positive ratings on the Internet from independent reviewers. These voluntary reviews could become negative if Amiable makes mistakes in design and production.	Continued positive endorsements create primary benefits. Primary damages can increase quickly as news of defective products spreads via the Internet. These damages can erode Amiable's reputation.

Risk Register for Amiable's "Speed-to-Market" Risks

Risk Register

Risk Owner ___Amiable Footwear___   Date ___

Item	Risk Owner (of component parts, if applicable)	Potential Impact (Opportunity/ Threat)	Risk Level 1=Minimum 2=Low 3=Medium 4=High 5=Maximum	Risk Treatment (Present)	Proposed Improvement Action	Next Review Date
A. Innovation	• Vice President of Research and Design • Vice President of Production • Research and Design Team	Opportunity: • Innovations that are difficult to duplicate • Increased reputation Threat: • Mistakes in design and inferior products • Decreased reputation	5 5	None None		
B. Unfinished Products/ Inventory	• Procurement Officer • Purchasing Department	Threat: • Scrapped inventory resulting from frequent changes	1	Currently controlled by just-in-time delivery of components for production		
C. Proprietary Information	• Vice President of Research and Design • Research and Design Team	Opportunity: • Sale/lease of patented designed	3	None		
	• Chief Risk Officer • Vice President of Research and Design • All employees	Threat: • Loss of proprietary information (designs, patents, trade secrets)	5	None		

Continued on next page ▶▶

D. Stakeholders' Support	• Vice President of Research and Design • Vice President of Production	Opportunity: • Cutting-edge product image to be gained • Increased reputation	4	None
	• Research and Design Team • Production Department • Vice President of Sales and Marketing	Threat: • Inferior product results in damages • Decreased reputation	4	None
E. Design/ Workmanship	• Vice President of Research and Design • Vice President of Production	Opportunity: • New products	5	None
	• Research and Design Team • Production Team	Threat: • Inferior product	5	None
F. Product Endorsements	• Vice President of Sales and Marketing • Sales managers	Opportunity: • Positive unsolicited endorsements	2	None
	• Sales teams	Threat: • Negative unsolicited endorsements	2	None

Risk Prioritization and Treatment—Amiable's "Speed to Market" Risks

Risks Identified	Potential Level of Disruption (Normal, Volatile, Rupture, Crisis) or Optimization of Capital (Risks Requiring Capital Allocation, Optimal Allocation for Those Capitalizations)	Prioritization for Treatment (Number) (Based on potential level of disturbance, degree of optimization for risk taking)	Risk Reduction Treatments (Avoidance, Mitigation,* Prevention, Reduction, Separation, Diversification, Duplication, Consolidation)	Risk Finance Treatments [Insurance Transfer, Noninsurance Transfer,** Alternative Risk Transfer (ART) Solutions, Resource Investments, Retention]
A. Innovation	Rupture possible Significant capitalization required for added engineering and design resources	1	Prevention through testing and quality control	Resource investments
B. Unfinished Products/ Inventory	Normal	6	Mitigation through supply chain control	
C. Proprietary Information	Volatile Significant capitalization required for added engineering and design resources Minimal changes to market/ lease patents	4	Mitigation through redeployment of marketing staff Diversification through related products	
D. Stakeholders' Support	Volatile Resources required for quality control	3	Mitigation through planning	Resource investments
E. Design/ Workmanship	Rupture Resources required for quality control	2	Mitigation through planning	Resource investments
F. Product Endorsements	Volatile	5	Mitigation through marketing redeployment	

*Continuity and redeployment plans, supply chain management

**Hold-harmless agreements, hedging

How will Amiable's chief risk officer prioritize the risks and choose the treatments?

Amiable's highest-rated threats and opportunities associated with its speed-to-market risks are (1) innovation risks related to its products and (2) design/workmanship risks. These two risks can create a rupture to the organization if efforts are unsuccessful or can optimize capital if efforts are successful. For these risks, resource investments are required to increase the rate at which Amiable applies expertise, creativity, and innovations to its designs in order to stay on the cutting edge with its products and make it difficult for the competition to replicate or compete with its designs. At the same time, resources must be dedicated to quality control in order to ensure that, as speed to market increases, the high quality of the product is maintained.

If Amiable effectively applies resources to stay on the cutting edge with its products, it will have the research systems in place to do more:

- Possibly generate additional designs and patents for lease, sale, or diversification (proprietary information)
- Safeguard stakeholders' support and product endorsements

Strategy 4: Monitor and Review Risks and Treatments

To be successful in managing its innovation and design/workmanship risks, Amiable must do more than invest capital in the Research and Design and Production departments. The entire organization must be aware of the possible threats to and opportunities for the organization, understand what risk criteria and thresholds are acceptable, and have opportunities to report changes to internal and external key performance indicators (KPIs). It will take the vigilance of all employees to detect, report, and act on issues that arise as Amiable increases the speed of its product to market.

For each prioritized risk identified, the chief risk officer next determines how the risks and treatments should be monitored and reviewed. Changes in risks should be compared to treatments in place, if any, to determine whether the current treatment is sufficient or whether a change in treatment is required. Included in this process are these considerations:

- Ethical and social responsibilities
- External requirements
- Risk criteria and thresholds
- The structure of the monitoring and reviewing functions for the company's "speed to market" risks and treatments
- Risk criteria and thresholds
- Data sources available to measure the thresholds and the frequency of data collection

Compliance with standards is not mandatory. However, applying ERM standards in the development of monitoring systems will prevent rework later if standards do become compulsory.

To deploy ERM for the selected risks, Amiable's chief risk officer defined the measurable risk criteria and the thresholds within the organization's risk appetite. The most highly prioritized risks are given aggressive goals to achieve. Responsibilities for data collection and reporting should be assigned to individuals in the organization who are accountable for that information. Also, employee reward programs are included to increase innovation and prompt action for competitors' abuse of Amiable's designs. This will require an information system to keep employees informed of the current priority demands by customers and product designs that can be compared to those of competitors.

All of the data collection, reporting, and dissemination of information can be improved if Amiable implements a business information (BI) system. Data can then be continually updated and visually available through heat maps or information dashboards.

Risk Monitoring and Reviewing—Amiable's "Speed-to-Market" Risks

Prioritized Risks	Note Ethical, Social, or External Requirements for Monitoring and Reviewing	Measurable Risk Criteria	Thresholds for Each Risk Criterion	Sources of Data for Collecting Measurements	Frequency of Collection
1. A. Innovation	Documentation to meet S&P's ERM criteria	Number of innovative changes per quarter	3	Management reports	Monthly
		Innovative changes measured by the priority of customer need satisfied and the degree to which the innovation meets that need measured by priority and degree of satisfaction achieved per quarter	At least 50% satisfaction to top 2 priorities	Management reports	Monthly
		Reward for employees who suggest innovations to priority customer needs	5 working days to honor reward recipients and communicate rewards internally	Employees' reporting system	Daily
		Earnings associated with increased sales	20% increase	Management and accounting reports	Monthly
2. E. Design/ Workmanship	Documentation to meet S&P's ERM criteria	Error rate	0.10% tolerance	Audit/quality control	Daily
3. D. Stakeholders' Support	Ensure that all communication is clear and factual	Communication media employed and frequency of communication	Monthly updates regarding innovation status distributed through 5 media	Management reports	Monthly
4. C. Proprietary Information	Documentation to meet S&P's ERM criteria	Controls in place to safeguard designs, patents, trade secrets—speed in addressing suspected abuse by competitors	1 working day from date of discovery to file injunction or take other legal action	Management reports	Monthly
		Reward for employees who discover suspected abuse by competitors	5 working days to honor reward and communicate rewards internally	Employees' reporting system	Daily
		Earning associated with patents leased/sold or diversified products developed	10% increase	Management and accounting reports	Annually

Prioritized Risks	Note Ethical, Social, or External Requirements for Monitoring and Reviewing	Measurable Risk Criteria	Thresholds for Each Risk Criterion	Sources of Data for Collecting Measurements	Frequency of Collection
5. F. Product Endorsements	Ensure that all communication and marketing that influences product endorsements is clear and factual	Communication media employed and frequency of communication	Monthly updates regarding innovation status distributed through 5 media	Management reports	Monthly
6. B. Unfinished Products/ Inventory	None	Value of scrap	<0.5% of components purchased	Management reports	Monthly

Questions to Answer to Develop an ERM Business Case—Amiable's "Speed-to-Market" Risks

Questions	Content Suggestions	Amiable's Business Case Content
Why does the organization need ERM?	• Benefits that other organizations in the same or similar industry have experienced • ERM compliance models adopted by other organizations in the same or similar industries • Strategies that should be driven from board level throughout the organization • ERM as a method of maintaining consistency in a changing environment	Our top two competitors have implemented ERM programs and have reported improved performance management, better pricing policies, and increased stock prices. Although ERM has not been mandated by reporting, emerging compliance models focus on an organization's adoption and integration of ERM. Therefore, compliance is a compelling reason for Amiable to view ERM as a strategic priority. Implementing ERM at this time may help us avoid a potential rating agency downgrade. Amiable can use ERM to implement and monitor cross-functional programs to more effectively address threats and opportunities. Implementing a company-wide program can ensure that decisions throughout the company are consistent with the stakeholders' risk appetite. It is apparent that we have not been successful in the past in adhering to company-wide quality control, as evidenced by our increased lawsuits related to product failures. Correcting these problems relates directly to our ability to achieve our business strategies and organizational goals. Consistency in risk monitoring that we will achieve through ERM will help us make informed decisions and improve our company's resilience in our competitive environment. A clear understanding of the potential gains or losses based on timely knowledge of the shifts in risk is crucial to our survival.
What resources must be committed to ERM?	• ERM compared to the existing traditional risk management program • Resources compared to key risks • Estimation of resources including infrastructure, capital expenses, changes issues, oversight, facilitation, and training	We have an existing risk management program that we can build on. With ERM, we will gain the ability to prioritize opportunities as well as threats and to act on both. A key resource that we must add is an information system that monitors the risk criteria compared to thresholds that we establish. This information system must be accessible to all employees so that they can react when results exceed thresholds and they can report information that allows others to react. This will require training, facilitation, and changes in performance measurements.
How will ERM success be measured?	• Success in addressing prioritized risks for action (risk criteria and thresholds) • Success in implementation of the ERM program	Success will be measured by the risk criteria and thresholds for each risk criterion. We have the ability to set the criteria and thresholds so that they are within our risk tolerance. Success can also be measured by our success in implementing the ERM program within our organization. Our degree of implementation can be compared to the Risk Maturity Model to identify our level of progression.

Who will be in charge of ERM?	• Senior executives, chief risk officers, executive managers	The effectiveness of ERM depends on the effectiveness of Amiable's information and communication. Information and communication about risk should be integrated throughout our company, by business unit, by functional unit, for product units, and by geographic marketing units. To make this possible, the chief risk officer will be responsible for the program. However, ERM must be supported by executive management and the board.
What can go wrong with ERM?	• Failure to secure strong board and executive management support derails the program. • Lack of communication, realistic goals, or a common vocabulary causes misunderstandings and a potentially narrow focus. • Lack of integration of the ERM program with other organizational processes paints ERM as an additional layer of bureaucracy. • Failure to clearly define the roles and responsibilities degrades the importance of ERM. • Failure to acknowledge individuals with developed risk management skills creates dissension. • Adopting a false sense of security because of ERM results in a failure to effectively collect risk information and identify risks. • Allowing regulations and compliance to define the conditions for success of an ERM program does not allow the organization to leverage the program effectively to gain benefits. • Overcomplicating data and reports can overwhelm the monitoring process, making it easier to overlook essential risk indications.	We have to be aware of the possible downsides to ERM and guard against those events: • Failure to demonstrate board and executive management support can undermine the program and make it irrelevant. • Lack of communication and realistic goals will create misunderstandings and reduce the chance of success. • Lack of integration of ERM with our processes will make ERM appear as a bureaucracy rather than a system essential to our survival. • Failure to clearly define the roles and responsibilities in the program will undermine the importance of the program. • Everyone in the organization must be involved with ERM, especially employees currently involved with risk management. We must include them in the ERM program and acknowledge their contributions to avoid dissension. • ERM is only as good as the information that we collect and how we use it. Failure to be diligent in the application of the program will render it ineffective. • The ERM information system that we develop must be user friendly or employees will avoid opportunities to access and use data.

Case Study Correct Answers

This solution might not be the only viable solution. Other solutions could be exercised if justified by the analysis. In addition, specific circumstances and organizational needs or goals may enter into the evaluation, making an alternative action a better option.

Strategy	Tools	Answers Applied
1. Establish the internal and external contexts		
• Determine the attributes of the organization's culture to assess stakeholders' appetite for risk.	Attributes of the Organization's Culture Questionnaire	From the senior- and mid-level managers' responses to the questionnaire, the chief risk officer gained an indication of their risk appetites as well as their willingness to embrace change.
• Conduct a SWOT analysis to examine the organization's internal and external environments.	SWOT Analysis Table	The SWOT analysis provided a snapshot of the organization's internal and external environment. Safeguards to the company's products were found missing as the company speeds products to market. The chief risk officer drafted a proposed corporate strategy to address that problem.
• Refine the organization's strategies by comparing them to the SWOT analysis to determine their feasibility.	Strategic Plan Drafting and Refining Questions	Questions helped the chief risk officer compare the results of prior tools to the newly proposed strategy. Overall, the proposed strategy was financially supportable, feasible, and acceptable.
2. Assess the risks		
• Determine for each risk the essential organizational resources at risk and events that could affect the organization.	Exposure Spaces Model	The risks associated with Amiable's drive to speed products to market were examined using the exposure spaces model regarding the resources at risk, events that can change the value of the resource, and impact. The company stands to gain from these risks as well as lose.
• Consolidate an organization's risks identified at the corporate level for treatment and monitoring.	Risk Register	The risks identified were placed in the risk register to allow for further examination of aspects of the risk owner, potential impacts, risk levels, and current treatments.
3. Treat the risks		
• Prioritize risks for treatment according to the level of disturbance that would result for the organization or opportunity for capital optimization, and identify appropriate treatments.	Risk Prioritization and Treatment/Optimization Table	Risks are prioritized for treatment according to their potential level of disturbance and degree of optimization. Risks associated with innovation and design/workmanship were the highest priority.

4.	Monitor and review risks and treatments		
	• Determine what, how, and when risk criteria (including ethical responsibilities, social responsibilities, and external requirements) will be monitored and reviewed.	Risk Monitoring and Reviewing Table	For each of the prioritized risks, measurable criteria, thresholds, data sources, and frequency of collection were required. Several treatments were determined for the highest priority risks, including employee involvement in innovation and protection of proprietary information.
5.	Communicate and consult		
	• Develop communication suitable for a board presentation that effectively responds to questions and provides a factual case for adopting ERM at the appropriate level of detail.	Responses to questions used to develop an ERM business case	The chief risk officer prepared a business case suitable for the senior executives and the board by responding to questions that provide a summary of the ERM program's costs and benefits.

Strategy 5: Communicate and Consult

To justify the value of the ERM program, Amiable's chief risk officer must provide the organization's senior managers and board members compelling information to support the allocation of resources required to implement the program. A business case or feasibility study should address what an organization must commit and what it can expect to receive in return. Because this is difficult to accomplish for ERM, responding to questions is an effective way to develop an ERM business case:

- To what questions should the chief risk officer respond to build the business case for ERM?
- What would responses to those questions look like?

The chief risk officer builds the case by responding to questions that senior managers are likely to ask when judging the value of a program. In unambiguous terms, the chief risk officer describes the benefits to be gained by the program and the cautions that are required.

SUMMARY

To demonstrate ERM implementation, a series of strategies with associated tools are applied to a hypothetical organization to demonstrate the progression of the development of an ERM plan:

- Establish the internal and external contexts and define risk criteria.
- Assess (identify, analyze, and evaluate) the upside and downside risks.
- Treat the risks deemed beyond the organization's risk appetite.
- Monitor and review risks and treatments.
- Communicate and consult with stakeholders.

Index

Page numbers in boldface refer to definitions of Key Words and Phrases.

A

Active directory, **4.13**
Alternate marketing stage, 7.27
Alternative risk transfer techniques
    advantages and disadvantages of, 10.12–10.13
    in risk financing, 10.3
    key features of, 10.3–10.4
    major benefits of, 10.4
    major types of, 10.4–10.5
AS/NZS 4360, 1.27–1.28
Assurance, risk management and, 12.6–12.9
At-risk metrics, 9.26–9.27

B

Bailment, **5.9**
Balcony financing, **10.7**
Basel II and Solvency II, 1.29–1.30
Bayesian networks, 6.20–6.23
BCM/BCP culture, building, 7.25–7.26
Benchmarking, **4.10**
BS 31100, 1.26
Business continuity planning
    information technology disaster recovery, and,
        4.30–4.31
    mitigating risk through, 7.22–7.26
Business intelligence, **4.15**
    analysis reports, 4.15
    data mining and risk notifications, 4.16
    external reports, 4.15
    information user roles, 4.13
    planning reports, 4.15
    program evaluation, 4.22–4.23
    reports, 4.14
Business intelligence systems
    elements of, 4.8
    enterprise-wide risk management implementation
        phases, 4.17–4.24
    information technology governance and outputs,
        4.24–4.31
    presenting the case for ERM, 4.31
Business model, **1.4**
Business strategies, types of, 3.6–3.7

C

Captive insurance (or reinsurance) companies, 10.9–10.12
Cash flow, **5.10**
Cash flow analysis, 9.3
Cash flow at risk (CFaR), 9.27–9.28
Catastrophe bond, **10.7**
Chief risk officer, **1.17**
Code of ethics, **11.15**
Co-dependencies, determining, 8.14–8.16
Communication ethics, 13.13
Communication problems, 13.13–13.14
Commutation, **10.21**
Compliance, 11.10
    levels of, 11.11
    reviews, 12.5–12.6
Context, **3.27**
Continuity plan
    developing, 7.24–7.25
    implementing, 7.25
Continuous change, **14.31**
    incorporating, 14.31
Co-opetition, **13.21**
Corporate governance, **4.8**
Correlation
    common misperceptions about, 9.24
Correlation/covariance matrices, 9.24–9.25
COSO II, 1.26–1.27
Cost of debt, **9.28**
Cost of equity, **9.28**
Counterparty risk, **10.4**
Crisis communication, 8.7–8.9
    benefits of, 8.9
    mitigating risk through, 8.7
Critical path, **14.8**
Cycle-time, 14.20

D

Data management/enterprise information modeling,
    4.28–4.29
Data masking, **4.30**
Data mining, **4.16**
Decision role analysis, **4.13**
Delphi technique, 6.18
Derivative, **10.3**

Development stage models, 3.7–3.8
Dimensional design, **4.14**
Discontinuous change, **14.31**
Discount rate, 9.3–9.4
Disruption, levels of, 7.3–7.7
Drivers of compliance, 11.10

E

Economic events, 5.12
Economic intelligence, **4.3**
    data gathering and, 4.4–4.5
    monitoring, 4.6
    risk investigation and, 4.5
    risk model testing and, 4.35–4.36
Empirical distribution, 6.13
Enterprise risk controls validation, 4.35
Enterprise risk identification, 4.18–4.19
Enterprise risk management
    compliance issues in, 11.9–11.15
    ethics and social responsibilities in, 11.15
    program assessment, 4.36
ERM
    business case, developing, 13.25–13.33
    communications, foundations of, 13.12
    emerging legal and regulatory requirements regarding, 1.10
    implementation plan, developing and implementing, 14.28
    in approaching business uncertainties, 1.20
    information compliance, 4.23–4.24
    rating levels, criteria behind, 12.11–12.13
    to meet financial rating agencies' expectations, 12.9–12.13
    traditional risk management versus, 1.11–1.18
Event, **5.5**
    classes of, 5.11
Expected value of utility, calculation of, 6.40–6.44
Exposure, 5.4
Exposure assessment tool, using an, 5.15
Exposure identification, 8.11
Exposure spaces model, 5.4
    applying, 5.22
External stakeholder communication channels, 13.15
Extreme events
    copulas and, 9.25
    stress scenarios and, 9.28
Extreme value theory, 6.15

F

FERMA, 1.30
Financial resources, 5.10
Finite risk insurance plan, 10.8
Foreign exchange rate risk, **10.7**
Forward contract, **10.6**
Frameworks, **14.28**

Free resources, 5.10
Fronting company, **10.11**
Futures contract, **10.7**
Fuzzy logic, 6.19–6.20

G

Gantt chart, **14.7**
Governance
    enterprise risk management, 11.5
    implementing, 11.8
    ownership of, 11.8

H

Hedging, **10.6**
Highly protected risk (HPR), **10.14**
Human events, 5.13

I

Impact, 5.3
    describing, 5.16
    measuring, 5.19
Industrial espionage, **5.9**
Industrial events, 5.12–5.13
Information resources, 5.9
Information systems, 6.5
Information technology
    application management/configuration services and, 4.27
    asset controls and, 4.26
    governance practices for enterprise risk information benchmarking and, 4.32
    investment management and, 4.26
Insurance derivative, **10.5**
Internal and external contexts, establishing, 14.13
Internal stakeholder communication channels, 13.15
ISO 31000:2009, 1.26

K

Key performance indicator (KPI), **4.6**
Key risk indicator (KRI), **4.6**
Knowledge management, **5.8**

L

Lagging indicator, **4.10**
Leading indicator, **4.10**
Loss exposure, **5.4**
Loss portfolio transfer, **10.22**

M

Management departments, 6.3–6.7
Margin, **10.8**
Master data management, **4.16**

Materiality, **3.32**
Maturity levels, 3.26
Maturity model format, 12.8
Metadata, **4.15**
Mission statement, **3.3**
Mitigation plans, 8.15
Modern portfolio theory (MPT), 9.17–9.28

N

Natural events, 5.12–5.13
Net present value, **9.3**
Nonverbal communications, 13.16
Notification log, **4.16**

O

Objective, **2.6**
Open source intelligence, 5.9

P

Partner resources, 5.10
Performance benchmarking, **4.15**
Performance management scorecards, 4.9
Performance metrics, 1.16
Political risk insurance, **14.17**
Portfolio selection, optimizing risk taking and, 9.17
Present value, 9.4
Primary impact, **5.18**
Process element format, 12.8
Program evaluation and review technique (PERT), **14.7**
Project
    constraint, 14.13
    life cycle, 14.11
    management disciplines, 14.4
    management plan development and implementation,
        14.3
    risks, 14.16
    scope, 14.3

Q

Qualitative impacts, 5.21

R

Rating agencies, role of, 12.10
Rebranding, **3.41**
Regression, 6.15
Reputation, **7.7**
Resource, **5.3**
Resources, classes of, 5.8–5.11
Risk appetite, **2.10**, 4.15, 9.15
Risk assessment, 14.13
Risk attitude, **2.10**
Risk categories, 1.11
Risk center, **6.7**

Risk centers method, 6.9
Risk criteria, **3.22**
Risk factors, **4.10**
Risk financing derivatives, major types of, 10.5
Risk governance structure, 3.22
Risk identification, 6.8
Risk information mapping, 4.20
Risk management
    as a value creation proposition versus a hindrance, 2.14
    criteria, 4.9
    culture accountability, 4.33
    culture, 12.10
    responses, 7.6
    role, 2.13
    within the context of a project, 14.12
Risk maturity model, 3.23
Risk owner, **6.7**
Risk ownership
    by the board, 13.9
    by employees, 13.10
    by management, 13.9
    by an organization's owners, 13.7
Risk perception, **3.27**
Risk position, **3.27**
Risk register, **5.15**
Risk taking in an organization, role of, 2.18
Risk to reputation, managing, 7.7
Risk tolerance, 2.10
Risk treatment, 14.13–14.14
Risk-adjusted return, **12.11**
Risk-avoiding attitude, 2.19
Risk management
    communication channels, 13.15
    communications with Stakeholders, 13.16
    reports, 13.17
Risk-optimizing attitude, 2.19
Risk-return relationship, 9.15–9.17
Risks to reputation, key sources of, 7.10
Risk-seeking attitude, 2.19

S

Scheduling tools, applying, 14.7
Scope creep, 14.11
    controlling, **14.11**
Scope statement, **14.15**
Securitization of insurance risks, 10.7
Segregation of duties, **4.13**
Self-assessments, 12.4
Simplified balance sheet method, 6.9
Slack time, **14.18**
Social and ethical responsibilities, practical considerations
        for, 11.18
Social license to operate, 11.6
Social responsibility, **11.16**
Special purpose vehicle (SPV), **10.7**

Stakeholder, **3.27**
    acceptance,1.24
    communications, 8.8
    concerns, 7.17
Stochastic differential equations, 6.14
Strategic integration, 1.12–1.13
Strategic management, **3.3**
Strategic redeployment planning stages, 7.27
Strategic risk management, 12.11
Strategy
    evaluation, 3.6
    formation, 3.4
    implementation, 3.6
Sub-frameworks, 1.31
Supply chain
    best practices, 8.5–8.6
    risk management, 8.3–8.6
    threats and opportunities inherent in, 8.4
Sustainable development, 2.20–2.23
    challenges posed by, 2.22
    defined, 2.21
Sustainable practices, 11.21
SWOT analysis, conducting, 3.34–3.41
System administration/security management, 4.30
System dynamics simulation, 6.19
System levels, 7.4–7.6

T

Tax shield, **9.28**
Technical resources, 5.9
Tertiary impact, **5.18**
Time-adjusted period of return, 9.4–9.5
Tone at the top, **4.24**
Triple bottom line, **3.30**

U

Uncertainty modeling, methods and limitations of,
    6.12–6.23
Upside of risk versus downside of risk, 5.17
Utility, **6.24**

V

Value at Risk (VaR), 9.26
Values, **3.27**
Verbal communications, 13.16
Vision, **14.20**
Vision statement, 3.3

W

Weighted average cost of capital (WACC), **9.28**